THE BRITISH ISLES

ORKNEY ISLANDS

OUTER HEBRIDES

Inverness
Loch Ness
▲ Ben Nevis
Highlands
SCOTLAND
Aberdeen

Glasgow
Firth of Forth
Edinburgh
Edinburgh Castle

Giant's Causeway
NORTHERN IRELAND
Belfast

ISLE OF MAN

Hadrian's Wall
Newcastle
Tyne
Lake District
Pennines

York
Hull
Humber

Irish Sea
Dublin
Liverpool   Manchester

St. George's Channel
▲ Snowdon
Cambrian Mountains
WALES
Nottingham   The Wash
Trent
ENGLAND

Birmingham
Severn
Cambridge
THE NETHERLANDS

Swansea
Cardiff

Oxford
London   Big Ben
Heathrow   Thames
North Sea

Stonehenge

Dover

EURO TUNNEL

BELGIUM

Devon
Cornwall
Plymouth
Penzance
ISLES OF SCILLY

Brighton
ISLE OF WIGHT

English Channel

FRANCE

CHANNEL ISLANDS

Scale:
0   100   200   300 km
0   100   200 miles

W0177580

Blue Line **3**

für Klasse 7

Das Lehrbuch versteht sich als Gesamtangebot. Welche Texte und Aufgaben verpflichtend sind, wird durch die schulinternen Curricula festgelegt.

1. Auflage
1 ⁵ ⁴ ³ ² | 20 19 18 17 16

Alle Drucke dieser Auflage sind unverändert und können im Unterricht nebeneinander verwendet werden.
Die letzte Zahl bezeichnet das Jahr des Druckes.

Herausgeber: Dr. Frank Haß, Kirchberg
Autorinnen und Autoren: David Brimage, Brighton; Geraldine Greenhalgh, Hamilton; Wolfgang Hamm, Marktredwitz; Melanie Ku, Hanau; Howard Rayner, London; Clare Treleaven, Castellón sowie Chris Caridia, Bangkok; Andrew Cowle, Glasgow; Jo Cummins, London; Michael Meisenzahl, Karlstadt; Karen Seekings, London; Konstanze Zander, Großenehrich
Beratung: Brunhilde Biek, Leonberg; Karin Braun, Dortmund; Wilma Brings, Bedburg; Amanda Chisnell, Lollar; Ulf Degen, Braunschweig; Tanja Frank, Ulm; Sandra Haberland, Recklinghausen; Wolfgang Hamm, Marktredwitz; Ulrike Heringhaus, Altheim; Michael Herrmann, Ludwigsfelde; Christa Kathmann-Fuhrmann, Bonn; Dr. Margitta Kuty, Greifswald-Eldna; Grit Machut, Berlin; Michael Meisenzahl, Karlstadt; Beatrix Pierce, Eppingen; Annegret Preker-Franke, Bielefeld; Dr. Hubert Schwandt, Parchen; Christian Straukamp, Nordhorn; Ines van Hove, Oldenburg; Dieter Vilimek, Helmstedt-Bargen

Redaktion: Ulrike Beutel, Joanne Popp; Dr. Susanne Dyka, Nürnberg; Birgit Piefke-Wagner, Korntal-Münchingen
Herstellung: Ulrike Wursthorn

Umschlaggestaltung und Gestaltungskonzept: know idea, Freiburg; Koma Amok, Stuttgart
Umschlagfoto: plainpicture GmbH & Co. KG (Ableimages/Jutta Klee), Hamburg; plainpicture GmbH & Co. KG (Bias), Hamburg
Fotografen: Thomas Weccard, Ludwigsburg
Illustrationen: Marek Blaha, Offenbach; Kirill Chudinskiy, Köln; Marcus Wilder, Hamburg; sowie Friederike Ablang, Berlin; Lars Benecke, Hannover; Thomas Binder, Magdeburg; Gilles Bonotaux, Paris; Vera Brüggemann, Bielefeld; Christian Dekelver, Weinstadt; Thorsten Droessler, Leipzig; Andreas Florian, Lübeck; Anke Fröhlich, Leipzig; Josef Hammen, Trierweiler; Christian Hansen, Berlin; Susann Hesselbarth, Leipzig; Carmen Hochmann, Bielefeld; Martin Hoffmann, Stuttgart; Hendrik Kranenberg, Drolshagen; Cleo-Petra Kurze, Berlin; Sven Leberer, Altenberge; Dorothee Mahnkopf, Berlin; Karin Mall, Berlin; Helga Merkle, Albershausen; Pawel Miedzinki, Kozieglowy; David Norman, Meerbusch; Katrin Oertel, Münster; Liliane Oser, Hamburg; Sven Palmowski, Barcelona; Katja Rau, Berglen; Bettina Reich, Zwenkau; Sandra Schmidt, Berlin; Carolin Ina Schröter, Berlin; Jaroslaw Schwarzstein, Hannover; Manfred Tophoven, Straelen; Jacqueline Urban, Eisenach; Ulrike Vetter, Leipzig; Aurel Voigt, Waiblingen; Martina Vollhardt, Kamenz; Sylvia Wolf, Wiesbaden; Steffen Wolff, Brohl-Lützing; Dorothee Wolters, Köln

Satz: Satzkiste GmbH, Stuttgart
Reproduktion: Schwabenrepro GmbH, Stuttgart
Druck: Stürtz GmbH, Würzburg

Printed in Germany
ISBN 978-3-12-547873-2 (fester Einband)
ISBN 978-3-12-548873-1 (flexibler Einband)

Blue Line 3

Herausgeber: Dr. Frank Haß

Ernst Klett Verlag
Stuttgart • Leipzig

Inhalt

L = Listening   S = Speaking   R = Reading   W = Writing   V = Viewing   I = Intercultural

L = Listening　S = Speaking　R = Reading　W = Writing　V = Viewing　I = Intercultural

Inhalt

L = Listening   S = Speaking   R = Reading   W = Writing   V = Viewing   I = Intercultural

Kompetenzen / Themen / **Ich kann …**	Fertigkeiten	Seite

So lernst du mit Blue Line

*Hier zeige ich dir, wie du dich
in deinem Buch gut zurechtfindest.
Das Buch hat fünf Units (Kapitel).
Jede Unit ist gleich aufgebaut.*

Way in

Hier steigst du in das neue Thema ein.
Dazu gibt es auch einen kurzen Film.

Im gelben Kasten siehst du, was du in
der *Unit* lernst.

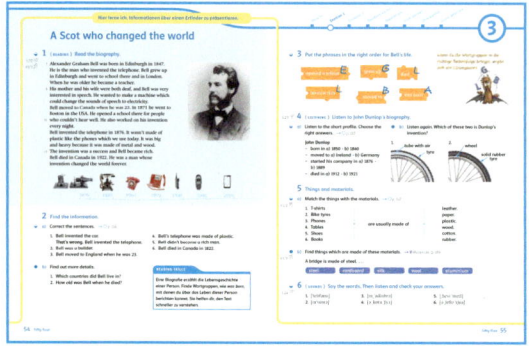

Stations

In jeder *Unit* gibt es zwei *Stations*,
in denen du viele neue Dinge lernst.
Diese Symbole zeigen dir, wie schwer
die Übung ist und ob es im Anhang
eine leichtere Variante gibt:

 → ○ p. 137, ●

In der *Your turn*-Aufgabe kannst du
zeigen, dass du alles verstanden hast,
und deine eigenen Ideen einbringen.

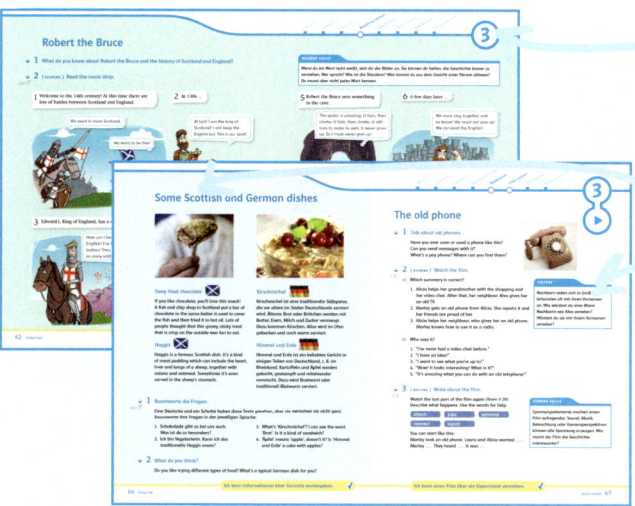

Reading corner

In der *Reading corner* gibt es verschiedene
Geschichten, Dialoge und andere Texte.

Mediation/Film corner

Auf der linken Seite geht es darum,
englische Informationen auf Deutsch
weiterzugeben oder umgekehrt.

In der *Film corner* geht es um einen
englischen Film.

Checkpoint

Auf dieser Seite kannst du überprüfen,
ob du in der *Unit* alles verstanden hast.
In der *Checklist* sind alle Lernziele noch
einmal aufgelistet.

Die Abschluss-Aufgabe (*task*) sollt ihr zu
zweit oder in der Gruppe lösen.

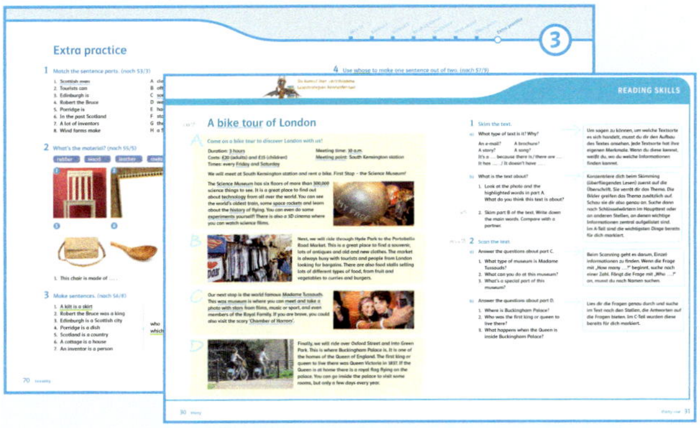

Extra practice

Hier findest du zwei Seiten mit Zusatz-Aufgaben, z. B. zur Vorbereitung auf die Klassenarbeit.

Skills

Auf einige *Units* folgt eine Doppelseite, auf der ihr eine bestimmte Fertigkeit (*skill*) besonders trainieren könnt, also z. B. das Lesen, Schreiben, Sprechen oder die Wörterbucharbeit.

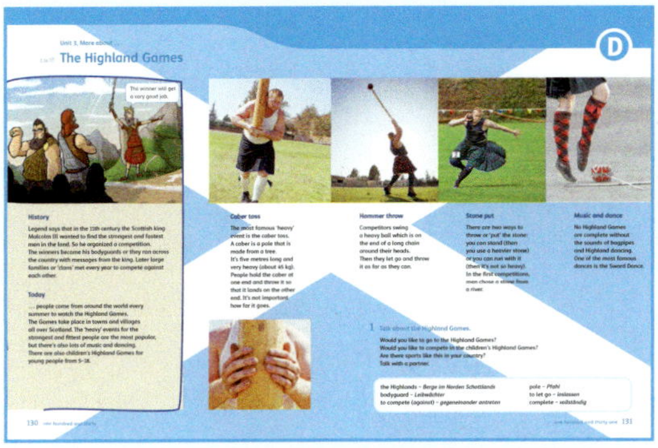

More about

Hier findest du interessante weiterführende Informationen zur Region der Unit.

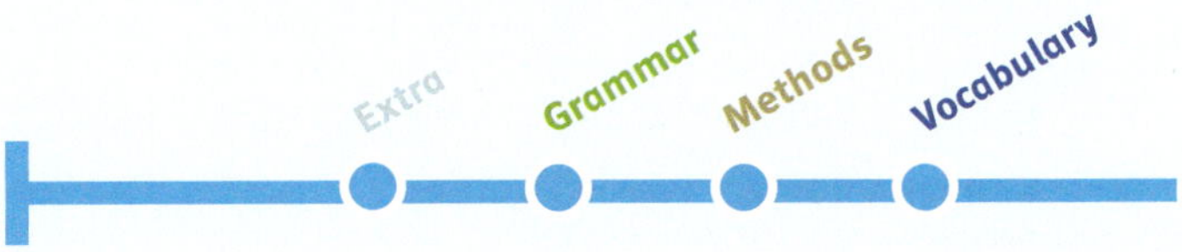

Im Anschluss an die fünf *Units* gibt es noch weitere nützliche Seiten:

Extra: Hier erwarten dich weitere Lesetexte: eine Geschichte, ein Theaterstück und vieles mehr.

Grammar: Hier findest du alle Regeln und Erklärungen zur Grammatik sowie weitere Übungen.

Methods: Manche Übungen könnt ihr auf eine bestimmte Art und Weise bearbeiten.
Das erkennt ihr an diesem Symbol: → M
Wie es genau funktioniert, kannst du hier nachlesen.

Vocabulary: Im *Vocabulary* findest du alle neuen Wörter in der Reihenfolge, in der sie in der *Unit* auftauchen, und die wichtigsten Arbeitsanweisungen.
Im *Dictionary* sind die Wörter noch einmal alphabetisch aufgelistet: zuerst Englisch–Deutsch und dann Deutsch–Englisch.

Am Schluss des Buches findest du noch
- Sätze, die du im Unterricht sagen kannst, z. B. bei der Gruppenarbeit
- Lösungen zu den Übungen der *Extra practice*-Seiten
- eine Liste mit den unregelmäßigen Verben

Symbol	Erklärung
○ ◒ ●	leicht/mittel/schwer (Niveaudifferenzierung)
✿	individualisierende Aufgabe (natürliche Differenzierung)
→ ○ p. 131	Verweis auf leichtere Parallelübung auf der *Diff corner*-Seite
OR	Aufgabe zur Auswahl (Wahldifferenzierung)
(Schlüssel)	Entwicklung von Schlüsselkompetenzen
P	Hier entsteht ein Produkt für das Portfolio.
4/1	Verweis auf eine Übung im *Workbook*
→ G13, p. 172	Verweis auf den Grammatikanhang (*Grammar*)
→ M	Verweis auf die Methodenseite (*Methods*)
→ V	Verweis zum Wortfeld im Vokabular (*Vocabulary*)
(Partner)	Partnerarbeit
(Gruppe)	Gruppenarbeit
(CD)	Verweis auf die Lehrer-CD (Audio)
(DVD)	Verweis auf die Lehrer-DVD (Film)
Find more online:	Code auf www.klett.de eingeben und Zusatzinformationen erhalten

Zoom in – The British Isles

The British Isles

Scotland

Northern Ireland

Republic of Ireland

England

Wales

- 🟠🟡🔵🟢🔴 The British Isles
- 🟡🔵🟢🔴 The United Kingdom (UK)
- 🔵🟢🔴 Great Britain (GB)

1 Do the British Isles quiz with a partner.

1. What are the names of the five countries of the British Isles?
2. Which is the biggest country in the United Kingdom (UK)?
3. Which is bigger, Northern Ireland or the Republic of Ireland?
4. Which is bigger, Scotland or Wales?
5. Which country is in the UK but not in Great Britain (GB)?
6. Which country has more people, Wales or Scotland?
7. Which is the biggest city in the UK?
8. Which country is not in the UK?
9. The Channel Tunnel goes from France to which country?

Sieh dir die Karte auf der Vorderseite an. Du kannst deine Antworten auf Seite 270 überprüfen.

England

Wales

Scotland

Northern Ireland

Ireland

1,1 🎧 **2** (LISTENING) **Listen to five teenagers from the British Isles.**

Make a table. Then listen and take notes.

Name	From?	Age?	Hobbies?	Plans?
Emily				
Dylan				
Lewis				
Sophie				
Patrick				

CULTURE

Die fünf Teenager kommen aus den verschiedenen Ländern der Britischen Inseln. Sie haben unterschiedliche Akzente. Welche Akzente findest du am einfachsten zu verstehen? Welche am schwierigsten?

⊕ Find more online:
fe76m3

1⎙ 1,2☞ ## Unit 1

England now and then

Stonehenge is an old stone circle in the south of England. It's more than **4,000 years old**. No one knows why it is there.

In **122** the Romans started to build **Hadrian's Wall** in the north of England. It took six years to build it.

1 **What's the oldest building or sight that you know?**

2 **Name the place.**

2/1-2 ⎘

1. There was lots of industry here during the Industrial Revolution. That's **Manchester**.
2. Some Vikings came to this town from Denmark in 866.
3. No one knows why this stone circle is there.
4. The Romans built this place in 122.
5. The Normans won a battle against the English there in 1066.

3

In **866** the Vikings invaded the English city of **York**. They came from Denmark, Norway and other countries. Some stayed in England and York became their home.

4

In **1066** the Normans came from France and invaded England. They won a battle against the English near **Hastings**. A Norman became king of England.

5

There was lots of industry in **Manchester** during and after the Industrial Revolution (**1780 – 1840**).
Now there are also shops, cafés and parks in the city.

---

 3 (LISTENING) **Stonehenge: Choose the right answers.**

1,3
2/3

1. The biggest stones weigh
   45 tonnes • 100 tonnes.
2. The biggest mystery is
   how old Stonehenge is • what Stonehenge was for.
3. Some people think the circle was
   a big clock • a big building.
4. Maybe people came there when they wanted to
   meet their friends • feel better.
5. Near Stonehenge there are
   graves • houses.

Diese Wörter helfen dir, den Hörtext zu verstehen.

tonne [tʌn] – Tonne
sun [sʌn] – Sonne
sick [sɪk] – krank
grave [greɪv] – Grab
million ['mɪljən] – Million

Ich kann Informationen über historische Orte in England herausfinden. ✔

Around York

1 Look at the pictures of York. What can you find in the city?

2 (READING) Read the dialogue.

1,4
3/1

1 **Sam:** Excuse me. I'm here on holiday. Do you know the way to the tourist information?
Mrs Jenkins: I do, but maybe I can help you. What are you interested in?
5 **Sam:** I would like to learn more about the history of the city.
Mrs Jenkins: Well, we are near the Viking Centre. It shows what the city was like about a thousand years ago. Just cross the road. After
10 that you can go to the tourist information. Walk past the post office and turn right at the end of the road. Then take the first road on the left.
Sam: OK. And do you know a good clothes shop?

15 **Mrs Jenkins:** Yes, I do. The best shops are on the Shambles. I often go there too. Why don't you go to the souvenir shop? It sometimes has cheap Viking helmets.
Sam: Brilliant! How do I get there?
20 **Mrs Jenkins:** That's easy. Turn right and walk down the road … it's on the left.
Sam: Is it far away?
Mrs Jenkins: No, it doesn't take long. It's just a five-minute walk.
25 **Sam:** Oh good. Thank you.
Mrs Jenkins: You're welcome.

3 Match the sentence parts.

1. The boy would like to know more about
2. The woman and the boy are very near
3. It shows what the city was like
4. The best shops are
5. The souvenir shop sometimes has
6. The souvenir shop is just

a five-minute walk away.
on the Shambles.
cheap Viking helmets.
the Viking Centre.
the history of the city.
about a thousand years ago.

4 (WRITING) Where can you buy these things?

a) Match the things with the right shops. Write them down. → ○ p. 112

3/2a)

 A   B   C    D   E

| shoe shop | clothes shop ✔ | card shop | baker's | sports shop |

1. You can buy jeans at the clothes shop. 2. You can buy …

b) Where can you buy these things? Copy the shopping list and complete it. → **V** Shops, p. 174

3/2b)

| newsagent's | greengrocer's |
| butcher's | pet shop |
| jeweller's |

Things to buy	Shop
sausages, ham	…
magazines, comics	…
fruit, vegetables, salad	…
…	…

5 (LISTENING) Find the way to the card shop.

1,5
3/3

a) Listen to the dialogue. Find the way on the map. Tell it to a partner.

| turn left | turn right |
| go straight on | walk past … |

b) What's the fastest way to the card shop? Tell a partner.

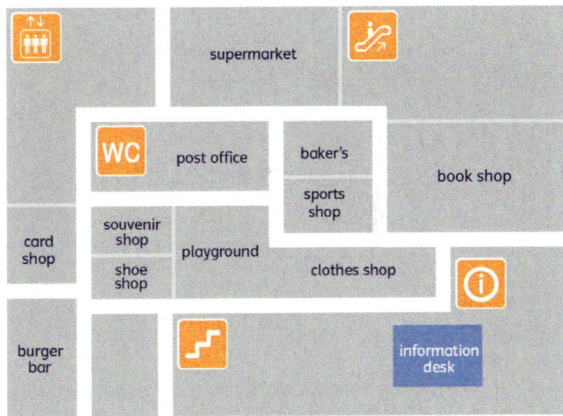

6 (SOUNDS) How quickly can you say this tongue twister?

1,6

Sharon sells shoes in the shoe shop. The shoes in the shoe shop aren't Sharon's size.

[s] [ʃ]

Language → G1, p. 150

Do you remember?

I often g<u>o</u> there.
It <u>doesn't take</u> long.
<u>Is</u> it far away?
<u>Do</u> you <u>know</u> a good clothes shop? - Yes, I do.

Schau dir die Sätze an. Welche Zeitform ist das? Wie wird sie gebildet?

7 **Complete the sentences with one of the verbs.**

He, she, it – das –s muss mit!

`go` ✔   `be (2x)`   `not arrive`   `have`   `prefer`

`wait`   `not like`   `meet`

1. I sometimes g<u>o</u> shopping with my friends at the weekend.
2. We always —— at 11 a.m.
3. My best friend usually —— before 11:30, but we always —— for him.
4. In the afternoon we often —— something to drink at a café.
5. My favourite shop —— The Busy Bookworm.
6. My friends —— it. They —— the sports shop.
7. Our favourite shops —— on the Shambles.

8 (SPEAKING) **Interview your partner.** → M Double circle, p. 167

a) Ask a partner. He or she answers. → ○ p. 112

A:				B:
	you		go to the cinema?	Yes, I do.
	your friends	sometimes	do your homework?	No, I don't.
Do +	they	+ often	+ play football?	Yes, he does.
Does	your dad	usually	watch TV?	No, he doesn't.
	he		go shopping?	Yes, they do.
				No, they don't.

b) Make more short dialogues. Use these words.

`buy clothes online`   `look for bargains`

`spend money on ...`   `get comics at a newsagent's`   `...`

A: Do you sometimes buy clothes online?
B: No, I don't. They don't usually fit.

9 (WRITING) Make questions.

a) Complete the dialogue. → ○ p. 112

5/6

1. (know) Do you know where the football stadium is? – Yes, I do.
2. (take) —— it —— long to get there? – Yes, it does. But there's a bus.
3. Where (be) —— the nearest bus stop? – It's just five minutes down that road.
4. When (leave) —— the buses ——? – I think it's every five minutes.
5. (be) —— bus tickets expensive? – No, they aren't. Just 90p.
6. Where (can) —— I buy a ticket? – On the bus.

b) Make three more questions and answers. Use the words for help.

> **toilets**   **food stalls**   **...**

Where are …? / Where can I find …?

✳10 (YOUR TURN) Directions → V Directions, p. 178

a) You are at X on the map. Work with your partner. Ask for directions to:

5/7

> **post office**   **swimming pool**   **café**   **...**

A: Excuse me, please. Is there a shoe shop near here?
B: Yes, there is. Go past the church. Then walk down the second street on the left. After that turn left. The shoe shop is opposite the cinema.
A: OK. Thanks for your help.
B: You're welcome.

> **turn right**   **go straight on**
> **cross the road**   **...**
> **left**   **next to the ...**   **...**

b) Present one of your dialogues in class.

> **Ich kann Wegbeschreibungen geben und verstehen.** ✔

Manchester and Bramford

1 (READING) **Read about where Hannah and Tom live.**

1,7
6/1

1 Hi! I'm Hannah and I'm from Manchester, in
the northwest of England. It's a large city with
more than half a million inhabitants. There's
lots of traffic. It's noisy too – I don't like that!
5 But there are many buses.

In the past Manchester had lots of industry.
There were dirty factories. There were coal
mines near Manchester too.

I live in a flat with my mum and my little
10 sister. It's in the centre of the city and it's very
small! Mum works in a supermarket. She often
has to work in the evening.

The best thing about Manchester? Football!
Manchester City is great!

My name is Tom and I live on a farm in   1
Bramford. That's a small village in the north
of England, near Hadrian's Wall. We used to
live in Newcastle, but my parents didn't like
the city. They wanted to live in the country.   5
Did they ask me? No, they didn't.

It's hard work on the farm. There are two
goats, Bert and Daisy, and a lot of cows.

It's quiet in the village. Only about 400
people live here. The country is boring, but   10
I like the animals on the farm!

The worst thing about our village? There
are only two buses a day. It's difficult to
see friends at the weekend! It's so unfair!

2 **Take notes about where they live.**

a) Make a table and put in the information.

	name of place	town, city or village?	where in England	good/bad things
Hannah	Manchester			
Tom				

b) What more can you remember? Close your book and write
one more sentence about Hannah and one about Tom.

3   Sort the words into groups.   → M Peer correction, p. 169

6/2   **a)   Copy the table. Put the words and phrases into the right groups.** → ○ p. 113

places	where	words for the size of places
village		

in the centre of	village ✔	miles away from	big

small	near	in the north/south/east/west of	town

large	city	in the mountains

b)   Add these words to your list.   → V Talking about places, p. 175

6/3

tiny	close to	a two-hour drive from	huge	on the coast

4   (SPEAKING)   Where would you like to live?   → M Think-pair-share, p. 171

6/4   **a)   Collect adjectives for the city and the country.**

city:	country:
exciting	…

b)   Talk with a partner.

A: I'd like to live in a city. Cities are exciting.
B: Yes, but they are noisy too!
    I'd like to live in the country.
A: Really? That's interesting.

town

quiet	small

near	in the mountains

That sounds boring/nice.

5   (SONG)   The City

1,8   Listen to the song. What does the singer think about his home?

1 This city never sleeps
   I hear the people walk by when it's late
   Sirens bleed through my windowsill
   I can't close my eyes
5 Don't control what I'm into
   This tower is alive
   The lights that blind keep me awake
   With my hood up and lace untied
   Sleep fills my mind
10 Don't control what I'm into

   London calls me a stranger
   A traveller
   This is now my home, my home
   I'm burning on the back street
15 Stuck here sitting in the backseat
   I'm blazing on the street
   What I do isn't up to you
   And if the city never sleeps
   Then that makes two

Language → G2, p. 151

Do you remember?

My parents <u>wanted</u> to live in the country.
They <u>didn't like</u> the city.

There <u>were</u> dirty factories.
<u>Did</u> they <u>ask</u> you?

Schau dir die Sätze an. Welche Zeitform ist das? Wie wird sie gebildet? Wann benutzt du sie?

7/5-6 **6** **Make Tom's story.**

a) Complete the sentences. → ◯ p. 113

1. Last Saturday morning things <u>went</u> a little crazy on our farm. (go)
2. I ⸺ a noise in the garden (hear) and I ⸺ . (get up)
3. I ⸺ my dad in the garden. (see)

4. He ⸺ to put Bert and Daisy, our goats, in his tractor. (want)
5. Suddenly he ⸺ in the mud, head first. (fall)
6. It ⸺ so funny. (be) I just ⸺ to laugh. (have)
7. Dad ⸺ very happy. (not be)

b) What happened next? Write an ending.

> shout at   be angry   help   . . .

7/7 **7** (WRITING) **What did Hannah and Kilkenny do on Saturday?**

a) Look at the pictures. Correct the sentences. → ◯ p. 113

1. Hannah walked to the baker's in the morning.

2. Hannah was in the living room at two o'clock.

3. Hannah did her homework in the afternoon.

4. She and her sister made jewellery at five o'clock.

5. Later she wrote a text message.

6. Hannah and her sister were at the cinema.

1. Hannah <u>didn't walk</u> to the baker's in the morning. She <u>watched</u> TV.

b) Look at the pictures again. What did Hannah's dog, Kilkenny, do?

Kilkenny <u>didn't watch</u> TV. He <u>played</u> with a ball.

8 (SPEAKING) **Talk to a partner about the weekend.** → M Milling around, p. 168

8/8-9

a) Make questions.

1. have • you • a nice weekend? • Did
   Did you have a nice weekend?
2. at home all weekend? • Did • stay • you
3. you • anything nice with your family? • Did • do
4. What • you • do together? • did
5. the weather like on Sunday? • What • was
6. did • What time • get home? • you
7. Were • tired on Sunday evening? • your parents

b) Talk to a partner. Use the questions from a).

> Did you have a nice weekend?

> Yes, I did, thanks! I visited my aunt and uncle.

| do your homework | go shopping |
| watch TV | be at home | … |

9 (YOUR TURN) **A short talk** → V Where I live, p. 179

Give a short talk about where you live.

9/1-2

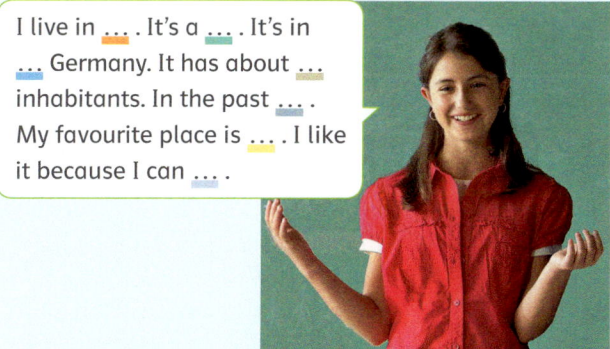

> I live in … . It's a … . It's in … Germany. It has about … inhabitants. In the past … . My favourite place is … . I like it because I can … .

name of place: Hamburg/…
size: small village/large town/city …
where: the north/the east/the south/ the west of …
number of inhabitants: 5,000/50,000/ a million/…
history: there was …/there were …/ we didn't have …/people worked in …/…
favourite place: cinema/…
what I can do there: play football/hang around/…

CULTURE

Auf englischen Straßenschildern stehen die Angaben für Entfernungen in Meilen (miles) statt in Kilometern. Eine Meile sind 1,6 Kilometer. Wie viele Meilen sind es von deinem Zuhause bis zur Schule?

Ich kann meinen Wohnort ausführlich vorstellen. ✔

A deadly silence

1 What do you know about Manchester – now and in the past? → M Think-pair-share, p. 171

2 (READING) Read the story.

1,9

The Rushy Park Coal Mine, near Manchester. September 1850

1.

1 My name is Jonas Fox. I'm twelve years old and I work in the
mines. I sit near a door in the tunnel every day. I open the door
when the coal arrives. Then I close the door again. I sit in the dark
every day, but I'm never scared because my friend Billy is there
5 with me. Billy sings all day long. He's yellow with black eyes. Billy
is a canary. I would love to sing too, but I can't even talk.

2.

Sometimes there is gas in the mine, and gas can explode. Last year
a gas explosion killed 30 miners and ten boys. A canary smells gas
sooner than a man. So when the canaries sing, the tunnels are
10 OK. But if they don't sing, there's gas in the mine. Everyone must
leave the tunnels very fast.

READING SKILLS

Dies ist eine längere Geschichte, aber sie ist in mehrere kurze Teile aufgeteilt. Lies dir jeden Teil kurz durch und versuche zu verstehen, worum es in diesem Teil der Geschichte geht.

Schau dir dann die Teile noch einmal genauer an und stelle **W**-Fragen. **Wer** kommt in diesem Teil der Geschichte vor?

Wo sind die Figuren, **was** passiert und **wann** passiert es?

3.
My brother, Bart, worked in the mine too. One day Bart started to cough. Bart coughed all the time after that. Soon he died. And I stopped talking. I don't know why, really. I
15 opened my mouth, but I couldn't speak. The men in the mine called me 'Silent Jonas' after that.

4.
Billy was singing like he always did. I heard the people in the tunnels and the noise of
20 the coal trucks. I opened the door. There was a cold wind in the tunnel. I closed the door. Billy stopped singing. There was gas in the mine!

5.
I had to tell everyone in the mine.
25 I opened my mouth and tried to say, "Gas." Nothing came out. I closed my eyes and opened my mouth again. Nothing. I had to speak! I tried again. This time I made a noise. I opened the door and suddenly
30 I could shout, "Gas. Gas. GAS!" A moment later I heard the miners in the tunnels. I took Billy's cage and ran too.

6.

I ran through the tunnel. My head hurt. I couldn't breathe in the gas. Suddenly I heard a voice. "Come
35 on, boy!" it said. One of the miners picked me up. He took me out of the mine. I had Billy's cage with me, but I was sure he was dead. At last we got out and I could breathe again.

7.

BOOM! The noise of the explosion was awful. My ears hurt.
40 I closed my eyes. Then I opened them again. I saw that the men and boys were all OK. A miner asked, "Who shouted?" "Me!" I said. They were so surprised! Then everyone said thank you. "Silent Jonas found his voice!" a miner shouted. But how could I feel happy? My friend Billy was dead. I
45 looked in his cage to say goodbye to him. Suddenly I heard a small 'Tweet'. Billy was alive! I opened the cage …

There were canaries in mines until 1987. Today miners use machines to find out if there is gas in the mine.

3 Did you like the story? Say why or why not.

| I liked/didn't like the story. | | I think the story was exciting/boring/interesting. |

| I like stories about the past. | | … |

4 Match each heading with a section of the story.

A Everything is OK if the canary sings.
B Gas in the mine!
C Jonas must find his voice.
D The explosion – and after
E Meet Jonas Fox – and Billy!
F Silent Jonas
G Can they get out?

5 Choose the right answer.

1. Jonas works in a **factory** • **mine**.
2. He is never scared because **his canary Billy** • **his brother Bart** is with him.
3. If the canary doesn't sing, **there's gas** • **there are people** in the mine.
4. When his brother died, Jonas **started** talking • **stopped** talking.
5. One day there was gas **in the mine** • **at home** and Billy stopped singing.
6. Jonas wanted to **tell everyone** • **run away** but he couldn't speak.
7. **Suddenly** • **A day later** Jonas shouted and the miners left the mine.
8. One of the miners took Jonas and Billy **out of the mine** • **into the tunnels**.

> **READING SKILLS**
>
> Du hast die Geschichte schon einmal gelesen, deshalb musst
> du dieses Mal nicht jedes Wort lesen.
> Schau dir jeden Teil kurz an. Lies genauer, wenn du die
> Informationen findest, nach denen du gesucht hast.

6 Look at the story again. Make a mind map about Jonas.

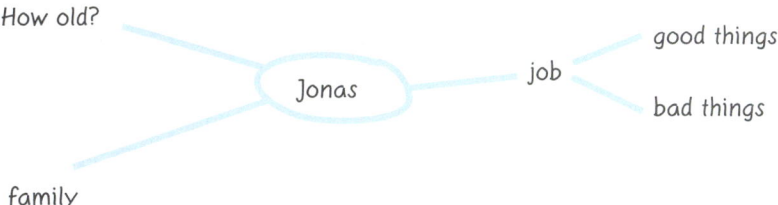

How old?

Jonas — job

good things

bad things

family

7 Choose one of these tasks.

10/1
11/2-4

a) Work in groups. Make freeze frames for
each part of the story. Let other groups
guess.

 OR

b) Work in groups. Practise the text.
Read it in class.
→ **M** Dramatic reading, p. 167

> **Ich kann eine Geschichte aus der Vergangenheit verstehen.** ✔

The history of football

INTERNET

Football now and then

1 Some people think the English invented football, but they didn't. More than 2,500 years ago the Chinese played a game with many similarities to football. Its name was cuju. The English did do one thing though: they wrote down the first
5 rules for the game.

Football was a popular sport in 19th-century England. When players from different schools played, there was one big problem: they all had different rules! For example, the players from Rugby School carried the ball; others used only their
10 feet. Players often disagreed about who won the game.

To make the game fair for everyone, they wrote down the rules. They were called the Cambridge Rules. The Football Association (FA) used these to make their own rules in 1863. This is when Association Football (called football in England
15 and soccer in the USA) and rugby became two different sports.

Nowadays it isn't just boys who play football in England. Many of the big English football clubs such as Arsenal, Liverpool and Chelsea have their own female teams and the
20 Women's National Team is one of the best in the world.

1 **Beantworte die Fragen.**

12/1-2

1. In welchem Land spielte man eine frühe Form von Fußball?
2. Warum wurde es nötig, die Fußballregeln niederzuschreiben?
3. Was erfährt man über Frauenfußball in England?

2 **What do you know about the history of football in Germany?**

Ich kann Informationen über die Geschichte eines Sports weitergeben. ✔

Girl from the past

1 **How did children live in Germany or England about 150 years ago?**

→ **M** Think-pair-share, p. 171

Think about these things.

work

school   children

home

CULTURE

Königin Viktoria war von 1837 bis 1901 britische Königin. Man nennt diese Zeit das „Viktorianische Zeitalter", und viele Gebäude in London stammen aus dieser Zeit. (Eine der wichtigsten Bahnhöfe in London ist z. B. Victoria Station.) Welche Königinnen kennst du?

Now watch the film. Was there anything new to you?

2 (VIEWING) **Watch the film.**

2 🎬

a) Which summary is correct?

1. Laura reads about the Victorian era in a book. Then she and Marley travel back in time.
2. Marley falls asleep in the library. He dreams that he meets a girl from the past.
3. Violet meets Laura in the library. Laura tells her about life in the 21st century.

b) Who says it?

1. I'd rather work than go to school.
2. I wish I could go to school!
3. Look, we've just travelled through time.
4. You've been asleep almost an hour.

Laura

Marley

Violet

3 (SPEAKING) **Talk about the film.**

a) Watch the film again from 1:30 to 3:25.

How does Marley feel?
First he is … .
Later he is … .
At the end he is … .

surprised   confused

happy   …

VIEWING SKILLS

Worte sind wichtig in einem Film, aber du solltest auch auf die Gesichter und die Körpersprache der Personen achten. Sie können dir viel darüber sagen, was passiert oder wie die Personen sich fühlen.

b) Would you like to travel back in time? Where would you like to go? Who would you like to meet?

Ich kann einen Film über Greenwich früher und heute verstehen. ✔

Checklist

Ich kann Informationen über historische Orte in England verstehen. ✔

13

Ich kann Wegbeschreibungen geben und verstehen. ✔

Excuse me. • Is there a shoe shop near here? • Go past the church. • Then walk down the second street on the left. • It's opposite the cinema. • Thanks for your help. • You're welcome.

13

Ich kann meinen Wohnort ausführlich vorstellen. ✔

I live in … . • It is a town/city/village. • It is in the north/south/… of Germany. • It has about … inhabitants. • In the past there was … .

14

Ich kann eine Geschichte aus der Vergangenheit verstehen. ✔

14

Ich kann Informationen über die Geschichte eines Sports weitergeben. ✔

15

Ich kann einen Film über Greenwich früher und heute verstehen. ✔

✿ (TASK) A film project

Work in groups of four to six students. Each group makes a short film about a sight in your home town or village.

Step 1

Collect ideas. → **M** Placemat, p. 169

First collect ideas and make a mind map of the sights you can film.

town hall
church
park
places
bus stop
café
swimming pool
?

Talk about the ideas. Choose a sight.
You can choose an old or a new sight or building.

Step 2

Find people for the different film jobs.

Who can:
- write 2–3 sentences about the sight?
- say the sentences (the presenter)?
- film the presenter and the sight?
- be a director?

STUDY SKILLS

Gib jeder Person die Möglichkeit zu sagen, welche Aufgabe sie gerne übernehmen oder nicht übernehmen möchte. Versucht euch in der Gruppe über eure Ideen für Drehbuch, Titel, Musik etc. zu einigen.

Step 3

Write the script and get ready.

a) Write two or three sentences about your sight.

b) Check the sentences and correct them if you need to.

c) The presenter must read the sentences in a clear voice. Practise this.
→ M Read and look up, p. 170

Step 4

Make your film.

Use a phone or a camera. Go to the sight and film the presenter there.
Wait until everyone is ready before you start, then say "Action!"
Make two or three versions ('takes') of the film. Keep cool if the presenter makes a mistake.

Step 5

Present your film.

Watch all the films together. Then make new groups.
The new group has one student from each film group.

Ask for feedback. Make a checklist like this.

Go back to the film group and look at the checklists. What would you do differently in your next film?
→ M Tip top, p. 171

Feedback checklist
The film is

O exciting   O easy to understand
O informative   O interesting
O fun   O not very interesting.

I like
O the presenter
O the …

Extra practice

1 Write the name of the places. (nach 11/3)

1. H — — — — — — — Wall

2. Y — — —

3. M — — — — — — ter

4. St — — — he — — —

5. H — — — — — — — —

2 Where do you go to . . . (nach 13/4)

1. buy bread?
2. buy some tennis balls?

3. look for a new coat?
4. buy a birthday card?

Which shop don't you need?

> sports shop card shop
> clothes shop shoe shop
> baker's

3 Write Ben's sentences. (nach 14/7)

> walk   fly   have   get up   eat   go

1. I never —— before 8 p.m.
2. I usually —— to different places.
3. But sometimes I also —— .
4. I always —— little animals for breakfast.
5. Cheese? No, I never —— that.
6. I usually —— to bed in the morning.

4 Do or Does? (nach 15/9)

1. Do / Does your friend sometimes buy T-shirts at the new clothes shop?
2. Do / Does you sometimes go shopping in the York Sweet Shop?
3. Do / Does they often play football after school?
4. Do / Does she usually buy bread at the baker's on the weekend?
5. Do / Does the new shoe shop always open at 10 p.m.?
6. Do / Does your family usually walk to the card shop?

5 Find the way. (nach 15/10)

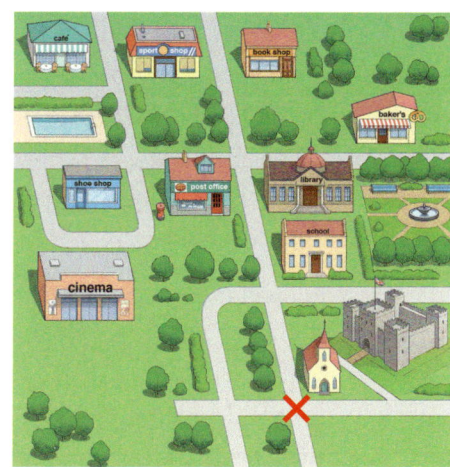

a) Start at the X on the map. Where do you go?

1. Walk down the second road on the left. It's on the right, opposite the shoe shop.
2. Walk down the first road on the right and walk past the school. It's on the left.
3. Go straight on and walk down the second road on the left. Turn right and then left. It's on the right.

b) Complete the sentences about the map.

1. The library is —— the baker's.
2. The church is —— the castle.
3. The school is on the —— of the first road on the right.
4. Go past the post office and —— the road. The shoe shop is on the —— .

6 Write sentences about Hannah. (nach 18/7)

| go + | meet + | get up – | go + | call – | go – |

1. Hannah —— at 9 a.m. So she was late.
2. She —— her friend on the bus.
3. They —— shopping and had lots of ice cream.
4. Hannah —— her mum at 4 p.m.
5. They —— back home at 5 p.m. Hannah's mum was angry.
6. So they —— to the cinema in the evening.

7 Write the questions. (nach 19/8)

1. you – forget – your mobile – Did   No, I forgot to call you. I'm sorry, mum.
2. a new T-shirt – Did – buy – you   No, I didn't like them.
3. to the library – you – Did – go   No, we met friends from school.
4. have – you – Did – a good time – together Yes, we had some ice cream. Yummy.
5. you – buy – cheese and tomatoes – Did   Yes, here you are.

Du kannst hier verschiedene Lesestrategien kennenlernen.

1,10

A bike tour of London

A

Come on a bike tour to discover London with us!

Duration: 3 hours
Costs: £20 (adults) and £15 (children)
Times: every Friday and Saturday

Meeting time: 10 a.m.
Meeting point: South Kensington station

We will meet at South Kensington station and rent a bike. First stop – the Science Museum!

The Science Museum has six floors of more than 300,000 science things to see. It is a great place to find out about technology from all over the world. You can see the world's oldest train, some space rockets and learn about the history of flying. You can even do some experiments yourself! There is also a 3D cinema where you can watch science films.

B

Next, we will ride through Hyde Park to the Portobello Road Market. This is a great place to find a souvenir, lots of antiques and old and new clothes. The market is always busy with tourists and people from London looking for bargains. There are also food stalls selling lots of different types of food, from fruit and vegetables to curries and burgers.

C

Our next stop is the world famous Madame Tussauds. This wax museum is where you can meet and take a photo with stars from films, music or sport, and even members of the Royal Family. If you are brave, you could also visit the scary 'Chamber of Horrors'.

D

Finally, we will ride over Oxford Street and into Green Park. This is where Buckingham Palace is. It is one of the homes of the Queen of England. The first king or queen to live there was Queen Victoria in 1837. If the Queen is at home there is a royal flag flying on the palace. You can go inside the palace to visit some rooms, but only a few days every year.

1 Skim the text.

a) What type of text is it? Why?

An e-mail?   A brochure?
A story?   A song?
It's a … because there is / there are …
It has … . / It doesn't have … .

> Um sagen zu können, um welche Textsorte es sich handelt, musst du dir den Aufbau des Textes ansehen. Jede Textsorte hat ihre eigenen Merkmale. Wenn du diese kennst, weißt du, wo du welche Informationen finden kannst.

b) What is the text about?

1. Look at the photo and the highlighted words in part A. What do you think this text is about?

2. Skim part B of the text. Write down the main words. Compare with a partner.

> Konzentriere dich beim Skimming (überfliegendes Lesen) zuerst auf die Überschrift. Sie verrät dir das Thema. Die Bilder greifen das Thema zusätzlich auf. Schau sie dir also genau an. Suche dann nach Schlüsselwörtern im Haupttext oder an anderen Stellen, an denen wichtige Informationen zentral aufgelistet sind. Im A-Teil sind die wichtigsten Dinge bereits für dich markiert.

19/1-4

2 Scan the text.

a) Answer the questions about part C.

1. What type of museum is Madame Tussauds?
2. What can you do at this museum?
3. What's a special part of this museum?

> Beim Scanning geht es darum, Einzelinformationen zu finden. Wenn die Frage mit „How many …?" beginnt, suche nach einer Zahl. Fängt die Frage mit „Who …?" an, musst du nach Namen suchen.

b) Answer the questions about part D.

1. Where is Buckingham Palace?
2. Who was the first king or queen to live there?
3. What happens when the Queen is inside Buckingham Palace?

> Lies dir die Fragen genau durch und suche im Text nach den Stellen, die Antworten auf die Fragen bieten. Im C-Teil wurden diese bereits für dich markiert.

⊕ Find more online:
fe76m3

Am Ende dieser Unit kann ich ...
- Informationen über Freizeitaktivitäten in Wales herausfinden.
- Informationen über eine Sportart präsentieren.
- den Rettungsdienst informieren.
- einen Bericht auf einer Schulwebsite verstehen.
- Informationen über eine Freizeitaktivität weitergeben.
- einen Film über ein Abenteuer in Wales verstehen.

3 🖥 1,11 ☞ Unit 2

Adventures in Wales

Bore da! –
Good morning!

1

Learn a language. Get ready and learn some Welsh!
We will read menus and road signs, and you will learn how
to get to know people.

2

Ride down a mountain. Mount Snowdon is the highe[st]
mountain in Wales (1,085 metres). The longest zip lin[e]
in Europe is near here. It's a mile long and you trave[l]
very fast! You can do skiing here too.

◖ **1** Look at the pictures.

20/1 ↗

a) Which activities would you /
wouldn't you like to do?

☺ I'd like to ... because ... .
☹ I wouldn't like to ... because I think ... .

b) Which activities do you do in your free time?

☺ I often/sometimes ... because ... .

◖ **2** (READING) Find the right words.

1. Canoeing and rafting are —— activities.
2. Cardiff is the —— of Wales.
3. We will read road —— .
4. Lifeboats help people in —— .
5. The highest mountain is —— .

Visit Cardiff Castle. The capital city of Wales is Cardiff. Visit Cardiff Castle in the city centre. It's almost two thousand years old! People often make films here too.

Try a water sport. Wales has a very long coast and many rivers, so you can try many different water sports. Canoeing and rafting are popular activities.

Be a volunteer. Lifeboats are very important in Wales. They help people in trouble at sea. The people on lifeboats are usually volunteers.

 3 (LISTENING) **Right or wrong?**

1,12
20/2

1. Teenagers learn Welsh until they are 15.
2. About 20 % of the Welsh people are fluent in Welsh.
3. A lot more people speak Welsh in the north and in the south.
4. There are no Welsh computer games.
5. The Welsh word 'plant' means children.

guest [gest] – Gast
fluent ['fluːənt] – fließend
plant [plɑːnt] – Pflanze
to mean [miːn] – bedeuten

Ich kann Informationen über Freizeitaktivitäten in Wales herausfinden. ✔

Outdoor activities

1 (READING) **Read the information.**

1,13

INTERNET

BLACK MOUNTAIN ACTIVITY CENTRE, POWYS, WALES
SUMMER ACTIVITIES

Take a canoeing trip on the river. We go slowly and the trip is six hours. We will have picnic lunch too.

If you like fast and tough sports, try rugby! It's a popular sport. We play in teams of girls and boys. You can learn the rules quickly.

The Welsh country is great for horse riding. Our team is friendly, and the horses are too!

We do outdoor rock climbing and we have an indoor wall – very good in wet Wales! You can borrow the equipment.

2 **Name the activities.**

21/1

a) Which activity is it?

1 **2**  **3**   **4**

b) Which activity …

1. … can you do on a wall?   2. … is with animals?   3. … is a water sport?   4. … is with a ball?

3 (READING) **Read the dialogue.**

1,14
21/2

1 **Beth:** I tried rugby myself for the first time last week. Why don't you come with me next time?
   Mark: Rugby? That's cool. But isn't it a tough sport? Are you big and strong enough for it?
5 **Beth:** Don't be cheeky! I'm small but I'm fit. I can run fast and I'm strong. I had lots of fun.
   Mark: *Rock climbing* is fun. I can climb quite well already. It isn't dangerous if you are careful, and you wear a helmet!
   Beth: No, thanks. I'm scared of heights. I'd like to try horse
10 riding.
   Mark: Horse riding? I did that last year and I hurt myself! That horse was dangerous!
   Beth: Oh dear! Well, you can go climbing and I'll try horse riding. We can tell each other about it later!

Language tip → G 3, p. 152
I hurt myself.

4 What is it?

a) Rugby, climbing or horse riding?

1. Mark thinks it's a tough sport.
2. Beth is scared of heights so she won't try this.
3. Mark hurt himself when he did this.

b) Which sports do Mark and Beth finally choose?

5 Find the words. → M Bus stop, p. 166

a) Find the opposites. → ○ p. 114

1. big ✔
2. slow
3. tough
4. friendly
5. strong
6. dangerous
7. wet
8. quiet

weak	unfriendly
dry	small ✔
easy	loud
safe	quick

b) Finish the sentences. → V Adjectives for sportspeople, p. 181

1. She can wait. She's very —— .
2. He's very tired. He's —— .
3. She has won lots of prizes. She's very —— .
4. He's going to be a star. He's young and —— .

| talented | patient |
| exhausted | successful |

6 (WRITING) Copy the text. Add the adjectives from the box. → M Peer correction, p. 169

21/3

Rafting is an interesting (1) sport for people from 12 to 99. Spend a —— (2) day on the river. Meet our —— (3) instructors and other —— (4) people. Rafting is —— (5) to learn but you won't stay —— (6). You'll love our —— (7) trips.

great	dry
interesting ✔	nice
exciting	easy
friendly	

WRITING SKILLS

Adjektive machen einen Text interessanter. Wenn du einen Entwurf schreibst, überlege:

Wo kannst du Adjektive ergänzen, um Personen oder Gegenstände zu beschreiben?

7 (SOUNDS) Listen, read and say.

1,15

Make a chart. Put the words into groups.

| popular ✔ | canoeing | adventure | difficult |
| equipment | interesting | instructor | horse riding |

Ooo	oOo
popular	…

→ G4, p. 153

Language detectives → G4, p. 153

Rugby is a <u>popular</u> <u>sport</u>.
You can <u>learn</u> the rules <u>quickly</u>.
We <u>go</u> <u>slowly</u> down the river.

Wann brauchst du die Endung <u>-ly</u>?

8 How did they do it? Complete the sentences.

22/4

1. I climbed the wall <u>slowly</u>. (slow)
2. We arrived —— . (safe)
3. The instructor called to us —— . (loud)
4. The rugby player ran —— . (quick)
5. The team won the game —— . (easy)
6. We rode our bikes —— . (careful)
7. They talked to each other —— . (quiet)

Sei vorsichtig bei Wörtern wie
careful und easy!
careful<u>ly</u>
easi<u>ly</u>

22/5-6
23/7

9 Complete the report.

a) Make adverbs. Add them to the text. → ◯ p. 114

| good | excited | fast | slow | heavy ✔ | hungry |

Last month Class 9G went on a camping trip to Snowdonia. It started to rain <u>heavily</u> (1) so we had to walk —— (2). At lunchtime we ate our picnics —— (3). On Sunday we went canoeing —— (4). We went down the river —— (5). Everything went —— (6) and no one got wet. Phew! We had lots of fun.

GRAMMAR → G4, p. 153

A <u>fast</u> game - she runs <u>fast</u>
A <u>hard</u> day - he works <u>hard</u>
A <u>good</u> song - they sing <u>well</u>

b) What does the coach tell the rugby team before the match? Make sentences. Use adverbs.

You have to play the ball quickly.
You have to …

| play | be | win | think |
| run | … |

| quick | good | clever |
| careful | fast | hard | … |

10 (WRITING) Adjective or adverb?

23/8

a) Complete the dialogue. → ○ p. 115

> Mark: Beth, how was horse riding today?
> Beth: It was **awful**/**awfully** (1). It was **wet**/**wetly** (2) and rained **terrible**/**terribly** (3).
> Mark: So you had to ride **careful**/**carefully** (4)?
> Beth: Yes, and there were lots of **crazy**/**crazily** (5) people on bikes too. Some of them rode **dangerous**/**dangerously** (6).
> Mark: Was your horse **nervous**/**nervously** (7) because of them?
> Beth: No, it wasn't. Look, here's a photo…

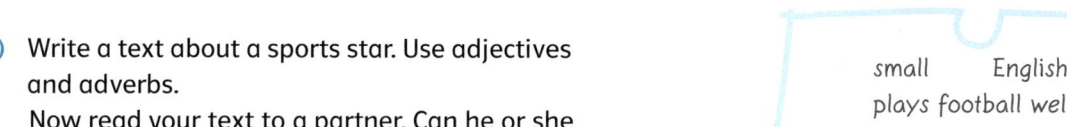

b) Write a text about a sports star. Use adjectives and adverbs.
Now read your text to a partner. Can he or she guess who it is?

> small   English
> plays football well
> runs fast   …

11 (YOUR TURN) A poster about your favourite activity or sport → V Sports and activities, p. 186

→ M Gallery walk, p. 168

a) Make a poster about your favourite sport or activity.
Make notes. Find more information. Add pictures.

– What's the sport like?
– What do you do?
– What must you be like?
– What equipment do you need?

b) Present your poster.

STUDY SKILLS

Schreibe deine Notizen auf Karten.
Übe, was du sagen willst, bevor du dein Poster präsentierst.
Sprich langsam und deutlich. Frage bei deinen Zuhörern nach, ob sie alles verstanden oder noch Fragen haben.

> Skiing is an exciting sport.
> It's easy. You can ski fast on beautiful mountains.
> You must be fit and careful.
> You can borrow equipment and special clothes.

Ich kann Informationen über eine Sportart präsentieren. ✔

Emergency on the beach

1 What do you do if you need help? Which number do you call?

2 (READING) Read the dialogue.

1,16

1 **Operator:** Hello, Emergency Services, which service?

Dylan: Hello, it's an emergency. I need an ambulance now! Please hurry!

5 **Operator:** OK, please wait a moment.

Janet: Hi, this is Janet from North Wales Ambulance Service. What's the problem?

Dylan: There's a man on the beach. His head is bleeding badly and his leg is too.

10 **Janet:** Tell me slowly what has happened.

Dylan: He has just had an accident. Maybe he fell over on the rocks. I think he has broken a leg.

Janet: OK, where are you?

Dylan: I'm on the north beach in Llandudno. 15

Janet: Good, the ambulance is coming. Is the man awake?

Dylan: Yes, he is.

Janet: Can you give me your name and your phone number, please? 20

Dylan: Dylan Adams. 07810 460 228.

Janet: Listen, Dylan. Stay with the man. The ambulance should arrive very soon. You've done the right thing.

Dylan: Thanks. Bye. 25

3 Right or wrong?

1. Dylan needs the police.
   That's wrong.
2. The man has hurt his head.
3. He has a problem with his leg too.
4. Dylan is on the south beach.
5. Dylan's family name is Thomas.
6. Dylan should stay with the man.

4 (LISTENING) Look at the list and listen.

1,17

Which of these things does the caller *not* say?

A good emergency call	
1. Say which service you need.	✔
2. Say what has happened.	☐
3. Say where you are.	☐
4. Give your name and phone number.	☐

CULTURE

In Großbritannien ist die Notrufnummer (Polizei, Feuerwehr, Krankenwagen oder Küstenwache) die 999. Man kann aber auch immer die 112 anrufen. Welche Nummer wählst du im Notfall in Deutschland?

5 (WRITING) **Match the sentences. Look at the pictures for help.**

24/1-2

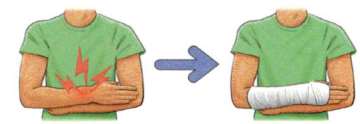

1. I've cut my finger. ✔

2. My tooth hurts.

3. You've broken your arm.

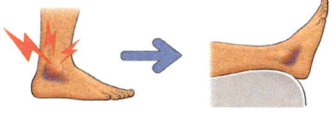

4. I've twisted my knee.

5. She's burnt her finger.

6. He's sprained his ankle.

A You need a cast.   B I'll put a bandage on it.   C Cool it with water.

D Take this tablet.   E Don't move it.   F Here's a plaster. ✔

24/3 **6** (SPEAKING) **Find excuses. Why can't you do PE?**

a) Make sentences. → ◯ p. 115

I'm so sorry. I can't do PE today. My head hurts
terribly. I have a sore throat too. I've also
twisted my knee. ...

I have cut ...   I have burnt ...

I have broken ...   My ... is bleeding

...

SPEAKING SKILLS

Wenn du sprichst, kannst du deine Stimme, dein Gesicht
und deine Hände benutzen. Das kann dir helfen, dich
besser verständlich zu machen.

b) What do you need? Add more sentences. → V Health and medicine, p. 182

I'm so ill. I think I need ... / Please bring me ...

some sleep   some medicine   a cuddly toy   an injection   an operation

Language → G5, p. 154

Do you remember?

He <u>has had</u> an accident.
He <u>has broken</u> his leg.
You've <u>done</u> the right thing.
What <u>has happened</u>?

Welche Zeitform ist das?
Wie bildest du sie?
Wie und wann benutzt du sie?

---

7 **What has happened? Make sentences.**

25/4

1. burn • hand

2. cut • finger

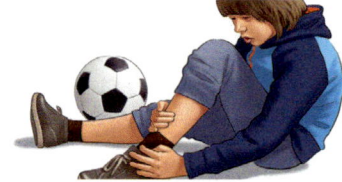

3. twist • ankle

4. break • leg

5. hit • head

6. have • accident

1. He <u>has burnt</u> his hand.

25/5 **8** (WRITING) **What has Megan already done? What hasn't she done yet?**

a) Make sentences. → ○ p. 115

What she has already done:
Put on her uniform
Open the door
Have lunch
Write a message

What she hasn't done yet:
Collect the bandages
Drink tea
Call the hospital

Megan <u>has</u> already <u>put on</u> her uniform.

b) Look at the picture again. Make more sentences.
Use <u>already</u> and <u>not yet</u> and the words from the right.

put on boots • close the window •
put on the helmet • get a torch

9 (SPEAKING) **Make dialogues.**

a) **Complete the dialogue with a partner.** → ○ p. 116

26/6

Kim: Hey, I —— your brother at football training last Monday. (not see) What's wrong with him?
Jamie: He —— in hospital last week. (be)
Kim: Oh, I'm sorry. He —— already —— his leg this year, right? (hurt)
Jamie: Yes, last time he and his friend —— to try some new cool skateboard tricks. (want)
Kim: When —— he —— home? (come)
Jamie: My parents —— just —— him back from the hospital. (bring)
Kim: That's great. —— his friend already —— the good news? (hear)
Jamie: No, I —— him yet. (not call)
Kim: OK, I'll have to go. See you.

Du musst dich hier zwischen dem simple past und dem present perfect entscheiden.
Die Signalwörter können dir helfen.

choose!

b) **Talk to a partner.**

26/7-8

Partner A:
Have you ever been in hospital?
Have you ever had an operation?
Have you ever had a cast?
When did it happen?
What happened? Where did it happen?
What was the problem?

Partner B:
Yes, I have been in hospital. / No, I haven't …
It happened in May/August/… .
It was on Monday/Tuesday/… .
It was on 23rd June.
…

✳10 (YOUR TURN) **A role play: Emergency!** → V Emergency, p. 187

27/1-2

1. Work with a partner. Write a list like this. Add your own ideas.
2. Exchange your list with another pair.
3. Practise the emergency call. Look at the checklist for help.
4. Act the role play.
5. Give feedback to the other pairs.
   → M Tip top, p. 171

Who? Lena
Where? In the swimming pool
How? fallen over
What's the problem? Arm

Ich kann den Rettungsdienst informieren. ✔

A trip to a Caldicot Castle

○ **1** Have you ever been to a castle? What castles do you know?

○ **2** (READING) Read the report.

1,18

YEAR 9 AT CALDICOT CASTLE

Story by school reporter Richard 'the Lionheart' Smith.

1 ### Castle of history

On a sunny Tuesday morning Year 9 visited
Caldicot Castle in Wales. When we arrived, we
saw that Caldicot Castle is a big building. It is
5 a stone castle and it is over 900 years old.
I said, "Wow, this castle is even older than
Mr Yeates, our History teacher!"
Everyone laughed. Mr Yeates didn't. ☹

Castle of adventure

We jumped when a big door opened 10
loudly. A knight came out of a cloud of
smoke!
He said, "I am Lancelot, a knight of this
castle. I travelled in time to tell you
kids about the castle." The castle had 15
dark corridors and tall towers. It was a
real adventure.
(I don't think Lancelot really was a
knight from the past - I saw him with a
mobile phone!) 20

○ **3** Find the information.

1. Who went on the trip?
2. When did they go?
3. Where did they go?

4. Who told them about the castle?
5. What did knights learn at 'knight schools'?
6. What did they do in the end?

READING SKILLS

Bevor du anfängst zu lesen, schaue dir die zwei Seiten an und überlege. Was für eine Art Text ist es? Wer könnte den Text geschrieben haben?

Für wen könnte der Text geschrieben worden sein? Können dir die Fotos helfen, den Text zu verstehen?

How to joust

Lancelot showed us how to put on armour and hold a sword (not a real one but still very heavy!). It made you feel like a real knight. It was the best!
The jousting was super cool and we all tried it. Even Ellie could do it in her wheelchair. In the old days there was a 'knight school' at the castle, and the knights learned how to joust there. When they were naughty, the knights had to go to the stocks!
We saw some real jousting. That was cool!

25

30

Lancelot goes back to the past

In the late afternoon we'd seen everything in the castle.
Lancelot said it was time for him to return to the past (I hope he remembered to take his phone!)
Before we left, Mr Yeates wanted to see the stocks. Why did he want to see them? Did he want something like that at our school?

35

No, of course he didn't. But we tried them out for fun and we took this photo as a souvenir.
We all loved the trip and learned lots about Caldicot Castle!

40

4 Choose one of these tasks.

28/1
29/2-4

a) Make a sound diary for the castle trip. Collect, make and record the sounds.

Play the recording to your class - can they guess the sounds?

 OR

b) Draw a plan of a castle you know. Label it in English and add some information (how old?, who lived there?, … ?)

Ich kann einen Bericht auf einer Schulwebsite verstehen.

The ride of your life!

Dos and Don'ts at Zip World

1 Zip World in Snowdonia has the fastest zip line in the world and the longest in Europe. And YOU can ride it! Get ready for the ride of your life!

DO wear the equipment we give you. It keeps you safe. The
5 helmet and goggles protect your head and eyes, and the red suit protects your skin, but also makes you travel more quickly!

DO listen to what your instructor says. You will get important information.

DO wear warm clothes and bring some gloves. Even if the weather is sunny, you will feel very
10 cold on the zip line.

DO check the website before you come. If the weather is bad (for example if it is raining heavily or is very windy), the zip line may not be safe and we may close it. You will get your money back.

DO book a place. If you don't, you may have to wait a long time.

15 DON'T wear sandals or flip flops. If you lose a shoe, we will not find it for you!

DON'T be afraid if you change your mind. We want you to have fun, and if you change your mind and don't want to ride, just let us know.

1 Beantworte die Fragen.

30/1-2

1. Welche Sicherheitsausrüstung gibt es?
2. Welche Kleidung solltest du tragen?
3. Was passiert bei schlechtem Wetter?
4. Was passiert, wenn du doch nicht mehr damit fahren willst?

2 Would you like to try an activity like this?

Would you like to try it? Say why or why not.
Have you ever done an activity like this (hot air balloon? roller coaster?) Talk about it.

Ich kann Informationen über eine Freizeitaktivität weitergeben. ✔

The briefcase

1 Look at the photo and guess.

Why are Laura and Alicia at the beach?
What time of the year is it?
Why is there a briefcase?
What's in it?

Now watch the film and check. Were you right?

2 (VIEWING) Watch the film. Right or wrong?

1. After the girls and Mr Becket had lunch, the girls go shopping.
2. A man answers his phone and then leaves his briefcase on the beach.
3. The girls cannot open the briefcase.
4. The man from the beach runs after the girls.
5. The girls find out that the briefcase is only a prop for a film.

> **CULTURE**
>
> Es gibt unterschiedliche Strände in Wales – wenn du Surfer bist, findest du im Westen perfekte Bedingungen. Aber es gibt auch Strände, wo du Seehunde und sogar Delfine beobachten kannst! Würdest du gerne an einen dieser Strände fahren?

3 (SPEAKING) Talk about the film.

Watch the last part of the film again (from 2:56).
Do you like the ending? Give reasons.

☺	☹
I like the ending because it's funny/... . I expected ... . I thought	I don't like the ending because it's boring ... . I expected something different. I thought ... .

> **VIEWING SKILLS**
>
> In jedem guten Film gibt es einen Wendepunkt.
> Das ist der Moment, in dem sich die Handlung plötzlich ändert.
> Was ist der Wendepunkt in diesem Film?

Ich kann einen Film über ein Abenteuer in Wales verstehen. ✔

Checklist

Ich kann Informationen über Freizeitaktivitäten in Wales verstehen. ✔

31

Ich kann Informationen über eine Sportart präsentieren. ✔

… is an exciting sport. • It's quite easy. • You can learn the rules quickly. • You must wear a helmet.

31

Ich kann den Rettungsdienst informieren. ✔

It's an emergency! • I need an ambulance. • I think he has broken a his leg. • His head is bleeding. • She's burnt her hand.

32

Ich kann einen Bericht auf einer Schulwebsite verstehen. ✔

32

Ich kann Informationen über eine Freizeitaktivität weitergeben. ✔

33

Ich kann einen Film über ein Abenteuer in Wales verstehen. ✔

(TASK) A photo story

Work in groups of three or four students. Each group makes a photo story. The groups can use the computer to make their stories as posters. Each group presents its story and gets feedback from the other groups.

Step 1

Find a good story.

Collect ideas and pictures. Your story can be about:
- a sport
- an emergency
- a trip
- …

Your pictures should have the same style. Don't mix comics with real life pictures. (You can also take your own photos.)

> **STUDY SKILLS**
>
> Wenn du mit einem Computer arbeitest, speichere deine Dateien in einen Ordner. Benenne die Dateien und den Ordner sinnvoll.

Step 2

Make a plan.

Put the pictures in a good order.
Remember:
Your story must have a beginning,
a middle and an ending.

> **STUDY SKILLS**
>
> Es gibt spezielle Computerprogramme,
> die dir helfen können, deine Fotos zu einer
> Geschichte zusammenzusetzen. Frage
> deinen Informatiklehrer, wenn du Hilfe
> brauchst.

Step 3

Add texts to your pictures.

You can have speech bubbles and / or captions.

The next day …

Hey! That's so cool!

Step 4

Check your draft. → **M** Peer correction, p. 169

Does it have all the important information? Check the spelling.
Ask a friend to read the story. What advice can he or she give you?

Step 5

Write the clean copy of your draft.

The clean copy should have no mistakes. Write or type as carefully as you can!

Step 6

Present your story to the other groups and get feedback. → **M** Tip top, p. 171

Which story was the best and why?

Extra practice

1 What's the word? (nach 34/1)

1. Cardiff is the … city of Wales. capital ✔
2. These are water sports.
3. You read them when you are in a car.
4. These can help people at sea.
5. A tough sport which is popular in Wales
6. You must know them when you play a game.
7. They don't get money for their work.
8. Not indoor
9. Not a good sport for you when you're scared of heights

a) canoeing, rafting
b) capital ✔
c) rock climbing
d) volunteers
e) lifeboats
f) outdoor
g) road signs
h) rugby
i) rules

2 What did the rock climbing instructor say? Adjective or adverb? (nach 37/10)

Good morning everybody! Now listen **careful** • carefully (1), please. Mark, if you talk **loud** • **loudly** (2), no one can hear me! The weather is **good** • **well** (3) for climbing today. We'll work **hard** • **hardly** (4) in the morning. Then we'll do some **easy** • **easily** (5) rock climbing in the afternoon. But please remember the rules: Always climb **slow** • **slowly** (6). You must be **careful** • **carefully** (7) if the rock is **wet** • **wetly** (8). I'm sure we'll have fun and you'll be **tired** • **tiredly** (9) this evening!

3 Match the parts of the dialogue. (nach 38/4)

1. Hello, Emergency Services, which service?
2. Hello, this is Sarah from Cardiff Ambulance Service. What's the problem?
3. Tell me slowly what has happened.
4. OK, where are you?
5. Right, the ambulance is coming.
6. Can you give me your name and phone number, please?
7. Listen, Pete. Stay with the girl. The ambulance should arrive soon.

A Great.
B I'm in East Street, near the bus stop.
C Of course. I'll wait here.
D She's just had an accident. She's fallen off her bike.
E There is a girl on the road. She's bleeding and …
F This is an emergency. I need an ambulance!
G Pete Brown. 077 386 941 23.

4 Write about accidents. (nach 39/5)

a) First write the words.

1. have an a ——
   have an <u>accident</u>
2. b —— my arm
3. cut my fi ——

4. twist my k ——
5. burn my f ——
6. sprain my an ——

b) Make sentences.

1. I've had an accident.
2. I've ... .

5 What have the people done? What haven't they done yet? (nach 40/8)

1

buy some tablets
not take them

2

burn his hand
not cool it

3

twist her knee
not put a bandage on
it

4

go to the doctor
not see the doctor

1. Claire <u>has bought</u> some tablets. She <u>hasn't taken</u> them yet.
2. Nick ... .   3. Molly ... .   4. Joe ... .

6 Complete the text. (nach 41/9)

Megan loves outdoor activities and sports. She
<u>has already tried</u> many things (1 already / try).
She —— (2 start) to play tennis when she
—— (3 be) ten years old. Two years ago she ——
(4 ride) her bike up Mount Snowdon. But
canoeing is her favourite and she ——
(5 already / win) lots of prizes. Last year she ——
(6 have) an accident and —— (7 break) her arm.
But it —— (8 get) better quickly and she ——
(9 already / be) on the river again this year. ——
(10 you / ever / go) canoeing?

The Baker – an interesting film?

1,19

Review 1 ★★★★☆

I really enjoyed *The Baker*.

This comedy has an interesting story about a murderer who runs away from London. He goes to Wales to hide when he has some problems. He becomes the town's new baker so he quickly has to learn how to make cakes and bread. No one knows his secret until his enemy arrives. The film finishes with a big, funny fight.

The stars are brilliant. The actors who play the Welsh people in the town are really funny. The location is very beautiful. There is also a great love story in the film.

Go and see this film! I give it four stars.

1. Introduction

2. Content

3. The writer's opinion

4. Conclusion

Review 2 ★☆☆☆☆

The Baker is one of the worst films I have ever seen.

It is the story of a murderer who gets a job wrong, so he moves to a small town in Wales and becomes a baker. Of course, he falls in love with a beautiful Welsh woman and doesn't want to be a murderer again, but the other people in the town find out his secret.

It is a really boring story and the film is very slow. The actors aren't very good and the ending is awful. It is a comedy, but it is more silly than funny.

Give this film a miss! I only give it one star.

Giving your opinion:

+

I really enjoyed this film.
This is one of the best films I've ever seen.
Go and see this film!
I give it four or five stars.

−

I didn't enjoy this film.
This is one of the worst films I've ever seen.
Give this film a miss!
I give it one or two stars.

1 Look at the first review.

Match these sentences with the parts of the review.

A The writer gives reasons why he or she likes the film.
B The writer rates the film and gives advice.
C The writer talks about the story of the film.
D The writer says which film he or she is writing about.

> Filmkritiken geben die persönliche Meinung des Verfassers wieder.
> Die Kritiken folgen stets demselben Aufbau. Sieh dir dazu das Beispiel an.

2 Read the second review.

1. Does the writer like the film or not? Why?
2. Find the parts of the structure in review 2.

> Um herauszufinden, wie die Meinung des Verfassers ist, sieh dir die Bewertungen an und achte auf die Wortwahl.

36/1-2
37/3

3 Write a film review.

a) Think about the last film you saw. Make notes about the story, actors and location.

The actors are … . The stars are … .
This film is a comedy / drama / romance.
The story / location / start / ending is … .

> Erstelle zuerst eine Stichwortsammlung zu allem, was dir zu diesem Film einfällt.

b) Write a draft of the review. Give the film a star rating.

> Wenn du deinen ersten Entwurf schreibst, beachte die richtige Reihenfolge. Eine Checkliste kann dir dabei helfen. Denke an das simple present.

c) Look at the review again. Where can you add some adjectives?

d) Write a clean copy of the review.

> Mache deine Kritik interessanter und benutze Adjektive, die deine Meinung unterstützen.

e) Read a partner's review and give feedback. Would you like to see the film he or she has written about?

> Wenn du die Filmkritik deines Partners oder deiner Partnerin gelesen hast, gib ihm oder ihr Feedback. War der Aufbau der Kritik in Ordnung? Hat die Kritik den Film gut erklärt? Ist die Meinung zu dem Film deutlich herausgekommen?

Find more online:
fe76m3

5 1,20

Unit 3

Made in Scotland

1

The capital of Scotland is Edinburgh. It is a very old city. Lots of inventors were born and worked in Edinburgh.

2

Robert the Bruce was born in 1274. Robert often fought against the English. Today Scotland is a part of the United Kingdom, but in the past it had its own king or queen.

1 What do you know?

a) Before you read, look at the pictures. What can you see? Talk to a partner.

I can see ... / There is ... / There are ...

b) Read the texts. What else can you find out?

| people | clothes | music |

| weather | food |

2 Right or wrong?

40/1-2

1. Many inventors were born in Edinburgh. **That's right.**
2. Robert the Bruce was born in 1375.
3. Scotland had a king or queen.
4. Scotland isn't a windy place.
5. Tourists can't stay in cottages.
6. A kilt is a skirt for men.

3

Scotland doesn't have much sun but it is a windy place. Now Scotland gets lots of clean electricity from wind farms.

4

Scotland has some beautiful mountains and lakes. Tourists can stay in modern cottages and enjoy the countryside.

5

There are lots of Scottish traditions, like the bagpipes and the kilt, a skirt for men. Scots often eat porridge for breakfast, a warm dish with oats and milk

3 (LISTENING) **Listen to the interview at Whitelee Wind Farm.**

1,21

Finish the sentences.

1. We're one of the —— wind farms in the UK.
2. Some turbines are 110 metres, others are —— metres tall.
3. Wind farms are important because they make —— electricity.
4. Are the turbines dangerous for —— ?
5. We have a special —— to protect them.

> (wind) turbine [ˈtɜːbaɪn] – Windrad
> to protect [prəˈtekt] – schützen
> nature [ˈneɪtʃə] – Natur
> dangerous [ˈdeɪndʒrəs] – gefährlich

Ich kann Informationen über Schottland herausfinden.

A Scot who changed the world

1 (READING) **Read the biography.**

1,22
41/1

1 Alexander Graham Bell was born in Edinburgh in 1847.
He is the man who invented the telephone. Bell grew up
in Edinburgh and went to school there and in London.
When he was older he became a teacher.

5 His mother and his wife were both deaf, and Bell was very
interested in speech. He wanted to make a machine which
could change the sounds of speech to electricity.
Bell moved to Canada when he was 23. In 1871 he went to
Boston in the USA. He opened a school there for people

10 who couldn't hear well. He also worked on his invention
every night.
Bell invented the telephone in 1876. It wasn't made of
plastic like the phones which we use today. It was big
and heavy because it was made of metal and wood.

15 The invention was a success and Bell became rich.
Bell died in Canada in 1922. He was a man whose
invention changed the world forever.

1876   1920   1960   1970   1980   2000   2010

2 **Find the information.**

a) Correct the sentences. → ○ p. 116

1. Bell invented the car.
   That's wrong. Bell invented the telephone.
2. Bell was a builder.
3. Bell moved to England when he was 23.

4. Bell's telephone was made of plastic.
5. Bell didn't become a rich man.
6. Bell died in Canada in 1822.

b) Find out more details.

1. Which countries did Bell live in?
2. How old was Bell when he died?

READING SKILLS

Eine Biografie erzählt die Lebensgeschichte
einer Person. Finde Wortgruppen, wie *was born*,
mit denen du über das Leben dieser Person
berichten kannst. Sie helfen dir, den Text
schneller zu verstehen.

3 Put the phrases in the right order for Bell's life.

opened a school **E**

grew up **G**

died **L**

became rich **L**

moved to **B**

was born **A**

Wenn du die Wortgruppen in die richtige Reihenfolge bringst, ergibt sich ein Lösungswort.

1,23 **4** (LISTENING) **Listen to John Dunlop's biography.**

a) Listen to the short profile. Choose the right answers. → ○ p. 117

John Dunlop
– born in a) 1850 • b) 1840
– moved to a) Ireland • b) Germany
– started his company in a) 1876 • b) 1889
– died in a) 1912 • b) 1921

b) Listen again. Which of these two is Dunlop's invention?

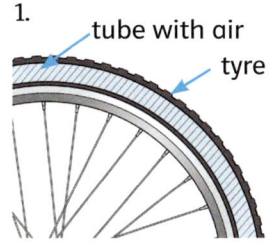

1.
tube with air
tyre

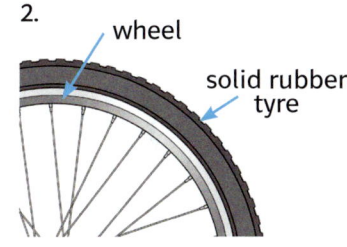

2.
wheel
solid rubber tyre

5 Things and materials.

41/2 a) Match the things with the materials. → ○ p. 117

1. T-shirts
2. Bike tyres
3. Phones
4. Tables
5. Shoes
6. Books

are usually made of

leather.
paper.
plastic.
wood.
cotton.
rubber.

41/3 b) Find things which are made of these materials. → **V** Materials, p. 189

A bridge is made of steel. ...

steel   cardboard   silk   wool   aluminium

6 (SOUNDS) Say the words. Then listen and check your answers.

1,24
1. [ˈtelɪfəʊn]
2. [ɪnˈventə]
3. [ɪnˌədinbrə]
4. [əˌkɒtn ˈʃɜːt]
5. [ˌhevi ˈmetl]
6. [əˌleθə ˈtʃeə]

Language detectives → G6, p. 155

Bell is the man who invented the telephone.
The school was for people who couldn't hear well.
He wanted to make a machine which could change the sounds of speech.
His telephone wasn't like the phones which we use today

Wann benutzt du who, wann benutzt du which?

---

7 **Match the sentence parts. Describe people and things.**

42/4

1. T-shirts and jeans are clothes
2. An inventor is a person
3. Dunlop was an inventor
4. A machine is something
5. Scots are people
6. Scotland is a country
7. Cars and bikes have tyres

+ which
who +

has had a lot of inventors.
are made of rubber.
made a tyre with air in it.
come from Scotland.
are usually made of cotton.
helps people with their work.
has ideas and makes new things.

---

8 (SPEAKING) **Talk about people and things.** → M Bus stop, p. 166

42/5

a) Ask your partner. Can he or she find the person or thing? → ○ p. 118

1. It's a thing —— goes on the wheel of a bike or car.
2. It's a person —— feeds animals at the zoo.
3. It's a person —— is the first player in a team.
4. It's a thing —— tells you the time.
5. It's a person —— works with machines.
6. It's a thing —— you use to cut food.

Du kannst that in Sätzen wie diesen benutzen:
It's a thing that … .
It's a person that … .

1. A: It's a thing which goes on the wheel of a bike or car.
   B: Is it a tyre?
   A: That's right!

b) Choose one of these pictures. Describe it. Can your partner guess what or who you are thinking of?

1  **2**  **3**

4  **5**  **6**

It's a person … / It's a thing …

9 Make sentences about Bell and Dunlop.

a) Use <u>whose</u> to make one sentence out of two. → ○ p. 118

43/6

1. Dunlop was an inventor.
   His invention made the bike better.
2. Bell was a teacher.
   His mother and wife were both deaf.
3. He was one of many Scottish inventors.
   Their work made Scotland famous.

> **GRAMMAR** → **G6**, p. 155
>
> Dunlop was an inventor <u>whose</u> <u>invention</u> made the bike better.

b) Choose <u>who</u> or <u>whose</u>?

43/7

1. People —— inventions are successful often become rich.
2. There are lots of Scots —— don't live in Scotland.

❋10 (YOUR TURN) A short biography → V Inventors and inventions, p. 193

a) Here are three inventions. Choose one. Find information in the library or on the internet.
Write a short biography of its inventor. Add photos. → M Writers' conference, p. 171

43/8

1 steam engine   2 blue jeans   3 light bulb

These phrases can help you to write your biography:

He / She was born in (place) in (year).   He / She grew up in ... .
He / She is the person who invented ... .   He / She died in (place) in (year).
It is a thing which ... . It is / was made of ... .

> **WRITING SKILLS**
>
> Eine kurze Biografie behandelt die wichtigsten Fakten aus dem Leben einer Person.
> Schreibe sie in chronologischer Reihenfolge auf. Sage auch, was an diesem Menschen
> besonders ist. Benutze das simple past.

b) Present your biographies. What information did you find interesting?
→ M 1-minute-presentation, p. 166

> Ich kann Informationen über einen Erfinder präsentieren.   ✔

Where can we stay?

1 (READING) **Read the dialogue.**

1,25

I don't want to go camping!

Dad! No way! If we go camping …

If nobody wants …

1 **Mum:** Katie, Jake, Harry. It's time to plan our trip to the Highlands. We'll have to decide where we want to stay. I'd love to stay in a cosy B & B in Inverness.
Dad: Abby, I thought we could go camping. You know
5 I love hiking. It's a simple and cheap way to spend our holidays. If we stay at a campsite, we'll be outside all day.
Jake: Dad! No way! We'll freeze if we go camping. And there'll be insects too.
Katie: Are you serious, Dad? I agree with Jake. No
10 camping! If we go to a hotel, there won't be any insects. And we'll have our own bathroom.
Jake: Katie is right. A hotel is great. And the buffets are fantastic. If we don't stay in a hotel, we won't get nice food!
15 **Mum:** I don't want to go camping either but I'm sorry, it won't be a hotel, kids. That's too expensive. We could rent a holiday cottage but spending a few days at a B & B is a better idea. Maybe we can get some tips about local food.
20 **Dad:** Yes, I think so too. If nobody wants to go camping, that's fine. But let's go to Loch Ness. Maybe we'll see Nessie, the Loch Ness monster …

2 Find the most important information. → M Bus stop, p. 166

44/1

a) Copy and complete the table.

Who?	Where?	Why?
Abby (Mum)	B & B	
Harry (Dad)		
Katie		
Jake		

b) Where would you like to stay? Why?

Language tip → G 7, p. 156

I love **hiking**.
Spending a few days in a B & B is a good idea.

CULTURE

Briten übernachten oft in einem B & B (bed and breakfast). Das sind Gästezimmer, die privat vermietet werden. Würdest du gerne in einem B & B übernachten? Weshalb?

3 Where do people stay on their holidays?

a) Match the words with the definitions. → ○ p. 118

44/2-
3a)

1. hotel
2. campsite
3. bed and breakfast
4. hostel
5. caravan

A It's a place where you go camping.
B It's a small home. Cars can take small ones from place to place.
C It's a big building which has a swimming pool and large buffets.
D It's a place that's almost like home.
E It's usually a place where young people stay. There's often a kitchen for everyone too.

b) Put the steps in the right order. → **V** Going on holiday, p. 190

44/3b)

| check out | ask about prices | pay the bill | make a reservation | check in |

1,26   **4** (LISTENING) Which picture is it?
45/4

a) Listen to Jim and Dianne. Look at the pictures. Where did they stay? → ○ p. 119

hotel   bed and breakfast   hostel

b) Why did you choose the picture? Give reasons.

I chose picture X because the … . And … .

> **LISTENING SKILLS**
>
> Bevor du den Text hörst, sieh dir die Bilder an.
> Welche Wörter fallen dir dazu ein? Achte beim Hören auf diese Wörter.

Language detectives → G8, p. 157 → G9, p. 158

We'll freeze if we go camping.
If we go to a hotel, there won't be any insects.
If we don't stay in a hotel, we won't get nice food!

Welche Satzhälfte steht für eine Bedingung?
Welche für eine Konsequenz?
Welche Zeiten werden in den Satzteilen verwendet?

5 Complete the sentences.

45/5

1. If Jake goes to Edinburgh, he —— (go) shopping.
   If Jake goes to Edinburgh, he'll go shopping.
2. If Dad has time, he —— (visit) the castle.
3. If I see a nice souvenir, I —— (buy) it.
4. If we stay at a campsite, maybe we —— (get) cold.
5. If I see the Loch Ness monster, I —— (take) a photo.
6. If we find Nessie, we —— (become) famous.

46/7 **6 Make sentences about a holiday in a hotel.**

a) Complete the sentences. → ○ p. 119

45/6

1. If everyone —— (agree), we'll stay in a hotel.
   If everyone agrees, we'll stay in a hotel.
2. If we —— (stay) in a hotel, we'll have a TV.
3. If I —— (have) a TV, it won't be boring.
4. If the son —— (watch) TV all day, he won't meet other kids.
5. If we —— (go) to a good hotel, I'll have internet too.
6. If we —— (not find) anything interesting online, we'll ask at the tourist information.

b) Make sentences.

1. get up early • go swimming before breakfast
   If I get up early, I'll go swimming before breakfast.

2. be hungry • eat at hotel restaurant
3. not rain • go horse riding
4. try haggis • like it
5. visit museum • be open on Tuesdays
6. not get cold • wear a jacket

*Pass auf! Welcher Satzteil
sollte das if haben?*

7 What will we do if … ?

a) Look at the pictures. Make sentences. → ○ p. 120

46/8a)

1. We'll go hiking in the mountains if … . (the weather / nice)

2. If we leave the hostel after ten o'clock, … . (pay)

3. If there's a party at the campsite, … . (have / barbecue)

4. If we go to the Highlands, … . (take / photo)

5. We'll have a problem with insects if … . (stay / tent)

6. We won't stay in that hotel if … . (no swimming pool)

b) What will happen if … ?

46/8b)

1. If we have a party at the hostel, we'll go to bed late. If we go to bed late, …

8 (SPEAKING) Play a game with wishes. → M Round robin, p. 170

Write a wish on a card. Put the cards in a box and take a wish. What will you do if it comes true?

| meet … | find a … |
| become rich | … |

A: If I get a phone for my birthday, I'll … .   B: If I meet …, I'll … .

✽ 9 (YOUR TURN) A role play → V Places to stay, p. 194

47/1-2

Act a role play with two others. Where can you go and stay? Use the cards and the phrases.

MacGowan Hotel *A*
Place: Glasgow
Activities: museums, food, theatre, shopping
Price: £275 for 2 people for 2 nights

Nessie's Nest (B & B) *B*
Place: Inverness
Activities: walking, canoeing, cycling, Loch Ness
Price: £420 for 4 people for 3 nights

No Tree Hostel *C*
Place: Isle of Skye
Activities: bird watching, boat trips, beach walks
Price: £25 for 1 person for 1 night

… is cheaper / more expensive.
If you like …, you will / won't like … .

I would like to … .
I think so too. / I agree / disagree.

Ich kann mich über Ausflugsmöglichkeiten unterhalten. ✔

Robert the Bruce

1 What do you know about Robert the Bruce and the history of Scotland and England?

2 (READING) Read the comic strip.

1,27

1 Welcome to the 14th century! At this time there are lots of battles between Scotland and England.

2 In 1306 …

We want to have Scotland.

We want to be free!

At last! I am the king of Scotland! I will keep the English out. This is our land!

3 Edward I, King of England, has a strong army …

4 After the sixth battle …

How can I beat the English? I've lost six battles! They have so many soldiers!

I shouldn't hide like this, but what can I do? I feel awful! Maybe it's impossible to beat the English.

READING SKILLS

Wenn du ein Wort nicht weißt, sieh dir die Bilder an. Sie können dir helfen, die Geschichte besser zu verstehen. Wer spricht? Wie ist die Situation? Was kannst du aus dem Gesicht einer Person ablesen? Du musst aber nicht jedes Wort kennen.

5 Robert the Bruce sees something in the cave.

6 A few days later …

The spider is amazing. It falls, then climbs, it falls, then climbs. It still tries to make its web. It never gives up. So I must never give up!

We must stay together and be brave! We must not give up! We can beat the English!

7 The Scots and the English fight a lot in the years after this. Robert the Bruce loses some battles, but he also wins some. Edward I, the English king, is angry …

This is crazy! Our king is too old and too ill …

I'm going to invade Scotland myself!

8 On the way to one battle Edward I dies.

My son, you are now king of England. You must finish what I started …

9 In 1314, at Bannockburn, near Stirling …

They have more soldiers than us. But we know this land. We have good tactics. Stay strong!

10 The ground at Bannockburn is very wet …

We can't beat them. The Scots know how to fight here. It's too difficult for us. We can't move …

3 Talk about the story.

Did you like the story? Talk about it with a partner and say why (or why not).

4 Answer the questions.

1. When did the story happen?
   in the 13th century • in the 14th century
2. Who is the hero of the story?
   Robert the Bruce • Edward II
3. Where did the Scottish win?
   at Culloden • at Bannockburn
4. What happened to the English?
   They ran away. • They stayed.

11 After two days …

Look, men! They're running away. We've won!

HOORAY!

HOORAY!

12 In the years after this Robert is a good king and the Scots are proud.

WE LOVE YOU!

I ❤ U

WE ❤ KING ROBERT

Hooray! The English are beaten!

We love you! Thank you!

13 In 1329 …

This is a sad day for Scotland!

Under Robert the Bruce there was peace in Scotland and it was a free country. He was a brave man and a great leader. He was Scotland's most successful king.

⚬ **5 Choose one of these tasks.**

48/1
49/2-3

a) A short biography of Robert the Bruce.

Search the internet about the life of Robert the Bruce. Then write a short biography. Add pictures.

→ **M** Peer correction, p. 169

 **OR**

b) Make a poster about the battle of Bannockburn.

Search the internet. Find pictures. Add some information.

> **STUDY SKILLS**
>
> Wenn du im Internet Informationen zu einer Person suchst, suche nur nach den wichtigsten Daten und Fakten. Schreibe dir diese als Stichpunkte auf. Benutze sie dann, um die Biografie zu schreiben.

Ich kann einen Comic über eine Schlacht verstehen.

Some Scottish and German dishes

Deep fried chocolate

If you like chocolate, you'll love this snack!
A fish and chip shop in Scotland put a bar of
chocolate in the same batter it used to cover
the fish and then fried it in hot oil. Lots of
people thought that this gooey, sticky treat
that is crisp on the outside was fun to eat.

Haggis

Haggis is a famous Scottish dish. It's a kind
of meat pudding which can include the heart,
liver and lungs of a sheep, together with
onions and oatmeal. Sometimes it's even
served in the sheep's stomach.

Kirschmichel

Kirschmichel ist eine traditionelle Süßspeise,
die vor allem im Süden Deutschlands serviert
wird. Älteres Brot oder Brötchen werden mit
Butter, Eiern, Milch und Zucker vermengt.
Dazu kommen Kirschen. Alles wird im Ofen
gebacken und noch warm serviert.

Himmel und Erde

Himmel und Erde ist ein beliebtes Gericht in
einigen Teilen von Deutschland, z. B. im
Rheinland. Kartoffeln und Äpfel werden
gekocht, gestampft und miteinander
vermischt. Dazu wird Bratwurst oder
traditionell Blutwurst serviert.

1 Beantworte die Fragen.

50/1

Eine Deutsche und ein Schotte haben diese Texte gesehen, aber sie verstehen sie nicht ganz.
Beantworte ihre Fragen in der jeweiligen Sprache.

1. Schokolade gibt es bei uns auch.
   Was ist da so besonders?
2. Ich bin Vegetarierin. Kann ich das
   traditionelle Haggis essen?

3. What's 'Kirschmichel'? I can see the word
   'Brot'. Is it a kind of sandwich?
4. 'Äpfel' means 'apple', doesn't it? Is 'Himmel
   und Erde' a cake with apples?

2 What do you think?

Do you like trying different types of food? What's a typical German dish for you?

Ich kann Informationen über Gerichte weitergeben. ✓

The old phone

1 **Talk about old phones.**

Have you ever seen or used a phone like this?
Can you send messages with it?
What's a pay phone? Where can you find them?

2 (VIEWING) **Watch the film.**

6 🎬

a) Which summary is correct?

1. Alicia helps her grandmother with the shopping and
   her video chat. After that, her neighbour Alva gives her
   an old TV.
2. Marley gets an old phone from Alicia. She repairs it and
   her friends are proud of her.
3. Alicia helps her neighbour, who gives her an old phone.
   Marley knows how to use it as a radio.

> **CULTURE**
>
> Nachbarn reden sich in Groß-
> britannien oft mit ihren Vornamen
> an. Wie würdest du eine ältere
> Nachbarin wie Alva anreden?
> Würdest du sie mit ihrem Vornamen
> anreden?

b) Who says it?

1. "I've never had a video chat before."
2. "I have an idea!"
3. "I want to see what you're up to!"
4. "Wow! It looks interesting! What is it?"
5. "It's amazing what you can do with an old telephone!"

3 (WRITING) **Write about the film.**

Watch the last part of the film again (from 3:20).
Describe what happens. Use the words for help.

attach   pipe   antenna

connect   signal

You can start like this:
Marley took an old phone. Laura and Alicia wanted … .
Marley … . They heard … . It was … .

> **VIEWING SKILLS**
>
> Spannungselemente machen einen
> Film aufregender. Sound, Musik,
> Beleuchtung oder Kameraperspektiven
> können alle Spannung erzeugen. Wie
> macht der Film die Geschichte
> interessanter?

Ich kann einen Film über ein Experiment verstehen. ✔

Checklist

Ich kann Informationen über Schottland verstehen. ✔

51

Ich kann Informationen über einen Erfinder präsentieren. ✔

… was born in (place) in (year). • He / She is a person who … . • … grew up • … invented the first … in … . • It was a … which … . • … died in (place) in (year).

51

Ich kann mich über Ausflugsmöglichkeiten unterhalten. ✔

Let's go to … . • … is cheaper / more expensive. • I like / don't like … , so … is better for me. • If you like / don't like … , you will / won't like … .

52

Ich kann einen Comic über eine Schlacht verstehen. ✔

52

Ich kann Informationen über Gerichte weitergeben. ✔

53

Ich kann einen Film über ein Experiment verstehen. ✔

✽ (TASK) An advert

Work in groups of three or four students. Each group thinks of a product and makes an advert (ad) for it. Each group presents the ad and gets feedback from the other groups.

Step 1

Look at the ads.

Do you like them? Discuss.

❶ A holiday you'll **never** forget in a **magical** tree house in the **beautiful** Scottish mountains!

From only **£595** for three wonderful nights! Other locations and offers available.

Book NOW at **www.holidaytreehouse.co.uk**

❷ FULL SERVICE
Mechanic On Duty!
GARAGE
Since 1960
TYRES • PETROLS • OILS
Free Coffee!

interesting   boring   funny   exciting

nice photos   lots of information   …

Step 2

What makes a good ad? → M Think–pair–share, p. 171

Look at the examples in Step 1 for help.
Look at the language, the photos and the information.

Step 3

Make and design your ad.

1. Choose your product.
2. Think: What is good about the product?
   What kind of people should buy the product?
3. Choose pictures or photos.
4. Write the text.
5. Make a draft of the ad. You can use a computer
   or a large piece of paper.

STUDY SKILLS

Wähle ein interessantes oder ungewöhnliches Produkt. Entscheide, für wen deine Werbung sein soll. Wähle ein Foto, das für sich selbst spricht. Der Text sollte einfach und klar sein und die Leser ansprechen. Benutze daher Fragen und Aufforderungen.

Step 4

Check your draft.

Does it have all the important information? Check the spelling too.

Step 5

Make your ad and show it to the other groups. → M Gallery walk, p. 168

Step 6

Get feedback from the other groups. → M Tip top, p. 171

What was good/not so good? Which ad was the best and why? Think about:

`the text`   `the design`   `the message`   `the photo(s)`   `who the ad is for`   `...`

Extra practice

1 Match the sentence parts. (nach 53/3)

1. <u>Scottish men</u>	A clean electricity for Scotland.
2. Tourists can	B often fought against the English.
3. Edinburgh is	C <u>sometimes wear a kilt.</u>
4. Robert the Bruce	D were born in Scotland.
5. Porridge is	E had its own king or queen.
6. In the past Scotland	F stay in a cottage.
7. A lot of inventors	G the capital of Scotland.
8. Wind farms make	H a Scottish breakfast dish.

2 What's the material? (nach 55/5)

rubber wood leather metal plastic paper cotton

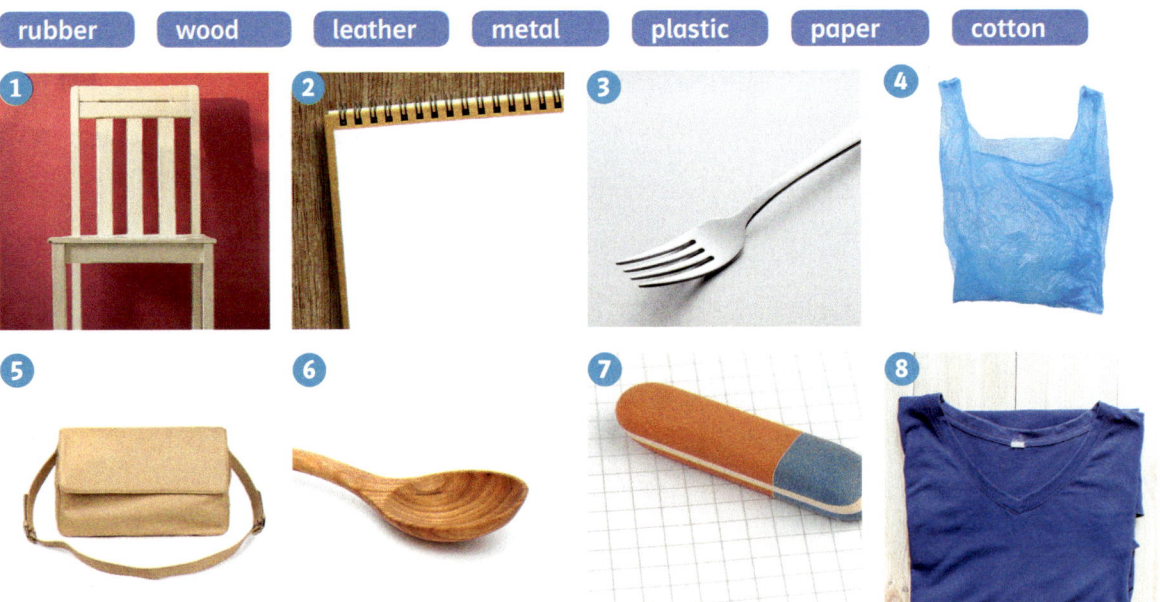

1. This chair is made of . . . .

3 Make sentences. (nach 56/8)

1. <u>A kilt is a skirt</u>
2. Robert the Bruce was a king
3. Edinburgh is a Scottish city
4. Porridge is a dish
5. Scotland is a country
6. A cottage is a house
7. An inventor is a person

who
which

<u>is for men.</u>
fought against the English.
is very old.
has oats in it.
doesn't have much sun.
is small and often in the country.
invents machines and other things.

4 Use <u>whose</u> to make one sentence out of two. (nach 57/9)

1. Inventors are important persons. Their ideas make life easier.
   Inventors are important persons whose ideas … .
2. Bell was a famous inventor. His wife and his mother were both deaf.
3. Bell was a teacher. His wish was to help people who couldn't hear well.
4. Bell became a famous man. His invention changed the world forever.

5 Complete the sentences. (nach 60/6)

1. If we —— (not want) to pay much, we —— (stay) at a campsite.
2. We —— (freeze) if we —— (stay) at a campsite.
3. There —— (not be) any insects if we —— (go) to a cosy B & B.
4. If we —— (be) in a hotel, we —— (have) our own bathroom.
5. We —— (not get) nice food if we —— (stay) at a campsite.
6. If we —— (choose) a hotel, we —— (not have) money for anything else.
7. We —— (take) a cottage if a hotel room —— (be) too expensive.
8. If we —— (see) the Loch Ness monster, everyone —— (be) happy.

6 Make sentences. (nach 61/8)

1. go …/visit Edinburgh   2. see …/take a photo   3. have …/go shopping

4. stay in a B & B/eat …   5. wet tomorrow/not go …   6. go …/learn about history

1. If I <u>go</u> to Scotland, I <u>will visit</u> Edinburgh.
2. If I see Nessie, I'll … .

On Ben Nevis

1,28

INTERNET

Avalanche hits rock climbers

10:35 published Monday 8th January

Four rock climbers who set off an avalanche in the Scottish highlands on Sunday 7th January were very lucky to <u>escape</u> with their lives.

The four young men, all from London, <u>were climbing</u> Ben Nevis, the highest mountain in the UK. At about 2 p.m. a huge <u>wave</u> of snow <u>swept</u> them 300 metres down the mountain.

In an interview later that day one of the men said, "I fell for a very long time. I didn't believe that I would survive. My friends and I, we all had safety equipment like red coats and red helmets. But still, we were really lucky to walk out. It was a very scary adventure. The rescue helicopter had already started to <u>look for</u> us. It took us to hospital, but we were all OK. Only one of my friends had a twisted ankle." Next year, the <u>climbers</u> will climb the highest mountain in Europe, Mont Blanc.

1 Look at the dictionary entry.

Use the entry for 'hit' to find the right German word(s) in these sentences:

1. The avalanche hit the climbers.
2. The car hit a tree.
3. The musical *Cats* is a real hit.
4. The boy hit the ball very hard.
5. There were 143 hits for this search.

Wenn Wörter in einem Wörterbuch aufgelistet werden, nennt man sie „Einträge". Jedes Wort wird in seiner Grundform angegeben. Suche zuerst immer danach.

Hier wird dir angezeigt, wie das Wort ausgesprochen wird.

Hier siehst du, ob das Wort ein Verb oder ein Substantiv ist.

Nützliche Redewendungen stehen unter dem Grundwort.

Viele Wörter haben mehr als eine Bedeutung. Es gibt jeweils eine Nummer für jede Bedeutung.

Diese Wörter helfen dir, die richtige Bedeutung zu finden.

hit hɪt| I. *n* ❶ Schlag *m* ❷ *(shot)* Treffer *m*; **to suffer a direct** direkt getroffen werden ❸ *(success)* Hit *m*; **to be a [big] ~ with sb** bei jdm gut ankommen ❹ INET Besuch *m* einer Webseite ❺ COMPUT *(match)* Treffer *m* II. *vt* <-tt-, hit, hit> ❶ schlagen ❷ *button* drücken ❸ *(collide)* **to ~ sth** gegen etw *akk* stoßen; *car* gegen etw *akk* krachen *fam* ❹ *(shoot)* **to be ~** getroffen werden ❺ *(occur)* **to ~ sb** jdm auffallen III. *vi* ❶ **to ~ hard** kräftig zuschlagen; **to ~ at sb** nach jdm schlagen ❷ *(attack)* **to ~ at sb** jdn attackieren *a. fig*
◆**hit back** *vi* zurückschlagen; **to ~ back at sb** jdm Kontra geben
◆**hit off** *vt* **to ~ it off [with sb]** *(fam)* sich prächtig [mit jdm] verstehen

56/1
57/2-4

2 Work with a dictionary.

a) Find the right German meaning for the underlined words in the text. Use an English-German dictionary.

b) What do the same words mean here?

1. The man waved wildly from the window.
2. A tornado swept through the town.
3. Can I have a look at that magazine?
4. The man escaped from prison in the night.
5. The plane went into a steep climb.

Du kannst auch Online-Wörterbücher benutzen. Pass aber auf. Nimm nicht gleich die erstbeste Bedeutung. Lies erst den gesamten Eintrag. Du kannst auch die Bedeutung in einem Deutsch-Englisch Wörterbuch gegenprüfen.

Am Ende dieser Unit kann ich ...
• **Informationen über Nordirland herausfinden.**
• **einem Freund oder einer Freundin einen Ratschlag geben.**
• **in einem Geschäft ein Gespräch führen und dort etwas einkaufen.**
• **einen Zeitungsartikel über eine Katastrophe verstehen.**
• **Informationen über ein B & B weitergeben.**
• **einen Film über eine Auseinandersetzung verstehen.**

7 ⏧ 2,1 ☞

Unit 4
In Northern Ireland

Hi! I'm Sarah Brown and I'm from Northern Ireland.

1
Belfast is the capital of Northern Ireland. You can see a lot of murals on the buildings. They are from the time of 'The Troubles', when there were problems between Protestants and Catholics.

2
My friend Julie and I visited the Giant's Causeway in the summer. That's on the coast of Northern Ireland. It was great!

1 **Match the headings with the photos or texts.**

A A lucky day for George
B A new town and job
C A small town shop
D Pictures on walls
E A great summer trip

2 **Answer the questions.**

58/1 ⏎

1. What can visitors see on the buildings in Belfast?
2. Where is the Giant's Causeway?
3. Why are Sarah's parents busy?
4. What is there in Randalstown?
5. Which ship was built in Belfast?

3

My dad lost his job in Belfast so we have just moved near Lough Neagh. My parents run a bed and breakfast there now.
They are very busy!

4

My aunt Maggie runs a shop in Randalstown, a small town northwest of Belfast. You can buy a lot of things there. And I always get free sweets!

5

Belfast was famous for ships. The Titanic was built here in 1912. My grandad's uncle George got a job as a waiter on it. He was sick on the day it left, so he didn't travel. Phew!

 3 (LISTENING) **Right or wrong?**

2,2
58/2

1. The man would like some information about Belfast.
   That's wrong. He would like . . . .
2. Buses go every 20 minutes.
3. The visitor centre tells the story of Mike O'Donnell.
4. An adult ticket costs £7.50.
5. A family ticket is £22.

outside [ˌaʊtˈsaɪd] – draußen
visitor centre [ˈvɪzɪtə ˌsentə] –
 Besucherzentrum
giant [dʒaɪənt] – Riese
to cost [kɒst] – kosten
adult [ˈædʌlt] – Erwachsene/r
probably [ˈprɒbəbli] –
 wahrscheinlich

 **Ich kann Informationen über Nordirland herausfinden.**

I'm really fed up!

1 (READING) **Read the e-mails.**

2,3
59/1

E-MAIL

1 Hi Julie,
   I need your advice. I'm really fed up.
   Mum and Dad never have any time for me any
   more. They're busy with their new B & B.
5 They work hard all day. And in the evenings
   they're tired. We had so much fun together
   when we lived in Belfast. But now?
   At the weekends Mum always nags me to tidy
   up the dining room. But Ashley helps me a lot!
10 Sometimes little brothers can be useful. ☺
   I don't like the B & B. We have new guests
   every day and they always ask the same
   questions. "Blah blah blah … ." It drives me crazy!
   I miss you so much!
15 If you were here, I wouldn't be so lonely.
   See you,
   Sarah ☹

E-MAIL

1 Hi Sarah,
   I miss you too. It's so boring here without you.
   Can't you talk to your parents? I think they
   would understand if you told them how you
5 feel. If I were you, I would speak to your dad
   first. He will listen.
   If I lived in a B & B, I'd probably hate it too.
   But think positive! Maybe your guests can tell
   you interesting stories?
10 If I visited you in our next holidays, you could
   show me Lough Neagh. I would probably ask
   the same silly questions as the tourists. But I
   have to go to Dublin with my family.
   Come to Belfast soon! If you were here now,
15 I would take you to the cool new milkshake
   place in town.
   I'll call you tomorrow.
   Julie XOX

2 Find the answers.

1. Does Sarah like the new place?
2. What are Sarah's problems?
3. Which advice does Julie give?

> She says …   She doesn't like …   There are …
>
> She feels …   She can …   She could …

3 (SPEAKING) **What do you think?**

a) Talk about these questions. → ○ p. 120
   → M Think–pair–share, p. 171

1. Can you understand how Sarah feels? Why?
   Why not?
2. Is Julie's advice OK? Why? Why not?

I think it's OK • a problem • not so easy
because …

b) Make questions.

Which questions may the guests at
the B & B have?

4 (LISTENING) Listen to the phone call. Choose the right answer.

2,4

1. Who called Sarah?
   Ashley • Julie
2. When was Sarah fed up?
   Yesterday • Two days ago
3. Who will Sarah talk to later that week?
   Her dad • Her mum
4. When will the girls talk again?
   Tomorrow morning • Tomorrow afternoon

5 Work with adjectives.

59/2

a) Make a chart. Sort the adjectives. → ○ p. 121 → M Bus stop, p. 166

| sad ✓ | furious | smart | confident | horrible | optimistic |

☺	☹
…	sad

Du brauchst für einige dieser Wörter ein Wörterbuch. Auf Seite 73 findest du Tipps, wie du mit einem Wörterbuch arbeitest.

59/3

b) Find words with the same meaning. Match the new words with the words from a).
→ V Adjectives for feelings, p. 195

1. down – sad
2. dreadful
3. hopeful
4. intelligent
5. sure of oneself
6. very annoyed

6 (WRITING) Describe an important person in your life. → M Peer correction, p. 169

60/4

Choose a person (family or friend) and write a short text.

What's good and not so good about him or her?

Use the example for help.
You can use the adjectives from Ex. 5 too.

> My best friend always listens to me. He's smart and knows a lot of things. He also … . But he's often late. That really makes me furious. Sometimes he … .

7 (SONG) Let your tears fall

2,5

Listen to the song. What advice does the singer give?

1 Watch your tears fall, let them fall, falling now,
Make the seas calm, take you in my arms, you
cry. (Let your tears fall …)
It's not a crime to fall apart sometimes,
5 It's not a crime to ask why, to ask why, you cry.
(Let your tears fall …)
I will come, no, I won't run,
I'm not scared, to care.

Come to me when you're in need,
10 Set it free, let the truth breathe.
(Chorus): Tell me all your secrets,
    tell me your fears,
I'm gonna push you away,
    then I'll pull you near,
15 No, I won't judge you, I'm gonna help
    you through.

Language detectives → G10, p. 159

If I lived in a B & B, I would hate it too.
If you were here, we'd go to the new place.
They would understand if you told them how you feel.

Sieh dir die Verben an. Was ist anders als in den if-Sätzen Typ I,
die du bereits kennst?

8 (WRITING) **Complete the sentences.**

60/5-6

If Sarah was 10 years older, …

| visit | work | live | move ✔ | meet | find |

1. she would move to Belfast.

2. … a job.

3. … in an office.

4. … in a flat.

5. … with Julie.

6. … her parents often.

9 What would happen?

a) Put in the verbs. → ○ p. 121 → **M** Peer correction, p. 169

61/7

1. If Sarah —— (go) to a sports club, she would make new friends.
   If Sarah went to a sports club, she would make new friends.
2. If Sarah —— (speak) to her parents about her problems, they would understand her better.
3. If Sarah and her friend Julie —— (meet) each other more often, they would be happier.
4. If Julie —— (not live) in Belfast, Sarah would see her best friend more often.
5. Sarah would spend more time in his room if Ashley —— (not listen) to that awful music.
6. Mum and dad wouldn't be so tired if they —— (not work) so hard.

b) Finish these sentences with your own ideas.

1. If Sarah —— (invite) a new friend home, her parents would … .
2. If Sarah's parents —— (not listen) to her, … .
3. If Sarah's brother —— (be) older, … .
4. If her parents —— (not work) in a B & B, … .

🗣💬 10 (SPEAKING) What would you do in this situation?

a) Make questions and answer them. Work with a partner. → ○ p. 121   → **M** Double circle, p. 167

61/8

Here are some ideas:

- you lose your phone   → ask friend / call my number
- you find a dog near your house   → take … home
- you meet your favourite singer   → take a photo
- you get a plane ticket to another country   → go to …
- you have a year without school   → …

A: What <u>would you do</u> if you <u>lost</u> your mobile phone?
B: I <u>would ask</u> a friend: "Can you call my number, please?"

b) Read the headlines. What you would do in each situation?

61/9

> School boy finds 200 year old coins in garden!   Woman wins big prize in art competition!

> Engineer invents time travel machine!

✳ 11 (YOUR TURN) An e-mail with advice → **V** Giving advice, p. 199

🅿
🔑 **a)** Read the e-mail. What is Steve's problem?

> **E-MAIL**
>
> Hi Julie,
> I've got a big problem. 'Tigerboy III' is in cinemas now. My mum hates these movies. But I really wanted
> to see it. Yesterday I told her: "I have to do homework together with Seb tonight." But Seb, Carol and I
> went to watch the movie. And what happened? We walked into the building and my mum's best friend
> was there. Of course she saw me.
> What should I do now? Mum will be furious …
> Please help me!
> See you,
> Steve

b) Write an e-mail to Steve and give advice. These phrases can help:

That sounds awful. / That's bad news.
Think positive. / I have a good idea. /
Why don't you …
If I were you, … / If you told your mum, … /
If you talked to your mum's friend, …
Call me later. / Let's speak soon. / …
→ **M** Writers' conference, p. 171

> **WRITING SKILLS**
>
> Folge diesen Schritten:
> - Denke an eine Anrede und einen Schluss.
> - Zeige, dass du das Problem verstanden hast.
> - Gib zwei Tipps.

Ich kann einem Freund oder einer Freundin einen Ratschlag geben.   ✔

Buy one, get one free

1 (**READING**) Read the dialogue in Maggie's shop in Randalstown.

2,6
62/1a)

1 **Maggie:** Hello! You're Ian Thompson's son, aren't you? How are you today?
Dan: Yes, that's right! I'm fine, thanks. I have to buy some things for my dad.
5 **Maggie:** What would you like?
Dan: I'd like some raspberry jam, please.
Maggie: Oh dear, we don't have any raspberry jam. But we have strawberry jam. Look, this one is the cheapest, but it's as tasty as the
10 others. There's a special offer. Buy one, get one free!
Dan: Strawberry is fine. I'll have two jars then. Do you have any brown bread?
Maggie: Yes, we do. There's some sliced bread
15 over there, and we have special farmer's bread. Our customers love it. But it's a little more expensive than the other one.
Dan: How much is a loaf?
Maggie: It's £1.20.
20 **Dan:** I'd like one loaf of farmer's bread, please. I have to post a letter for my dad too. Can I have four stamps, please?
Maggie: Of course. Where is the letter for? Oh, Ballyronan? That's where my niece lives.
25 **Dan:** Really?
Maggie: Yes. Her family moved there from Belfast. They have a B & B there now. Of course, Ballyronan isn't as big as Belfast,

and it's less exciting than the big city too. Well, that's £2.52 for the stamps. Anything 30 else?
Dan: I think I have everything. Thanks.
Maggie: OK. That will be £5.27, please.
Dan: Sorry, can you repeat that, please? I didn't get that. 35
Maggie: Yes, of course. £5.27, please.
Dan: Sorry, I've only got a twenty pound note.
Maggie: That's OK. So that's £14.73 change. Here you are. 40
Dan: Thanks. Bye now.
Maggie: You're welcome. Bye!

2 Find out about the shopping trip.

a) Which is Dan's shopping list?

A raspberry jam
  bread
  one stamp for letter

B strawberry jam
  bread
  four stamps

C raspberry jam
  bread
  four stamps

b) How much does the jam cost?

3 **Find the phrases in the dialogue. Look at the beginning and the ending.**

What can you say …

1. to check that a person is OK?
2. when you don't hear or understand?
3. when you give something to a person?
4. when a person says thank you?

4 **Work with shopping phrases.**

a) Put the phrases in A in the right order. The phrases in B can help you. → ○ p. 122
   → M Peer correction, p. 169

A
A That will be £3.63.
B Goodbye!
C That's £1.37 change.
D Anything else?
E Hi!
F What would you like?

B
1. Hello!
2. I'd like … .
3. Yes, … ./ No, thanks.
4. Here you are.
5. Thank you.
6. See you.

b) Who can say these phrases, the customer or the shop assistant?

> Sorry, we've run out of that.   Do you have another brand?   I can order some for you.
>
> Do you have the exact change?   Sorry, I've changed my mind.

5 (LISTENING) **Listen to two more customers in Maggie's shop.**

2,7

a) Look at the things and listen. Who buys which thing(s)?

Customer 1 buys …

b) Listen again. How many do the customers buy? How much is it?

a jar of peanut butter

a packet of tissues

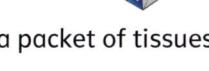

a bottle of mineral water

6 (PUZZLE) **What's more money, A or B?**

> **CULTURE**
>
> Alle britischen Münzen und Banknoten haben auf einer Seite das Bild des Königs oder der Königin. Welche Menschen oder Dinge sind auf eurem Geld zu sehen?

Language → G11, p. 160

Ballyronan isn't as big as Belfast.
It's less exciting than the big city.
This one is the cheapest.
It's more expensive than the other one.

Wie sagen wir, dass zwei Dinge gleich sind?
Wann benutzen wir more / most und wann benutzen wir -er / -est?
Was bedeutet das Wort than?

Erinnerst du dich, wie du Dinge auf Englisch vergleichst?

7 Compare the things on the shelf.

63/3-4a)

1. The loaf of sliced bread is bigger than the brown loaf. (big)
2. The brown box of tea is —— the red one. (cheap)
3. The raspberry jam is —— the peanut butter. (expensive)
4. The jar of jam is —— the jar of peanut butter. (big)
5. The tissues in the green packet are not —— the tissues in the blue packet. (cheap)
6. The mineral water from Northern Ireland is —— the Scottish water. (expensive)

8 (SPEAKING) What do you think? Talk with a partner.

63/4b)

a) Compare the things. → ○ p. 122

1. chocolate or strawberry? (tasty)
   A: I think chocolate is tastier than strawberry. Do you agree?
   B: Yes, I think you're right.
2. winter or summer? (good)
3. picnic or restaurant? (cheap)
4. speaking any language or talking to animals? (interesting)
5. doing homework or tidying your room? (exciting)
6. having a camel or being a camel? (funny)

| as ... as | not as ... as | -er than | more ... than | less ... than |

b) Compare these things. Do you agree?

dogs or cats?   football or tennis?   small shops or big shops?

Language detectives → G 12, p. 161

I have to buy <u>some</u> things for my dad.
Oh dear, we don't have <u>any</u> raspberry jam.
Do you have <u>any</u> brown bread?

Wann benutzen wir <u>some</u> und wann benutzen wir <u>any</u>?
Finde weitere Beispiele im Text auf Seite 80.

64/5 **9 <u>Some</u> or <u>any</u>?**

a) Put in <u>some</u> or any. → ○ p. 122

1. I'd like to buy <u>some</u> comics.
2. Sorry, we don't have —— tissues.
3. Do you have —— sweets in your bag?
4. Oh dear! We don't have —— change!
5. Let's eat —— cake!
6. Sorry, I didn't buy —— orange juice. I forgot!

b) Make the second sentence. Use the ideas on the right.

1. I can't go out today. I have to do <u>some</u> homework.
2. Oh dear, my nose! …
3. I'm very hungry. …
4. Are you thirsty? …

> be / sandwiches in the kitchen ?
>
> have / tissues ?   have / homework + ✔
>
> give you / mineral water +

10 (YOUR TURN) A shopping dialogue → V Shopping, p. 200

64/6-7
65/1

a) Write notes for a shopping dialogue with a partner. You can use the phrases from Ex. 4 on page 81.
Here are some more ideas:

Assistant:
Ask friendly questions. (How are you? / …?)
Say what is cheaper, more/less …
Say that there is a special offer.
Say that you have some new/cool/…

Customer:
Answer the assistant's questions. (Be friendly!)
Say that you need some … and why.
Ask: "Do you have any …?"
Say: "No thanks, I don't need any …"

SPEAKING SKILLS

Höre deinem Gegenüber zu, wenn er oder sie mit dir spricht. Zeige Interesse an dem, was er oder sie sagt. Wenn du etwas nicht verstehst, sage: „Sorry, can you repeat that, please?" Versuche zu helfen, wenn jemand stecken bleibt.

b) Practise and act the dialogue. → M Read and look up, p. 170

> Ich kann in einem Geschäft ein Gespräch führen und dort etwas einkaufen. ✔

The Titanic disaster

● **1** **What do you already know about the Titanic?** → M Think-pair-share, p. 171

● **2** (READING) **Read the newspaper report.**

2,8

The Belfast News
Wednesday, 17th April 1912

Titanic hits iceberg and sinks

TWO DAYS AFTER – MORE FACTS
The Titanic was built here in Belfast's shipyard. It hit an iceberg shortly before midnight on 14th April. A few hours later it sank. It was on its way from Southampton to New York on its first voyage. There were more than 2,200 passengers and crew on board. Only about 700 people survived the accident.

WORLD'S LARGEST SHIP
The Titanic was the largest and most expensive ship in the world. It had a swimming pool, a gymnasium and two libraries. The ship's builders, The White Star Line, said that their ship was safe. So it only had 20 lifeboats. That was only enough for half of the people on board.

● **3** **Talk about the report.**

Was there anything new to you? What did you find most interesting?

● **4** **Find the facts.**

1. time and date of accident?
2. from where to where?
3. number of people on board?

4. number of people who survived?
5. number of lifeboats?
6. number of crew members from Northern Ireland?

Auf die Bedeutung mancher englischer Wörter kannst du selbst kommen, weil du sie so ähnlich schon im Deutschen kennst, wie etwa iceberg, optimistic und passenger. Findest du weitere Beispiele im Text?

LOCAL MEN DIE AT SEA

Twenty of the crew were from Northern Ireland. The ship's doctor, Dr John Simpson, 37, was born in Belfast. His mother was optimistic when a letter from him arrived at her home yesterday. However, we now know that Dr Simpson did not survive.

Dr John Simpson

DOG SAVES LIVES

Some of the dogs on board were lucky. One of the dogs on board saved the lives of the people in one of the lifeboats. A ship only found the lifeboat because they heard the dog.

HOW COULD IT HAPPEN?

Why did no one see the iceberg? Why were there only 20 lifeboats for the 2,200 people on board? And how can we make sure that something like will never happen again?

Some ships today have over 6,500 passengers and crew. All ships must have one lifeboat place for every person on board.

Dr Simpson's last letter to his mother is now in the Belfast Titanic museum.

5 Choose one of these tasks.

66/1
67/2-4

a) A letter

Imagine you are on board the Titanic when it leaves Southampton. Write a letter for 13th April 1912 (100 words). Think about these questions:

OR

> **How do you feel?**

> **What is it like on board?**

> **What can you do there?**   **. . .**

b) A diary entry

Imagine you survived the disaster. Write the diary entry for 15th April 1912 (100 words). Think about these questions:

> **Where are you now?**

> **How do you feel?**

> **What was it like on the lifeboat?**

> **. . .**

Ich kann einen Zeitungsartikel über eine Katastrophe verstehen. ✔

At a bed and breakfast

1 Beantworte die Fragen.

68/1-2

Du übernachtest mit deiner Familie im „Browns Bed & Breakfast" in der Nähe von Lough Neagh. Dort siehst du diese Schilder.

1. Wer darf hier parken? Was passiert mit Falschparkern?
2. Wann soll man die Klingel betätigen? Was meinst du, warum wurde der Text auf dem Schild geändert?
3. Bekommen die Gäste im B & B wirklich Frühstück ans Bett?
4. Was müssen die Gäste bei der Ankunft machen?
5. Was machst du mit den nassen Handtüchern, wenn du dieses Schild im Bad siehst?
6. Was bedeutet dieses Schild?

> **CULTURE**
>
> In britischen B & B gibt es oft lustige Schilder. Was ist das lustigste Schild, das du jemals gesehen hast?

2 What rules would you have?

If you ran a B & B, what rules would you have? Make signs for two of them.

Ich kann Informationen über ein B & B weitergeben. ✔

The cousin from Northern Ireland

1 Talk about the photos.

Nathan and Laura are with their cousin, Sean. Look at the photos from the film.
What do you think is happening?

2 (VIEWING) Watch the film.

8

a) Right or wrong? Correct the wrong sentences.

1. Sean is very good at sport.
2. There are some good basketball teams in Northern Ireland.
3. Nathan is not very good at computers.
4. Sean can't help Nathan with his computer problems.
5. The boys want to cook a meal together.

b) Watch for details.

1. What colour is Sean's shirt?
2. What's behind the basketball court?
3. How many bottles of water are there?
4. What colour is the bench that they sit on?

> **CULTURE**
>
> Viele (Nord)Iren sind in der Vergangenheit ins Vereinigte Königreich gezogen. Heute haben etwa sechs Millionen Menschen im Vereinigten Königreich zumindest einen (nord)irischen Vorfahren. Hast du Familienmitglieder, die in anderen Ländern wohnen?

3 (SPEAKING) Talk about the film.

Watch the film again from the start to 1:00.
How do the kids feel? Match the feelings with the names and tell your partner.

`Sean` `Nathan` `Laura` `Marley` `angry` `proud` `unhappy` `sorry` `. . .`

> **VIEWING SKILLS**
>
> An einem Filmdreh sind viele Personen beteiligt, z. B. ein Drehbuchautor, ein Regisseur, ein Kameramann oder Make-up artists. Würdest du gerne bei einer Filmproduktion mitmachen?

Ich kann einen Film über eine Auseinandersetzung verstehen. ✔

Checklist

Ich kann Informationen über Nordirland verstehen. ✔

69 ↗

Ich kann einem Freund oder einer Freundin einen Ratschlag geben. ✔

Think positive. • I have a good idea. • If I were you, … • If you told …, …

69 ↗

Ich kann in einem Geschäft ein Gespräch führen und dort etwas einkaufen. ✔

How are you today? • I'd like … . • This … is less expensive than that one. • Here's your change.

70 ↗

Ich kann einen Zeitungsartikel über eine Katastrophe verstehen. ✔

70 ↗

Ich kann Informationen über ein B & B weitergeben. ✔

71 ↗

Ich kann einen Film über eine Auseinandersetzung verstehen. ✔

(TASK) A newspaper report

Work in groups of three or four students. Each group thinks about an interesting, fun, or scary event during their last school year. Each group writes a report about it.

Step 1

Collect ideas.

Choose an event. Collect ideas. Make a mind map.

Who? What? When? Where? Why? event

Step 2

Look at the example.

It shows the most important features of a newspaper report.

1 Headline
2 Date, author
3 Introduction
4 Main part
5 Ending

① Film crew visits local school

② 7th April 2016, by Jamie Smith

③ A film crew was at Hollywell School on Saturday. But nobody knows what the film will be!

④ Students heard the news yesterday from the headteacher, Lucy Green. Mrs Green told us: "A film company came to the school on Saturday and they filmed in the morning and the afternoon. We are all very excited, but we don't know the name of the film yet."

"No children or teachers were at the school. The caretaker opened the doors at 9 o'clock but left after that," she added.

⑤ Film companies often work in Northern Ireland, of course, but Hollywell School has never been in a film before.

Hollywell School

Step 3

Write the introduction, the main part and the ending.

a) Introduction:
Write one or two sentences.
Answer the Wh-questions.

It took place in … on … . • … were there. •
… because … .

b) Main part:
Write more details about the event.

First … •
Then … . • After that … . • …

c) Ending:
Write one or two sentences to finish your report.

In the end … . • Finally … . • …

Step 4

Find one or two photos.

Write captions for the photos.
Find a headline.
Headlines are always very short.
Only use about five words.
Say who wrote the report and when.

Step 5

Check your report. → M Writers' conference, p. 171

Are there any spelling mistakes?
Did you write clearly?
Do you have a headline?
Did you add a date?
…

WRITING SKILLS

Wenn du einen Computer benutzt, kann dir die
Rechtschreibprüfung helfen, Fehler zu vermeiden.
Damit sich dein Text flüssiger liest, verwende
Bindewörter (but, and, after that). Ergänze Adjektive.

Step 6

Present your report. Give feedback to other groups. → M Tip top, p. 171

Extra practice

1 Find the places. (nach 75/5)

| Northern ✓ | bed | Lough | breakfast | Giant's | Neagh |
| fast | Maggie's | Causeway | Ireland ✓ | and | shop | Bel |

1. Northern Ireland   2. …

2 Find the adjectives and make a word. (nach 77/5)

| sad | furious | smart | confident | horrible | optimistic | fed up |

1. It means clever. (fifth letter)
2. You are … when you know that you are good at something. (second letter)
3. Sarah was really … . (first letter of second word)
4. It means very angry. (third letter)
5. It means very bad. (fifth letter)
6. It's the opposite of happy. (first letter)
7. It means that you feel good about the future. (third letter)
8. The new word is … .

Aus den Hinweisen in den Klammern ergibt sich ein neues Wort.

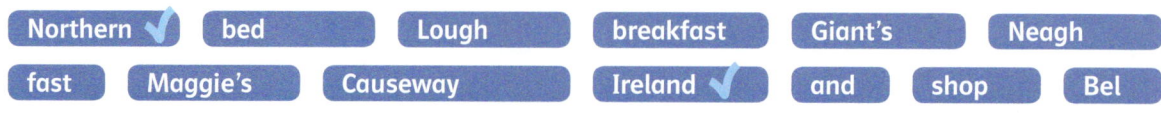

3 What would they do? (nach 78/9)

1. If Julie —— (live) in a B & B, she would talk to the tourists.
   If Julie <u>lived</u> in a B & B, she <u>would talk</u> to the tourists.
2. If Sarah's parents had more time, it —— (be) more fun.
3. If Sarah's mum didn't nag her, Sarah —— (feel) better.
4. If Ashley —— (not help) Sarah, it would be horrible.
5. If Julie —— (live) nearer, Sarah —— (not miss) her.
6. If Julie —— (visit) Sarah, she —— (ask) silly questions.
7. If Sarah and her family —— (live) in Belfast, Sarah —— (see) her friend more often.

4 Complete the shopping dialogue. (nach 81/4)

1. Shop assistant: Hello. What would you —— ?
2. Customer: Hi. I'd like a —— of strawberry jam and a bottle of mineral water, please.
3. Shop assistant: That will be £3.30. Anything —— ?
4. Customer: No, thanks. Here you —— .
5. Shop assistant: Here's 70p —— . Bye now.
6. Customer: See —— .

5 Write a shopping list. (nach 81/5)

– two bottles of …

6 Compare the things. (nach 82/8)

| is as … as | isn't as … as | is -er/more … than |

1. Northern Ireland 13,843 km² – Scotland 78,387 km² (big)
   Northern Ireland isn't as big as Scotland.
2. the train: takes an hour – the car: takes 75 mins (fast)
3. rice: ✔ – pasta: ✔ (good)
4. rugby: ☺ ☺ – football: ☺ ☺ ☺ (popular in Northern Ireland)
5. Belfast: 19°C – Berlin: 22°C (warm today)
6. orange juice: 1L, £2.75 – mineral water: 1L, £1.85 – (expensive)

74/1-2
75/3-4

7 Complete the dialogue in the supermarket. (nach 83/9)

Some or any?
1. Customer 1: I can't see any peanut butter. Can you?
2. Customer 2: Yes, it's here. They have —— jars on special offer.
3. Customer 1: Tissues are on our list too. There are —— over there.
4. Customer 2: Great. Can you see —— brown bread?
5. Customer 1: No, but they have —— white bread. It looks very nice.
6. Customer 2: Oh! There aren't —— more cakes. Maybe they've sold them all!
7. Customer 1: I haven't eaten —— chocolate today.
8. Customer 2: Really? Let's buy —— now!

A day in Lisburn

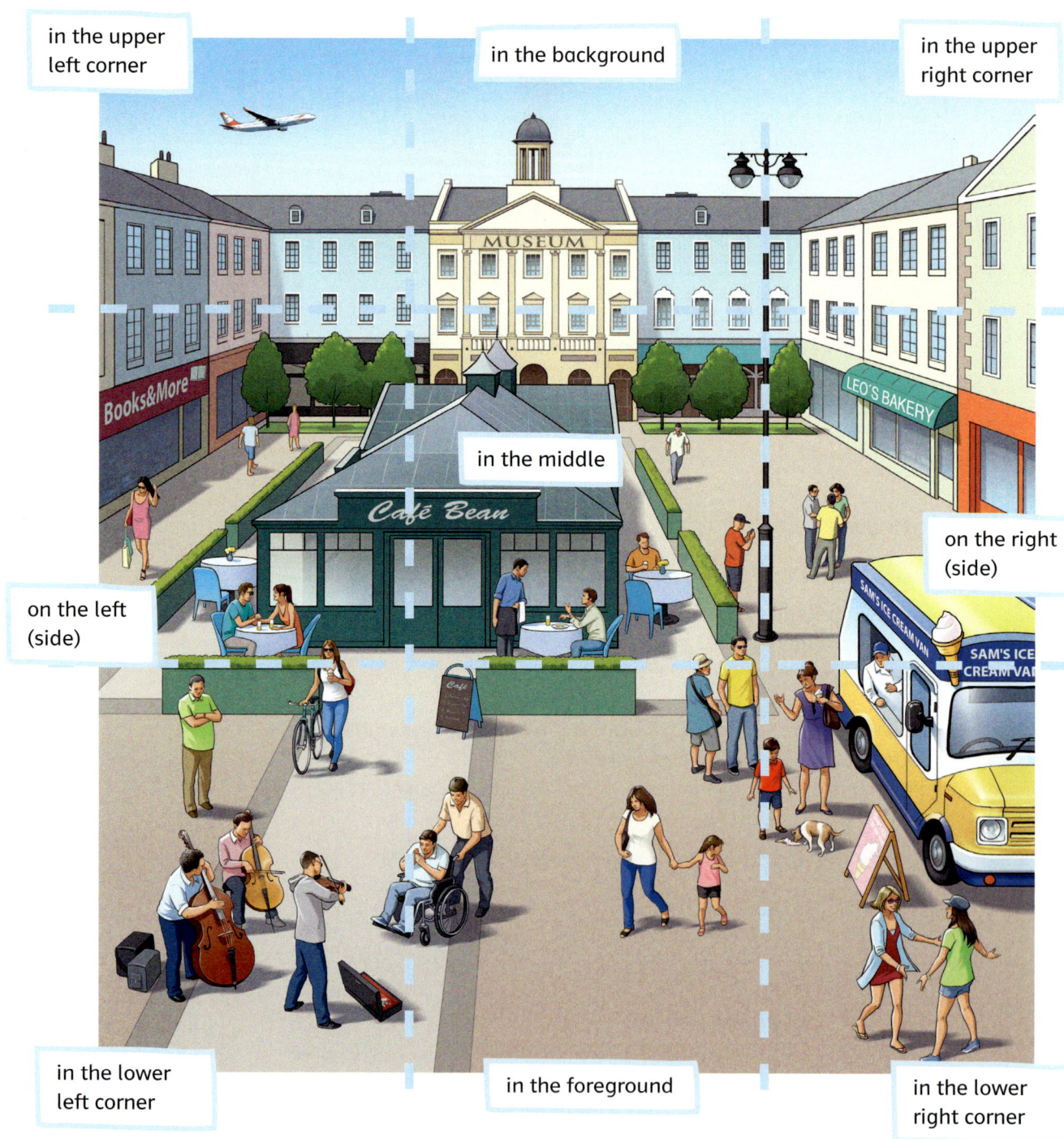

in the upper left corner

in the background

in the upper right corner

in the middle

on the right (side)

on the left (side)

in the lower left corner

in the foreground

in the lower right corner

1 What, who, where?

Answer the questions about the picture.

1. What can you see?
2. Who can you see?
3. Where is it?

> Bevor du anfängst, sieh dir das Bild genau an. Sage zuerst sehr allgemein, was du siehst. Beantworte dazu kurz die drei Fragen.

2 Describe the picture.

a) Add more details.

In the upper left corner there is … .
On the left (side) I can see … .
In the lower left corner there are … .
In the background I can see … .
In the middle there is … .

> Halte eine von dir vorher festgelegte Reihenfolge ein. Beginne z. B. von links oben und gehe dann nach rechts unten.

b) Look at the picture again.
Where are the people or the things?

In front of the ice cream van there are … .
Next to the book shop there is … .

> Sage, wo sich die Personen aufhalten oder wo sich Gegenstände befinden. Nutze dazu folgende Präpositionen: next to, between, behind, over, in, on, in front of, under.

3 What are the people doing?

Look at the people and say what they are doing.

In front of the café some people are having lunch.
The dog is eating the boy's ice cream.

> Ergänze, was die Personen tun.
> Benutze das present progressive.

74/1-2
75/3-4

4 Describe your own picture.

Choose a picture or photo and describe it.

Find more online:
fe76m3

Am Ende dieser Unit kann ich ...
- Informationen über Irland herausfinden.
- mich mit meiner Gastfamilie unterhalten.
- eine Reise mit öffentlichen Verkehrsmitteln planen.
- eine Geschichte über einen Umzug in ein anderes Land verstehen.
- Informationen über eine Schauspielerin weitergeben.
- einen Film über Musikunterricht verstehen.

9 ⎙ 2,9 ☞   Unit 5

Welcome to Ireland

The green republic

1

Welcome to Ireland! The Republic of Ireland is in the European Union and it uses the euro. But it isn't part of the United Kingdom.

2

There are lots of famous Irish bands, and people often pl music in pubs. Many cities have a youth orchestra too. Orchestras from other countries often come to play conce

1 Choose one picture. Describe it to a partner.

78/1-2

You can use these phrases:

- In the foreground there is ...
- In the middle there are ...
- In the background I can see ...
- ...

You can also look for help on the skills pages 92–93.

2 Right or wrong?

1. The Irish use the pound to pay.
2. There are many youth orchestras in Ireland.
3. Keith Hanley won in a competition for singers.
4. The arts programmes in Dublin have courses in sports like tennis and football.
5. The Irish colour is blue.

3

Keith Hanley is an Irish singer from a small town near Cork. He is a winner of 'The Voice of Ireland' competition. Keith's favourite musical style is hip hop.

4

Dublin, the capital of Ireland, has lots of arts programmes for young people. There are courses in music and acting, dancing and making films.

5

Every year on 17th March the Irish celebrate St Patrick's Day. The people wear green, the Irish colour. There are many parties.

🔵 **3** (LISTENING) **Which statement about Keith Hanley is right? A or B?**

2,10 ⌕

A
– 19 years old
– cares for animals
– hobbies: singing, dancing and playing the saxophone

B
– 19 years old
– cares for children with special needs
– hobbies: singing, dancing and playing the guitar

to care for [tə ˈkeə ˌfɔː] – sich kümmern um
sign language [ˈsaɪn ˌlæŋgwɪdʒ] – Zeichensprache
with special needs [wɪθ ˈspeʃl ˌniːdz] – mit Behinderung
guitar [gɪˈtɑː] – Gitarre

Ich kann Informationen über Irland herausfinden. ✔

At home with the O'Brians

🔵 **1** (READING) **Read the dialogue.** → M Dramatic reading, p. 167

2,11 ☞

1

1 Conor: Here we are. I'll show you the house. Just leave your bags here. You don't have to take off your shoes. … Here's the kitchen. There's the fridge. Just help yourself. We don't
5 usually have breakfast together during the week but we all meet for dinner around 6:30.
Leo: Could we have an Irish breakfast one day, please?
Conor: No problem. We can have it at the
10 weekend. But on weekdays I often just have cereal.
Leo: That's fine with me. Some people have bread with ham or cheese. But I prefer a sweet breakfast.

3

15 Conor: That's Maddy's bedroom. That's Jamie's. OK. Just make yourself at home. Are you hungry? Would you like some tea?
Leo: No, thanks. I don't drink tea.
Conor: Ha. I don't mean the drink but the
20 meal. Mum is preparing a snack in the kitchen now. Just come down when you're ready and join us.
Leo: Thanks a lot.

2

Conor: This is the bathroom. Mum put some towels for you over there. You can use all 25
the shampoo, except Maddy's. She hates to share hers with others. Maddy isn't at home at the moment. She's practising with her school band. Are you nervous about your own concert? It'll be great. You can put your 30
toothbrush and other things over here. Did you bring an adaptor?
Leo: Err, I think I didn't.
Conor: Don't worry, we often have guests from other countries. We always have one at 35
home. You can use ours.
Leo: Great. Thanks.
Conor: Oh, the phone is ringing. Just a second.

Leo Kurz (14), from Hanau in Germany

Conor O'Brian (14), from Cork in Ireland

🔵 **2** **Answer the questions.**

1. Which rooms does Conor show Leo?
2. When does the family meet for dinner?
3. What would Leo like to try for breakfast?
4. What doesn't Maddy like to do?
5. Why does Conor's family have an adaptor?
6. What does Conor mean when he says "Would you like some tea"?

CULTURE BOX

Die meisten Briten und Iren essen abends warm. Einige nennen das 'tea', andere 'dinner'. Esst ihr abends warm? Wann esst ihr Abendbrot?

3 (LISTENING) **Complete Leo's and Mrs O'Brian's sentences.**

2,12

1. Do you have —— you need?
2. I couldn't find out how to —— the window.
3. Would you like some —— and sausages for dinner?
4. I'm sorry. I thought of —— .
5. Would you please get the —— ?
6. I brought some —— for you.

4 (WRITING) **Make a mind map with things for a trip.** → M Think-pair-share, p. 171

79/1

things for the bathroom

charger   **things for a trip**   raincoat

ID

personal things   ?   clothes

5 **What would you take on a trip?**

a) Match the things for a trip with the words. Add them to your mind map. → ○ p. 123

79/2

1. nail scissors
2. comb
3. toothpaste
4. hairdryer
5. shower gel
6. body lotion

b) When do you need …? → V In the bathroom, p. 201

79/3

| hair gel | soap | perfume | mirror | hairbrush |

1. You need hair gel when you hair is a mess.

6 (SPEAKING) **Play the game: I'm going to take …**

80/4

A: I'm going to take a toothbrush.
B: I'm going to take a toothbrush and an umbrella.
C: I'm going to take a toothbrush, an umbrella and … .

SPEAKING SKILLS

Wenn dir ein Wort nicht so schnell einfällt, benutze Pausenfüller, z. B. Well … / I think … / Uhm … .

→ G13, p. 162

Language detectives

We usually have breakfast together.
Mum is preparing a snack in the kitchen now.

Die Signalwörter helfen dir, die richtige Zeitform zu finden.

Was ist der Unterschied zwischen den beiden Situationen?

7 **Choose the right form.** → M Peer correction, p. 169

80/5-6
81/7

1. **Conor:** Hi Leo, what **do you do** • **are you doing** right now?
2. **Leo:** **I listen** • **I'm listening** to some new songs.
3. **Conor:** I usually **listen** • **am listening** to rock music. What do you like?
4. **Leo:** I always **enjoy** • **am enjoying** hip hop music a lot. This is Torch OneTwo, a new German rapper. **He** usually **writes** • **is writing** about his life.
5. **Conor:** The music sounds OK. What **does he talk** • **is he talking** about now?
6. **Leo:** **He sings** • **is singing** about his city, Heidelberg.
7. **Conor:** **We** never **hear** • **are hearing** about German hip hop artists.

8 **Complete the text messages.**

a) Simple present or present progressive? → ○ p. 123

81/8

1 **Leo Germanguy**
I'm in the bathroom right now and I —— (look for / towels). Where are they?

2 **Conor O'Brian**
We always —— (put / in cupboard). Let me know if you can't find them there.

3 **Conor O'Brian**
I'm going to be home late. I am at school and I —— (finish / Art project). Will u tell mum?

4 **Mad O'Brian**
I'll tell her. But she —— (hate / it) when you're late.

5 **Mad O'Brian**
I'm here and I —— (wash / hair). And now my shampoo isn't here. Grrrrrh!!! M

6 **Conor O'Brian**
Boy, Maddy is angry. She never —— (share / shampoo). Did you take it???

b) Write Leo's text messages for these situations:
   – You wait at bus stop. There's no school bus.
   – You have dinner with the family. You like the food.

81/9 **9** **Rewrite the sentences.**

a) Rewrite the sentences. Use possessive pronouns. → ○ p. 124

1. It's Dad's chocolate pudding. – It's his.
2. It's Maddy's tea cup. – It's … .
3. It's my rain coat. – It's … .
4. It's Mum's and Dad's room. – It's … .
5. It's your shirt. – It's … .
6. It's our cat. – It's … .
7. It's Conor's bike. – It's … .

GRAMMAR	→ **G14**, p. 163
my – mine	your – yours
his – his	her – hers
our – ours	their – theirs

b) Leo has forgotten many things. Who can he borrow things from?

Mr O'Brian
Conor
Mr and Mrs O'Brian
Jamie
Maddy

10 (YOUR TURN) **A text message dialogue** → **V** Things for a trip, p. 206

You are staying with a host family: Your partner is in town and you are at home. Write a text message dialogue.

A (at home)

1. Say hi. Ask what your partner is doing and where he or she is.

3. Answer. Say that you have forgotten … / you can't find … / you would like to borrow … .

5. Answer: It's a good / bad idea because … .

B (in town)

2. Answer your partner. Ask: Is he or she OK?

4. Answer your partner. Ask: Can he or she meet for an ice cream (where, when)?

6. Finish the dialogue.

WRITING SKILLS

Wenn du Wörter in einer Textnachricht in Großbuchstaben schreibst, „schreist" du dein Gegenüber an. Bleib höflich.

Ich kann mich mit meiner Gastfamilie unterhalten. ✔

Getting around in Dublin

1 (READING) Read the flyer and the dialogue. → M Read and look up, p. 170

2,13
82/1

1 Jamie: I can't wait to go to the Striking Moves workshop tomorrow. I'm sure they'll teach us some new moves there.
Lisa: I think so too. We should plan our journey.
Jamie: Where is the workshop?
5 Lisa: It's in Sackville Place. It's not far from The Spire on O'Connell Street.
Jamie: How do we get there? I don't use public transport very often!
Lisa: Here, I've brought the timetables. All right, let's see
10 what we can find out. We can take the number 9 bus to Goldenbridge. We must get off the bus there and change to the tram. Then it's ten stops on the Red Line to Abbey Street.
Jamie: How long does the journey take?
Lisa: About an hour. Maybe longer. The bus may not be on
15 time. It usually isn't.
Jamie: Well, the workshop starts at 10, so we must leave by 8:30. We really mustn't be late. Why don't we meet at the bus stop near my house? There's a bus at 8:25.
Lisa: That sounds good to me.
20 Jamie: OK. How much is the fare?
Lisa: We can get tickets that are valid all day for three fifty each. But we needn't spend that much money. A single ticket costs one forty each. And then it's the same for the way back.
Jamie: Great. See you tomorrow, then I won't be late …

STRIKING MOVES
Dance and drumming workshop

Take part in our exciting project
Learn the coolest moves!

Saturdays 21st, 28th June and 5th, 12th July
10 a.m. – 5 p.m.

14 Sackville Place, Dublin

For ages 15–35

2 Answer the questions.

a) Find the information.

1. Where do Lisa and Jamie want to go?
2. Which tram do they take?
3. How many stops are there to Abbey Street?
4. What's special about the buses?
5. How long is the workshop?
6. Who can take part in the workshop?

b) When would you choose a day ticket and when single tickets?

3 Find the odd one out.

82/2

a) Which word doesn't go with the others? Why? → ○ p. 124

1. train • bus • ticket
2. fare • receipt • present
3. stop • line • museum

4. on time • sure • late
5. date • timetable • map
6. plan • change • get off

82/3

b) What are these tickets valid for? → **V** Public transport, p. 203

| daily | weekly | monthly | single | return |

A daily ticket is valid for one day.

83/4

4 (SPEAKING) Find the way. → **M** Milling around, p. 168

a) Look at the map and find the best way to get from James's to … → ○ p. 124

– George's Dock
– Connolly train station
– Milltown

To get from James's to George's Dock, take the Red Line. It's eight stops. Get off the tram and you're there.

b) Make a list with three places. Partner A's list are the starting points and partner B's list is where you want to go. Give each other directions.

5 (SONG) Luminous

2,14

Listen to the song by the Irish group, Jedward: What will the singer always know, and why?

1 We see the day, tryin' to fight it.
It's all in vain, 'cause we know the night wins,
But we don't care,
We're lighting up like a flare.

5 It's so unreal,
The light that you're shining.
You make me feel like
The darkness won't matter,

'Cause you and I,
10 Don't care where the day has gone.
We don't need the break of dawn,
We don't need the break of dawn.

(Chorus): And I will always know where you are,
15 'Cause I can see you glow in the dark.
We got the stars, and moon in us,
We're always gonna be luminous.

Language detectives → G15, p. 164

We <u>must</u> get off the bus.
We <u>needn't</u> buy tickets for the journey back.
We <u>mustn't</u> be late.
We <u>can</u> take the number 9 bus.
The bus <u>may not</u> be on time.

<u>Must</u>, <u>mustn't</u>, <u>needn't</u>, <u>can</u> und <u>may</u>, <u>may not</u> sind besondere Verben. In welchen Situationen benutzt du sie?

6 What <u>can</u> kids do at a dance workshop? What <u>mustn't</u> they do?

83/5

1. They **can** • **mustn't** be late.
2. They **can** • **mustn't** eat during the dance classes.
3. They **can** • **mustn't** stop dancing when they need a break.
4. They **can** • **mustn't** talk when the teachers dance.
5. They **can** • **mustn't** drink water when they are thirsty.
6. They **can** • **mustn't** learn new dance steps.

7 (SPEAKING) What <u>must</u> you do on a bus? What <u>mustn't</u> you do?

84/6a)

a) Explain these school bus rules. → ○ p. 125

FOLLOW THE SCHOOL BUS RULES

You read:

1. Talk quietly.
2. Don't eat ice cream.
3. Don't talk to the driver.
4. Don't bring pets.
5. Keep your head, hands and feet inside.
6. Don't push other students.

You say:

1. You must talk quietly.
2. You …

b) Think of other bus rules. Then talk with a partner. Are your partner's rules OK?

84/6b)

8 Make sentences. Choose <u>must</u> or <u>needn't</u>. → **M** Peer correction, p. 169

84/7

1. <u>I have two tickets. So you</u>		<u>buy one. You can have one of mine.</u>
2. Do you really think we	**must**	take our coats? It's a warm day!
3. It's already four o'clock! We		go now or we won't get our bus.
4. Alan is at the workshop. So we	**needn't**	wait for him at the bus stop. Let's go.
5. I can hear you very well. You		talk loudly.
6. Do you know where Kate is? We		call her. We can meet her at the station.

9 (WRITING) <u>Must</u>, <u>needn't</u> or <u>mustn't</u>?

a) Put in the right verb. → ○ p. 125

84/8

1. Dogs travel free. You —— buy an extra ticket.
2. Your dog —— be with you all the time.
3. Your dog —— hurt people.
4. It —— be nice to other people.
5. You —— carry a small dog in a bag. It's OK to hold it.
6. You —— play with your dog when you're on the bus.

b) Find rules for a pet at home. Write a list.

sleep   eat   play   go out   sit

✳10 (YOUR TURN) A journey by public transport → **V** Public transport, p. 207

P

a) Find out how to get from the airport or train station to your house on public transport.

85/1

b) Write an e-mail to a friend from another country. Give him or her advice how to get to your house from the airport or train station.

E-MAIL

Hi Helen,

Let me tell you how to get to my house from the airport. You should take the train …
Best wishes,

…

You should take … .
Then … .
It's … stops.
The journey takes … .
You must buy … .
You needn't … .
It costs … .

Ich kann eine Reise mit öffentlichen Verkehrsmitteln planen. ✔

A different kind of gold

1 Have you ever moved to another place? How did you feel?

2 (READING) Read the story.

2,15

1 It was St Patrick's Day yesterday. And I wished I was back home in Ireland. My Dad and I moved here two months ago and I still miss my Irish friends and our nice little
5 home in Donegal.

Oh, I should introduce myself to you. My name is Niamh. That's an old Irish girl's name. You say it 'neve', like 'leave'. I always have to explain it to people here in
10 Northampton in England. That's where we moved. Dad worked in a factory in Donegal until it closed last year. He tried to find another job in the area, but lots of other factories were closing too. He finally found a
15 job but that meant that we had to move to England.

So yesterday it was my favourite holiday, St Patrick's Day. Back home there are lots of parades and parties. Everyone wears green
20 clothes. In fact the whole city is green. We send cards with shamrocks and rainbows on and give each other sweets in gold paper. The shamrock is our national flower. The rainbows and the sweets are from an old
25 Irish story. It says there's a pot of gold at the end of the rainbow.

There were parties here in Northampton too. It almost felt like being home, but I still don't know a lot of people and places. So I stayed
30 at home. That's why the day just made me feel very lonely and homesick. I got even sadder because the netball girls Sonya, Billy and Nisha, who I really like, didn't answer any of my calls.

3 Talk about feelings.

a) Make a list of adjectives and verbs that describe how Niamh feels. Compare with a partner.

b) How does Niamh's feelings change in the last paragraph? Give reasons.

First Niamh feels / is ... because ...   Then she feels ... because ...   She is ...

4 Talk about St Patrick's Day.

Look at the third paragraph (lines 16 to 25). What did you learn about St Patrick's Day that you didn't know before?

In manchen Geschichten muss man auf die Hinweise achten, wie sich Menschen fühlen oder was passiert ist. Man nennt das „zwischen den Zeilen lesen".

35 When Dad came home from work that afternoon, I was just sitting at the window. "Are you OK, Niamh?" he asked me. "Yes," I said.
But Dad didn't believe me. So he tried to
40 cheer me up with this old poem (don't ask me where he got that one from):

At the end of the rainbow is a pot of gold,
My dad would say to me.
We packed our bags, our house was sold,
45 *We crossed the Irish Sea.*
But until the fable once foretold
Actually comes to be,
The wealth of friends and family old
Is gold enough for me.

50 He wasn't very successful. I still felt miserable and just wanted to feel sorry for myself. Do you know what I mean?

Later that day, in the late afternoon, our doorbell rang. Dad said: "You can go to the
55 door." When I opened it I couldn't believe my eyes. The netball girls. All three dressed in green clothes and big green party hats on. I couldn't help but laugh. "Surprise!" they said. "Your dad says it's OK to take you to a
60 St Patrick's Day party at our youth centre. Do you want to join us?" I rushed into my room and grabbed my Paddy's Day outfit as fast as I could. Maybe this was the beginning of something wonderful.

5 Choose one of these tasks.

a) Some singers and bands have left Ireland to become successful in Britain or the USA. Others come from a family which moved to these countries a long time ago.

Find information and photos on the internet for a short presentation about one of them.
→ M 1-minute-presentation, p. 166

86/1
87/2-4

b) Write your own poem. Choose one of these titles:

Friends   **Leaving home**

1. Make a list of words that match the title.
2. Make an outline of an object or shape. It should be big enough to write ten words into it.
3. Write them into the shape. Share your poems with the class.

fun holiday
Ireland
happy green parades
party shamrock dance
celebrate

Ich kann eine Geschichte über einen Umzug in ein anderes Land verstehen. ✓

A German star

INTERNET

Emilia Schüle

Emilia Schüle

1 Die Schauspielerin Emilia Schüle kam als Ein-
jährige 1993 aus Russland nach Deutschland.
Bereits mit acht Jahren begann sie, Ballett-
stunden und Unterricht in Hip-Hop und Street
5 Dance zu nehmen. Mit 13 Jahren nahm sie am
Theaterworkshop „Talents Getting Started" teil
und beeindruckte die Jury mit ihrem Können.
Danach erhielt sie erste Rollen als Schauspielerin
und spielte auch in einigen Werbefilmen mit.

10 Ihre erste Hauptrolle hatte sie 2007 in dem Film
„Manatu – Nur die Wahrheit rettet dich", in dem
es um ein magisches Brettspiel geht. Auch in der
bekannten Serie „Tatort" spielte sie schon mit.
Bekannt wurde sie schließlich durch die beiden
15 Filme „Freche Mädchen" und Freche Mädchen 2",
in denen sich alles um Teenagerfreundschaften
und erste Liebesprobleme dreht.

Emilia hat in dieser kurzen Zeit ihrer Schauspieler-
karriere schon einige Preise verliehen bekommen:
Im Jahr 2014 erhielt sie die „Goldene Kamera" 20
und den „Deutschen Schauspielerpreis" in der
Kategorie „Beste Schauspielerin Nachwuchs".
Trotz dieser frühen Erfolge war es ihr sehr wichtig,
die Schule abzuschließen. Während des letzten
Schuljahres arbeitete sie sogar nebenher als 25
Schauspielerin.

1 Talk about Emilia Schüle.

88/1-2

You are on an exchange visit in Ireland. Your exchange partner sees the article
and is interested in acting. Tell her about Emilia Schüle. Say:

1. who she is
2. how she became an actor
3. what TV and film work she has done

2 And you?

Would you like to be an actor? Say why or why not.

Ich kann Informationen über eine Schauspielerin weitergeben. ✔

The guitar lesson

1 Talk about music. → M Think-pair-share, p. 171

What is music good for? What can you do with music? Collect words.

dance

impress

music

listen to

...

> **CULTURE**
>
> Musik spielt im Leben vieler Menschen überall auf der Welt eine große Rolle. Die meisten Länder haben besondere Instrumente. Einige der traditionellen irischen Instrumente sind die Harfe und das Bodhran (eine Art Trommel). Kennst du traditionelle Instrumente in anderen Ländern?

2 (VIEWING) Watch the film.

10 a) Watch the film from the beginning to 1:45. Find the right answer.

1. Where does Ciara (the music teacher) want to go?
   a) Victoria Station • b) Greenwich
2. Where did Hayley work?
   a) in a café and on a pineapple farm • b) at a restaurant and on a wind farm
3. What does Hayley mean when she says, "I go wherever the wind takes me."
   a) She'll go to a very windy place next. • b) She doesn't know where she'll go next.

b) Watch the film from 1:45 to the ending.

1. Where does Marley find out about the guitar lessons?
2. What does Alicia think about Marley's idea at the end?
3. Why does Marley want to have guitar lessons?

3 (SPEAKING) Talk about the film.

a) Which places are not in the film?

bus station   café   supermarket

streets in Greenwich   music school

> **VIEWING SKILLS**
>
> Es ist schwierig, einen Film im Freien zu drehen. Wenn man in einer belebten Straße dreht, können fremde Personen durchs Bild laufen oder die Hintergrundgeräusche stören. In geschlossenen Räumen zu drehen ist aber auch nicht einfach. Das Team braucht viel Platz für Kameras und Mikrofone. Daher drehen viele Produktionsfirmen im Studio.

b) What do you think: why did the filmmakers choose the places to shoot the film?

Ich kann einen Film über Musikunterricht verstehen. ✓

Checklist

Ich kann Informationen über Irland verstehen.

89 ↗

Ich kann mich mit meiner Gastfamilie unterhalten.

I didn't pack any .... • You can put your ... here. • We usually eat at half past six.

89 ↗

Ich kann eine Reise mit öffentlichen Verkehrsmitteln planen.

You can take a number 9 bus to .... • You must change at .... • The journey takes ... minutes. • The tickets cost ....

90 ↗

Ich kann eine Geschichte über einen Umzug in ein anderes Land verstehen.

90 ↗

Ich kann Informationen über eine Schauspielerin verstehen.

91 ↗

Ich kann einen Film über Musikunterricht verstehen.

✳ (TASK) A quiz

Work in groups and write questions for a quiz about the five countries of the British Isles. Each group writes eight questions for one country. The groups are the teams when you do the quiz.

Collect ideas and decide on your questions.

a) Collect ideas for questions about your country.

England | Northern Ireland | Wales | Scotland | The Republic of Ireland

Here are some ideas for questions (you can ask about things that were in the units in this book):
- food?
- sport?
- town?
- famous person?
- flag?
- transport?
- ...

CULTURE

 Diese Flagge wird normalerweise mit Nordirland in Verbindung gebracht. Man nennt sie St Patrick's Cross. (Offiziell hat Nordirland keine eigene Flagge. Man benutzt die Flagge Großbritanniens.)

b) Make a long list with everyone's ideas. Then look at all the ideas together and agree on a short list.
→ M Placemat, p. 169

STUDY SKILLS

Hört euch alle Ideen gut an. Gebt allen eine Chance, zu erklären, was er oder sie gemeint hat. Einigt euch auf eure Ideen für die Fragen.

Step 2

Write your questions and check the answers.

a) Each student writes a card with one question and the answer on the back.

b) Another student checks the English. A third student checks that the answer is correct.

c) Each student in the team has to read one or more questions. Decide on the order of the questions and practise before you do the quiz.

Step 3

Get ready for the quiz.

1. When can you do the quiz?
2. Who can be the umpire and start/finish the quiz?
3. Which team reads its questions first?

Jedes Team kann eine Flagge vorbereiten. Ihr könnt auch ein Maskottchen mitbringen. Viel Glück!

Step 4

Do the quiz.

Each team reads its questions. The other teams write the answers.

SPEAKING SKILLS

Lest die Fragen laut und deutlich vor. Seht die anderen Teams an, wenn ihr eure Fragen vorlest. Wenn ihr eine Frage nicht versteht, fragt höflich nach. (Wenn ihr die Antwort wisst, behaltet sie zunächst für euch).

Can you say that again please?

Sorry, I didn't understand that!

Can you speak louder, please?

One student from each team checks the answers at the end and gives the results to the umpire. The umpire says who the winner is.

Step 5

Talk about the quiz. → M Round robin, p. 170

Did you enjoy the quiz? What was good/not so good about it?

Extra practice

1 Find the words. (nach 95/3)

1. There is a —— for singers in Ireland every year.
2. —— is on 17th March. Everybody wears —— clothes.
3. People often play music in —— in Ireland.
4. Teenagers can learn how to —— at special —— in Dublin.
5. Ireland isn't part of the United Kingdom, but it is in the ——.
6. Many Irish cities have a youth ——.

2 What is it? (nach 97/5)

1. You put it on a toothbrush.
2. This is where you have breakfast.
3. This is where you sleep in.
4. It's a cold place for milk or cheese.
5. You need it when your hair is dirty.
6. It's a hot drink and a meal.
7. It's for when your hair is wet. It needs electricity.

3 Put in the right forms. Simple present or present progressive? (nach 98/8)

1. I can't talk now. I —— (do) my homework.
   I can't talk now. I'm doing my homework.
2. Conor sometimes —— (cook) for the family.
3. We usually —— (have) breakfast at eight o'clock. And you?
4. Maddy —— (practise) with the school band at the moment.
5. Look at that woman! She —— (wear) the same T-shirt as me.
6. Conor often —— (use) Maddy's shampoo.
7. What's that noise? Oh, it's Leo. He —— (shout) at his sister.
8. You'll need an umbrella in Ireland. It often —— (rain) there.

4 Match and make sentences. (nach 100/2)

a) Match the words.

get   public   bus   plan ✓   pay

the journey ✓   the fare   timetable   transport   off

b) Put in the words from a).

1. The workshop is tomorrow. We must plan the journey.
2. Don't —— here – this isn't our stop.
3. You must —— when you travel on a bus or a train.
4. The —— tells you when the bus leaves and arrives.
5. I don't understand buses. I don't use —— very often.

5 Concert rules. Must or mustn't? (nach 102/7)

1. You —— bring glass bottles.
2. You —— buy a ticket.
3. You —— make films with your mobile.
4. You —— push other people.
5. You —— leave big bags outside.
6. You —— bring your own food.
7. You —— sit on the stairs.
8. You —— put rubbish on the floor.

6 Put in the right words. (nach 103/9)

1. It's raining now. We —— take an umbrella.
2. Our tickets are valid. You —— worry.
3. That bus is always on time. We —— be late.
4. Ssh, not so loud. We —— talk quietly.
5. I've heard that joke already. You —— tell me.
6. What's the next stop? I'll ask the driver.
   No, you —— talk to the driver.
7. Look, here's a plan. You —— ask.
8. Come on. We —— get off here.

must (3x)

mustn't (2x)

needn't (3x)

Diff corner

Unit 1, p.13

○ **4** (WRITING) **Where can you buy these things?**

Complete the sentences.

card		clothes ✓		sports
shoe		baker's		

A You can buy jeans at the clothes shop.
B You can buy bread at the … .
C You can buy a football at the … shop.
D You can buy a birthday card at the … shop.
E You can buy shoes at the … shop.

Unit 1, p.14

○ **8** (SPEAKING) **Interview your partner.** → M Double circle, p. 167

Ask a partner questions. He or she gives short answers.

A:
Do you
Do your friends
Does your dad
Do they
Does he

sometimes
often
usually

go to the cinema?
do your homework?
play football?
watch TV?
go shopping?

B:
Yes, I do.
No, I don't.
Yes, he/she does.
No, he/she doesn't.
Yes, they do.
No, they don't.

Do you often go shopping?   Yes, I do. / No, I don't.

Unit 1, p.15

○ **9** (WRITING) **Make questions and answers.**

Match the questions and answers.

1. Do you know where the football stadium is?
2. Does it take long to get there?
3. Where is the nearest bus stop?
4. When do the buses leave?
5. Are bus tickets expensive?
6. Where can I buy a ticket?

A On the bus.
B I think it's every five minutes.
C Yes, I do.
D No, they aren't. Just 90p.
E It's just five minutes down that road.
F Yes, it does. But there's a bus.

Unit 1, p.17

3 **Sort the words into groups.** → **M** Peer correction, p. 169

Copy the table. Put the words and phrases into the right groups.

words for the size	where	sorts of places

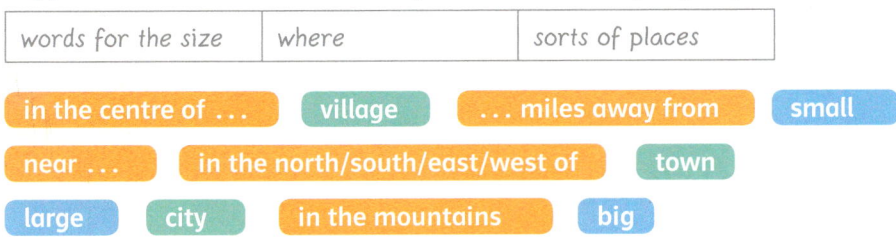

in the centre of …   village   … miles away from   small

near …   in the north/south/east/west of   town

large   city   in the mountains   big

Unit 1, p.18

6 **Make Tom's story.**

Complete the sentences.

went   wasn't   fell   got up   wanted   heard   was   had   saw

1. Last Saturday morning things <u>went</u> a little crazy on our farm. (go)
2. I —— a noise in the garden (hear) and I —— . (get up)
3. I —— my dad in the garden. (see)
4. He —— to put Bert and Daisy, our goats, in his tractor. (want)
5. Suddenly he —— in the mud, head first. (fall)
6. It —— so funny. (be) I just —— to laugh. (have)
7. Dad —— very happy. (not be)

Unit 1, p.18

7 (WRITING) **What didn't Hannah and Kilkenny do on Saturday?**

Make sentences with <u>didn't</u>, <u>wasn't</u> or <u>weren't</u>.

1. Hannah <u>didn't walk</u> to the baker's in the morning.
2. Hannah —— (not be) in the living room at two o'clock.
3. Hannah —— (not do) her homework in the afternoon.

p.113

4. She and her sister —— (not make) jewellery at five o'clock.

5. Later she —— (not write) a text message.

6. Hannah and her sister —— (not be) at the cinema.

Unit 2, p. 35

○ **5 Find the words.** → **M** Bus stop, p. 166

Find the opposites.

1. big – small
2. slow – q——
3. tough – e——
4. friendly – u——
5. strong – w——
6. dangerous – s——
7. wet – d——
8. quiet – l——

weak   unfriendly   dry
small ✓   easy   loud
safe   quick

Unit 2, p. 36

○ **9 Complete the report.**

Add these words to the text.

well   excitedly   fast   slowly   heavily   hungrily

Last month Class 9G went on a camping trip to Snowdonia. It started to rain <u>heavily</u> (1) so we had to walk —— (2). At lunchtime we ate our picnics —— (3). On Sunday we went canoeing —— (4). We went down the river —— (5). Everything went —— (6) and no one got wet. Phew! We had lots of fun.

GRAMMAR   → G4, p. 153

A <u>fast</u> game – she runs <u>fast</u>
A <u>hard</u> day – he works <u>hard</u>
A <u>good</u> song – they sing <u>well</u>

Unit 2, p. 37

○ **10** (WRITING) **Adjective or adverb?**

Complete the dialogue.

Nach den Formen von „to be" („was", „were") benutzt du immer nur Adjektive!

Mark: Beth, how was horse riding today?
Beth: It was <u>awful</u>/awfully (1). It was wet/wetly (2) and rained terrible/terribly (3).
Mark: So you had to ride careful/carefully (4)?
Beth: Yes, and there were lots of crazy/crazily (5) people on bikes too. Some of them rode dangerous/dangerously (6).
Mark: Was your horse nervous/nervously (7) because of them?
Beth: No, it wasn't. Look, here's a photo of us …

Unit 2, p. 39

○ **6** (SPEAKING) **Find excuses. Why can't you do PE?**

Make sentences. Use the words in the box.

Dear teacher,
I'm so sorry. I can't do PE today.
My head hurts terribly. I have a sore throat too. I've also twisted my knee.
… I just don't feel well. ☹

I have cut my finger / hand / . . . .

I have burnt my finger / hand / arm / . . . .

I have broken my finger / hand / arm / foot / leg . . .

My . . . is bleeding . . .

Unit 2, p. 40

○ **8** (WRITING) **What has Megan already done? What hasn't she done?**

Make sentences.

What she has already done:
Put on her uniform
Opened the door
Had lunch
Written a message

What she hasn't done yet:
Collected the bandages
Drunk tea
Called the hospital

Megan <u>has</u> already <u>put on</u> her uniform. Megan <u>hasn't collected</u> … <u>yet</u>.

Unit 2, p. 41

9 (SPEAKING) Make a dialogue.

Complete the dialogue. Use the simple past (last) or the present perfect (already, yet, just).

Kim: Hey, I —— your brother at football training last Monday. (not see) What's wrong with him?
Jamie: He —— in hospital last week. (be)
Kim: Oh, I'm sorry. He —— already —— his leg this year, right? (hurt)
Jamie: Yes, last time, he and his friend —— to try some new cool skateboard tricks. (want)
Kim: When —— he —— home? (come)
Jamie: My parents —— just —— him back from the hospital. (bring)
Kim: That's great. —— his friend already —— the good news? (hear)
Jamie: No, I —— him yet. (not call)
Kim: OK, I'll have to go. See you.

Unit 3, p. 54

2 (READING) Find the information.

1 Alexander Graham Bell was born in Edinburgh in 1847.
He is the man who invented the telephone. Bell grew up
in Edinburgh and went to school there and in London.
When he was older, he became a teacher.
5 His mother and his wife were both deaf, and Bell was very
interested in speech. He wanted to make a machine which
could change the sounds of speech to electricity.
Bell moved to Canada when he was 23. In 1871 he went to
Boston in the USA. He opened a school there for people
10 who couldn't hear well. He also worked on his invention
every night.
Bell invented the telephone in 1876. It wasn't made of
plastic like the phones which we use today. It was big and
heavy because it was made of metal and wood.
15 The invention was a success and Bell became rich.
Bell died in Canada in 1922. He was a man whose
invention changed the world forever.

Correct the sentences.

1. Bell invented the car.
   That's wrong. Bell invented the telephone.
2. Bell was a builder.
3. Bell moved to England when he was 23.

4. Bell's telephone was made of plastic.
5. Bell didn't become a rich man.
6. Bell died in Canada in 1822.

Unit 3, p. 55

○ **4** (LISTENING) **Listen to John Dunlop's biography.**

1,23

Listen to the profile. Choose the right answer.

1 John Dunlop was born in Ayrshire on the west of Scotland in 1840.
He went to school there and in 1859 he started work as a vet in Edinburgh.
5 In 1867 he moved to Ireland and worked as a vet there. Dunlop often had to go to farms. This was difficult because the roads in Ireland were awful.
One day in 1887 he noticed that his young
10 son's tricycle was very uncomfortable. Its tyres were made of solid rubber. Dunlop took a garden hose and used it as a kind of tube. He put air in it and put it around the wheels. Riding the tricycle was much nicer with air
15 in the tyres.

Dunlop wasn't the first person to invent a tyre like this. Another Scot, Robert Thomson, had the same idea in 1845. But Dunlop's tyres were cheaper. In 1889 he started the Dunlop Rubber Company. The 20 company was a success, but Dunlop didn't really get rich. He sold his part of the company in 1896. After that the Dunlop Rubber Company made tyres for the new cars, and Dunlop's name became famous all 25 around the world. Dunlop lived quietly in Ireland and bought part of a clothes company. He died in 1921.

John Dunlop
– born in a) 1850 • b) 1840
– moved to a) Ireland • b) Germany
– started his company in a) 1876 • b) 1889
– died in a) 1912 • b) 1921

Unit 3, p. 55

○ **5** **Things and materials.**

What is the right material?

1. T-shirts are usually made of cotton • wood.
2. Bike tyres are usually made of **paper** • **rubber.**
3. Mobile phones are usually made of **wood** • **plastic.**
4. Tables are usually made of **wood** • **cotton.**
5. Shoes are usually made of **leather** • **paper.**
6. Books are usually made of **metal** • **paper.**

Unit 3, p.56

8 (SPEAKING) Talk about people and things. → M Bus stop, p.166

Ask your partner. Can he or she find the person or thing?

1. It's a thing —— goes on the wheel of a bike or car.
2. It's a person —— feeds animals at the zoo.
3. It's a person —— is the first player in a team.
4. It's a thing —— tells you the time.
5. It's a person —— works with machines.
6. It's a thing —— you use to cut food.

 clock   tyre ✔   engineer   captain   knife   zookeeper

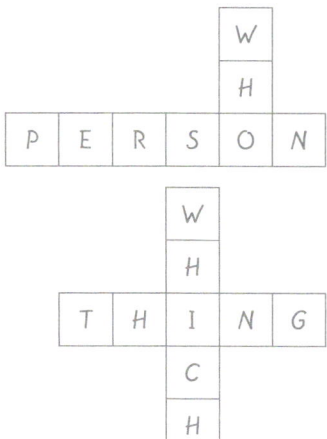

1. A: It's a thing which goes on the wheel of a bike or car.
   B: Is it a tyre?
   A: That's right!

Unit 3, p.57

9 Make sentences about Bell and Dunlop.

Use whose to make one sentence out of two.

1. Dunlop was an inventor ——. His invention made the bike better.
2. Bell was a teacher ——. His mother and wife were both deaf.
3. He was one of many Scottish inventors ——. Their work made Scotland famous.

Unit 3, p.59

3 Where do people stay on their holidays?

Match the words with their definitions.

A It's a place where you go camping.
B It's a small home. Cars can take small ones from place to place.
C It's a big building which has a swimming pool and large buffets.
D It's a place that's almost like home.
E It's usually a place where young people stay.
  There's often a kitchen for everyone too.

p.119

1. hotel
2. campsite
3. bed & breakfast
4. hostel
5. caravan

Unit 3, p. 59

4 (LISTENING) Which picture is it?

1,26

Listen to Jim and Dianne. Look at the pictures. Where did they stay?

Look at the windows, chairs, shelves, pictures and lamps.

hotel

bed and breakfast

hostel

Unit 3, p. 60

6 Make sentences about a holiday in a hotel.

"he", "she", "it" – das "s" muss mit.

Complete the sentences.

1. If everyone —— (agree), we'll stay in a hotel.
   If everyone <u>agrees</u>, we'll stay in a hotel.
2. If we —— (stay) in a hotel, we'll have a TV.
3. If I —— (have) a TV, it won't be boring.
4. If the son —— (watch) TV all day, he won't meet other kids.
5. If we —— (go) to a good hotel, I'll have internet too.
6. If we —— (not find) anything interesting online, we'll ask at the tourist information.

Unit 3, p.61

○ **7** **What will we do if …?**

Look at the pictures. Make sentences.

1. We'll go hiking in the mountains if … .

2. If we leave the hostel after ten o'clock, … .

3. If there's a party at the campsite, … .

4. If we go to the Highlands, … .

5. We'll have a problem with insects if … .

6. We won't stay in that hotel if … .

we'll have a barbecue we'll take a photo stay in a tent

we'll pay fifty pounds there's no swimming pool the weather is nice

Unit 4, p.76

○ **3** (SPEAKING) **What do you think?** → M Think-pair-share, p. 171

Talk about these questions.

1. Can you understand how Sarah feels? Why? Why not?

I can understand how she feels	because	her parents don't have time for her. she's new. she doesn't know a lot of people. she moved to an interesting place. she will meet new people. …
I can't understand how she feels		

2. Is Julie's advice OK? Why? Why not?

I think it's OK	because	Sarah's dad is OK. Sarah will learn a lot from the guests. …
I think it's a problem / not so easy		her parents are very busy. there are new guests every day. …

Unit 4, p.77

○ **5 Work with adjectives.** → M Bus stop, p. 166

Make a chart. Sort the adjectives.

sad ✔   **furious**   **smart**   **confident**   **horrible**   **optimistic**

☺	☹
s...	sad
c...	f...
o...	h...

Du brauchst für einige dieser Wörter ein Wörterbuch. Auf Seite 73 findest du Tipps, wie du mit einem Wörterbuch arbeitest.

Unit 4, p.78

○ **9 What would happen?** → M Peer correction, p. 169

Put in the verbs.

didn't work   **spoke**   **didn't live**   **went**   **didn't listen**   **met**

1. If Sarah —— (go) to a sports club, she would make new friends.
   If Sarah <u>went</u> to a sports club, she would make new friends.
2. If Sarah —— (speak) to her parents about her problems, they would understand her better.
3. If Sarah and her friend Julie —— (meet) each other more often, they would be happier.
4. If Julie —— (not live) in Belfast, Sarah would see her best friend more often.
5. Sarah would spend more time in his room if Ashley —— (not listen) to that awful music.
6. Mum and dad wouldn't be so tired if they —— (not work) so hard.

Unit 4, p.79

○ **10 (SPEAKING) What would you do in this situation?** → M Double circle, p. 167

Make questions and answer them. Work with a partner.

What would you do if ...
- you lost your phone
- you found a dog near your house
- you met your favourite singer
- you got a plane ticket to another country
- you had a year without school

I would ...
→ ask friend / call my number
→ take / home
→ take / photo
→ go to / ...
→ ...

A: What <u>would you do</u> if you <u>lost</u> your phone?
B: I <u>would ask</u> a friend to call my number.

Unit 4, p. 81

○ **4** **Work with shopping phrases.** → **M** Peer correction, p. 169

Complete the dialogue.

| What would you like? | That will be £3.63. | Goodbye! |

A
1. Hi!
2. …
3. Anything else?
4. …
5. That's £1.37 change.
6. …

B
1. Hello!
2. I'd like … .
3. Yes, … . / No thanks.
4. Here you are.
5. Thank you.
6. See you.

Unit 4, p. 82

○ **8** (SPEAKING) **What do you think? Talk with a partner.**

Compare the things with a partner.

1. chocolate or strawberry? (tasty)
   A: I think chocolate is tastier than strawberry. Do you agree?
   B: Yes, I think you're right.
2. winter or summer? (better)
3. picnic or restaurant? (cheaper)

4. speaking any language or talking to animals? (more interesting)
5. doing homework or tidying your room? (more exciting)
6. having a camel or being a camel? (funnier)

| as … as | not as … as | -er than | more … than | less … than |

Unit 4, p. 83

○ **9** **Some or any?**

Put in some or any.

1. I'd like to buy some comics.
2. Sorry, we don't have —— tissues.
3. Do you have —— sweets in your bag?
4. Oh dear! We don't have —— change!
5. Let's eat —— cake!
6. Sorry, I didn't buy —— orange juice. I forgot!

In verneinten Aussagen und Fragen steht „any"!

Unit 5, p. 97

○ **5** **What would you take on a trip?**

Match the things.

1. nail scissors
2. comb
3. toothpaste
4. hairdryer
5. shower gel
6. body lotion

Unit 5, p. 98

○ **8** **Finish their text messages.**

Simple present or present progressive?

1
Leo Germanguy
I'm in the bathroom right now and I … (look for / am looking for) towels. Where are they?

2
Conor O'Brian
We always … (put / are always putting) them in the cupboard. Let me know if you can't find them there.

3
Conor O'Brian
I'm going to be home late. I am at school and I … (finish / am finishing) my Art project. Will u tell mum?

4
Mad O'Brian
I'll tell her. But she (hate / is hating) it when you're late.

5
Mad O'Brian
I'm here and I … (wash / am washing) my hair. And now my shampoo isn't here. Grrrrh!!! M

6
Conor O'Brian
Boy, Maddy is angry. She never … (share / is never sharing) her shampoo. Did you take it???

Unit 5, p. 99

○ **9 Rewrite the sentences.**

Rewrite the sentences. Use possessive pronouns.

1. It's **Dad's** chocolate pudding. – It's his.
2. It's **Maddy's** tea cup. – It's . . . .
3. It's **my** rain coat. – It's . . . .
4. It's **Mum's** and **Dad's** room. – It's . . . .
5. It's **your** shirt. – It's . . . .
6. It's **our** cat. – It's . . . .
7. It's **Conor's** bike. – It's . . . .

GRAMMAR	→ **G14**, p. 163

my – mine	your – yours
his – his	her – hers
our – ours	their – theirs

Unit 5, p. 101

○ **3 Find the odd one out.**

Which word doesn't go with the others? Why?

Think of times, prices, transportation, verbs.

1. train • bus • ticket
2. fare • receipt • present
3. stop • line • museum

4. on time • sure • late
5. date • timetable • map
6. plan • change • get off

Unit 5, p. 101

○ **4 (SPEAKING) Find the way.** → **M** Milling around, p. 168

Look at the map and find the best way to get from James's to …

– George's Dock
– Connolly train station
– Milltown

To get from James's to
George's Dock, take the
Red Line. It's eight stops.
Get off the tram and
you're there.

> Stay on the tram for . . . stops.   Take the Green Line.

> Take the Red Line to . . . .   Change at . . . and walk to . . . .

Unit 5, p.102

○ **7** (SPEAKING) What <u>must</u> you do on a bus? What <u>mustn't</u> you do?

Explain these school bus rules.

FOLLOW THE SCHOOL BUS RULES

You read:

1. Talk quietly.
2. Don't eat ice cream.
3. Don't talk to the driver.
4. Don't bring pets.
5. Take your rubbish with you.
6. Keep your head, hands and feet inside.
7. Don't push other students.

You say:

1. You must talk quietly.
2. You mustn't eat … .
3. You mustn't … .
4. You mustn't … .
5. You must … .
6. You … .
7. …

Unit 5, p.103

○ **9** (WRITING) <u>Must</u>, <u>needn't</u> or <u>mustn't</u>?

Put in the right verb.

1. Dogs travel free. You —— buy an extra ticket.
2. Your dog —— be with you all the time.
3. Your dog —— hurt other people.
4. It —— be nice to other people.
5. You —— carry a small dog in a bag. It's OK to hold it.
6. You —— play with your dog when you're on the bus.

must = müssen
needn't = nicht müssen
mustn't = nicht dürfen

one hundred and twenty-five 125

2,16

The Norman conquest

1

The old king of England, Edward, died in 1066. He had no children and both his Anglo-Saxon brother-in-law, Harold, and his French cousin, William, Duke of Normandy, wanted to be the next king of England. Harold made himself king, and William was very angry. So what did he do next? He sailed to England with his army . . .

2

Harold and William fought the battle on Senlac Hill, near Hastings. William's men were knights and they were better trained. They fought on horses and were good archers. Harold's men fought on foot and they were already tired from an earlier battle at Stamford Bridge, 200 miles away in the north of England. (Yes, they had to walk those 200 miles!)

conquest – *Eroberung*
the Anglo-Saxons – *die Angelsachsen*
(das Volk, das schon vor 1066 in England lebte)
brother-in-law – *Schwager*
duke – *Herzog*

army – *Heer; Armee*
knight – *Ritter*
archer – *Bogenschütze; Bogenschützin*
tapestry – *Wandteppich*
surname – *Nachname; Familienname*

3

How do we know what happened during the battle? Well, we have the 70-metre long Bayeux Tapestry to tell us! The tapestry is like a comic and it tells the story of the battle. It tells us that Harold died when he got an arrow in his eye, but we don't know if this really happened.

4

William became king of England on Christmas Day 1066. He was a big castle fan and built lots of them in England, including part of the Tower of London. He also took land from the Anglo-Saxons and gave it to his Norman friends.

5

Did the Normans change England? Yes, of course they did! For example, they brought many new words to the English language. Words like 'pork' and 'garden' come from this time. Guess what? There are still many English people who have Norman surnames, like Archer or Darcy. Before the Normans came to England, most people didn't even have surnames. They lived in small villages, so a first name or a nickname was often enough.

1 **What did you find most interesting in the text? Talk about it with a partner.**

The RNLI: Volunteers on the coast

Did you know?

- The RNLI is the Royal National Lifeboat Institution. It's a charity and it saves lives at sea.
- The RNLI has 237 lifeboat stations and about 4,600 crew members in the UK and Ireland.
- The RNLI rescues about 8,000 people per year.
- The RNLI has saved about 140,000 lives since 1824.
- Many of the lifeboat crew members are volunteers.
- The RNLI gets money from fundraising.

2,17 ✆ A rescue – boys in trouble

18th June 2016, by Simon Spade. **Yesterday the RNLI rescued two teenage boys who got into trouble when they were kayaking near Llandudno.**

The two 14-year-old boys went out too far in their kayaks and could not get back to the beach because of strong winds. A tourist spotted the boys and called the RNLI. The lifeboat crew got to the kayaks very quickly. Lifeboat helm Howard Link called the ambulance to meet them on the beach.

Both boys were very weak and seasick. They both spent the night in Llandudno hospital but are back home now.

Rules to remember

There are some rules to remember when you go to the beach:

S pot the dangers.

A lways go with a friend or adult.

F ind and follow the safety signs and flags.

E mergency – put up your hand and shout or call 999/112.

RNLI profiles

Most lifeboat crew members are volunteers. Let's meet some.

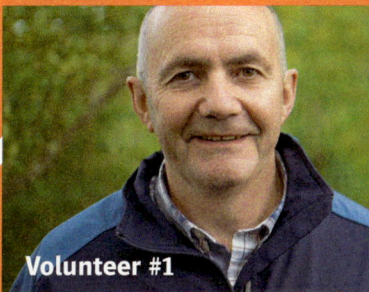

Volunteer #1

Name: Howard Link
Job: Postman

Lifeboat helm
I lead the rescue. It is my job to make sure that everyone on the boat stays safe while we are at sea.

Volunteer #2

Name: Susan Merchant
Job: Teacher

Lifeboat crew member
I grew up in Wales near the sea, so I have been in boats for many years. I help during the rescue and look after the rescued person.

Volunteer #3

Name: John Taylor
Job: Student

Lifeboat youth volunteer
I'm only 16 so I'm too young to join the lifeboat crew, but I work at the station. I look after the equipment and help at fundraising events.

Fundraising Calendar, Llandudno RNLI

January 25th:
10k run around Llandudno

March 17th:
Cake sale at the lifeboat station

April 4th:
Talent show at Llandudno High School

September 13th:
Fun boat race at West Beach

1 Talk about the RNLI.

1. Does Germany have a charity like the RNLI?
2. Would you join the RNLI? Why? Why not?

---

charity – *Wohltätigkeitsorganisation*
to save – *retten; bergen*
crew – *Crew; Besatzung*

to rescue – *retten*
fundraising – *Spendenaktionen*
to join – *Mitglied in / bei etwas werden*

2,18 🎧 **The Highland Games**

The winner will get a very good job.

History

Legend says that in the 11th century the Scottish king Malcolm III wanted to find the strongest and fastest men in the land. So he organized a competition. The winners became his bodyguards or they ran across the country with messages from the king. Later large families or 'clans' met every year to compete against each other.

Today

… people come from around the world every summer to watch the Highland Games. The Games take place in towns and villages all over Scotland. The 'heavy' events for the strongest and fittest people are the most popular, but there's also lots of music and dancing. There are also children's Highland Games for young people from 5–18.

Caber toss

The most famous 'heavy' event is the caber toss. A caber is a pole that is made from a tree. It's five metres long and very heavy (about 45 kg). People hold the caber at one end and throw it so that it lands on the other end. It's not important how far it goes.

Hammer throw

Competitors swing
a heavy ball which is on
the end of a long chain
around their heads.
Then they let go and throw
it as far as they can.

Stone put

There are two ways to
throw or 'put' the stone:
you can stand (then
you use a heavier stone)
or you can run with it
(then it's not so heavy).
In the first competitions,
men chose a stone from
a river.

Music and dance

No Highland Games
are complete without
the sounds of bagpipes
and Highland dancing.
One of the most famous
dances is the Sword Dance.

1 Talk about the Highland Games.

Would you like to go to the Highland Games?
Would you like to compete in the children's Highland Games?
Are there sports like this in your country?
Talk with a partner.

the Highlands – *Berge im Norden Schottlands*
bodyguard – *Leibwächter*
to compete (against) – *gegeneinander antreten*

pole – *Pfahl*
to let go – *loslassen*
complete – *vollständig*

The Troubles and after

2,19

Murals

If you go to Belfast, you'll see lots of large pictures on the sides of the buildings. These are called murals. They show events and people from the past which are important to people who live in the city. A lot of these murals are from the time that we call 'The Troubles'.

Different schools

Catholic and Protestant children in Northern Ireland often go to separate schools. Even in small towns there are often two schools – one for the children of each religion.

The background

Many Scottish and English Protestant people arrived and settled in what is now Northern Ireland about 400 years ago. Since then, there have often been problems between the Catholic and Protestant people who lived there. Some people (usually Protestants) want Northern Ireland to stay part of the UK. Others (usually Catholics) want it to be part of the Republic of Ireland. This disagreement has often caused fighting.

'The Troubles' (late 1960s–1998) were a very violent time in Northern Ireland's history. There was a lot of terrorism and more than 3,500 people died. When British soldiers came to help in 1969, people welcomed them, but many Catholics soon felt the soldiers were not on their side.

Belfast – then and now

During the Troubles, high walls separated Protestants and Catholics. These walls were called 'peace walls'. A lot has changed since then. Now everyone is working for a future without violence. Today Belfast is a very friendly city for tourists. Many of the walls are still there, but now you can walk from one side to the other. And you can write your own message on one of the 'peace walls'. More 'mixed' schools, for children from Protestant and Catholic families, open every year too.

New chances

Did you know that 30,000 people worked in Belfast's shipyards in the past? When we didn't need as many ships, many people lost their jobs. During the Troubles, not many businesses wanted to come to Northern Ireland and unemployment was high. This has changed and there are new jobs now in making films and TV series.

1 **Talk about the text.**

What did you find most surprising and interesting in the text? Talk about it with a partner.

to settle (in) – *besiedeln*	to separate – *trennen*
to cause – *verursachen*	peace – *Frieden*
violent – *gewalttätig; brutal*	business – *Unternehmen*
separate – *getrennt; verschieden*	unemployment – *Arbeitslosigkeit*

Highlights of Irish history

about 500 BC

I'm a Celt. The Celtic people are the early settlers of the island of Ireland.

9th century

I'm a Viking from Denmark. We invaded Ireland and our people lived here for about 300 years!

12th century

I'm Henry II, King of England. I invaded Ireland with a huge army.

16th century

I'm Henry VIII, King of England and Ireland. The English own 90% of Ireland now. Many Irish people don't like me.

Saint Patrick

Saint Patrick is the patron saint of Ireland. He lived about 1,500 years ago and brought Christianity to Ireland. There are many stories about his life. One of the most famous is that he drove all the snakes in Ireland into the sea where they drowned. St Patrick's Day is on 17th March every year.

settler – *Siedler, Siedlerin*
century – *Jahrhundert*
to own – *besitzen*
famine – *Hungersnot*
to emigrate – *auswandern*
to split – *teilen; spalten*
to sign – *unterschreiben; unterzeichnen*
patron saint – *Schutzheiliger, Schutzheilige*
to drive – *treiben*
economy – *Wirtschaft*
financial crisis – *Wirtschaftskrise*

1845

was the year of the Great Famine.
One million people died and one million emigrated.
I wanted to emigrate to America.

20th century

We split Ireland into Northern Ireland and the Republic of Ireland. There were many problems after this.

1998

I'm Bertie Ahern, prime minister of Ireland.
I signed an agreement which was a big step in the peace process.

2002

I'm the euro! Ireland began to use me in 2002. Ireland has been a member of the EU since 1973.

Celtic Tiger

When Ireland joined the EU in 1973, it was a poor country. Between 1995 and 2000, Ireland's economy grew very quickly and people said it was as strong as a tiger. Many companies moved their European offices to Ireland. After the European financial crisis in 2008, however, people said that the 'Celtic Tiger' was dead.

1 Talk about the text.

What did you find most surprising and interesting in the text about Ireland? Talk about it with a partner.

Extra

Be a better photographer[1].

1 **Do you take a lot of pictures? How many pictures do you take a day?**

Taking pictures is a fun hobby for many people. You probably take pictures almost every day with your phone too. Some people are professional photographers. They have very good cameras and know all the tricks. But even with your own phone you can get better results.

2 **Look at the pictures. Do you think they are OK? Why? Why not?**

☺ I like picture 1 because it is … .
☺ I think picture 1 is great/OK because it has … .
☹ I don't like picture 1 because it is … .
☹ I think picture 1 isn't OK because … .

nice colours • funny • interesting • great • …
too light • too dark • blurred[2] • boring • …

You have the perfect subject and the light couldn't be better. Just when you press the shutter[3], somebody jumps into the picture and makes a funny face. That's what's called a **photobomb**.

3 **Find funny photobombs on the internet and show them to the class. What's funny about them?**

1 photographer [fəˈtɒɡrəfə] – *Fotograf/Fotografin*; 2 blurred [blɜːd] – *unscharf*; 3 shutter [ˈʃʌtə] – *Auslöser*

Three simple tips for better pictures

1. Be creative. Change perspectives and angles[1]. Sometimes the world looks different then.

A front   B low angle   C birds-eye view

2. Always check the background. Sometimes the picture might be embarrassing[2] for someone.

That's wrong.   That's right.

3. Try to zoom with your camera. Or just move forward a foot or two. Sometimes details can be more interesting than the whole person or thing.

A Medium shot   B Close up   B Extreme close up

4 Choose an interesting subject and take three pictures. Use the tips.
Show your pictures to the class and discuss them.

1 angle ['æŋgl] – *Winkel*; 2 embarrassing [ɪm'bærəsɪŋ] – *unangenehm*

How the heart works

1   **Look at the sentences. Do you know any German sayings with the word 'heart'?**

I know the words by heart.

I have a broken heart.

He has a heart of stone.

Follow your heart.

You're close to my heart.

2   **Read the facts about the heart. What do you find most interesting?**

The heart begins beating four weeks after conception[1] and does not stop until death[2].

Every day, the heart produces[3] enough energy to drive a truck 20 miles (about 32 km). In a lifetime, that is like driving to the moon[4] and back.

During an average[5] lifetime, the heart will pump nearly 1.5 million tons of blood[6] – enough to fill 200 wagons.

Take a tennis ball and squeeze[7] it tightly[8]: that's how hard the beating heart works to pump blood.

The heart beats 100,000 times a day.

The heart has its own electrical impulse[9]. It can beat even when it is outside of the body. But it must get enough oxygen[10].

3   **What keeps your heart healthy?**

A healthy heart is a happy heart. But what can you do to keep it happy? Make sentences.

1 conception [kənˈsepʃn] – *Empfängnis*; 2 death [deθ] – *Tod*; 3 produce [prəˈdjuːs] – *erzeugen*; 4 moon [muːn] – *Mond*;
5 average [ˈævrɪdʒ] – *durchschnittlich*; 6 blood [blʌd] – *Blut*; 7 squeeze [skwiːz] – *drücken*; 8 tight [taɪt] – *fest*;
9 impulse [ˈɪmpʌls] – *Impuls*; 10 oxygen [ˈɒksɪdʒən] – *Sauerstoff*

4 Read about the anatomy[1] of the heart

The heart is your strongest muscle. It's a little to the left in your chest[2] and about the size of your fist[3]. Your heart pumps blood through your body to provide you with oxygen and other useful things. Your blood moves through tubes (arteries[4] and veins[5]). Your heart has four different chambers[6] – two chambers in each side. The chambers on top are called atria[7], the ones on the bottom ventricles[8].

Anatomy of the Human Heart

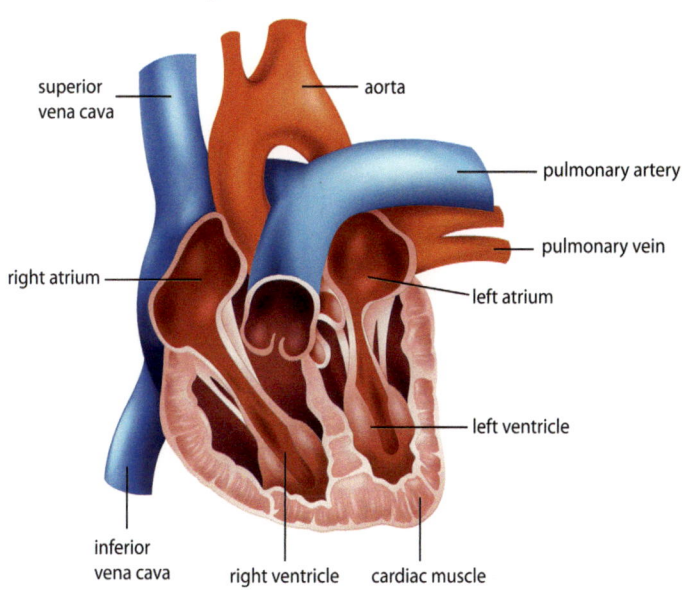

superior vena cava
aorta
pulmonary artery
pulmonary vein
right atrium
left atrium
left ventricle
inferior vena cava
right ventricle   cardiac muscle

5 Find out your pulse[9].

Check your pulse in different situations.
Count the beats for one minute.

What's your pulse when you are sitting?
What's your pulse when you have just run for a minute?

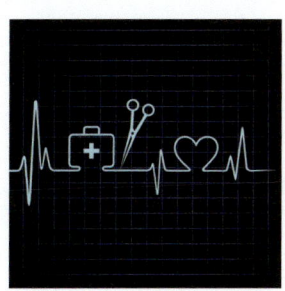

---

1 anatomy [əˈnætemi] – *Anatomie (Lehre vom Aufbau der Organismen)*; 2 chest [tʃest] – *Brust*; 3 fist [fɪst] – *Faust*;
4 artery [ˈɑːtri] – *Arterie*; 5 vein [veɪn] – *Vene*; 6 chamber [ˈtʃeɪmbə] – *Kammer*; 7 atrium [ˈeɪtriəm] – *Vorhof (des Herzens)*;
8 ventricle [ˈventrɪkl] – *Herzkammer*; 9 pulse [pʌls] – *Puls*

The London Eye Mystery by Siobhan Dowd (2007)

1 *My name is Ted. I live in London with my sister Kat and my parents. One day, my cousin*
Salim and his mum, my Aunt Gloria, come to stay. We go into town and we visit the
London Eye. I think it looks like a bike wheel up in the clouds. Salim rides on the London
Eye. Kat and I wait for him. But the pod[1] comes down again and Salim isn't in it any
5 *more. What has happened to Salim?*

"Let's lie[2]," said Kat. "About taking that ticket from a stranger[3]." She grabbed[4]
my arm.
"Lie," I repeated[5]. "Uhm. Lie."
"We could say Salim got lost in the crowds, say he …" She let my arm go. "Oh,
10 forget it," she said. "You can't lie."
We walked over to Aunt Gloria and Mum in the café.
We didn't say anything.
"There you are," Aunt Gloria said. "Have you got the tickets?"
Kat waited for me to say something.
15 I waited for Kat to say something.
"Where's Salim?" asked Mum. "Is he still in the queue?"
"Uhm," I said. "No."
"Where is he?"
"We don't know!" Kat said. "This man gave us his ticket. For free. He bought it,
20 but he didn't want to go on the ride."
"He had claustrophobia[6]," I said.
"That's right. And the queue was awful. So we took the ticket. And gave it to
Salim. And Salim went up alone. And he didn't come down."
Aunt Gloria looked up at the London Eye. "So he's still up there," she said.
25 Kat had a strange look on her face. "No," she said.
"He went up some time ago. Ted and I watched his pod. But when it came
down – he wasn't on it."

---

1 pod [pɒd] – *Gondel*; 2 lie [laɪ] – *lügen*; 3 stranger ['streɪndʒə] – *Fremder*; 4 grab sth. [græb] – *nach etw. greifen*;
5 repeat [rɪ'piːt] – *wiederholen*; 6 claustrophobia [ˌklɔːstrə'fəʊbiə] – *Platzangst*

Mum's face scrunched up[1], so I knew she was a) confused[2] or b) angry or c) both[3].

"What are you trying to say: He wasn't on it?!"

30 "He went up, Mum," I repeated. "But he didn't come down."

Mum's mouth became like an O.

"He went against the law of gravity[4], Mum. He went up but he didn't come down. Uhm."

Mum looked more angry than confused now. But Aunt Gloria looked calm[5].

35 "I think I know what happened," she said and smiled.

"I bet he went around one more time."

Yes, that's it, I thought.

"That's it," said Kat. "He just stayed on."

I looked at the big clock on the wall. "So … he'll land at … twelve thirty-two."

40 We went back to the Eye with Mum. Aunt Gloria stayed at the café so Salim would find her if he came back.

We watched a lot of pods open and close, but no Salim. 12:32 came and went. No Salim.

Mum asked a woman from customer services[6] but she couldn't help.

45 "Kat," Mum said, "It was wrong to take that ticket and let Salim go up alone."

Kat started crying[7]. "It's always my fault[8]. Never Ted's. Ted never does anything wrong."

"You're older, Kat. But really not much wiser." Mum stared[9] angrily at Kat and Kat stared back.

50 "Why don't we call his mobile?" I said.

"Of course! Ted," Mum said, "You're a genius. Why didn't we think of that before?"

We went back to Aunt Gloria in the café. There was no sign[10] of Salim.

,21 "Call him on his mobile!" said Mum.

"OK," Aunt Gloria said. "Yes, maybe he's near us."

55 She called his number and put the phone to her ear with a smile. Then she looked confused.

"His phone isn't on." she whispered. "Why?"

---

1 scrunch up [ˈskrʌnʃʌp] – *verziehen*; 2 confused [kənˈfjuːzd] – *verwirrt*; 3 both [bəʊθ] – *beides*; 4 against the law of gravity [əˈgenst ðə lɔːˌəv ˈgrævəti] – *gegen das Gesetz der Schwerkraft*; 5 calm [kaːm] – *ruhig*; 6 customer service [ˌkʌstəmə ˈsɜːvɪs] – *Kundenservice*; 7 cry [kraɪ] – *weinen*; 8 fault [fɔːlt] – *Schuld*; 9 stare [ˈsteə] – *anstarren*; 10 sign [saɪn] – *Zeichen*

We called the police.

A police officer took our names and addresses. Could Salim find his way back to our house? he asked. Yes, we said. Then he told us to do three things: a) keep[1] trying his phone, b) go home and wait and c) try not to worry. And if Salim wasn't home in a few hours, a police officer would visit us.

The officer said, "Children don't disappear[2]! He will be back soon."

So then we did b) and went home to wait. And Aunt Gloria did a): She called Salim again and again. Mum and Kat tried to do c). Mum made tea. Kat brought in a plate of my favourite biscuits, chocolate fingers. But no one ate any. We all tried not to worry but it didn't really work.

I looked at Aunt Gloria.

"What are you staring at?" she cried out. "You wanted to go to the London Eye – now this has happened! You and your silly bike wheel up in the clouds!" She sat down on the sofa.

A bit later she said, "Oh, Ted. I'm sorry. I didn't mean[3] that."

"Gloria!" Mum said and sat down next to her. "Calm down, love."

She made a sign at me to say she didn't want me in the room.

So I went up to my room.

I got out my encyclopaedia[4] and sat on my bed, looking at some interesting pages. The door opened and Kat came in. She sat on the bed next to me.

I looked up. "The dodo[5] disappeared, Kat," I said.

"What?"

"The dodo. It disappeared from the evolutionary path[6]."

"Right. The dodo. So?"

"Darwin would say it wasn't adaptable[7] enough to survive[8], so it didn't."

"I don't think Salim's disappeared from the evolutionary path, Ted."

"No, I know," I said. "But there's lots more about disappearing in my encyclopaedia."

"Oh, yeah?" "There was Lord Lucan. People think he killed himself. Maybe he did. But they never found his body, Kat. Maybe he wanted it to look that way, but really disappeared … went away, say, to India and became a hippie."

---

1 keep trying sth. [kiːp ˈtraɪɪŋ] – *etwas immer wieder versuchen*; 2 disappear [ˌdɪsəpɪə] – *verschwinden*; 3 mean [miːn] – *meinen*; 4 encyclopaedia [ɪnˌsaɪkləˈpiːdɪə] – *Lexikon*; 5 dodo [ˈdəʊdəʊ] – *Dodo (ausgestorbener, großer, flugunfähiger Vogel)*; 6 evolutionary path [ˌiːvəˌuːʃnri ˈpɑːθ] – *Evolutionsgeschichte*; 7 adaptable [əˈdæptəbl] – *anpassungsfähig*; 8 survive [səˈvaɪv] – *überleben*

"I don't see what that's got to do with –" There was a long silence[1].

90 "That's not very helpful, Ted."

"And there was the Mary Celeste, a big ship from New York. It turned up[2] near Gibraltar. Nobody was on board, like … like aliens beamed them up!"

"Ted, stop joking. It's not funny."

I closed my book and looked at Kat.

95 "OK," she said. "It wasn't a joke. I should know you never joke. So what do you mean?"

I didn't really know what I meant. But Kat looked really sad and I wanted to say something nice.

"Kat," I said, "you and I are together in this. People disappear. And things. Most of 100 them reappear[3]."

Kat put her hand on mine and I saw the tears[4] on her face.

"Ted," she said, shaking[5] her head, "the Mary Celeste people never reappeared. Nor[6] the dodo. Nor Lord What's-His-Name. That police officer was right. People don't just disappear. Salim must be somewhere[7]. I have to find him. But I need your help. I 105 need your brain[8], Ted. No one is better at thinking than you."

That was Kat's first compliment to me ever. I put my hands into my jacket pockets[9] and went, "Uhm."

Then I felt something in one of the pockets – something surprising. I took it out and Kat and I stared at it.

110 "Salim's camera!"

How will the story go on? Will Salim return?

---

1 silence ['saɪləns] – *Schweigen*; 2 turn up [ˌtɜːn ˈʌp] – *erscheinen*; 3 reappear [ˌriːəˈpɪər] – *wieder auftauchen*; 4 tear [tɪə] – *Träne*; 5 shake [ʃeɪk] – *schütteln*; 6 nor [nɔː] – *und auch nicht*; 7 somewhere ['sʌmweə] – *irgendwo*; 8 brain [breɪn] – *Grips, Verstand*; 9 pocket ['pɒkɪt] – *(Jacken-)Tasche*

Ivanhoe

Characters:
Narrator
Rowena
Cedric
Athelstane
Rebecca
Isaac
Prince John
Three Norman knights
Five Anglo-Saxon knights
Ivanhoe (The Disinherited)
Crowd (5 – 8 people)
King Richard (The Black Knight)
Robin Hood
Robin's men (5 – 8 people)

2,23

Scene 1

1 NARRATOR: This is a story about brave[1] men and women. It is a story about hate[2] and about love. It is a story about power and great kindness[3]. Our story is old, but hate, love, power and kindness are still a big part of our lives today. The date is 1194. The place is England. But at this time the Normans ruled[4] England. The good King Richard is in another country. He was fighting in a

5 war[5], but now he is in prison far from his country. His awful brother, the Norman Prince John, now rules England and the Anglo-Saxons that live there are not happy.
(A trumpet[6] plays). Ah! Hear that. It is the start of the famous competition between Norman and Anglo-Saxon knights. Look, there sits Cedric, an Anglo-Saxon. He looks after the beautiful Rowena. Listen, they are having an argument.

10 *(Narrator leaves. Cedric and Rowena are sitting in the crowd – a semi-circle[7] of chairs are in front of the audience[8].)*
ROWENA: *(Angry)* No, I will not get married to him!
CEDRIC: But Rowena, Athelstane is an Anglo-Saxon and a good man! I am your father and I say you will get married to him!

15 ROWENA: *(Very angry)* You are not my father!
CEDRIC: But Rowena, I love you like my own child. I have looked after you.
ROWENA: Yes, it is true, you have. I had no mother or father, but you looked after me. But what about Ivanhoe, your real child?
CEDRIC: *(Angry now)* Today Ivanhoe is not my child! He went away to fight with the Normans

20 and King Richard. He is not a true Anglo-Saxon. Do not say his name again!

---

1 brave [breɪv] – *mutig;* 2 hate [heɪt] – *Hass;* 3 kindness ['kaɪndnəs] – *Güte;* 4 rule [ruːl] – *regieren;* 5 war [wɔː] – *Krieg;* 6 trumpet ['trʌmpɪt] – *Trompete;* 7 semi-circle ['semi 'sɜːkl] – *Halbkreis;* 8 audience ['ɔːdiəns] – *Zuschauer*

ROWENA: But I love Ivanhoe and I will only get married to HIM!

CEDRIC: *(angry)* Stop, girl!

(Rowena looks unhappy, but she doesn't say anything. She looks around. An old man and a young woman come on stage and sit near Rowena and Cedric).

25 **ROWENA:** *(To Cedric)* Who is that man and the beautiful woman over there?

CEDRIC: Ah, that is Isaac and his daughter Rebecca. Isaac is a great businessman[1]. He has a lot of money.

REBECCA: *(Speaks to her father)* Father, do you think the Anglo-Saxon knights will win the competition?

30 **ISAAC:** I'm not sure, Rebecca.

(The trumpet plays again; someone who is not on stage calls 'Prince John'. Prince John walks to his place and sits down. The crowd cheers[2].)

PRINCE JOHN: Let's start the competition!

(Trumpet plays again. Three knights on horses come from the right. They have a flag that says 'Normans'.
35 *Five knights on horses come from the left. They have a flag that says 'Anglo-Saxons'. All the knights have lances[3].)*

PRINCE JOHN: *(Stands up)* Let the first knights start!

(One Norman and one Anglo-Saxon knight attack[4] each other. The Norman hits the Anglo-Saxon with his lance and the Anglo-Saxon falls from his horse. Half the crowd cheer and half boo[5]. Prince John is laughing.
40 *Cedric, Rowena, Isaac and Rebecca look unhappy.*
The next Norman knight wins against the next Anglo-Saxon. The third Norman also wins. The knights who fall leave the stage. Two Anglo-Saxon knights are on stage.)

FIRST NORMAN KNIGHT: Who will fight us next?

(The two Anglo-Saxon knights are scared. Suddenly a new knight comes from the left. He holds a flag that
45 *says 'The Disinherited[6]'. This knight fights against the three Norman knights. He wins every time. He holds his flag up to Prince John.)*

PRINCE JOHN: Very good, brave knight. You call yourself the Disinherited. Do you have a real name?

IVANHOE: I am the Disinherited. My father does not want to call me his child. I fought with
50 your brother King Richard in the great war.

(Sounds of surprise from the crowd. Prince John looks very unhappy.)

PRINCE JOHN: All right, Disinherited. You are the winner of the first part of the competition. You can choose the woman who you believe is the most beautiful. She will be our competition queen.

55 *(Prince John puts a crown[7] on Ivanhoe's lance. Ivanhoe sees Rowena and gives the crown to her. She puts it on her head. The crowd cheers. Ivanhoe leaves the stage.)*

---

1 businessman ['bɪznɪsmæn] – *Geschäftsmann;* 2 cheer [tʃɪə] – *jubeln;* 3 lance [lɑːns] – *Lanze;* 4 attack [ə'tæk] – *angreifen;*
5 boo sb. [buː] – *jdn. ausbuhen;* 6 disinherited [ˌdɪsɪn'herɪtɪd] – *der Enterbte;* 7 crown [kraʊn] – *Krone*

Scene 2

1   *(Music is playing. The crowd is talking and laughing.)*
NARRATOR: *(On stage)* It is the second day of the competition. The knights fight with swords[1].
This is very dangerous. Some knights may get hurt. Look! The knights are coming. *(Trumpet plays. Narrator leaves.)*

5   *(Three Norman knights come from the right with a Norman flag. Two knights and Ivanhoe come from the left with an Anglo-Saxon flag. All the knights are on horses and have swords.)*
PRINCE JOHN: *(Stands up)* Let the second part of the competition start! *(Trumpet plays.)*
(There is a big fight: Ivanhoe is hit badly on his left side, but he still fights. The two Anglo-Saxon knights fall and cannot fight. Suddenly a new knight arrives from the side. This knight is wearing black. The crowd
10   *makes sounds of surprise. The Black Knight fights two of the Norman knights. Ivanhoe fights the last Norman knight. Ivanhoe and The Black Knight win against the Normans. They get off their horses and walk to each other.)*
IVANHOE: *(Whispers[2])* There is only one man in England who can fight like this. Is it really you?
KING RICHARD: *(Whispers back)* Yes, Ivanhoe. I am back. Meet me in the forest[3] in five days and
15   I will be King of England again. *(King Richard leaves the stage on his horse.)*
PRINCE JOHN: Disinherited! Come and get your prize. You are the winner! I give you this crown, but take off[4] your helmet.
(IVANHOE takes off his helmet. Sounds of surprise from the crowd)
PRINCE JOHN: Ah, it is you, Ivanhoe! The son of Cedric.
20   *(Prince John puts the crown on Ivanhoe's head. Ivanhoe falls. He is hurt badly.)*
ROWENA: *(Stands up)* We must help him! He is hurt. Come on!
CEDRIC: Sit down, Rowena! He is not part of my family. King Richard can help him.
ROWENA: King Richard is in prison in another country. He cannot help Ivanhoe. We must help him. He is your son and I love him. *(She starts to leave.)*
25   CEDRIC: *(Angry)* You will not help him!
ROWENA: But he was so brave and now he really needs our help. Please, Cedric, let's help him.
(Cedric pushes her back into her seat.)
REBECCA: *(Speaks to her father)* Father! We must help him. Come, father.
ISAAC: Wait, child, be careful! If we help him now, the Prince will hate us.
30   REBECCA: I don't care[5]! I will help him. (She looks at Isaac) Will you help me take that man home? *(Isaac nods[6]. He and Rebecca go to Ivanhoe. Rebecca talks to Ivanhoe.)* You are a brave man. I can help you. I will take you home and give you medicine[7].
IVANHOE: Thank you.
(Rebecca and Isaac carry Ivanhoe off stage.)

---

1 sword [sɔːd] – *Schwert*; 2 whisper [ˈwɪspə] – *flüstern*; 3 forest [ˈfɒrɪst] – *Wald*; 4 take off [ˌteɪkˈɒf] – *abnehmen*;
5 I don't care! [aɪ dəʊnt keə] – *Es ist mir egal!*; 6 nod [nɒd] – *nicken*; 7 medicine [ˈmedsn] – *Medizin*

2,25

Scene 3

1 *(In the forest. Robin's men are sitting around a fire. They are eating, drinking and laughing. King Richard is still wearing black. He is talking to Robin Hood.)*

ROBIN HOOD: Your plan is good, King Richard. We can fight Prince John and win.

KING RICHARD: When Cedric knows that the famous Robin Hood is fighting with me against

5 Prince John, he and the other Anglo-Saxons will join[1] us too.

ROBIN HOOD: Yes, I have sent one of my men to tell Cedric to meet us here. Listen! *(Robin's men stop talking and eating and listen carefully.)* I think I hear someone coming.

IVANHOE: *(Just his voice)* This must be the place, my friends.

(Isaac, Rebecca and Ivanhoe come on stage.)

10 IVANHOE: *(Very happy)* It is you, my King! *(Ivanhoe and King Richard hug.)*

KING RICHARD: It is good to see you too, my great friend. I escaped[2] from prison and now I am back in England with my brave army [3]. Robin and I have a plan to chase[4] Prince John and his men out of this country and I will rule England again. *(Robin's men cheer and start eating and drinking again.)*

15 Who is this man and lovely woman with you? *(He looks at Isaac and Rebecca.)*

IVANHOE: This beautiful woman is Rebecca. She gave me medicine and made me well. And this is her father.

ROBIN HOOD: Listen, I hear voices again.

CEDRIC: *(Just his voice)* Come! Robin Hood and his men must be here.

20 *(Cedric and Rowena come on stage.)*

ROWENA: *(Suddenly sees Ivanhoe)* Oh, Ivanhoe! *(She runs to Ivanhoe and they hug.)*

ROBIN HOOD: Cedric, this is King Richard. He was The Black Knight at the competition.

KING RICHARD: Your son, Ivanhoe, is a brave man, Cedric. He won the competition. I believe the brave Ivanhoe and the lovely Rowena want to get married.

25 CEDRIC: *(Looks at his feet)* I … I thought Athelstane … *(Cedric doesn't know what to say. He looks at Ivanhoe and Rowena and then at King Richard.)* You are right, King Richard. I have a brave son and I am proud of him. He and Rowena WILL get married. *(Everyone cheers and Rowena and Ivanhoe hug again.)*

ROBIN HOOD: Now let's use your plan; King Richard; and take action against[5] the awful Prince

30 John. Cedric, will you join us?

CEDRIC: Of course, Robin. Long live King Richard! *(Everyone says 'long live King Richard' together.)*

NARRATOR: *(Comes on stage)* Together, these brave men and women chased Prince John and his men out of England. King Richard ruled England once more and the Anglo-Saxons were very happy – so were Rowena and the great Ivanhoe. Long live King Richard!

---

1 join [dʒɔɪn] – *sich anschließen;* 2 escape [ɪˈskep] – *entkommen;* 3 army [ˈɑːmi] – *Armee;* 4 chase [tʃeɪs] – *verfolgen;*
5 take action against sb. [teɪkˌˈækʃn əˈɡenst] – *gegen jdn. vorgehen*

Grammar

G4

Mit **G** sind die Grammatikkapitel gekennzeichnet und der Reihe nach durchnummeriert. Eine Übersicht über alle Themen in diesem Band findest du auf der nächsten Seite.

Language tip **G7**

Die Seiten kennzeichnen zusätzliche Grammatik-kapitel. Du kannst dir die neuen Formen dort wie neue Vokabeln merken oder – wenn du es genau wissen willst – ein paar Regeln dazu lernen.

Hier stehen Besonderheiten und Tipps.

(TEST YOURSELF)

Hier kannst du üben.
Die Lösungen findest du auf S. 165.

(FÜR PROFIS)

Hier findest du knifflige Extras zum Thema.

R = Revision (Wiederholung)

	Englisch	Deutsch	Beispiel	Seite
G1	R: simple present	einfache Gegenwart	I (don't) know. • He doesn't know her. • Do you know?	150
G2	R: simple past	einfache Vergangenheit	They worked a lot. • She was in York. • I didn't go. • Did you go?	151
G3	reflexive pronouns, each other	Reflexivpronomen	I have hurt myself. • You should help each other.	152
G4	adjectives and adverbs	Adjektive und Adverbien	slow – slowly	153
G5	R: present perfect	Perfekt	I have already read the book. • He hasn't been to Wales yet. • Have you ever gone skiing?	154
G6	relative clauses	Relativsätze	This is my friend who goes climbing with me. • Edinburgh is a town which is very old.	155
G7	gerund	Gerundium	Swimming is great! • I love running too.	156
G8	R: will-future	Zukunft mit will	The weather will be fine tomorrow. • I'll help you.	157
G9	If-clauses I	Bedingungssätze Typ I	If it's sunny, I'll go swimming.	158
G10	If-clauses II	Bedingungssätze Typ II	If I had a holiday, I would go to the mountains.	159
G11	clauses of comparison	Vergleichssätze	Travelling is more interesting than staying at home. • Water is less expensive than juice. • London is as nice as Paris.	160
G12	some and any	some und any	I must drink some water. • They don't sell any bread.	161
G13	simple present and present progressive	Gegenwartszeiten	They eat porridge every day. • I can't go with you, I'm doing my homework now.	162
G14	possessive pronouns	Possessivpronomen	Is this your pen? Yes, it's mine.	163
G15	modal auxiliaries	modale Hilfsverben	They must / mustn't / needn't / may take the car.	164

Unit 1

G1 R: Die einfache Gegenwart

Revision: The simple present

Do you remember?

Wenn du einen Zustand beschreiben möchtest oder sagen willst, dass jemand etwas gewohnheitsmäßig tut oder dass etwas häufig oder regelmäßig geschieht, verwendest du das **simple present**.

Signalwörter	
every Monday	jeden Montag
always	immer
often	oft
usually	normalerweise
sometimes	manchmal
never	nie

I **like** computer games.	Ich mag Computerspiele.
He never **goes** to a fast food restaurant.	Er geht nie in ein Fastfood-Restaurant.
The new shop **sells** Indian food.	Der neue Laden verkauft indisches Essen.

 He, **she**, **it** – das **s** muss mit!

Mit **don't** oder **doesn't** (bei he, she, it) kannst du sagen, was man **nicht** macht.

I **don't know** where the best shops are.	Ich weiß nicht, wo die besten Geschäfte sind.
She **doesn't have** much time.	Sie hat nicht viel Zeit.

Und so kannst du fragen und kurz darauf antworten:

Do you sometimes **go** to the cinema?	Yes, I **do**.	No, I **don't**.
Does your brother **read** comics?	Yes, he **does**.	No, he **doesn't**.

Aussagen und Verneinungen mit **be** bildest du so:

I **am** (I'**m**)	I **am not** (I'**m not**)
you **are** (you'**re**)	you **are not** (you **aren't**)
he / she / it **is** (he'**s** / she'**s** / it'**s**)	he / she / it **is not** (he / she / it **isn't**)
we **are** (we'**re**)	we **are not** (we **aren't**)
they **are** (they'**re**)	they **are not** (they **aren't**)

Fragen und Kurzantworten mit **be** bildest du so:

Are you from York?	Yes, I **am**.	No, I'**m not**.
Is the park far away?	Yes, it **is**.	No, it **isn't**.

(TEST YOURSELF) Put the verbs in the simple present.

1. I sometimes —— (buy) clothes online.
2. She —— (do) her shopping every Friday.
3. The buses —— (not go) after 9 p.m.
4. —— you —— (go) to school by bus?
5. The girls —— (be) near the Viking Centre.
6. —— (be) Sam from Bristol?

G

G2 R: Die einfache Vergangenheit

Revision: The simple past

Um über Dinge zu sprechen, die in der Vergangenheit passiert und vorbei sind, verwendest du die einfache Vergangenheit (**simple past**).

> **Signalwörter**
> **yesterday**
> **last month**
> **a week ago**
> **in 2015**

gestern
letzten Monat
vor einer Woche
(im Jahr) 2015

Das simple past bildest du so:
Hänge die Endung **-ed** an das Verb.
Achte auf unregelmäßige Verben, z. B. do → **did**; fall → **fell**; get → **got**; go → **went**; have → **had**; hear → **heard**; make → **made**; see → **saw**; write → **wrote**

Eine Liste der unregelmäßigen Verben findest du auf Seite 210.

I **helped** my aunt last Sunday.	Letzten Sonntag half ich meiner Tante.
Hannah **bought** a coat yesterday.	Hannah kaufte gestern eine Jacke.

Um zu sagen, was in der Vergangenheit nicht passiert ist, setzt du **didn't** (= did not) vor das Verb.

I **didn't watch** TV yesterday.	Ich schaute gestern nicht fern.
Tom's parents **didn't like** Bramford.	Toms Eltern gefiel Bramford nicht.

Und so kannst du im **simple past** Fragen stellen:

Did you **have** a nice weekend?	Yes, I **did**.	No, I **didn't**.
When **did** your sister **visit** you?	At the weekend.	

 Im Deutschen gibt es verschiedene Möglichkeiten, Vergangenes auszudrücken:

Tim met Sarah.	Tim hat Sarah getroffen. / Tim traf Sarah.

Aussagen und Verneinungen mit **be** bildest du so:

I **was** in York. I **wasn't** in London.	Ich war in York. Ich war nicht in London.
Sue **wasn't** at the zoo. She **was** at home.	Sue war nicht im Zoo. Sie war zu Hause.
The students **were** at the theatre. They **weren't** at the cinema.	Die Schüler waren im Theater. Sie waren nicht im Kino.

Fragen und Kurzantworten mit **be** bildest du so:

Were you at home?	Yes, I **was**.	No, I **wasn't**.
Was it funny?	Yes, it **was**.	No, it **wasn't**.

(TEST YOURSELF) **Put the verbs in the simple past.**

1. Hannah —— (have) a great time.
2. I —— (not hear) a noise.
3. —— you —— (have) a nice day?
4. What —— you —— (do) yesterday?
5. Last Friday Tom —— (not be) at home.
6. —— (be) you in Italy last summer?

Unit 2

Language tip

G3 Reflexivpronomen und each other

Reflexive pronouns and each other

I have hurt myself.

Ich habe mich verletzt.

Im Englischen werden die Reflexivpronomen mit **-self** oder **-selves** gebildet. Im Deutschen werden sie meist mit „mir" oder „mich", „dir" oder „dich", „sich" usw. übersetzt.

I bought **myself** a new T-shirt.	Ich habe mir ein neues T-Shirt gekauft.
Can you see **yourself** in the window?	Kannst du dich im Fenster sehen?
He cut **himself** with a knife.	Er hat sich mit einem Messer geschnitten.
She asked **herself** why it happened.	Sie fragte sich, warum es passiert ist.
The cat hurt **itself**.	Die Katze hat sich verletzt.
We built **ourselves** a tree house.	Wir haben uns ein Baumhaus gebaut.
Help **yourselves**!	Bedient euch!
They hurt **themselves** during the sports lesson.	Sie haben sich beim Sportunterricht verletzt.

 Achtung: Beachte den Unterschied zwischen **themselves** und **each other**.

Ben and his sister are looking at **themselves**.	Ben und seine Schwester schauen sich an (= jeder sich selbst).
Ben and his sister are looking at **each other**. (= Ben looks at his sister and she looks at him.)	Ben und seine Schwester schauen sich gegenseitig an (= jeder den anderen).

(TEST YOURSELF) **Put in the correct word.**

1. I saw —— (myself / himself) in the newspaper.
2. Did you buy —— a present (itself / yourself)?
3. Grandma cut —— (herself / himself) with a knife.
4. We saw —— (yourselves / ourselves) on TV.
5. Sam and Ben always tell —— (each other / themselves) jokes.
6. The dog cut —— (itself / himself).

(FÜR PROFIS)

Du kannst mit den Reflexivpronomen auch betonen, dass jemand etwas selbst gemacht hat:

He made the cake **himself**.	Er hat den Kuchen selbst gebacken.

G4 Adjektive und Adverbien

Adjectives and adverbs

That was easy.
I won the race easily.

Das war leicht.
Ich hab' das Rennen leicht gewonnen.

Ein **Adjektiv** (Eigenschaftswort) beschreibt eine Person oder eine Sache.

Beth is a **good** student.	Beth ist eine gute Schülerin.
Climbing is a **dangerous** sport.	Klettern ist ein gefährlicher Sport.

Ein **Adverb** beschreibt, wie jemand etwas tut oder wie etwas geschieht. Im Englischen erkennt man Adverbien durch ein angehängtes **-ly**.

He ran **slowly**.	Er rannte langsam.
It happened **quickly**.	Es geschah schnell.

 Achtung Schreibweise: easy → eas**ily**; careful → carefu**lly**

Es gibt aber auch unregelmäßige Adverbien:

That's a **good** song.	(Adjektiv)	Das ist ein gutes Lied.
She can sing **well**.	(Adverb)	Sie kann gut singen.

Manche Adverbien verändern sich nicht:

Rugby is a **fast** game.	(Adjektiv)	Rugby ist ein schnelles Spiel.
Look, the players are running **fast**.	(Adverb)	Schau, die Spieler rennen schnell.
This was a **hard** exercise.	(Adjektiv)	Das war eine schwierige Übung.
Mum works **hard** every day.	(Adverb)	Mama arbeitet jeden Tag schwer.

(TEST YOURSELF) **Use adjectives or adverbs.**

1. You must always ride —— (careful).
2. Max is a —— (good) tennis player.
3. Lucy speaks English —— (good).
4. Sherlock is a —— (clever) dog.
5. They walked home —— (slow).
6. Don't run so —— (fast).

G5 R: Das Perfekt

Revision: The present perfect

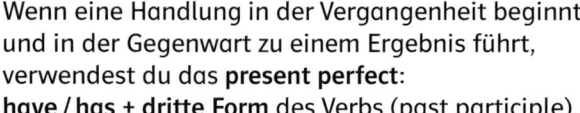

Do you remember?

Wenn eine Handlung in der Vergangenheit beginnt und in der Gegenwart zu einem Ergebnis führt, verwendest du das **present perfect**:
have / has + dritte Form des Verbs (past participle).

Signalwörter	
already	schon
just	gerade
not ... yet	noch ... nicht
ever (in Fragen)	jemals

Bei den meisten Verben hängst du für die dritte Form ein **-ed** an das Verb: help → help**ed**

| I **have** just **played** football. | Ich habe gerade Fußball gespielt. |
| He **has** already **had** his lunch. | Er hat schon zu Mittag gegessen. |

Achtung: Einige Verben haben unregelmäßige dritte Formen, z. B.:
break → broke → **broken**; do → did → **done**; be → was / were → **been**

Eine Liste der unregelmäßigen Verben findest du auf S. 210.

Um die Sätze zu verneinen, benutzt du **haven't** oder **hasn't** (bei he, she, it):

| I **haven't called** the hospital yet. | Ich habe das Krankenhaus noch nicht angerufen. |
| She **hasn't been** to London yet. | Sie ist noch nicht in London gewesen. |

Fragen und Kurzantworten bildest du so:

Have you ever **broken** your arm?	Yes, I **have**.	No, I **haven't**.
Has your brother ever **won** a prize?	Yes, he **has**.	No, he **hasn't**.
Have the girls **been** to the party?	Yes, they **have**.	No, they **haven't**.

Bei Fragen mit Fragewörtern stellst du das Fragewort an den Satzanfang.

| What **has happened**? | Was ist passiert? |
| Where **have** you **been**? | Wo bist du gewesen? |

(TEST YOURSELF) **Put the verbs in the present perfect.**

1. Where —— you —— (be), Dylan?
2. Sue —— already —— (do) her homework.
3. We —— just —— (have) an accident.
4. I —— (not ask) him yet.
5. —— you —— (forget) your mobile again?
6. Why —— she —— (not call) the ambulance yet?

G6 Relativsätze mit Relativpronomen

Relative clauses with relative pronouns

This is the coat which is best for tonight.

Das ist die Jacke, die für heute Abend am besten ist.

Wenn du eine Person oder eine Sache genauer beschreiben willst, verwendest du die Relativpronomen **who**, **which** oder **that**.

who → Personen
which → Dinge
that → Personen und Dinge

Bell was **the man who / that** invented the telephone.	Bell war der Mann, der das Telefon erfand.
He invented **machines which / that** changed the world.	Er erfand Geräte, die die Welt veränderten.

Willst du Zugehörigkeit oder Besitz ausdrücken, verwendest du bei Personen und Dingen **whose**.

That's the **boy whose** parents are doctors.	Das ist der Junge, dessen Eltern Ärzte sind.
Edinburgh is a **city whose** centre is very old.	Edinburgh ist eine Stadt, deren Zentrum sehr alt ist.

(TEST YOURSELF) **Put in <u>who</u>, <u>whose</u> or <u>which</u>.**

1. Bell was a man —— had lots of fantastic ideas.
2. He even built a machine —— could fly.
3. One day he opened a school for people —— couldn't hear.
4. The phones —— people used fifty years ago are in museums now.
5. Many people —— are famous inventors come from Scotland.
6. This is the girl —— parents are from India.

(FÜR PROFIS)

Folgt <u>nach</u> who, which oder that ein Personalpronomen wie **I**, **you**, **he**, **she**, **it**, **we**, **they**, kannst du who, which oder that auch weglassen. Diesen Satz nennt man **contact clause**.

The lady (who) **we** saw on TV last night is my cousin.	Die Frau, die wir gestern im Fernsehen gesehen haben, ist meine Kusine.
Scotland is the country (which) **I** want to visit next year.	Schottland ist das Land, das ich nächstes Jahr besuchen möchte.

Language tip

G7 Das Gerundium

Gerund

Spending a few days in Scotland is always a great idea.
I love looking at the sheep.

Ein paar Tage in Schottland zu verbringen ist immer eine tolle Idee.
Ich liebe es, die Schafe anzuschauen.

Ein Gerundium bildet man, indem man **-ing** an ein Verb anhängt. Dadurch wird das Verb zu einem Nomen (Hauptwort). Mit dem Gerundium kann man über Tätigkeiten und Aktivitäten sprechen. Es steht am Satzanfang und ist **Subjekt / Satzgegenstand** des Satzes.

Watching TV can be interesting.   Fernsehen kann interessant sein.
Playing football is my favourite sport.   Fußballspielen ist mein Lieblingssport.

Das Gerundium kann aber auch nach dem Verb stehen und ist dann **Objekt / Satzergänzung** des Satzes. Das gilt besonders für Verben wie **love**, **(not) like** und **hate**.

I like **swimming**.   Ich schwimme gerne.
I don't like **cleaning** my shoes.   Ich putze meine Schuhe nicht gerne.
Tim hates **tidying** his room.   Tim hasst es, sein Zimmer aufzuräumen.

 Das Gerundium darf man nicht mit dem **present progressive** verwechseln. Vergleiche:

I **am** walk**ing** on the beach.   Ich gehe gerade am Strand spazieren.
I **love** walk**ing** on the beach.   Ich mag es, am Strand spazieren zu gehen.

(TEST YOURSELF) **Use the verbs to make the gerund.**

1. —— (walk) with a dog can be fun.
2. —— (meet) friends is my favourite activity.
3. Rock —— (climb) can be very exciting.
4. Jane likes —— (stay) on a farm.
5. I hate —— (work) in the garden.
6. I don't like —— (write) tests.

(FÜR PROFIS)

Ein Gerundium kann auch nach Ausdrücken wie **be good at …** oder **What about …?** stehen.

I'm good at playing frisbee.   Ich bin gut im Frisbeespielen.
What about dancing?   Wie wär's mit Tanzen?

G8 R: Die Zukunft mit will

Revision: The will-future

Do you remember?

Mit dem **will-future** sprichst du über die Zukunft. Oft drückst du damit Hoffnungen, Wünsche und Vorhersagen aus. Dann beginnen diese Sätze mit **I hope**, **I think**, **I'm sure** oder **maybe**.
Du bildest das **will-future** mit **will** oder **won't** und der **Grundform des Verbs**. Häufig wird die Kurzform verwendet: I **will** go → I'll go

We'll **stay** at a campsite.	Wir werden auf einem Campingplatz übernachten.
Maybe we'll **see** Nessie.	Vielleicht sehen wir Nessie.
I hope it **won't rain** tomorrow.	Ich hoffe, es wird morgen nicht regnen.

Im Deutschen kann man über Zukünftiges mit der Zukunft oder der Gegenwart sprechen:

We'll **wait** for you.	Wir werden auf dich warten.
	Wir warten auf dich.

Auch wenn du dich in einer Situation ganz spontan für etwas Bestimmtes entscheidest, verwendest du das **will-future**.

I don't understand this exercise.	Ich verstehe diese Aufgabe nicht.
– Don't worry, I'll **help** you.	– Keine Sorge, ich helfe dir.
Look, it's sunny. I **won't take** a coat.	Schau, es ist sonnig. Ich nehme keine Jacke mit.

 Achtung! Verwechsle **will** (werden) nicht mit **want to** (wollen):

I **will** buy some souvenirs.	Ich **werde** ein paar Souvenirs kaufen.
I **want to** buy some souvenirs.	Ich **will** ein paar Souvenirs kaufen.

(TEST YOURSELF) **Complete the sentences.**

1. Maybe we —— (stay) in a cosy B&B in Inverness this summer.
2. I hope you —— (not be) ill on holiday.
3. Look, that's real Scottish food. – Great, I —— (have) that.
4. I don't have a map. – I —— (show) you the way.
5. Can you help us? – We —— (do) our best.
6. You can give her the money, she —— (not lose) it.

G9 Bedingungssätze Typ I

If-clauses type I

If it stops raining soon, I'll take a photo.

Wenn es bald aufhört zu regnen, mache ich ein Foto.

If-Sätze benutzt man, um Bedingungen und Folgen auszudrücken. Im if-Satz steht das **simple present**. Im Hauptsatz steht das **will-future**. Geht der **if**-Satz voran, steht am Ende des **if**-Satzes ein Komma.

Bedingung	Folge	
If it **rains**,	we**'ll stay** at home.	Wenn es regnet, bleiben wir zu Hause.
If it**'s** too dark,	I **won't take** any photos.	Wenn es zu dunkel ist, mache ich keine Fotos.

 Im **if**-Satz steht nie **will / won't**!

Bedingungssätze können auch mit dem Hauptsatz beginnen. Dann entfällt das Komma.

I**'ll be** unhappy if you **don't come** to my party.	Ich werde unglücklich sein, wenn du nicht zu meiner Party kommst.

(TEST YOURSELF) **Complete the sentences.**

1. If I —— (meet) Nancy, I —— (tell) her about the new swimming pool.
2. If Jake —— (go) to Scotland, he —— (not visit) a museum.
3. If Olivia —— (have) time on Saturday, she —— (go) shopping.
4. If Katie —— (not do) her homework, she —— (not be) good at Maths.
5. You —— (become) famous if you —— (take) a good photo of Nessie.
6. We —— (be) very unhappy if you —— (not visit) us at the weekend.

G10 Bedingungssätze Typ II

If-clauses type II

If I had a lot of money, I would buy a castle.

Wenn ich viel Geld hätte, würde ich ein Schloss kaufen.

Du kennst schon die Bedingungssätze Typ I. Bei Typ I steht die Bedingung im simple present und die Folge im will-future. (S. 158)
Bei Bedingungssätzen Typ II ist eine Bedingung unwahrscheinlich oder nicht erfüllbar. Du verwendest im if-Satz **simple past**. Im Hauptsatz steht **would / wouldn't + Grundform des Verbs**.

Bedingung	Folge	
If I **had** a dog,	I **would go** for a walk every day.	Wenn ich einen Hund hätte, würde ich jeden Tag spazieren gehen.
If it **rained**,	I **would take** my umbrella.	Wenn es regnen würde, würde ich meinen Regenschirm mitnehmen.

 Im if-Satz steht nie **would / wouldn't**.

Bedingungssätze können auch mit dem Hauptsatz beginnen. Dann entfällt das Komma.

I **would be** very sad if I **didn't find** my mobile again.	Ich wäre sehr traurig, wenn ich mein Handy nicht mehr finden würde.

 Achtung Besonderheit: Statt **If I was** … wird oft **If I were** … gebraucht.

If I **were** you, I **would call** her.	Wenn ich du wäre, würde ich sie anrufen.

Im Deutschen verwendet man in beiden Satzteilen **würde**, **wäre** oder **hätte (Konjunktiv)**.

If your mum **didn't work** so hard, she **wouldn't be** so tired.	Wenn deine Mutter nicht so schwer arbeiten **würde**, **wäre** sie nicht so müde.

(TEST YOURSELF) Complete the sentences.

1. If I —— (have) more time, I —— (go) camping with my friends.
2. If Sue —— (be) older, she —— (understand) the film.
3. If I —— (be) in Northern Ireland, I —— (visit) the Giant's Causeway.
4. I —— (hear) you better if you —— (speak) louder.
5. Your grandparents —— (be) very sad, if you —— (not visit) them.
6. Kate —— (not stay) at home if she —— (not be) ill.

G11 Steigerung und Vergleiche von Adjektiven

Clauses of comparison

My eyes are bigger than your eyes.

Meine Augen sind größer als deine Augen.

Adjektive mit **einer Silbe** steigerst du mit **-er / -est**:

| cheap | cheap**er** | the cheap**est** | billig, billiger, am billigsten |

Zweisilbige Adjektive, die auf **-y** enden, wie z. B. **happy**, **easy**, **crazy**, steigert man auch mit **-er / -est**.

| happy | happ**ier** | the happ**iest** | glücklich, glücklicher, am glücklichsten |

Alle anderen Adjektive **mit zwei und mehr Silben** steigerst du, indem du **more** und **the most** davor setzt.

| expensive | **more** expensive
the most expensive | teuer, teurer,
am teuersten |

Und so kannst du ausdrücken, dass etwas weniger oder am wenigsten ist:

| interesting | **less** interesting
the least interesting | interessant, weniger interessant,
am wenigsten interessant |

So kannst du Dinge miteinander vergleichen:

| My big sister is **as nice as** my little brother. | Meine große Schwester ist genauso nett wie mein kleiner Bruder. |
| Mineral water is **not as** expensive **as** juice. | Mineralwasser ist nicht so teuer wie Saft. |

 Achtung: Um ungleiche Dinge zu vergleichen, benutzt du **than**.

| London is **bigger than** Berlin. | London ist größer als Berlin. |

(TEST YOURSELF) **Compare these things.**

1. Northern Ireland is —— (small) than England.
2. Speaking English is —— (easy) than speaking French.
3. Watching a film can be —— (interesting) than surfing the internet.
4. Belfast is the —— (exciting) city in Northern Ireland.
5. A bike is —— (expensive) than a car.
6. Look, the black shoes are as —— (nice) as the white shoes.

G12 Some und any

Some and any

I *need some milk but I don't need any cheese.*

Ich brauche Milch, aber ich brauche keinen Käse.

Some oder **any** bedeuten im Deutschen **etwas**, **einige** oder **ein paar**.

In positiven Aussagen benutzt du **some**. Es muss nicht immer übersetzt werden.

I'd like **some** fruit.	Ich möchte gerne (etwas) Obst.
I must buy **some** carrots.	Ich muss (ein paar) Karotten kaufen.

In verneinten Aussagen und in den meisten Fragen steht **any**. Es wird nicht immer übersetzt.

Do you have **any** milk at home?	Hast du Milch zu Hause?
Sorry, we don't have **any** bread.	Es tut mir leid, wir haben kein Brot.

Wie **some** und **any** werden auch ihre Zusammensetzungen verwendet:

something und **anything**	(irgend)etwas
somebody und **anybody**	(irgend)jemand
someone und **anyone**	(irgend)jemand
somewhere und **anywhere**	irgendwo

He told me **something**.	Er hat mir etwas gesagt.
Did he tell you **anything**?	Hat er dir etwas gesagt?
No, he didn't tell me **anything**.	Nein, er hat mir nichts gesagt.

Achte auf folgende Übersetzungen:
not … anything → nichts; not … anybody / anyone → niemand; not … anywhere → nirgendwo

(TEST YOURSELF) **Put in <u>some</u> or <u>any</u>.**

1. Do you know —— facts about Northern Ireland?
2. Look, there are —— funny dancers in the street.
3. Let's buy —— food for the party.
4. Mr Taylor asked me —— questions about Belfast.
5. Do you have —— strawberries?
6. Sorry, we don't have —— strawberries today.

Unit 5

G13 Gegenüberstellung: Simple present und present progressive

Simple present and present progressive

*I usually don't drink juice, but today
I'm drinking green juice because it's
St Patrick's Day.*

Normalerweise trinke ich keinen Saft,
aber heute trinke ich grünen Saft, weil
St. Patrick's Day ist.

Present progressive

Wenn du sagen möchtest, was gerade passiert
oder was jemand im Augenblick tut, verwendest
du das **present progressive**.
So bildest du Aussagen im **present progressive: am / are / is + Verb + -ing.**
So verneinst du die Sätze: **am / are / is <u>not</u> + Verb + -ing.**
Bei Fragen stellst du **am / are / is** an den Satzanfang.

Signalwörter	
now	jetzt, nun
at the moment	im Moment

> Listen, your mobile **is** ring**ing**.   Hör' mal, dein Handy klingelt gerade.
> We **are not** us**ing** the computer at the moment.   Wir benutzen den Computer gerade nicht.
> **Are** you prepar**ing** a snack?   Bereitest du gerade einen Imbiss vor?

Simple present

Wenn du einen Zustand beschreiben möchtest
oder sagen willst, dass jemand etwas
gewohnheitsmäßig tut oder dass etwas häufig
oder regelmäßig geschieht, verwendest du das
simple present.

Signalwörter	
every ...	jede / r / s
always	immer
usually	normalerweise
often	oft
sometimes	manchmal
never	nie

 He, **she**, **it** – das **s** muss mit!

Mit **don't** oder **doesn't** (bei he, she, it) kannst du sagen, was man **nicht** macht.
Bei Fragen mit Vollverben (z. B. sing, write, play etc.) musst du **do** oder **does** verwenden.

> Every year Keith celebrate**s** St Patrick's Day.   Jedes Jahr feiert Keith den St. Patrick's Day.
> Sue **doesn't** speak German.   Sue spricht kein Deutsch.
> **Do** you often eat fish?   Isst du oft Fisch?

(TEST YOURSELF) **Use simple present or present progressive.**

1. Simon often —— (help) his grandma.
2. Listen, Maddy —— (practise) with her band.
3. —— you sometimes —— (eat) eggs?
4. Keith —— (not listen to) music now.
5. —— (you) —— (watch) TV at the moment?
6. Leo —— (not drink) tea every day.

G14 Possessivpronomen

Possessive pronouns

I found a mobile. Is it yours?

Ich habe ein Handy gefunden. Ist es deins?

Du kennst bereits die Possessiv**begleiter** (**my**, **your**, **his**, **her**, **our**, **their**). Sie stehen **vor** einem Nomen. Mit den Possessiv**pronomen** kannst du sagen, wem etwas gehört, wenn **kein** Nomen **folgt**.

Possessive determiner	Possessivbegleiter	Possessive pronoun	Possessivpronomen
That's **my** umbrella.	Das ist **mein** Schirm.	It's **mine.**	Das ist **meiner.**
Is that **your** coat?	Ist das **deine** Jacke?	Is it **yours?**	Ist das **deine?**
This is **his** toothbrush.	Das ist **seine** Zahnbürste.	It's **his.**	Das ist **seine.**
This is **her** shampoo.	Das ist **ihr** Shampoo.	It's **hers.**	Es ist **ihrs.**
Look at the cat and **its** ball.	Schau dir die Katze und **ihren** Ball an.	It's **its.**	Das ist **ihrer.**
They are **our** bags.	Es sind **unsere** Taschen.	They are **ours.**	Es sind **unsere.**
Are they **your** towels?	Sind das **eure** Handtücher?	Are they **yours?**	Sind das **eure?**
This is **their** new car.	Das ist **ihr** neues Auto.	It's **theirs.**	Das ist **ihrs.**

(TEST YOURSELF) **Put in the correct word.**

1. Your mobile just looks like —— (my / mine).
2. Have you put —— (your / yours) scarf in the bag, Leo?
3. Is that Maddy's bag? – Yes, it's —— (theirs / hers).
4. Their towels are white, —— (our / ours) are brown.
5. Is this the O'Brians' new car? – No, it isn't —— (their / theirs).
6. I think it's Conor's bike. – Well, I don't think it's —— (his / yours) bike.

G15 Modale Hilfsverben

Modal auxiliaries

You mustn't walk.

Du darfst nicht gehen.

Modale Hilfsverben verändern die Art und Weise eines Verbs. **Can**, **can't**, **must**, **needn't**, **mustn't**, **may**, **may not** kommen immer zusammen mit einem anderen Verb vor.

I **can** play tennis.	Ich kann Tennis spielen.
	(Ich habe es gelernt.)
I **can't** play tennis now.	Ich kann jetzt nicht Tennis spielen.
	(Ich muss meine Hausaufgaben machen.)
You **must** play tennis with Amy.	Du musst mit Amy Tennis spielen.
He **needn't** play tennis.	Er braucht nicht Tennis (zu) spielen.
	(Wir sind genug Spieler.)
She **mustn't** play tennis.	Sie darf nicht Tennis spielen.
	(Sie ist krank.)
We **may** play tennis later.	Wir spielen vielleicht später Tennis.
	(Jetzt ist der Platz besetzt.)
They **may not** play tennis then.	Sie spielen dann vielleicht nicht Tennis.
	(Also können wir spielen.)

 Aufgepasst bei **mustn't** (nicht dürfen) und **needn't** (nicht brauchen, nicht müssen):

You **mustn't** talk so loud.	Du darfst nicht so laut sprechen.
You **needn't** wait for me.	Du brauchst nicht auf mich (zu) warten.
	oder: Du musst nicht auf mich warten.

(TEST YOURSELF) **Choose the right word.**

1. —— (can / mustn't) I use your pen?
2. You —— (mustn't / needn't) eat ice cream in the classroom.
3. Sara —— (must / mustn't) do her homework.
4. You —— (may not / mustn't) have time to come to the party.
5. We —— (must / needn't) go now. It's already 7 o'clock.
6. You —— (can / needn't) worry. The children will be OK.

Lösungen

TEST YOURSELF

G1
1. buy
2. does
3. don't go
4. Do … go
5. are
6. Is

G2
1. had
2. didn't hear
3. Did … have
4. did … do
5. wasn't
6. Were

G3
1. myself
2. yourself
3. herself
4. ourselves
5. each other
6. itself

G4
1. carefully
2. good
3. well
4. clever
5. slowly
6. fast

G5
1. have … been
2. has … done
3. have / 've … had
4. have not / haven't asked
5. Have … forgotten
6. has … not / hasn't … called

G6
1. who
2. which
3. who
4. which
5. who
6. whose

G7
1. Walking
2. Meeting
3. climbing
4. staying
5. working
6. writing

G8
1. 'll / will stay
2. won't / will not be
3. 'll / will have
4. 'll / will show
5. 'll / will do
6. won't / will not lose

G9
1. meet, 'll / will tell
2. goes, won't / will not visit
3. has, 'll / will go
4. doesn't do, won't / will not be
5. 'll / will become, take
6. 'll / will be, don't visit

G10
1. had, would go
2. was, would understand
3. were, would visit
4. would hear, spoke
5. would be, didn't visit
6. wouldn't / would not stay, wasn't

G11
1. smaller
2. easier
3. more / less interesting
4. most exciting
5. less expensive
6. nice

G12
1. any
2. some
3. some
4. some
5. any
6. any

G13
1. helps
2. is practising
3. Do … eat
4. isn't listening to
5. Are … watching
6. doesn't drink

G14
1. mine
2. your
3. hers
4. ours
5. theirs
6. his

G15
1. Can
2. mustn't
3. must
4. may not
5. must
6. needn't

Methods

1-minute-presentation

Step 1
Nimm ein Blatt DIN A4-Papier quer und falte es so, dass das untere Drittel nach hinten wegknickt.

Step 2
Schreibe den Vortragstext auf die oberen zwei Drittel.

Step 3
Streiche nun die wichtigsten Stichpunkte im Text an. Notiere sie noch einmal auf dem unteren Drittel. Das ist dein Spickzettel.

Step 4
In deiner Präsentation verwendest du nur den Spickzettel. Wenn du steckenbleibst, darfst du ihn umknicken und kurz auf den Text oben schauen.

Bus stop
(Lerntempoduett)

Step 1
Bearbeite die Aufgabe zunächst allein. Schreibe deine Lösungen auf.

Step 2
Wenn du fertig bist, gehe zum „bus stop". Warte dort auf die nächste Person bzw. triff die Person, die dort schon wartet. Vergleicht und korrigiert eure Ergebnisse.

Step 3
Gehe danach wieder zu deinem Platz zurück. Bearbeite die nächste Aufgabe.

Double circle

(Kugellager)

Step 1

Teilt euch in zwei Gruppen A und B.
Gruppe A bildet den inneren Kreis. Gruppe B bildet den
äußeren Kreis. Steht dabei so, dass ihr euch anseht.

Step 2

Wenn ein Signal ertönt, sprecht ihr mit der Person,
die euch gegenübersteht.

Step 3

Beim nächsten Signal rückt der mittlere Kreis zwei
Plätze weiter nach links. Wiederholt den Vorgang.

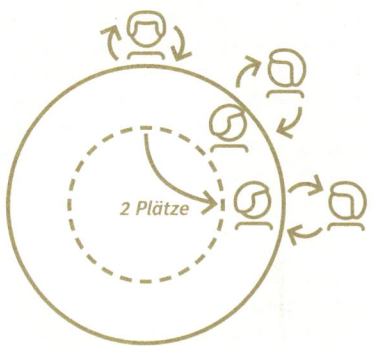

Dramatic reading

(Szenisches Lesen)

Step 1

Verteilt die Rollen innerhalb eurer Gruppe.

Step 2

Lies dir deinen Text lautlos oder ganz leise immer
wieder vor, bis du ihn gut kennst.

Step 3

Übt euren Text in der Gruppe mit der Methode
„Read and look up" (Seite 170).

Step 4

Überlegt euch, wie ihr euch in der Rolle fühlt und
wie ihr euch bewegen würdet. Tragt euren Text so
frei wie möglich vor.

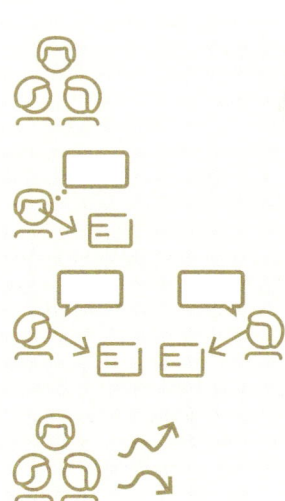

Gallery walk

Step 1

Hängt nach eurer Gruppenarbeit euer Produkt
gut sichtbar im Klassenzimmer auf.

Step 2

Einer von euch, der „Experte", bleibt bei eurem
Produkt stehen und erklärt es den anderen.
Die anderen gehen herum. Nach jedem Durchgang
wechselt der Experte.

Step 3

Seht euch die Produkte der anderen an und
bewertet sie.

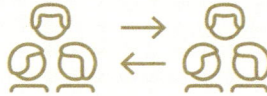

Step 4

Wertet im Anschluss eure Ergebnisse in der Klasse aus.

Milling around
(Marktplatz)

Step 1

Bearbeite die Aufgabe zunächst allein.
Auf ein Zeichen vom Lehrer oder der Lehrerin
steht ihr auf und geht durch den Raum.
Nimm die Aufgabe und einen Stift mit.

Step 2

Wenn ein Signal ertönt, bleibt ihr stehen.
Besprecht mit der Person die Aufgabe,
die euch am nächsten steht.

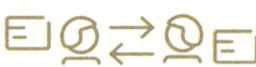

Step 3

Beim nächsten Signal trennt ihr euch und geht
weiter durch den Raum. Wiederholt den Vorgang.

Peer correction

(Partnerkontrolle)

Step 1
Bearbeite die Aufgabe zunächst selbstständig.

Step 2
Tausche deine Lösungen mit einem Partner/einer Partnerin.
Kontrolliere seine oder ihre Lösungen.

Step 3
Tauscht euch danach zu der Aufgabe aus und korrigiert den Text.

Placemat

(Platzdeckchen)

Step 1
Bildet Virergruppen.

Step 2
Teilt ein großes Blatt Papier in fünf Bereiche ein.

Step 3
Setzt euch so hin, dass alle in eine Ecke des Blattes
schreiben können.

Step 4
Jedes Gruppenmitglied denkt allein über das Thema nach
und schreibt Ideen auf seinen Teil des Blattes.

Step 5
Tauscht euch über die Ideen aus. Einigt euch auf die besten
Ideen und schreibt diese in die Mitte des Blattes.

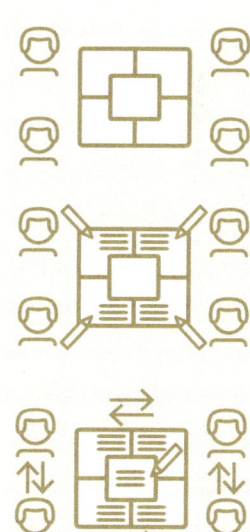

Read and look up

(Lesen und Aufschauen)

Step 1

Schaue auf deinen Text und präge dir die erste Zeile oder den ersten Satz ein. Schaue hoch und sprich deine Zeile/ deinen Satz lautlos oder leise vor dich hin. Nimm dir die nächste Zeile/den nächsten Satz vor.

Step 2

Übe nun mit einer Partnerin/einem Partner. Erzähle deinen Text, Zeile für Zeile oder Satz für Satz. Dazwischen schaust du immer wieder nach unten auf deinen Text.

Step 3

Wiederhole alles, bis es gut klappt. Überlege dir, wo du stehen und wie du dich bewegen willst.

Round robin

(Blitzlicht)

Step 1

Bildet Gruppen und setzt euch in einen Kreis.

Step 2

Jedes Gruppenmitglied überlegt sich kurz einen Satz, der seine persönliche Meinung zum Thema ausdrückt.

Step 3

Wenn alle bereit sind, sagen die Gruppenmitglieder der Reihe nach ihre Meinung.

Step 4

Die anderen Gruppenmitglieder dürfen die Sätze nicht kommentieren.

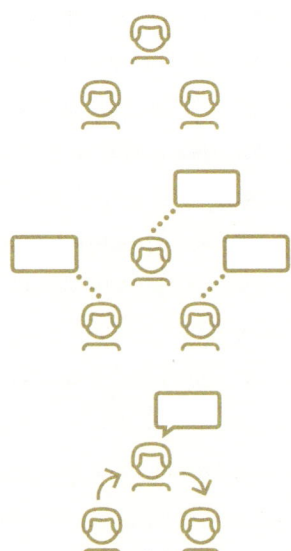

Think – pair – share

Step 1
Schreibe deine Ideen, Gedanken oder Lösungen zur Aufgabe auf.

Step 2
Tauscht eure Notizen zu zweit aus und besprecht sie.

Step 3
Präsentiert euer Ergebnis anderen Paaren oder der gesamten Klasse.

Tip top

Step 1
Sage zunächst, was dir gut gefallen hat – was „top" war.

Step 2
Sage nun, was noch nicht so gut war, und gib einen Tipp, was man noch verbessern könnte.

Writers' conference
(Schreibwerkstatt)

Step 1
Bildet Vierergruppen.

Step 2
Lest euch eure Sätze/Texte gegenseitig vor.

Step 3
Die anderen sagen, was ihnen gefallen hat.

Step 4
Die Zuhörer machen Verbesserungsvorschläge.

Step 5
Jede Gruppe wählt den besten Text aus und liest ihn der Klasse vor.

Vocabulary

Das Vocabulary enthält alle neuen Wörter und Wendungen. Sie stehen in der Reihenfolge, wie sie im Buch vorkommen.

Die Wortliste ist in drei Spalten aufgeteilt:

Links findest du das englische Wort mit der Lautschrift in Klammern. (Die Lautschrift wird ganz unten auf jeder Seite im *Dictionary* erklärt.)

In der mittleren Spalte steht die deutsche Übersetzung.

Rechts findest du Beispielsätze, Hinweise und Tipps, die dir beim Lernen helfen.

Die **fett** gedruckten Wörter musst du lernen.
Die blau gedruckten Wörter kannst du lernen, musst du aber nicht.
Die Wörter aus den Checkpoints musst du nicht lernen.

Symbole und Abkürzungen:

⬄	Achte auf die Aussprache!	=	entspricht
✐	Achte auf die Schreibung!	*(sg)*	Einzahl (Singular)
↔	ist das Gegenteil von	*(pl)*	Mehrzahl (Plural)
→	ist verwandt mit	R	ähnlich wie im Russischen
sth	something	T	ähnlich wie im Türkischen

Die *Word bank*-Seiten helfen dir, die *Your turn*-Aufgaben in den *Units* zu bearbeiten.
Du findest dort nützlichen individuellen Wortschatz zum Thema der *Unit*, der dir hilft, über deine eigene Situation zu sprechen oder zu schreiben. Diese Wörter findest du auch im *Dictionary*.

Wenn du ein Wort nicht weißt und im Wörterbuch nachschlagen willst, schau auf den *Dictionary*-Seiten ab S. 212 nach. Oder bei den *Instructions* auf S. 208.

Zoom in – The British Isles

p. 8	**The British Isles** [ðə ˌbrɪtɪʃ ˈaɪlz]	die Britischen Inseln
	Northern Ireland [ˌnɔːðn ˈaɪələnd]	Nordirland
	The Republic of Ireland [ðə rɪˌpʌblɪk əv ˈaɪələnd]	Irland
	Wales [weɪlz]	Wales
	The United Kingdom [ðə juːˌnaɪtɪd ˈkɪŋdəm]	Vereinigtes Königreich von Großbritannien und Nordirland
	Great Britain [ˌgreɪt ˈbrɪtn]	Großbritannien
p. 9	**hobby** [ˈhɒbi]	Hobby

R хобби T hobi

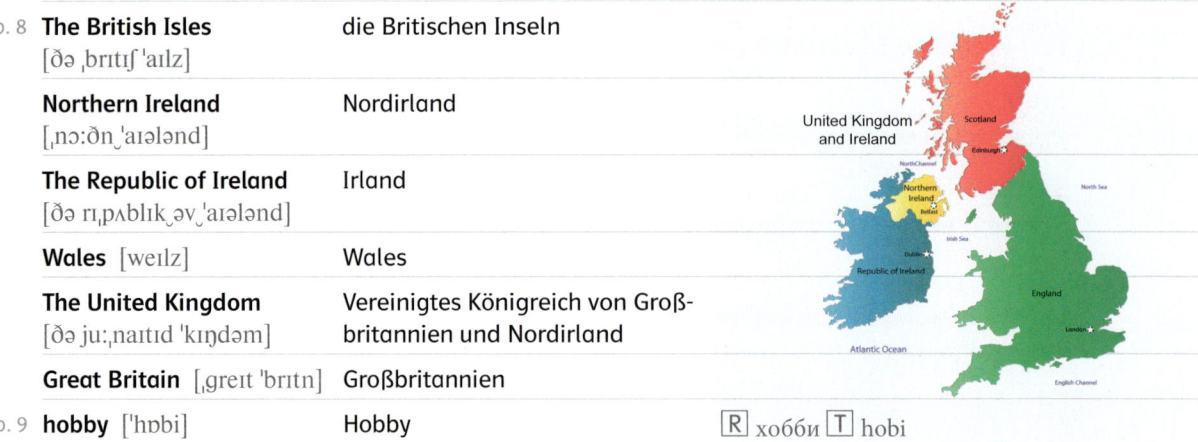

Unit 1 England now and then

p. 10 | **then** [ðen] | damals | We lived in Wales **then**.

Way in

stone [stəʊn]	Stein	
circle [ˈsɜːkl]	Kreis; Ring	
in the south of [ˌɪn ðə ˈsaʊθ ˌəv]	im Süden von	Stonehenge is **in the south of** England.
the Romans [ðə ˈrəʊmənz]	die Römer	**The Romans** built Hadrian's Wall.
north [nɔːθ]	Norden	**north** ↔ south
to **take** [teɪk]	dauern	It **takes** two hours by train.

p. 11 | **the Vikings** [ðə ˈvaɪkɪŋz] | die Wikinger | **The Vikings** went to York. |
to **invade** [ɪnˈveɪd]	einmarschieren (in); eindringen (in)	The Vikings **invaded** York.
Denmark [ˈdenmaːk]	Dänemark	**Denmark** is in the north of Europe.
Norway [ˈnɔːweɪ]	Norwegen	Ⓡ Норвегия Ⓣ Norveç
the Normans [ðə ˈnɔːmənz]	die Normannen	In 1066 **the Normans** came from France.
France [fraːns]	Frankreich	Ⓣ Fransa Ⓡ Франция
battle [ˈbætl]	Schlacht; Kampf	The Normans won a **battle**.
against [əˈgenst]	gegen	I fell **against** the tree.
the English [ði ˈɪŋglɪʃ]	die Engländer	**The English** lost a battle near Hastings.
Norman [ˈnɔːmən]	Normanne; Normannin	A **Norman** became king of England.
king [kɪŋ]	König	
industry [ˈɪndəstri]	Industrie	There is lots of **industry** in England.
during [ˈdjʊərɪŋ]	während	I ate my lunch **during** the break.
Industrial Revolution [ɪnˌdʌstriəl revlˈuːʃn]	industrielle Revolution	The **Industrial Revolution** was from 1780 to 1840.
sun [sʌn]	Sonne	
sick [sɪk]	krank	She isn't at school because she is **sick**.
grave [greɪv]	Grab	People found **graves** near Stonehenge.
million [ˈmɪljən]	Million	**1 million** = 1,000,000

Station 1

> **Shops**
>
> | | | | |
> |---|---|---|---|
> | **souvenir shop** ['su:vnɪə ˌʃɒp] | Souvenirladen | **butcher's** ['bʊtʃəz] | Metzgerei |
> | **baker's** ['beɪkəz] | Bäckerei | **jeweller's** ['dʒu:ələz] | Juwelierladen |
> | **newsagent's** ['nju:zˌeɪdʒnts] | Zeitschriftenladen | **greengrocer's** ['gri:nˌgrəʊsəz] | Obst- und Gemüseladen |
> | | | **pet shop** ['pet ˌʃɒp] | Tierhandlung |

p. 12	**way** [weɪ]	Weg; Art und Weise	Do you know the **way** to the shops?
	to **be interested in** [bi: 'ɪntrəstɪd ˌɪn]	sich interessieren für; interessiert sein an	**to be interested in** = to like sth
	to **learn about sth** [ˌlɜ:n ə'baʊt]	etwas erfahren über	I'd like to **learn about** the city.
	history ['hɪstri]	Geschichte	R история
	what sth was like [ˌwɒt … 'wəz laɪk]	wie etwas war	It shows you **what the city was like** before.
	to **cross** [krɒs]	überqueren	We have to **cross** the road to get there.
	past [pɑ:st]	vorbei (an)	Walk **past** the cinema, then cross the road.
	right [raɪt]	rechts	Turn **right** at the end of the road.
	left [left]	links	**left** ↔ right
	How do I get there? [ˌhaʊ du aɪ 'get ðeə]	Wie komme ich dahin?	Ganze Sätze am besten als Einheit lernen.
	down [daʊn]	entlang; herunter; hinunter	**down** ↔ up
	far [fɑ:]	weit	**far** ↔ near
	a five minute walk [ə 'faɪv mɪnɪt ˌwɔ:k]	fünf Minuten zu Fuß	It's just **a five minute walk** from here.
p. 13	to **sell** [sel], **sold** [səʊld], **sold** [səʊld]	verkaufen	**to sell** ↔ to buy
p. 15	**near** [nɪə]	nah	Excuse me, where's the **nearest** book shop?
	ticket ['tɪkɪt]	Fahrschein; Eintrittskarte	
	library ['laɪbri]	Bibliothek; Bücherei	
	street [stri:t]	Straße	Walk down the second **street** on the left.

Station 2

Talking about places

northwest [ˌnɔːˈθwest]	Nordwesten		**tiny** [ˈtaɪni]	klein; winzig
in the centre of [ˌɪn ðə ˈsentər ˌəv]	in der Mitte von		**close** [ˈkləʊs]	in der Nähe; nahe
			drive [draɪv]	Fahrt; Autofahrt
quiet [ˈkwaɪət]	ruhig; leise; still		**huge** [hjuːdʒ]	riesig; riesengroß
noisy [ˈnɔɪzi]	laut		**on the coast** [ˌɒn ðə ˈkəʊst]	an der Küste
east [iːst]	Osten			
west [west]	Westen			

p. 16	**half a million** [ˌhɑːf ə ˈmɪljən]	eine halbe Million	More than **half a million** people live there.
	inhabitant [ɪnˈhæbɪtnt]	Einwohner; Einwohnerin; Bewohner; Bewohnerin	**inhabitants** of a town = people who live in a town
	traffic [ˈtræfɪk]	Verkehr	It's a busy city with lots of **traffic**.
	past [pɑːst]	Vergangenheit	In the **past** Manchester had lots of industry.
	factory [ˈfæktri]	Fabrik; Werk	
	coal [kəʊl]	Kohle	**Coal** is black stones you use on a fire.
	mine [maɪn]	Bergwerk	You get coal from a coal **mine**.
	village [ˈvɪlɪdʒ]	Dorf	There are not many houses in a **village**.
	used to (live) [ˈjuːst tə]	(wohnte) früher	We **used to** live in Newcastle.
	goat [gəʊt]	Ziege	
	a lot of [ə ˈlɒt ˌəv]	viel; eine Menge	**a lot of** = lots of
	cow [kaʊ]	Kuh	
	only [ˈəʊnli]	nur; bloß; erst	**Only** about 400 people live there.
	worst [wɜːst]	schlimmste; schlechteste	That is the **worst** thing about our village.
	unfair [ʌnˈfeə]	unfair	I can't see my friends. It's so **unfair**!
p. 17	**mountain** [ˈmaʊntɪn]	Berg	
p. 18	**head first** [ˈhed fɜːst]	kopfüber	He fell into the mud, **head first**.
p. 19	**around** [əˈraʊnd]	herum; umher	I hang **around** with my friends.

Reading corner

p. 20	**deadly** ['dedli]	tod-; tödlich	It was **deadly** quiet in the house.
	silence ['saɪləns]	Stille; Schweigen; Ruhe	**silence** = no noise
	tunnel ['tʌnl]	Tunnel	R тоннель T tünel
	the dark [ðə 'dɑːk]	Dunkelheit	I sit in **the dark** every day.
	canary [kə'neəri]	Kanarienvogel	
	gas [gæs]	Gas	R газ T gaz
	to **explode** [ɪk'spləʊd]	explodieren	The gas in a mine can **explode**.
	explosion [ɪk'spləʊʒn]	Explosion	There was a big **explosion**.
	to **kill** [kɪl]	töten	An explosion **killed** 30 men.
	miner ['maɪnə]	Bergarbeiter; Bergarbeiterin	A **miner** works in a mine.
	to **smell** [smel], **smelt** [smelt], **smelt** [smelt]	riechen	A canary **smells** gas in the coal mine.
p. 21	**one day** [wʌn 'deɪ]	eines Tages	**One day** I stopped talking.
	to **cough** [kɒf]	husten	Bart **coughed** all the time.
	to **die** [daɪ]	sterben	He was really ill and **died**.
	could [kʊd]	konnte	I **couldn't** talk.
	to **speak** [spiːk], **spoke** [spəʊk], **spoken** ['spəʊkn]	sprechen	I opened my mouth, but couldn't **speak**.
	silent ['saɪlənt]	stumm; schweigsam	**silent** → silence
	truck [trʌk]	Wagen; Karre	
	nothing ['nʌθɪŋ]	nichts	**nothing** ↔ something
	time [taɪm]	Mal	This **time** I made a noise.
p. 22	to **breathe** [briːð]	atmen	I couldn't **breathe** in the mine.
	voice [vɔɪs]	Stimme	I could hear the miners' **voices**.
	to **pick up** [ˌpɪkˈʌp]	aufheben	One of the miners **picked** me **up**.
	dead [ded]	tot	I thought Billy was **dead**.
	to **get out** [ˌget 'aʊt]	herauskommen	We had to **get out** of the mine quickly.
	that [ðæt]	dass	I saw **that** everyone was OK.
	alive [ə'laɪv]	am Leben	**alive** ↔ dead

Film corner

p. 25	**Victorian era** [vɪkˌtɔːriən ˈɪərə]	viktorianisches Zeitalter	This was when Queen Victoria was the Queen.
	to **fall asleep** [ˌfɔːl əˈsliːp]	einschlafen	I **fell asleep** at ten o'clock.
	to **dream** [driːm], **dreamt** [dremt], **dreamt** [dremt]	träumen	I **dreamt** that I was a teacher.
	century [ˈsenʃri]	Jahrhundert	a **century** = 100 years
	I'd rather [aɪd ˈrɑːðə]	ich würde lieber	**I'd rather** eat vegetables than meat.
	to **wish** [wɪʃ]	wünschen	I **wish** every day was Saturday.
	to **be asleep** [biː əˈsliːp]	schlafen	You have **been asleep** all day.
	almost [ˈɔːlməʊst]	fast; beinahe	55 minutes is **almost** an hour.
	confused [kənˈfjuːzd]	verwirrt; wirr	I was **confused**, I didn't know where I was.

▬ Checkpoint ▬

project [ˈprɒdʒekt]	Projekt	**informative** [ɪnˈfɔːmətɪv]	**informativ**
presenter [prɪˈzentə]	Moderator; Moderatorin		

Reading skills

p. 31	**type** [taɪp]	Sorte; Typ; Art	What **type** of text is it?
	brochure [ˈbrəʊʃə]	Broschüre; Prospekt	R брошюра T broşür
	to **be about** [biː əˈbaʊt]	gehen um; handeln von	The text **is about** a bike tour.
	queen [kwiːn]	Königin	
	inside [ˌɪnˈsaɪd]	in; innen in; im Innern	The Queen is **inside** the palace.

Word bank: Directions

on the left

on the right

beside / next to

opposite

on the corner

at the traffic lights

our house is on
the right / left

turn right

turn left

go straight on

cross the road

walk down the road

go / walk past
(a book shop)

Asking for help:	Getting help:
Excuse me, please.	Can I help you?
Do you know where there is a … ?	Yes, I do.
	No, I don't.
Can I walk there?	Yes, it's just a five minute walk.
	Yes, it isn't far.
	No, I'd take the bus / underground.
Are there buses?	Yes, every five minutes.
	No, there aren't.
Does it take long?	Yes, about 30 minutes.
	No, it doesn't take long.
Is it far away?	Yes, it is.
	No, it isn't.

Word bank: **Where I live**

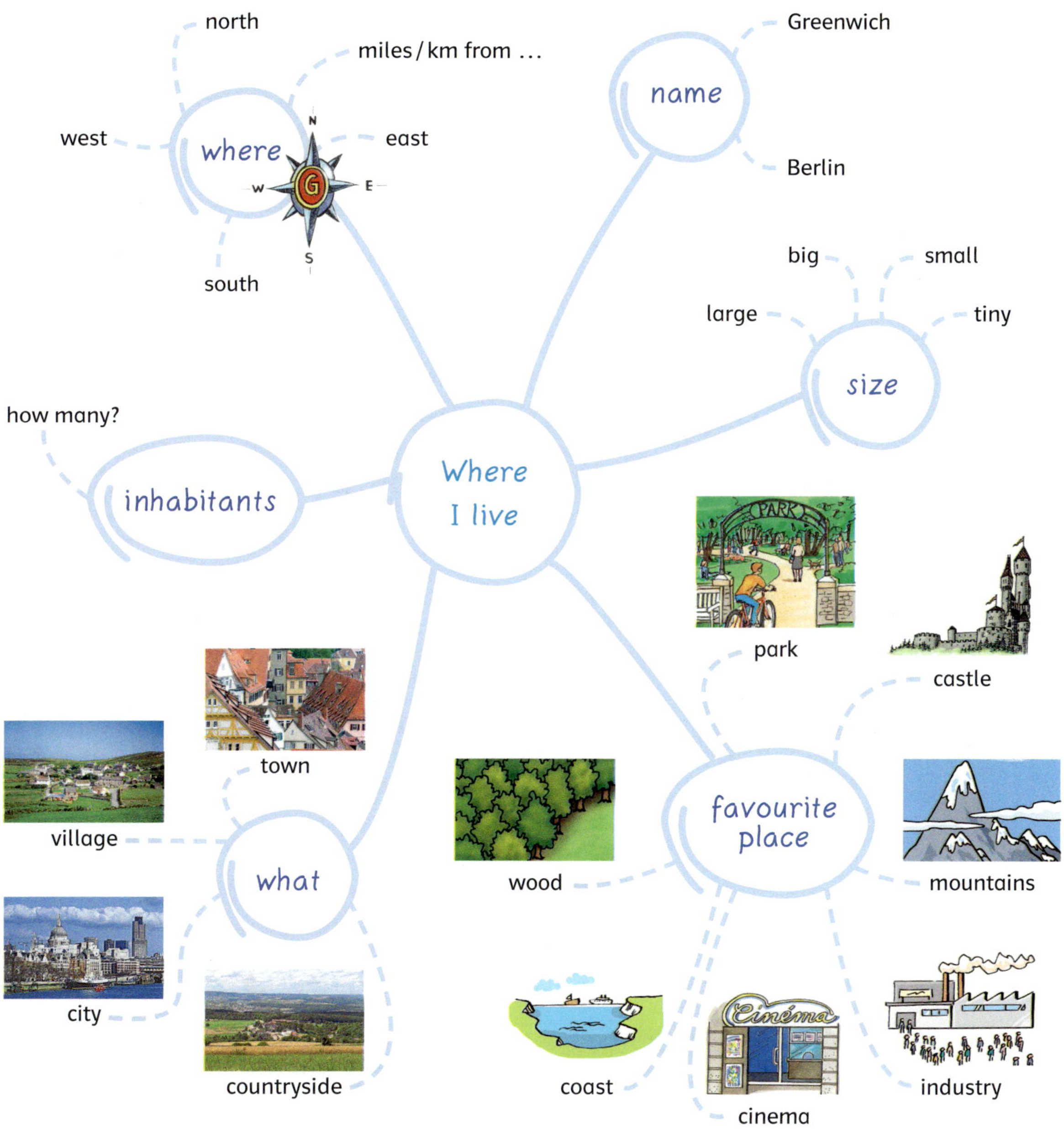

north

miles/km from …

Greenwich

name

Berlin

west

where

N

W · G · E

S

east

south

big small

large tiny

size

how many?

inhabitants

Where I live

park

castle

town

village

what

wood

favourite place

mountains

city

countryside

coast

cinema

industry

Unit 2 Adventures in Wales

p. 32	**adventure** [əd'ventʃə]	Abenteuer	We'll have lots of **adventures** in Wales.

Way in

	Welsh [welʃ]	Walisisch; walisisch; Waliser; Waliserin	**Welsh** is a very old language.
	sign [saɪn]	Schild; Zeichen	✍ Achtung Schreibweise! si**gn**
	zip line ['zɪp ˌlaɪn]	Seilrutsche	The longest **zip line** in Europe is in Wales.
	skiing ['ski:ɪŋ]	Skifahren	
p. 33	**capital (city)** ['kæpɪtl (ˌsɪti)]	Hauptstadt	The **capital** of England is London.
	city centre [ˌsɪti 'sentə]	Stadtzentrum; Stadtmitte	There are lots of shops in the **city centre**.
	to try [traɪ]	ausprobieren	Have you ever been canoeing? **Try** it!
	water ['wɔ:tə]	Wasser	Penguins like **water**.
	sport [spɔ:t]	Sportart	®︎ спорт Ⓣ spor
	coast [kəʊst]	Küste	England has a lot of **coast**.
	rafting ['rɑ:ftɪŋ]	Rafting	You can do **rafting** in the sea or on a river.
	popular ['pɒpjələ]	beliebt	Canoeing and rafting are **popular** sports.
	volunteer [ˌvɒlən'tɪə]	Freiwilliger; Freiwillige; ehren-amtlicher Helfer; ehrenamtliche Helferin	**Volunteers** help people and don't get any money.
	lifeboat ['laɪfbəʊt]	Rettungsboot	**Lifeboats** are very important in Wales.
	important [ɪm'pɔ:tnt]	wichtig; einflussreich	Don't forget. It's very **important**!
	trouble ['trʌbl]	Schwierigkeiten; Problem; Ärger	They help people in **trouble**.
	teenager ['ti:nˌeɪdʒə]	Teenager; Teenagerin; Jugend-liche; Jugendlicher	A **teenager** is between 13 and 19 years old.
	fluent ['flu:ənt]	fließend; flüssig	I'm German, but can speak **fluent** English.
	plant [plɑ:nt]	Pflanze	
	to mean [mi:n], **meant** [ment], **meant** [ment]	bedeuten; meinen	'Wurst' **means** 'sausage' in English.
	guest [gest]	Gast	We have **guests** for the weekend.

Station 1

Adjectives for sportspeople

slow [sləʊ]	langsam	**safe** [seɪf]	sicher; ungefährlich
tough [tʌf]	hart	**unfriendly** [ʌnˈfrendli]	unfreundlich
quick [kwɪk]	schnell	**small** [smɔːl]	klein
strong [strɒŋ]	stark	**loud** [laʊd]	laut
fit [fɪt]	fit; in Form	talented [ˈtæləntɪd]	begabt; talentiert
friendly [ˈfrendli]	freundlich; nett	exhausted [ɪgˈzɔːstɪd]	erschöpft
weak [wiːk]	schwach	patient [ˈpeɪʃnt]	geduldig
dry [draɪ]	trocken	successful [səkˈsesfl]	erfolgreich

p. 34	**outdoor** [ˌaʊtˈdɔː]	Freiluft-; Outdoor-	Kayaking is an **outdoor** sport.
	activity centre [ækˈtɪvəti ˌsentə]	Jugendzentrum	The **activity centre** looks really good.
	to **take a trip** [ˌteɪk ə ˈtrɪp]	eine Fahrt machen	We **took** a canoeing **trip** down the river.
	rugby [ˈrʌgbi]	Rugby	Ⓡ perби Ⓣ rugbi 
	rule [ruːl]	Regel	You can learn the **rules** quickly.
	indoor [ˌɪnˈdɔː]	Hallen-; Innen-	**indoor** ↔ outdoor
	equipment [ɪˈkwɪpmənt]	Ausrüstung	**equipment**: helmet, special clothes, …
	myself [maɪˈself]	selbst; selber	It's nice. I often go there **myself**.
	enough [ɪˈnʌf]	genug; genügend	I'm strong **enough** for it.
	cheeky [ˈtʃiːki]	frech	Mark was **cheeky** to Beth.
	to **climb** [klaɪm]	klettern; steigen; besteigen	✐ Achtung Schreibweise! clim**b**
	quite [kwaɪt]	ziemlich; ganz; völlig	I can climb **quite** well already.
	dangerous [ˈdeɪndʒrəs]	gefährlich	**dangerous** ↔ safe
	to **be scared** [bi ˈskeəd]	Angst haben; erschrocken sein	I'm **scared** of dogs.
	each other [ˌiːtʃ ˈʌðə]	einander; sich; sich gegenseitig	We can tell **each other** about it later!
	self [self]	selbst; sich	**self**: myself, yourself, himself, herself, itself, ourselves, yourselves, themselves
p. 35	**instructor** [ɪnˈstrʌktə]	Lehrer; Lehrerin	All our **instructors** are friendly.
p. 36	**class** [klɑːs]	Klasse	Our **class** went on a trip last week.
	camping [ˈkæmpɪŋ]	Camping; Zelten	We went on a **camping** trip to Wales.
p. 37	**because of** [bɪˈkɒz əv]	wegen	I was late **because of** the weather.

What must you be like? [wɒt ˌmʌst ju ˈbiː laɪk]	Wie musst du sein?	Ganze Sätze am besten als Einheit lernen.

Station 2

Health and medicine

to **bleed** [bliːd], **bled** [bled], **bled** [bled]	bluten	**cast** [kɑːst]	Gips
to **cut** [kʌt], **cut** [kʌt], **cut** [kʌt]	(sich) schneiden	to **put on** [ˌpʊt ˈɒn]	anlegen; anziehen
		bandage [ˈbændɪdʒ]	Verband
finger [ˈfɪŋgə]	Finger	to **cool** [kuːl]	kühlen
tooth (sg) [tuːθ], **teeth** (pl) [tiːθ]	Zahn	to **move** [muːv]	(sich) bewegen
		plaster [ˈplɑːstə]	Pflaster
knee [niː]	Knie	**sleep** [sliːp]	Schlaf
to **burn** [bɜːn], **burnt** [bɜːnt], **burnt** [bɜːnt]	verbrennen; brennen	**medicine** [ˈmedsn]	Medikamente; Medizin
to **sprain** [spreɪn]	verstauchen; verrenken	**injection** [ɪnˈdʒekʃn]	Spritze
		operation [ˌɒprˈeɪʃn]	Operation

p. 38	**emergency** [ɪˈmɜːdʒnsi]	Notfall	Help! It's an **emergency**.
	operator [ˈɒpreɪtə]	Vermittlung	You get the **operator** when you call 999.
	emergency service [ɪˈmɜːdʒnsi ˌsɜːvɪs]	Notdienst; Rettungsdienst	You call 999 for the **emergency services** in the UK.
	service [ˈsɜːvɪs]	Dienst	Which **service** do you need?
	ambulance [ˈæmbjələns]	Krankenwagen	
	to **hurry** [ˈhʌri]	sich beeilen	I need an ambulance. Please **hurry**!
	bad [bæd]	schlimm; böse; schlecht	His head doesn't look as **bad** as his leg.
	accident [ˈæksɪdnt]	Unfall	The man has had an **accident**.
	to **fall (over)** [ˌfɔːl ˈəʊvə]	fallen; hinfallen; umfallen	I think he **fell** over on the beach.
	rock [rɒk]	Fels; Stein	
	awake [əˈweɪk]	bei Bewusstsein; wach	Is the man **awake**?
	phone number [ˈfəʊn ˌnʌmbə]	Telefonnummer	Give me your **phone number**, please!
	should [ʃʊd]	sollte	You **should** try something new this year.

to **do the right thing** [ˌduː ðə ˈraɪt θɪŋ]	das Richtige tun	It's OK. You've **done the right thing**.
police [pəˈliːs]	Polizei	R полиция T polis
caller [ˈkɔːlə]	Anrufer; Anruferin	**caller** → to call
emergency call [ɪˈmɜːdʒnsi ˌkɔːl]	Notruf	The phone number for **emergency calls** is 999.
p. 39 **cuddly toy** [ˈkʌdli ˌtɔɪ]	Kuscheltier	My little sister has lots of **cuddly toys**.
p. 40 **hand** [hænd]	Hand	
to **hit** [hɪt]	(sich) stoßen; anstoßen	He **hit** his head on the table.
p. 41 **training** [ˈtreɪnɪŋ]	Training	On Friday I have football **training**.
skateboard [ˈskeɪtbɔːd]	Skateboard	R скейтборд T skateboard
trick [trɪk]	Kunststück	I want to try some skateboard **tricks**.
back [bæk]	zurück	I have just sent it **back** to the shop.

Reading corner

p. 42 **reporter** [rɪˈpɔːtə]	Reporter; Reporterin	A **reporter** writes stories for magazines.
to **jump** [dʒʌmp]	zusammenzucken; erschrecken	The loud noise made us **jump**.
knight [naɪt]	Ritter	⌁ Achtung Schreibweise! k̲night
cloud [klaʊd]	Wolke	
smoke [sməʊk]	Rauch	
corridor [ˈkɒrɪdɔː]	Gang; Flur; Korridor	There are lots of **corridors** at school.
p. 43 to **joust** [dʒaʊst]	einen Turnierzweikampf austragen; turnieren	We learned how to **joust**.
armour [ˈɑːmə]	Rüstung	
to **hold** [həʊld], **held** [held], **held** [held]	halten; festhalten	I **held** the door open for the film star.
sword [sɔːd]	Schwert	
still [stɪl]	dennoch	It wasn't real but it was **still** heavy.
to **make sb feel like sth** [ˌmeɪk … ˈfiːl laɪk]	jmdm. das Gefühl geben, etw. zu sein	It **made you feel like a real knight**.
jousting [ˈdʒaʊstɪŋ]	Turnierzweikampf	The **jousting** was super cool.

wheelchair [ˈwiːltʃeə]	Rollstuhl	
naughty [ˈnɔːti]	frech; böse	**naughty** ↔ good
stocks [stɒks]	Pranger	He put me in the **stocks**.
to **try out** [ˌtraɪˈaʊt]	ausprobieren	We **tried out** the stocks.
for fun [fə ˈfʌn]	zum Spaß	We did it just **for fun**.
lots [lɒts]	viel; jede Menge	We learned **lots** about Caldicot Castle.

Film corner

p. 45	**briefcase** [ˈbriːfkeɪs]	Aktenkoffer; Aktentasche	My dad puts things in his **briefcase**.
	to **answer the phone** [ˌɑːnsə ðə ˈfəʊn]	ans Telefon gehen	I **answered the phone** when you called.
	cannot [ˈkænɒt]	nicht können	The girls **cannot** open the briefcase.
	prop [prɒp]	Requisit	You need **props** for films and plays.
	ending [ˈendɪŋ]	Schluss; Ende	I didn't like the **ending**.
	to **expect** [ɪkˈspekt]	erwarten	I **expected** a happy ending.

Writing skills

p. 50	**review** [rɪˈvjuː]	Kritik	Read this **review** about the new book.
	to **enjoy** [ɪnˈdʒɔɪ]	*hier:* mögen	I really **enjoyed** the film.
	introduction [ˌɪntrəˈdʌkʃn]	Einleitung; Einführung	The **introduction** is very short.
	comedy [ˈkɒmədi]	Komödie	R комедия T komedi
	murderer [ˈmɜːdrə]	Mörder; Mörderin	You don't see the **murderer** until the end.
	to **run away** [ˌrʌn əˈweɪ]	weglaufen	She was scared and **ran away**.
	to **hide** [haɪd], **hid** [hɪd], **hidden** [ˈhɪdn]	(sich) verstecken	She ran away and **hid** behind the car.
	baker [ˈbeɪkə]	Bäcker; Bäckerin	
	enemy [ˈenəmi]	Feind; Feindin	**enemy** ↔ friend
	fight [faɪt]	Kampf; Streit	**fight** → to fight
	content [ˈkɒntent]	Inhalt	The **content** is about the film.
	writer [ˈraɪtə]	Verfasser; Verfasserin; Autor; Autorin	The **writer** of the review liked the book.
	location [ləʊˈkeɪʃn]	Drehort; Lage	The **location** of the film was beautiful.
	opinion [əˈpɪnjən]	Meinung	I gave my **opinion** and said what I thought.

star [stɑː]	Stern	In her review she gave the film four **stars**.
conclusion [kənˈkluːʒn]	Schlussfolgerung; Schluss	The **conclusion** is at the end.
to **get a job wrong** [ˌget ə dʒɒb ˈrɒŋ]	einen Auftrag vermasseln	The murderer **gets a job wrong**.
to **fall in love (with)** [ˌfɔːl ɪn ˈlʌv]	sich verlieben (in)	I **fell in love** with the actor in the film.
to **give sth a miss** [ˌgɪv sʌmθɪŋ ə ˈmɪs]	auf etw. verzichten; etw. bleiben lassen	**Give** the film **a miss**.
to **give reasons** [ˌgɪv ˈriːznz]	Gründe nennen; Gründe angeben	**Give** the **reasons** for your opinion.
to **rate** [reɪt]	bewerten; einstufen	The writer **rates** the film.
advice [ədˈvaɪs]	Rat; Ratschlag	Nichola gave me some good **advice**.
drama [ˈdrɑːmə]	Drama	Ⓡ драма Ⓣ dram
romance [ˈrəʊmæns]	Liebesgeschichte	**Romance** is also a type of film.
start [stɑːt]	Start; Anfang	**start** ↔ ending

p. 51 (to give reasons)

Word bank: Sports and activities

Water sports

 swimming

 surfing

 windsurfing

 canoeing

 rafting

Ball sports

 rugby

 football

 netball

 handball

 basketball

Winter sports

 skiing

 snowboarding

 ice skating

Athletics

 high jump

 long jump

 javelin

Racket sports

 tennis

 badminton

 squash

Equipment

 boat

 racket

 paddle

 waterproofs

 ball

 goggles

 helmet

Activities

 ride a bike

 go rock climbing

 do skateboard tricks

 go jogging

 go hiking

Word bank: Emergency

Emergency services

police

ambulance

fire brigade

coastguard

cast

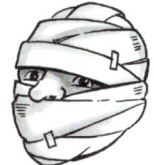

bandage

plaster

cut

Useful verbs the operator says

to cool

to move

to sit

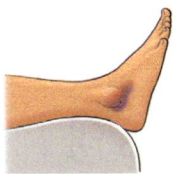

bruise

Useful verbs the caller says

to cut

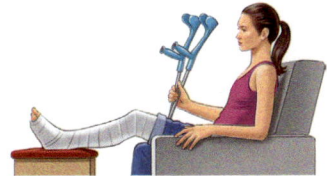

to break

poison

to fall

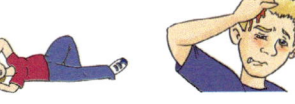

to hurt to bleed

to sprain to breathe

wound

Unit 3 Made in Scotland

Way in

p. 52	**inventor** [ɪnˈventə]	Erfinder; Erfinderin	Lots of **inventors** are from Scotland.
	to be born [biː ˈbɔːn]	geboren werden	I **was born** in Germany.
	to fight [faɪt], **fought** [fɔːt], **fought** [fɔːt]	kämpfen; (sich) streiten	⌀ Achtung Schreibweise! fi**gh**t
	its [ɪts]	sein; ihr	The dog has **its** leg stuck in the mud.
p. 53	**clean** [kliːn]	sauber	**clean** ↔ dirty
	electricity [ˌelɪkˈtrɪsəti]	Strom; Elektrizität	Scotland has clean **electricity**.
	wind farm [ˈwɪnd fɑːm]	Windpark	A **wind farm** makes lots of electricity.
	lake [leɪk]	See	
	cottage [ˈkɒtɪdʒ]	Häuschen	
	to enjoy [ɪnˈdʒɔɪ]	genießen	I **enjoy** my garden in the summer.
	countryside [ˈkʌntrɪsaɪd]	Landschaft; Land	Tourists can enjoy the **countryside**.
	Scottish [ˈskɒtɪʃ]	schottisch	**Scottish** → Scotland
	tradition [trəˈdɪʃn]	Tradition	There are many **traditions** in Scotland.
	bagpipes *(pl)* [ˈbægpaɪps]	Dudelsack	In Scotland people play the **bagpipes**.
	kilt [kɪlt]	Schottenrock; Kilt	A **kilt** is a Scottish skirt, usually for men.
	Scot [skɒt]	Schotte; Schottin	**Scot** → Scotland
	porridge [ˈpɒrɪdʒ]	Haferbrei	Scots often eat **porridge** for breakfast.
	oat [əʊt]	Hafer	Porridge is made with **oats**.
	(wind) turbine [(wɪnd) ˈtɜːbaɪn]	Windrad	The **turbines** are very tall.
	to protect [prəˈtekt]	schützen	We must **protect** the animals.
	nature [ˈneɪtʃə]	Natur	Animals and plants are **nature**.

Station 1

Materials

plastic [ˈplæstɪk]	Plastik; Kunststoff		**cotton** [ˈkɒtn]	Baumwolle
metal [ˈmetl]	Metall		**steel** [stiːl]	Stahl
wood [wʊd]	Holz		**cardboard** [ˈkɑːdbɔːd]	Pappe; Karton
rubber [ˈrʌbə]	Gummi		**silk** [sɪlk]	Seide
leather [ˈleðə]	Leder		**aluminium** [ˌæljəˈmɪniəm]	Aluminium
paper [ˈpeɪpə]	Papier			

p. 54	**who** [huː]	der; dem; den; die	There's the man **who** was in the film.
	to **change** [tʃeɪndʒ]	verändern; (sich) ändern	He was a Scot who **changed** the world.
	to **invent** [ɪnˈvent]	erfinden	to **invent** → inventor
	telephone [ˈtelɪfəʊn]	Telefon	®телефон ⊤ telefon
	to **grow up** [ˌɡrəʊ ˈʌp], **grew up** [ˌɡruː ˈʌp], **grown up** [ˌɡrəʊn ˈʌp]	aufwachsen	She **grew up** in London.
	deaf [def]	gehörlos; schwerhörig; taub	She can't hear you. She's **deaf**.
	speech [spiːtʃ]	Sprache; Rede	Bell was very interested in **speech**.
	which [wɪtʃ]	die; der; dem; den; das	That's the dog **which** ate the food.
	sound [saʊnd]	Laut; Ton; Geräusch	Listen to the **sounds** of speech.
	Canada [ˈkænədə]	Kanada	**Canada** is north of America.
	USA (United States of America) [ˌjuːesˈeɪ (juːˌnaɪtɪd ˌsteɪts əv əˈmerɪkə)]	USA (Vereinigte Staaten von Amerika)	Boston is in the **USA**.
	invention [ɪnˈvenʃn]	Erfindung	**invention** → to invent → inventor
	to **be made of** [biː ˈmeɪd əv]	hergestellt sein aus	The house **is made of** stone.
	success [səkˈses]	Erfolg	Bell's telephone was a **success**.
	rich [rɪtʃ]	reich	He has a lot of money. He is **rich**.
	whose [huːz]	dessen; deren	He is a man **whose** invention saves time.
p. 55	to **start** [stɑːt]	gründen	He **started** a company in 2012.
	tube [tjuːb]	Schlauch; Rohr	There's a **tube** in the tyre.
	air [eə]	Luft	You have to put **air** in the tyres.

tyre [taɪə]	Reifen		
wheel [wiːl]	Rad		
solid [ˈsɒlɪd]	fest	They were made of **solid** rubber.	
tyre [taɪə]	Reifen	**Tyres** are usually black.	
p. 57	steam engine [ˈstiːm ˌendʒɪn]	Dampfmaschine	
	light bulb [ˈlaɪt ˌbʌlb]	Glühbirne	

Station 2

Going on holiday

campsite [ˈkæmpsaɪt]	Campingplatz; Zeltplatz	to **check out** [ˌtʃek ˈaʊt]	auschecken
bed and breakfast (B & B) [ˌbed ˌən ˈbrekfəst]	Frühstückspension	to **pay the bill** [ˌpeɪ ðə ˈbɪl]	die Rechnung bezahlen
hostel [ˈhɒstl]	Herberge	to **make a reservation** [ˌmeɪk ə ˈrezəveɪʃn]	reservieren
caravan [ˈkærəvæn]	Wohnwagen	to **check in** [ˌtʃek ˈɪn]	einchecken
tent [tent]	Zelt		

p. 58	trip [trɪp]	Reise	It's time to plan our **trip**.
	to **decide** [dɪˈsaɪd]	(sich) entscheiden	We have to **decide** where to go.
	cosy [ˈkəʊzi]	gemütlich	This hotel looks nice and **cosy**.
	could [kʊd]	könnten	You **could** show me the sights.
	hiking [ˈhaɪkɪŋ]	Wandern	You know I love **hiking**.
	simple [ˈsɪmpl]	einfach	**simple** = easy
	outside [ˌaʊtˈsaɪd]	draußen; im Freien	We'll be **outside** every day.
	all day [ˌɔːl ˈdeɪ]	den ganzen Tag	They work **all day**.
	No way! [ˌnəʊ ˈweɪ]	Auf keinen Fall!; Was?!; Echt?!	**No way!** I'm not going camping.
	to **freeze** [friːz], **froze** [frəʊz], **frozen** [ˈfrəʊzn]	frieren; gefrieren	We'll **freeze** in a tent.
	insect [ˈɪnsekt]	Insekt	
	Are you serious? [ˌɑː ju ˈsɪəriəs]	Im Ernst?	Ganze Sätze am besten als Einheit lernen.
	buffet [ˈbʊfeɪ]	Büfett	R буфет T büfe

nice [naɪs]	*hier:* lecker; gut	The food is **nice** in a hotel.
not ... either [nɒt ... 'aɪðə]	auch nicht	I don't want to go camping **either**.
to **rent** [rent]	mieten	We could **rent** a holiday cottage.
a **few** [ə 'fjuː]	ein paar; wenige; einige	I looked again **a few** hours later.
tip [tɪp]	Tipp	We can get some **tips** about sights.
local ['ləʊkl]	hiesig; örtlich; lokal	I love the **local** food.
nobody ['nəʊbədi]	niemand	If **nobody** wants to go camping, fine.
monster ['mɒnstə]	Ungeheuer; Monster	Ⓡ монстр

p. 60	to **get cold** [ˌget 'kəʊld]	frieren	We will **get cold** if it rains.
	early ['ɜːli]	früh	I get up **early** at the weekend.
	haggis ['hægɪs]	Haggis *(schottisches Gericht aus Schafsinnereien)*	**Haggis** is a Scottish dish.

p. 61	walking ['wɔːkɪŋ]	Wandern	**Walking** in the mountains is fun.
	cycling ['saɪklɪŋ]	Radfahren	My favourite activity is **cycling**.
	bird watching ['bɜːd ˌwɒtʃɪŋ]	Vogelbeobachtung	**Bird watching** is an activity you can do.
	walk [wɔːk]	Spaziergang	A **walk** in the afternoon is nice.

Reading corner

p. 62	to **keep out** [ˌkiːp 'aʊt]	draußen halten	I will **keep** the English **out**.
	army ['ɑːmi]	Armee; Heer	Edward I has a strong **army**.
	to **beat** [biːt], beat [biːt], beaten ['biːtn]	besiegen; schlagen	We can't **beat** the English.
	soldier ['səʊldʒə]	Soldat; Soldatin	They have so many **soldiers**.
	like this [laɪk 'ðɪs]	so; auf diese Weise	I shouldn't hide **like this**.
	impossible [ɪm'pɒsəbl]	unmöglich	I think it's **impossible** to win.
p. 63	spider ['spaɪdə]	Spinne	
	amazing [ə'meɪzɪŋ]	erstaunlich; unglaublich; toll	This spider is **amazing**.
	web [web]	Spinnennetz; Netz	Look at its **web**.
	to **give up** [ˌgɪv 'ʌp]	aufgeben	The spider never **gives up**.
	must not/never [ˌmʌst 'nɒt/'nevə]	nicht/nie dürfen	I **must never** give up.
	brave [breɪv]	tapfer; mutig	We must be **brave**.

p. 64	**son** [sʌn]	Sohn	**son** ↔ daughter
	tactic ['tæktɪk]	Taktik; Vorgehensweise	We have good **tactics**. We can win.
	ground [graʊnd]	Boden; Erdboden	The **ground** is very wet.
p. 65	**proud (of)** [praʊd (əv)]	stolz (auf)	The Scots are **proud** of Robert the Bruce.
	peace [piːs]	Frieden	There was **peace** in Scotland.
	leader ['liːdə]	Führer; Führerin; Anführer; Anführerin	Robert the Bruce was a great **leader**.
	sad [sæd]	traurig	**sad** ↔ happy
p. 64	**hero** *(sg)* ['hɪərəʊ], **heroes** *(pl)* ['hɪərəʊz]	Held	He was the **hero** in the story.

Film corner

p. 67	**pay phone** ['peɪ fəʊn]	Münztelefon	I need some money for the **pay phone**.
	video chat ['vɪdiəʊ ˌtʃæt]	Video-Chat	We can talk about it on the **video chat**.
	neighbour ['neɪbə]	Nachbar; Nachbarin	Our **neighbours** live next to us.
	to **repair** [rɪ'peə]	reparieren	Alicia **repairs** everything.
	radio ['reɪdiəʊ]	Radio	Ⓡ радио }radyo
	to **be up to** [bi: 'ʌp tə]	vorhaben	I want to see what you'**re up** to.
	to **attach** [ə'tætʃ]	verbinden	You have to **attach** the two wires.
	pipe [paɪp]	Rohr	The machine has a water **pipe** in it.
	antenna [æn'tenə]	Antenne	The radio has an **antenna** on it.
	to **connect** [kə'nekt]	verbinden	**Connect** the wire to the radio.
	signal ['sɪgnl]	Empfang; Signal; Zeichen	Have you got a **signal**?

Checkpoint

advert (ad) ['ædvɜːt]	Anzeige	on duty [ɒn 'djuːti]	im Dienst
magical ['mædʒɪkl]	zauberhaft; magisch	garage ['gærɑːʒ]	Werkstatt; Tankstelle
wonderful ['wʌndəfl]	wunderbar	since [sɪns]	seit
offer ['ɒfə]	Angebot	petrol ['petrl]	Benzin
available [ə'veɪləbl]	erhältlich; verfügbar	free [friː]	kostenlos
full service [ˌfʊl 'sɜːvɪs]	Komplettservice	coffee ['kɒfi]	Kaffee
mechanic [mə'kænɪk]	Mechaniker; Mechanikerin	design [dɪ'zaɪn]	Design; Gestaltung
		message ['mesɪdʒ]	Botschaft

Word bank: Inventors and inventions

Talking about inventors

… was born in …	… invented …
… grew up in …	… also invented …
… moved to …	… was rich …
… died in … (place / year)	… was famous because …

Talking about inventions

is made of …

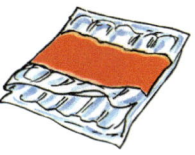

wood   plastic   metal   glass

is used for …

mirrors

trolley suitcases   tyres   light bulbs   tables

… is good because …

it is light	it is slow
it is heavy	it is recyclable
it is fast	it is washable

Word bank: Places to stay

B&B

hotel

guest house

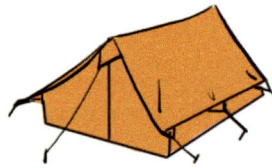
tent

campsite

hostel (youth hostel)

caravan

camper

static caravan

holiday flat

holiday cottage

farm

town

village

city

countryside

Words for describing places to stay

cheap	small
comfortable	clean
cosy	near …
big	good for …

Unit 4 In Northern Ireland

Way in

p. 74	**mural** [ˈmjʊərəl]	Wandgemälde	That **mural** on the building is great.
	Protestant [ˈprɒtɪstnt]	Protestant; Protestantin; protestantisch	There were problems between the **Protestants**
	Catholic [ˈkæθlɪk]	Katholik; Katholikin; katholisch	and the **Catholics**.
p. 75	**to run** [rʌn]	*hier:* betreiben; leiten; führen	My parents **run** a hotel.
	northwest of [ˌnɔːθˈwest ˌəv]	nordwestlich	It is a town **northwest of** Belfast.
	free [friː]	kostenlos	The tickets are **free**.
	grandad [ˈgrændæd]	Opa	
	every [ˈevri]	alle	Buses go **every** 30 minutes.
	adult [ˈædʌlt]	Erwachsene; Erwachsener	**adult** ↔ child
	to cost [kɒst], **cost** [kɒst], **cost** [kɒst]	kosten	The tickets **cost** a lot of money.
	giant [dʒaɪənt]	Riese	
	probably [ˈprɒbəbli]	wahrscheinlich	We will **probably** go there in the summer.

Station 1

> **Adjectives for feelings**
>
> | | | | |
> |---|---|---|---|
> | **useful** [ˈjuːsfl] | nützlich; hilfreich | **optimistic** [ˌɒptɪˈmɪstɪk] | optimistisch |
> | **lonely** [ˈləʊnli] | einsam | **down** [daʊn] | deprimiert |
> | **positive** [ˈpɒzətɪv] | positiv | **dreadful** [ˈdredfl] | furchtbar |
> | **silly** [ˈsɪli] | dumm; doof | **hopeful** [ˈhəʊpfl] | hoffnungsvoll |
> | **furious** [ˈfjʊəriəs] | wütend | **intelligent** [ɪnˈtelɪdʒnt] | intelligent; klug; vernünftig |
> | **smart** [smɑːt] | schlau; klug; intelligent | | |
> | **confident** [ˈkɒnfɪdnt] | selbstsicher; selbstbewusst | **sure of oneself** [ˈʃʊər ˌəv ˌwʌnself] | selbstsicher |
> | | | **annoyed** [əˈnɔɪd] | verärgert |
> | **horrible** [ˈhɒrəbl] | schrecklich; furchtbar | | |

p. 76	**to be fed up (with)** [bi: fed ˈʌp (wɪð)]	die Nase voll haben (von); sauer sein	I'm **fed up** with school and homework.

not … any more [ˌnɒt … eni ˈmɔː]	nicht mehr	They aren**'t** friends **any more**.
in the evenings [ɪn ði ˈiːvnɪŋz]	abends	**In the evenings** they don't have time.
to **nag** [næg]	nörgeln; meckern	They always **nag** me about my jobs.
to **drive sb crazy** [ˌdraɪv … ˈkreɪzi]	jmdn. verrückt machen	The guests sometimes **drive me crazy**.
so much [ˌsəʊ ˈmʌtʃ]	so sehr	I miss my friends **so much**.
without [wɪˈðaʊt]	ohne	I don't like it **without** you.
to **hate** [heɪt]	hassen; nicht mögen	I **hate** snakes, but I love bears.
milkshake [ˈmɪlkˌʃeɪk]	Milchmischgetränk; Milchshake	

p. 79

coin [kɔɪn]	Münze	
time travel [ˈtaɪm ˌtrævl]	Zeitreise	He has invented a **time travel** machine.
competition [ˌkɒmpəˈtɪʃn]	Wettbewerb; Turnier	Dave won a prize in a **competition**!

Station 2

Shopping

special offer [ˌspeʃl ˈɒfə]	Sonderangebot		**brand** [brænd]	Marke
customer [ˈkʌstəmə]	Kunde; Kundin		**exact** [ɪgˈzækt]	exakt; genau
to **repeat** [rɪˈpiːt]	wiederholen		to **change one's mind** [ˌtʃeɪndʒ wʌnz ˈmaɪnd]	seine Meinung ändern
to **run out of** [ˌrʌn ˈaʊt ˌəv]	ausgehen (Ware)			

p. 80

raspberry [ˈrɑːzbri]	Himbeere	
jam [dʒæm]	Marmelade; Konfitüre	I like raspberry **jam** on my toast.
one(s) [wʌn(z)]	*Platzhalter für ein Nomen*	This scarf is nice, but that **one** is nicer.
tasty [ˈteɪsti]	lecker; schmackhaft	This jam is **tastier** than that jam.
jar [dʒɑː]	Glas	**Jars** are made of glass.
sliced bread [ˌslaɪst ˈbred]	in Scheiben geschnittenes Brot	In England you buy **sliced bread**.
loaf (sg) [ləʊf], **loaves** (pl) [ləʊvz]	Brotlaib	I'd like one **loaf** of farmer's bread, please.
to **post** [pəʊst]	aufgeben (einen Brief); abschicken (einen Brief)	I have to **post** this to my aunt.
letter [ˈletə]	Brief; Buchstabe	We don't write **letters**, we write e-mails.

	stamp [stæmp]	Briefmarke	
	niece [ni:s]	Nichte	Sarah is her aunt's **niece**.
	less [les]	weniger	**less** ↔ more
	to get [get]	*hier:* verstehen	Sorry, I didn't **get** that.
p. 81	**to check** [tʃek]	überprüfen; kontrollieren	Can you **check** my homework, please?
	peanut butter [ˌpiːnʌt ˈbʌtə]	Erdnussbutter	
	tissue [ˈtɪʃuː]	Taschentuch	tissue →
	mineral water [ˈmɪnrl ˌwɔːtə]	Mineralwasser	I drink juice with **mineral water**.
p. 82	**camel** [ˈkæml]	Kamel	
p. 83	**assistant** [əˈsɪstnt]	Verkäufer; Verkäuferin	The **assistant** helped me in the shop.

Reading corner

p. 84	**disaster** [dɪˈzaːstə]	Katastrophe; Desaster; Unglück	My holiday was a **disaster**.
	to hit [hɪt]	gegen etw. fahren	The car **hit** the bike.
	iceberg [ˈaɪsbɜːg]	Eisberg	R айсберг
	to sink [sɪŋk], **sank** [sæŋk], **sunk** [sʌŋk]	untergehen; sinken	The Titanic hit an iceberg and **sank**.
	after [ˈaːftə]	danach; später	Two days **after** there were more facts.
	shipyard [ˈʃɪpjaːd]	Werft	It was made in a Belfast **shipyard**.
	shortly [ˈʃɔːtli]	kurz	It happened **shortly** after the start.
	midnight [ˈmɪdnaɪt]	Mitternacht	**Midnight** is at twelve o'clock at night.
	voyage [ˈvɔɪdʒ]	Reise; Fahrt	The **voyage** started on April 15th.
	crew [kruː]	Crew; Besatzung; Mannschaft	The **crew** is the team who works on a ship.
	on board [ˈɒn bɔːd]	an Bord	Achtung Schreibweise! **on board**
	to survive [səˈvaɪv]	überleben	**to survive** ↔ to die
	gymnasium [dʒɪmˈneɪziəm]	*hier:* Fitnessraum	**gymnasium** ≠ Gymnasium
	ship builder [ˈʃɪp ˌbɪldə]	Schiffsbauer; Schiffsbauerin	The **ship's builders** said the ship was safe.
	half *(sg)* [haːf], **halves** *(pl)* [haːvz]	(die) Hälfte	**half** a lemon
p. 85	**Dr** [ˈdɒktə]	Dr. *(Anrede)*	My doctor is **Dr** Smith.

| however [haʊ'evə] | jedoch | **However**, we found out he was wrong. |
| to **save** [seɪv] | retten; bergen | The dog **saved** the people. |

Film corner

p. 87	**court** [kɔːt]	Spielfeld	You play tennis and basketball on a **court**.
	bench [benʃ]	Bank; Sitzbank	
	to **be sorry** [bi: 'sɒri]	leid tun	I **was sorry** when I heard what happened.

Checkpoint

| author ['ɔːθə] | Autor; Autorin | headteacher [ˌhed'tiːtʃə] | Schulleiter; Schulleiterin |
| main [meɪn] | Haupt- | to **take place** [ˌteɪk 'pleɪs] | stattfinden |

Speaking skills

p. 92	**upper** ['ʌpə]	obere	In the **upper** left corner there is a bird.
	corner ['kɔːnə]	Ecke	
	in the background [ɪn ðə 'bækgraʊnd]	im Hintergrund	The tree is **in the background**.
	in the middle [ɪn ðə 'mɪdl]	in der Mitte	The car is **in the middle** of the road.
	lower ['ləʊə]	untere	In the **lower** left corner there is a man.
	in the foreground [ɪn ðə 'fɔːgraʊnd]	im Vordergrund	The dog is **in the foreground**.
p. 93	**van** [væn]	Lieferwagen; Transporter	

Word bank: **Giving advice**

I have a good idea.

That's great.

Think positive.

That's good news.

That's a good idea.

That sounds good.

That's nice.

That's bad news.

That's terrible.

That's horrible.

That's a bad idea.

That sounds awful.

That's not very nice.

Suggestions:

Why don't you …
You can always …
Maybe you should …
How about you …
If I were you, I would …

If you told your mum / dad, …
If you talked to your mum's / dad's friend, …
If you …
Call me later.
Let's speak soon.

Word bank: Shopping

a bottle of

| water | juice | ketchup | milk | lemonade |

a bar of

chocolate

a can of

pet food   tomatoes   peaches

a jar of

jam   honey   peanut butter

a box of

tea bags   eggs

a bag of

flour   crisps   nuts   apples

a packet of

tissues   biscuits   tea   candles   sugar

a loaf of

bread

Where is …, please?
Where can I find …, please?
Have you got …, please?
Can you repeat that, please?
Sorry, I didn't understand / hear you.

How much is …, please?
Have you got this in a bigger size / box, please?
Have you got a different flavour, please?
Are these / Is this on special offer?
Could I have a …, please?

Unit 5 Welcome to Ireland

Way in

p. 94	**republic** [rɪˈpʌblɪk]	Republik	Ireland is called the green **republic**.
	euro [ˈjʊərəʊ]	Euro *(Währung)*	Ⓡ евро Ⓣ euro
	Irish [ˈaɪrɪʃ]	irisch; Irisch	There are many famous **Irish** bands.
	pub [pʌb]	Kneipe; Gasthaus	People often play music in **pubs**.
	youth *(no pl)* [juːθ]	Jugend-; Jugend	There are lots of **youth** groups in my town.
	orchestra [ˈɔːkɪstrə]	Orchester	Ⓡ оркестр Ⓣ orkestra
p. 95	**competition** [ˌkɒmpəˈtɪʃn]	Wettbewerb; Turnier	Dave won a prize in a **competition**!
	musical [ˈmjuːzɪkl]	Musik-; musikalisch	**musical** → music
	style [staɪl]	Stil	My favourite **style** is rock music.
	hip hop [ˈhɪphɒp]	Hip-Hop *(Musik)*	Keith's favourite style is **hip hop**.
	course [kɔːs]	Kurs	We have lots of different **courses**.
	acting [ˈæktɪŋ]	Schauspielen; Schauspielerei	There are courses in **acting** and dancing.
	to **care (for)** [ˈkeə (fɔː)]	sich kümmern (um)	He **cares** for old people.
	with special needs [wɪθ ˌspeʃl ˈniːdz]	mit Behinderung; mit besonderen Bedürfnissen	He helps children **with special needs**.
	guitar [ɡɪˈtɑː]	Gitarre	
	sign language [ˈsaɪn ˌlæŋɡwɪdʒ]	Gebärdensprache; Zeichensprache	Keith knows **sign language**.

Station 1

In the bathroom			
towel [ˈtaʊəl]	Handtuch	**shower gel** [ˈʃaʊə ˌdʒel]	Duschgel
shampoo [ʃæmˈpuː]	Shampoo	**body lotion** [ˈbɒdi ˌləʊʃn]	Körperlotion
toothbrush [ˈtuːθbrʌʃ]	Zahnbürste	**hair gel** [ˈheə ˌdʒel]	Haargel
nail scissors *(pl)* [ˈneɪl ˌsɪzəz]	Nagelschere	**soap** [səʊp]	Seife
comb [ˈkəʊm]	Kamm	**perfume** [ˈpɜːfjuːm]	Parfüm
toothpaste [ˈtuːθpeɪst]	Zahnpasta	**mirror** [ˈmɪrə]	Spiegel
hairdryer [ˈheəˌdraɪə]	Fön	**hairbrush** [ˈheəbrʌʃ]	Haarbürste

p. 96	to **take off** [ˌteɪk ˈɒf]	ausziehen	You don't have to **take off** your shoes.
	fridge [frɪdʒ]	Kühlschrank	
	to **help oneself** [ˌhelp wʌnˈself]	sich bedienen	**Help yourself** to food and drinks.
	around [əˈraʊnd]	gegen; ungefähr um	We all meet for dinner **around** 6:30.
	on weekdays [ɒn ˈwiːkdeɪz]	unter der Woche; an Werktagen	**On weekdays** I have toast with jam.
	cereal [ˈsɪərɪəl]	Müsli; Cornflakes	I eat **cereal** for breakfast.
	sweet [swiːt]	süß	Leo likes a **sweet** breakfast.
	except [ɪkˈsept]	außer	You can use all of them, **except** Maddy's.
	to **share** [ʃeə]	teilen	I'll **share** my room with you.
	to **practise** [ˈpræktɪs]	üben; trainieren	Today I have to **practise** with the band.
	adaptor [əˈdæptə]	Adapter	I can't find my **adaptor**.
	ours [aʊəz]	unsere	This room is for you and me. It's **ours**.
	to **prepare** [prɪˈpeə]	zubereiten; vorbereiten	Mum is **preparing** a snack for us.
	to **join** [dʒɔɪn]	sich anschließen	**Join** us when you're ready.
p. 97	**charger** [ˈtʃɑːdʒə]	Ladegerät	I need a **charger** for my phone.
	ID [ˌaɪˈdiː]	Ausweis; Personalausweis	You need your **ID** to visit another country.
	personal [ˈpɜːsnl]	persönlich	I have lots of **personal** things in my bag.
	raincoat [ˈreɪnkəʊt]	Regenmantel	I have a blue **raincoat**.
p. 98	**right now** [ˌraɪt ˈnaʊ]	gerade; jetzt gleich; sofort	I'm listening to music **right now**.
	German [ˈdʒɜːmən]	deutsch; aus Deutschland	I really like this **German** music.
	rapper [ˈræpə]	Rapper; Rapperin	Listen to this new German **rapper**.
	artist [ˈɑːtɪst]	Künstler; Künstlerin	Do you like the new hip hop **artist**?
	project [ˈprɒdʒekt]	Projekt	R проект T proje
	to **wash** [wɒʃ]	(sich) waschen; spülen	I **wash** my hair with shampoo.
	hair [heə]	Haar; Haare	
	cupboard [ˈkʌbəd]	Schrank	We always put the towels in the **cupboard**.
p. 99	**theirs** [ðeəz]	ihre	This is Dave's and Ann's room. It's **theirs**.
	partner [ˈpɑːtnə]	Partner; Partnerin	Ask what your **partner** is doing.

Station 2

Public transport

timetable [ˈtaɪmˌteɪbl]	Fahrplan	
to **change** [tʃeɪndʒ]	umsteigen	
tram [træm]	Straßenbahn	
stop [stɒp]	Haltestelle; Halt	
line [laɪn]	Linie	
on time [ɒn ˈtaɪm]	pünktlich	
fare [feə]	Fahrpreis	
valid [ˈvælɪd]	gültig	

single ticket [ˈsɪŋgl ˌtɪkɪt]	einfache Fahrkarte
station [ˈsteɪʃn]	Bahnhof; Haltestelle; Station
daily [ˈdeɪli]	täglich
weekly [ˈwiːkli]	wöchentlich
monthly [ˈmʌnθli]	monatlich
return ticket [rɪˈtɜːn ˌtɪkɪt]	Hin- und Rückfahrkarte

p. 100	to **get around** [ˌget əˈraʊnd]	herumkommen	It's very easy to **get around** the city.
	striking [ˈstraɪkɪŋ]	bemerkenswert; auffallend	He is a **striking** actor.
	move [muːv]	Bewegung	We will learn lots of new **moves**.
	dance [dɑːns]	Tanz	**dance** → to dance → dancer
	drumming [ˈdrʌmɪŋ]	Trommel-	Let's try the **drumming** workshop.
	to **take part (in)** [ˌteɪk ˈpɑːt]	teilnehmen (an)	We can **take part** in the workshop.
	I can't wait [aɪ ˌkɑːnt ˈweɪt]	ich kann es kaum erwarten	**I can't wait** to go on holiday.
	journey [ˈdʒɜːni]	Fahrt; Reise	It's a long **journey** to London from here.
	public transport [ˌpʌblɪk ˈtrænspɔːt]	öffentliche Verkehrsmittel	**public transport**: buses, trams, trains
	by [baɪ]	bis (spätestens)	We must leave **by** 8:30 a.m.
	mustn't [ˈmʌsnt]	nicht dürfen	You **mustn't** forget to buy a ticket.
p. 102	**class** [klɑːs]	Unterricht	You can't eat during **class**.
	step [step]	Schritt	You must learn the new **steps**.
	to **follow** [ˈfɒləʊ]	befolgen; folgen	Please **follow** the rules.
	driver [ˈdraɪvə]	Fahrer; Fahrerin	Don't talk to the **driver**!
	to **push** [pʊʃ]	schubsen; drängeln	Don't **push** other people!
p. 103	to **travel** [ˈtrævl]	fahren	Dogs **travel** free.
	to **carry** [ˈkæri]	tragen	I can **carry** the heavy bag for you.

Reading corner

p. 104	**gold** [gəʊld]	Gold	My jewellery is made of **gold**.
	to **explain** [ɪk'spleɪn]	erklären	I always have to **explain** my name.
	parade [pə'reɪd]	Parade; Umzug	There are lots of **parades** and parties.
	shamrock ['ʃæmrɒk]	Kleeblatt	
	rainbow ['reɪnbəʊ]	Regenbogen	
	gold [gəʊld]	golden; Gold-	The sweets are in **gold** paper.
	national ['næʃnl]	National-; national	Look! There is the **national** team.
	flower ['flaʊə]	Blume	
	pot [pɒt]	Topf	The flower is in a **pot**.
	to **be homesick** [bi: 'həʊmsɪk]	Heimweh haben	It made me **be homesick**.
	call [kɔ:l]	Anruf; Ruf	They didn't answer my **calls**.
p. 105	to **cheer sb up** [ˌtʃɪər'ʌp]	jmdn. aufheitern; jmdn. aufmuntern	He tried to **cheer** me **up**.
	poem ['pəʊɪm]	Gedicht	I read a nice **poem** about summer.
	fable ['feɪbl]	Fabel; Märchen	A **fable** is a kind of story.
	once [wʌns]	einst; einmal	at a time in the past
	to **foretell** [fɔ:'tel]	vorhersagen	She **foretold** my life.
	actually ['æktʃuəli]	tatsächlich; wirklich; eigentlich	**Actually**, I like your new dress.
	wealth [welθ]	Reichtum	My **wealth** is my family and friends.
	miserable ['mɪzrəbl]	elend; armselig; jämmerlich	I feel **miserable** today.
	to **feel sorry for** [ˌfi:l 'sɒri fə]	Mitleid haben mit; bedauern	Niamh **felt sorry for** herself.
	I couldn't believe my eyes. [aɪ ˌkʊdnt bɪˌli:v maɪˈaɪz]	Ich traute meinen Augen nicht.	Ganze Sätze am besten als Einheit lernen.
	dressed [drest]	angezogen (wie); verkleidet (als)	They were all **dressed** in green clothes.
	I couldn't help but ... [ˌaɪ kʊdnt 'help bʌt]	Ich konnte nicht anders als …	**I couldn't help but** laugh.
	to **rush** [rʌʃ]	eilen; sich beeilen; stürzen	I **rushed** into my room.
	to **grab** [græb]	schnappen; greifen; ergreifen	Lucy was angry and **grabbed** her bag.
	outfit ['aʊtfɪt]	Outfit; Kleidung	I grabbed my Paddy's Day **outfit**.
	beginning [bɪ'gɪnɪŋ]	Anfang; Beginn	**beginning** ↔ end
	wonderful ['wʌndəfl]	wunderbar	**Wonderful!** = Great! = Fantastic!

Film corner

p. 107	to **impress** [ɪmˈpres]	beeindrucken	We **impressed** our English teacher.
	pineapple [ˈpaɪnæpl]	Ananas	
	wherever [weəˈrevə]	wo(hin) auch immer; egal wo(hin); überall wo(hin)	I go **wherever** the wind takes me.

Word bank: **Things for a trip**

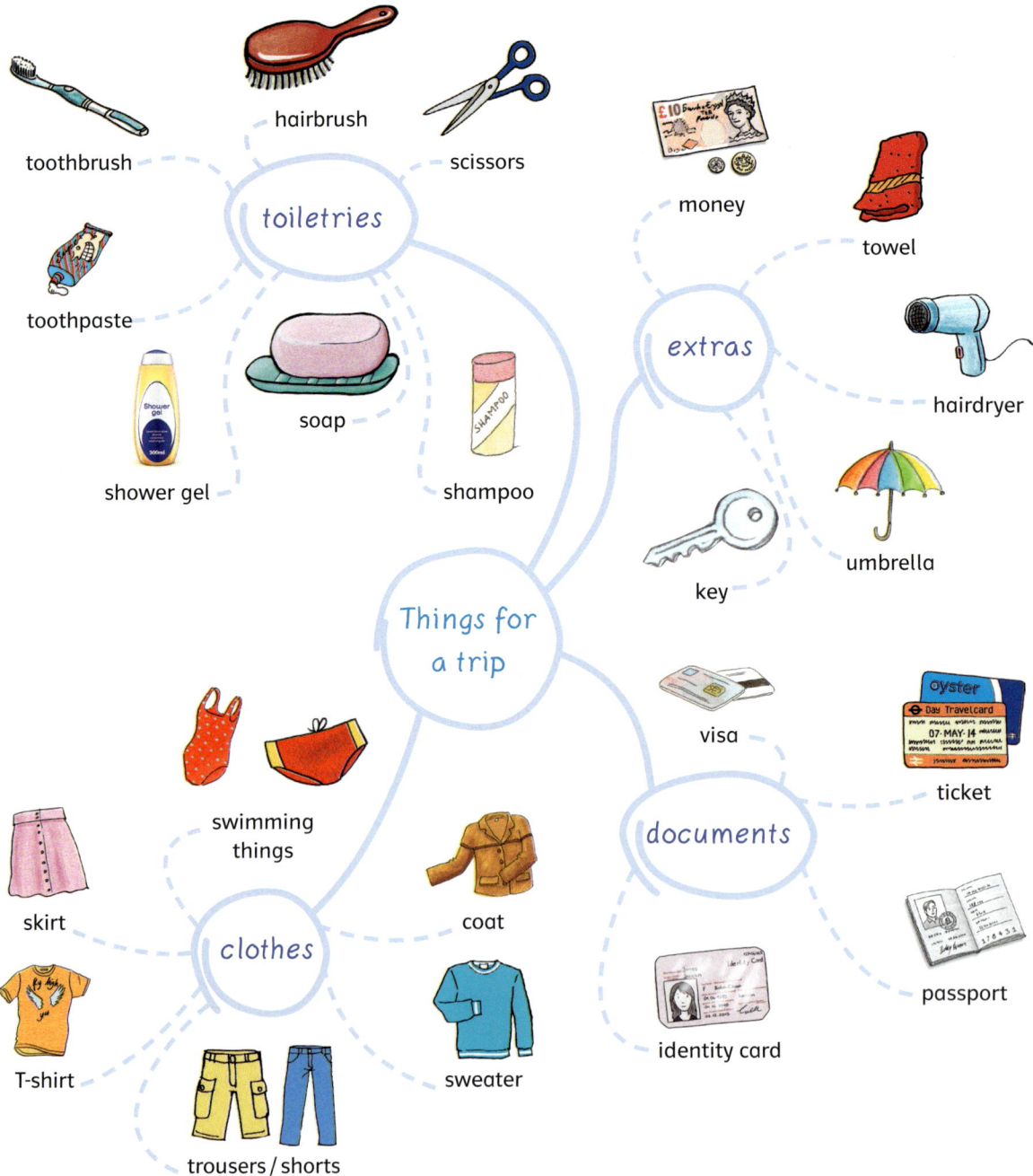

toothbrush

hairbrush

scissors

money

towel

toiletries

toothpaste

extras

hairdryer

shower gel

soap

shampoo

key

umbrella

Things for
a trip

visa

ticket

swimming
things

coat

documents

skirt

clothes

passport

T-shirt

sweater

identity card

trousers / shorts

Word bank: **Public transport**

airport

plane

helicopter

station / stop

underground

train

bus

tram

other transport

skateboard

taxi

car

boat

motorbike / moped

bike / bicycle

ferry

You should take …
Use the … line.
Travel northbound / southbound / westbound / eastbound.
Then …
It's … stops.
It stops at …

You must / have to buy …
You needn't / don't have to …
It costs …
You can buy a single ticket / a return ticket.
Change buses / trains at …

Instructions

Arbeitsanweisungen mit Operatoren

Act the dialogue • the role play.	**Spielt** den Dialog • das Rollenspiel.
Add more words.	**Ergänze** mehr Wörter.
Answer the questions.	**Beantworte** die Fragen.
Ask a partner.	**Frage** eine Partnerin/einen Partner.
Check the sentences.	**Überprüfe** die Sätze.
Choose one of the tasks • the right answer.	**Wähle** eine der Aufgaben • die richtige Antwort **aus**.
Collect ideas.	**Sammle** Ideen.
Compare with your partner.	**Vergleicht** zu zweit.
Complete the sentences • the dialogue.	**Vervollständige** die Sätze • den Dialog.
Copy the list.	**Schreibe** die Liste **ab**.
Correct the wrong sentences.	**Verbessere** die falschen Sätze.
Decide on the best order.	**Entscheide dich für** die beste Reihenfolge.
Describe the picture.	**Beschreibe** das Bild.
Discuss in groups.	**Besprecht euch** in Gruppen.
Draw a picture.	**Zeichne** ein Bild.
Exchange your lists.	**Tauscht** eure Listen **aus**.
Explain the rules.	**Erkläre** die Regeln.
Finish the sentences.	**Vervollständige** die Sätze.
Give feedback.	**Gib** Rückmeldung.
Give reasons.	**Gib Gründe an**.
Guess.	**Überlege**.
Interview your partner.	**Interviewe** deine Partnerin/deinen Partner.
Label the picture.	**Beschrifte** das Bild.
Listen to the dialogue.	**Höre** dir den Dialog **an**.
Look at the photos • pictures (again).	**Schau** dir die Fotos • Bilder (noch einmal) **an**.
Make a list • a chart • a mind map.	**Erstelle** eine Liste • eine Tabelle • ein Wörternetz.
Make notes.	**Mache** dir **Stichpunkte**.
Make up more verses.	**Denke dir** weitere Strophen **aus**.
Match the sentences with the pictures.	**Ordne** den Bildern die richtigen Sätze **zu**.
Name the place.	**Nenne** den Ort.
Plan your role play.	**Plant** euer Rollenspiel.
Practise with a partner.	**Übe** mit einer Partnerin/einem Partner.
Present your profile to the class.	**Stelle** dein Profil deiner Klasse **vor**.
Put in the right verbs.	**Setze** die richtigen Verben **ein**.
Put the words **in the right order**.	**Bringe** die Wörter **in die richtige Reihenfolge**.
Read the story **again**.	**Lies** die Geschichte **noch einmal**.
Record your dialogue.	**Nehmt** euren Dialog **auf**.
Rewrite the sentences.	**Schreibe** die Sätze **um**.

Say how you feel.	Sage, wie du dich fühlst.
Show your text to a partner.	Zeige deinen Text einer Partnerin/einem Partner.
Sort the words into groups.	Sortiere die Wörter in Gruppen.
Take notes.	Mache dir Notizen.
Talk about the photos.	Rede über die Fotos.
Tell the class.	Erzähle es der Klasse.
Think about the story.	Denke über die Geschichte nach.
Think of a number.	Denke dir eine Nummer aus.
Use your own ideas.	Benutze deine eigenen Ideen.
Watch the film.	Schau den Film an.
Write a poem • a heading • a draft.	Schreibe ein Gedicht • einen Titel • einen Entwurf.

Classroom phrases

You and your teacher

I'm sorry I'm late.	Tut mir leid, dass ich mich verspätet habe.
I'm sorry I don't have my exercise book.	Tut mir leid, ich habe mein Heft nicht dabei.
What's the homework?	Was haben wir als Hausaufgabe auf?
Can you help me, please?	Können Sie / Kannst du mir bitte helfen?
Can you say that again, please?	Können Sie / Kannst du das bitte wiederholen?
Can I go to the toilet, please?	Kann ich bitte auf Toilette gehen?
Mr / Mrs / Miss …, I don't feel well.	Herr / Frau …, mir geht es nicht gut.
What page is it, please?	Auf welcher Seite ist das?
What's the German / English word for …?	Was ist das deutsche / englische Wort für …?
How do you spell …?	Wie schreibt man …?
What does that mean?	Was heißt / bedeutet das?
Sorry, I don't understand/ I don't know.	Tut mir leid, ich verstehe das nicht/ ich weiß es nicht.

Working together

Can we work in pairs / groups?	Können wir zu zweit / in Gruppen arbeiten?
Do you want to work with me / us?	Willst du / Wollt ihr mit mir / uns arbeiten?
Let's make a / draw a …	Lass(t) uns ein … machen / zeichnen.
Whose turn is it? – It's my / your turn.	Wer ist dran? – Ich bin dran. / Du bist dran.

Your teacher can say …

Turn to page …	Schlagt Seite … auf.
Look at the board.	Schaut an die Tafel.
Put your hands up, please!	Meldet euch, bitte!
Try again!	Versuche es noch einmal.

List of irregular verbs

Hier findest du alle unregelmäßigen Verben, die im Buch vorkommen. Die Liste enthält jeweils alle drei Formen, auch wenn sie noch nicht alle in den Units vorgekommen sind.

infinitive	simple past	past participle	German
be [biː]	was, were [wɒz, wɜː]	been [biːn]	sein
beat [biːt]	beat [biːt]	beaten [ˈbiːtn]	schlagen; besiegen
become [bɪˈkʌm]	became [bɪˈkeɪm]	become [bɪˈkʌm]	werden
bleed [bliːd]	bled [bled]	bled [bled]	bluten
break [breɪk]	broke [brəʊk]	broken [ˈbrəʊkn]	brechen
bring [brɪŋ]	brought [brɔːt]	brought [brɔːt]	bringen; mitbringen
build [bɪld]	built [bɪlt]	built [bɪlt]	bauen
burn [bɜːn]	burned/burnt [bɜːnt]	burned/burnt [bɜːnt]	brennen
buy [baɪ]	bought [bɔːt]	bought [bɔːt]	kaufen
choose [tʃuːz]	chose [tʃəʊz]	chosen [ˈtʃəʊzn]	auswählen; wählen
come [kʌm]	came [keɪm]	come [kʌm]	kommen
cost [kɒst]	cost [kɒst]	cost [kɒst]	kosten
cut [kʌt]	cut [kʌt]	cut [kʌt]	(sich) schneiden
do [duː]	did [dɪd]	done [dʌn]	machen; tun
draw [drɔː]	drew [druː]	drawn [drɔːn]	zeichnen
dream [driːm]	dreamed/dreamt [dremt]	dreamed/dreamt [dremt]	träumen
drink [drɪŋk]	drank [dræŋk]	drunk [drʌŋk]	trinken
eat [iːt]	ate [eɪt]	eaten [ˈiːtn]	essen
fall [fɔːl]	fell [fel]	fallen [ˈfɔːln]	fallen; hinfallen
feed [fiːd]	fed [fed]	fed [fed]	füttern; ernähren
feel [fiːl]	felt [felt]	felt [felt]	(sich) fühlen
fight [faɪt]	fought [fɔːt]	fought [fɔːt]	kämpfen; streiten
find [faɪnd]	found [faʊnd]	found [faʊnd]	finden
fly [flaɪ]	flew [fluː]	flown [fləʊn]	fliegen
forget [fəˈget]	forgot [fəˈgɒt]	forgotten [fəˈgɒtn]	vergessen
freeze [friːz]	froze [frəʊz]	frozen [ˈfrəʊzn]	frieren; gefrieren
get [get]	got [gɒt]	got [gɒt]	bekommen; werden
give [gɪv]	gave [geɪv]	given [ˈgɪvn]	geben
go [gəʊ]	went [went]	gone [gɒn]	gehen; fahren
grow up [ˌgrəʊˈʌp]	grew up [ˌgruːˈʌp]	grown up [ˌgrəʊnˈʌp]	aufwachsen
hang [hæŋ]	hung [hʌŋ]	hung [hʌŋ]	hängen
have [hæv]	had [hæd]	had [hæd]	haben; besitzen
hear [hɪə]	heard [hɜːd]	heard [hɜːd]	hören
hide [haɪd]	hid [hɪd]	hidden [ˈhɪdn]	verstecken
hit [hɪt]	hit [hɪt]	hit [hɪt]	schlagen; treffen
hold [həʊld]	held [held]	held [held]	halten; festhalten
hurt [hɜːt]	hurt [hɜːt]	hurt [hɜːt]	verletzen; weh tun
keep [kiːp]	kept [kept]	kept [kept]	halten
know [nəʊ]	knew [njuː]	known [nəʊn]	wissen; kennen

infinitive	simple past	past participle	German
lay [leɪ]	laid [leɪd]	laid [leɪd]	legen; (den Tisch) decken
leave [li:v]	left [left]	left [left]	verlassen; lassen; abfahren
lend [lend]	lent [lent]	lent [lent]	leihen; verleihen
lose [lu:z]	lost [lɒst]	lost [lɒst]	verlieren
make [meɪk]	made [meɪd]	made [meɪd]	machen; tun; bilden
mean [mi:n]	meant [ment]	meant [ment]	bedeuten; meinen
meet [mi:t]	met [met]	met [met]	kennen lernen; (sich) treffen
pay [peɪ]	paid [peɪd]	paid [peɪd]	bezahlen
put [pʊt]	put [pʊt]	put [pʊt]	setzen; legen; stellen
read [ri:d]	read [red]	read [red]	lesen
ride [raɪd]	rode [rəʊd]	ridden ['rɪdn]	fahren; reiten
ring [rɪŋ]	rang [ræŋ]	rung [rʌŋ]	klingeln; läuten
run [rʌn]	ran [ræn]	run [rʌn]	laufen; rennen
say [seɪ]	said [sed]	said [sed]	sagen; sprechen
see [si:]	saw [sɔ:]	seen [si:n]	sehen
sell [sel]	sold [səʊld]	sold [səʊld]	verkaufen
send [send]	sent [sent]	sent [sent]	schicken; senden
show [ʃəʊ]	showed [ʃəʊd]	shown [ʃəʊn]	zeigen
sing [sɪŋ]	sang [sæŋ]	sung [sʌŋ]	singen
sink [sɪŋk]	sank [sæŋk]	sunk [sʌŋk]	untergehen; sinken
sit [sɪt]	sat [sæt]	sat [sæt]	sitzen
sleep [sli:p]	slept [slept]	slept [slept]	schlafen
smell [smel]	smelled/smelt [smelt]	smelled/smelt [smelt]	riechen
speak [spi:k]	spoke [spəʊk]	spoken ['spəʊkn]	sprechen
spell [spel]	spelled/spelt [spelt]	spelled/spelt [spelt]	buchstabieren
spend [spend]	spent [spent]	spent [spent]	ausgeben; verbringen
stand [stænd]	stood [stʊd]	stood [stʊd]	stehen
sweep [swi:p]	swept [swept]	swept [swept]	fegen
swim [swɪm]	swam [swæm]	swum [swʌm]	schwimmen
take [teɪk]	took [tʊk]	taken ['teɪkn]	nehmen; mitnehmen
tell [tel]	told [təʊld]	told [təʊld]	erzählen; sagen
think [θɪŋk]	thought [θɔ:t]	thought [θɔ:t]	denken; glauben
throw [θrəʊ]	threw [θru:]	thrown [θrəʊn]	werfen
understand [ˌʌndə'stænd]	understood [ˌʌndə'stʊd]	understood [ˌʌndə'stʊd]	verstehen
wake up [weɪk 'ʌp]	woke up [wəʊk 'ʌp]	woken up [ˌwəʊkn 'ʌp]	aufwachen
wear [weə]	wore [wɔ:]	worn [wɔ:n]	tragen
win [wɪn]	won [wʌn]	won [wʌn]	gewinnen; siegen
write [raɪt]	wrote [rəʊt]	written ['rɪtn]	schreiben

Dictionary

Im *Dictionary* sind alle wichtigen Wörter aus deinem Buch enthalten. Die Wörter stehen in alphabetischer Reihenfolge. Englische Wörter schlägst du ab S. 212 nach, deutsche Wörter ab S. 247.

Die Abkürzungen geben an, wo das Wort zum ersten Mal im Buch erscheint.

across	[əˈkrɒs]	über	III	U1	11
englisches Wort	Aussprache	deutsche Übersetzung	Band 3	Unit 1	Seite

Die mit einem Sternchen (*) gekennzeichneten Verben sind unregelmäßige Verben (→ *List of irregular verbs*, S. 210 – 211).

Manche Wörter haben verschiedene Bedeutungen. Am besten liest du alle, bevor du dich für eine entscheidest.

practice [ˈpræktɪs] Training; Übung I[1]
to **accept** [əkˈsept] akzeptieren
  <III U4, 86>[3]

*to **spend** [spend] ausgeben; verbringen II[1]

actually [ˈæktʃuəli] tatsächlich; wirklich; eigentlich III U5, 105[2]
address [əˈdres] Adresse II[2]

1 Lernwortschatz für alle: schwarz; 2 Differenzierungswortschatz: blau; 3 kein Lernwortschatz: < >

A

a [ə] ein; eine I
  a bit [ə ˈbɪt] ein bisschen; ein wenig II
  a few [ə ˈfjuː] ein paar; wenige; einige III U3, 58
  a little [ə ˈlɪtl] ein bisschen II
  a lot [əˈlɒt] viel I; sehr II
  a lot of [ə ˈlɒt ˌəv] eine Menge; viel I; viel; eine Menge III U1, 16
  a pair of [ə ˈpeər ˌəv] ein Paar II
  a/one hundred [ˈhʌndrəd] einhundert; hundert I
  a/one thousand [ə/wʌn ˈθaʊznd] eintausend; tausend II
  a five minute walk [ə ˈfaɪv mɪnɪt ˌwɔːk] fünf Minuten zu Fuß III U1, 12
a.m. [ˌeɪˈem] vormittags II
about [əˈbaʊt] ungefähr; circa; etwa II
  to be about [bi: əˈbaʊt] gehen um; handeln von III U1, 31

about [əˈbaʊt] über II
  out and about [ˌaʊt ˌən əˈbaʊt] unterwegs I
to accept [əkˈsept] akzeptieren
  <III U4, 86>
accident [ˈæksɪdnt] Unfall III U2, 38
stomach **ache** [ˈstʌmək ˌeɪk] Bauchweh; Bauchschmerzen II
across [əˈkrɒs] über II
to act [ækt] spielen II
  acting workshop [ˈæktɪŋ ˌwɜːkʃɒp] Schauspielworkshop II
acting [ˈæktɪŋ] Schauspielen; Schauspielerei III U5, 95
Action! [ˈækʃn] Achtung Aufnahme!
  <III U1, 27>
activity [ækˈtɪvəti] Aktivität I
  activity centre [ækˈtɪvəti ˌsentə] Jugendzentrum III U2, 34
actor [ˈæktə] Schauspieler; Schauspielerin II
actually [ˈæktʃuəli] tatsächlich; wirklich; eigentlich III U5, 105

adaptor [əˈdæptə] Adapter III U5, 96
to add [æd] hinzufügen II
address [əˈdres] Adresse II
adjective [ˈædʒɪktɪv] Adjektiv; Eigenschaftswort I
adult [ˈædʌlt] Erwachsene; Erwachsener III U4, 75
adventure [ədˈventʃə] Abenteuer III U2, 32
adverb [ˈædvɜːb] Adverb <III U2, 36>
advert (ad) [ˈædvɜːt] Anzeige
  <III U3, 68>
advice [ədˈvaɪs] Rat; Ratschlag III U2, 51
afraid [əˈfreɪd] ängstlich II
  to be afraid [bi: əˈfreɪd] sich fürchten; Angst haben II
after [ˈɑːftə] nach I; danach; später III U4, 84
  after that [ˌɑːftə ˈðæt] danach I
afternoon [ˌɑːftəˈnuːn] Nachmittag I
  in the afternoon [ɪn ðiˌɑːftəˈnuːn] am Nachmittag I

again [əˈgen] wieder; noch einmal II
Can you say that again, please?
[kæn ju: ˌseɪ ðæt əˈgen pliːs] Könntest du das bitte wiederholen? I

against [əˈgenst] gegen III U1, 11

age [eɪdʒ] Alter I

ago [əˈgəʊ] vor II

to **agree** [əˈgriː] zustimmen II
to agree (on) [əˈgriː (ɒn)] sich einigen (auf) <III U5, 108>

agreement [əˈgriːmənt] Vereinbarung <III U5, 135>

air [eə] Luft III U3, 55

airport [ˈeəpɔːt] Flughafen II

alarm clock [əˈlɑːm ˌklɒk] Wecker I

alien [ˈeɪliən] Außerirdische; Außerirdischer I

alive [əˈlaɪv] am Leben <III U1, 17>; III U1, 22

all [ɔːl] alle I
all day [ɔːl ˈdeɪ] den ganzen Tag III U3, 58

all right [ɔːl ˈraɪt] in Ordnung; alles klar II

allergic to [əˈlɜːdʒɪk tə] allergisch gegen II

allergy [ˈælədʒi] Allergie II

almost [ˈɔːlməʊst] fast; beinahe III U1, 25

along [əˈlɒŋ] entlang I

alphabet [ˈælfəbet] Alphabet I

already [ɔːlˈredi] schon; bereits II

aluminium [ˌæljəˈmɪniəm] Aluminium III U3, 55

always [ˈɔːlweɪz] immer I

am [æm] bin I

amazing [əˈmeɪzɪŋ] erstaunlich; unglaublich; toll III U3, 63

ambulance [ˈæmbjələns] Krankenwagen III U2, 38

an [ən] ein; eine I

and [ænd] und I

Anglo-Saxon [ˌæŋgləʊˈsæksn] angelsächsisch <III U1, 126>

the **Anglo-Saxons** [ði ˌæŋgləʊˈsæksnz] die Angelsachsen <III U1, 127>

angry [ˈæŋgri] wütend; zornig; verärgert; böse II

animal [ˈænɪml] Tier I
animal rescue shelter [ˌænɪml ˈreskju: ˌʃeltə] Tierheim I

ankle [ˈæŋkl] Fußgelenk; Fußknöchel II

announcement [əˈnaʊnsmənt] Durchsage; Ankündigung II

annoyed [əˈnɔɪd] verärgert III U4, 77

another [əˈnʌðə] ein andere; noch ein II

answer [ˈɑːnsə] Antwort I

to **answer** [ˈɑːnsə] antworten; beantworten I
to answer the phone [ˌɑːnsə ðə ˈfəʊn] ans Telefon gehen III U2, 45

antenna [ænˈtenə] Antenne III U3, 67

antique [ænˈtiːk] Antiquität <III U1, 30>

any [ˈeni] irgendwelche; irgendein II
Any idea? [ˌeni ˈaɪdɪə] Irgendeine Idee? I
not … any [ˌnɒt … eni] kein II

anything [ˈeniθɪŋ] irgendetwas II
Anything else? [ˌeniθɪŋ ˈels] Darf es sonst noch etwas sein? I
anything to drink [ˈeniθɪŋ tə ˈdrɪŋk] etwas zu trinken II

apple [ˈæpl] Apfel I
apple crumble [ˌæpl ˈkrʌmbl] Apfelauflauf (mit Streuseln bedeckt) II

April [ˈeɪprl] April I

archer [ˈɑːtʃə] Bogenschütze; Bogenschützin <III U1, 126>

archive [ˈɑːkaɪv] Archiv II

are [ɑː] bist; sind I
Are you serious? [ɑː ju ˈsɪəriəs] Im Ernst? III U3, 58

argument [ˈɑːgjəmənt] Auseinandersetzung; Streit II

armour [ˈɑːmə] Rüstung III U2, 43

army [ˈɑːmi] Armee; Heer III U3, 62

around [əˈraʊnd] herum; umher III U1, 19
to get around [ˌget əˈraʊnd] herumkommen III U5, 100

around [əˈraʊnd] gegen; ungefähr um III U5, 96

around the house [əˌraʊnd ðə ˈhaʊs] zu Hause I

to **arrive** [əˈraɪv] ankommen II

arrow [ˈærəʊ] Pfeil <III U1, 127>

Art [ɑːt] Kunst I

article [ˈɑːtɪkl] Artikel; Bericht <III U5, 106>

artist [ˈɑːtɪst] Künstler; Künstlerin III U5, 98

as … as [əz … əz] so … wie II

as [æz] als II; so <III U4, 133>

as [æz] wie II

to **ask** [ɑːsk] fragen I
to ask about [ˈɑːsk əˌbaʊt] sich erkundigen nach; fragen nach II
asking the way [ˈɑːskɪŋ ðə ˈweɪ] nach dem Weg fragen I

*to be **asleep** [bi: əˈsliːp] schlafen III U1, 25
to fall asleep [fɔːl əˈsliːp] einschlafen III U1, 25

assistant [əˈsɪstnt] Verkäufer; Verkäuferin III U4, 83
shop assistant [ˈʃɒp əˌsɪstnt] Verkäufer; Verkäuferin II

association football [əˈsəʊsieɪʃn ˌfʊtbɔːl] Assoziationsfußball (offizieller Name von Fußball) <III U1, 24>

at [æt] auf; an; in; um; bei; am I
at break [ət ˈbreɪk] in der Pause I
at home [ət ˈhəʊm] zu Hause I
at last [ət ˈlɑːst] endlich; zu guter Letzt II
at school [ət ˈskuːl] in der Schule I
at the seaside [ət ðə ˈsiːsaɪd] am Meer I
at the weekend [ət ðə ˌwiːkˈend] am Wochenende I

ate [eɪt] simple past von to eat II

athletics [æθˈletɪks] Leichtathletik <III U2, 186>

to **attach** [əˈtætʃ] verbinden III U3, 67

attic [ˈætɪk] Dachboden I

audition [ɔːˈdɪʃn] Vorspielen; Vorsprechen; Vorsingen; Vortanzen II

August [ˈɔːgəst] August I
in August [in ˈɔːgəst] im August I

aunt [ɑːnt] Tante II

s six • **z** zoo • **ʃ** she • **ʒ** revision • **h** her • **m** me • **n** no • **ŋ** sing • **iə** hear • **l** let • **r** red • **j** yes

213

aunt

author ['ɔ:θə] Autor; Autorin
<III U4, 88>

available [ə'veɪləbl] erhältlich; ver-
fügbar <III U3, 68>

avalanche ['ævlɑ:nʃ] Lawine
<III U3, 72>

awake [ə'weɪk] bei Bewusstsein;
wach III U2, 38

away [ə'weɪ] weg; entfernt II

awful ['ɔ:fl] schrecklich; furchtbar I

B

back [bæk] Rückseite <III U5, 109>

back street ['bæk stri:t] Hinterhof
<III U1, 17>

*__to get back__ [ˌget ˈbæk] zurückkom-
men <III U2, 128>

back [bæk] zurück III U2, 41

back home [bæk 'həʊm] zu Hause II

background ['bækgraʊnd] Hintergrund III U4, 92
in the background [ɪn ðə
'bækgraʊnd] im Hintergrund
III U4, 92

backseat ['bæksi:t] Rücksitz
<III U1, 17>

bad [bæd] schlimm; böse; schlecht
III U2, 38

badminton ['bædmɪntən] Badminton
<III U2, 186>

bag [bæg] Tasche; Tüte; Sack I
tea bag ['ti: ˌbæg] Teebeutel
<III U4, 200>

bagpipes (pl) ['bægpaɪps] Dudelsack
III U3, 53

pasta bake [ˌpæstə 'beɪk] Nudelauf-
lauf II

baker ['beɪkə] Bäcker; Bäckerin
III U2, 50

baker's ['beɪkəz] Bäckerei III U1, 13

ball [bɔ:l] Ball II
cannon ball ['kænən ˌbɔ:l] Kanonenkugel II

balloon [bə'lu:n] Luftballon I
hot air balloon [ˌhɒt ˌeə bə,lu:n]
Heißluftballon <III U2, 44>

banana [bə'nɑ:nə] Banane I

band [bænd] Band; Musikgruppe II
to start a band [ˌstɑ:t ˌə 'bænd] eine
Band gründen II

bandage ['bændɪdʒ] Verband III U2, 39

a bar of chocolate [bɑ:r ˌəv 'tʃɒklət]
eine Tafel Schokolade I

barbecue ['bɑ:bɪkju:] Grill I

bargain ['bɑ:gɪn] Schnäppchen II

laundry basket ['lɔ:ndri ˌbɑ:skɪt]
Wäschekorb <III U4, 86>

basketball ['bɑ:skɪtbɔ:l] Basketball II

bat [bæt] Fledermaus I

bathroom ['bɑ:θrʊm] Bad(ezimmer) I

batter ['bætə] Bierteig <III U3, 66>

battle ['bætl] Schlacht; Kampf
III U1, 11

BC (= before Christ) [bi:'si:] vor Chris-
tus <III U5, 134>

*__to be__ [bi:] sein I
to be about [bi: ə'baʊt] gehen um;
handeln von III U1, 31
to be afraid [bi: ə'freɪd] sich fürchten; Angst haben II
to be asleep [bi: ə'sli:p] schlafen
III U1, 25
to be born [bi: 'bɔ:n] geboren
werden III U3, 52
to be called [bi: 'kɔ:ld] heißen;
genannt werden II
to be careful [bi: 'keəfl] vorsichtig
sein II
to be fed up (with) [bi: fed ˌ'ʌp
(wɪð)] die Nase voll haben (von);
sauer sein III U4, 76
to be good at [bi 'gʊd ˌət] gut sein
in; gut sein bei I
to be homesick [bi: 'həʊmsɪk]
Heimweh haben III U5, 104
to be interested in [bi: 'ɪntrəstɪd ˌɪn]
sich interessieren für; interessiert
sein an III U1, 12
to be lucky [bi: 'lʌki] Glück haben
<III U3, 72>
to be made of [bi: 'meɪd ˌəv] hergestellt sein aus III U3, 54
to be right [bi: 'raɪt] recht haben II
to be scared [bi: 'skeəd] Angst
haben; erschrocken sein III U2, 34

to be sick [bi 'sɪk] sich übergeben I
to be sorry [bi: 'sɒri] leid tun
III U4, 87
to be up to [bi: 'ʌp tə] vorhaben
III U3, 67

beach [bi:tʃ] Strand I
to go beach combing [gəʊ 'bi:tʃ
ˌkəʊmɪŋ] den Strand nach Strandgut absuchen II

*__to beat__ [bi:t] besiegen; schlagen
III U3, 62

beat [bi:t] simple past von to beat
III U3, 62

beaten ['bi:tn] past participle von to
beat III U3, 62

beautiful ['bju:tɪfl] schön; hübsch I

became [bɪ'keɪm] simple past von to
become II

because [bɪ'kɒz] weil; da I
because of [bɪ'kɒz ˌəv] wegen
III U2, 37

*__to become__ [bɪ'kʌm] werden II

become [bɪ'kʌm] past participle von
to become II

bed [bed] Bett I
bed and breakfast (B & B) [ˌbed ˌən
'brekfəst] Frühstückspension
III U3, 58
to go to bed [ˌgəʊ tə 'bed] ins Bett
gehen I

bedroom ['bedrʊm] Schlafzimmer;
Kinderzimmer I

beef [bi:f] Rindfleisch II

been [bi:n] past participle von to be II

before [bɪ'fɔ:] vorher; zuvor II

before [bɪ'fɔ:] bevor; bis zu II

*__to begin__ [bɪ'gɪn] beginnen; anfan-
gen <III U5, 135>

beginning [bɪ'gɪnɪŋ] Anfang; Beginn
III U5, 105

behind [bɪ'haɪnd] hinter II

to believe [bɪ'li:v] glauben II
I couldn't believe my eyes [aɪ
ˌkʊdnt bɪˌli:v maɪ ˌaɪz] Ich traute
meinen Augen nicht. III U5, 105

bell [bel] Glocke II

bench [benʃ] Bank; Sitzbank III U4, 87

beside [bɪ'saɪd] neben <III U1, 178>

best [best] beste II

the best [ðə ˈbest] die besten II

Best wishes, [ˌbest ˈwɪʃɪz] Mit den besten Wünschen, I

between [bɪˈtwiːn] zwischen II

bicycle [ˈbaɪsɪkl] Fahrrad <III U5, 206>

big [bɪg] groß I

big wheel [ˌbɪg ˈwiːl] Riesenrad II

bike [baɪk] Fahrrad I

bill [bɪl] Rechnung III U3, 59

to pay the bill [ˌpeɪ ðə ˈbɪl] die Rechnung bezahlen III U3, 59

billion [ˈbɪlɪən] Milliarde II

biography [baɪˈɒgrəfi] Biografie <III U3, 54>

Biology [baɪˈɒlədʒi] Biologie I

bird [bɜːd] Vogel III U3, 61

bird watching [ˈbɜːd ˌwɒtʃɪŋ] Vogelbeobachtung III U3, 61

birthday [ˈbɜːθdeɪ] Geburtstag I

Happy birthday! [ˌhæpi ˈbɜːθdeɪ] Alles Gute zum Geburtstag! I

biscuit [ˈbɪskɪt] Keks II

dog biscuit [ˈdɒg ˌbɪskɪt] Hundekeks II

a bit [ə ˈbɪt] ein bisschen; ein wenig II

black [blæk] schwarz I

to blaze [bleɪz] brennen; lodern <III U1, 17>

bled [bled] simple past, past participle von *to bleed* III U2, 38

***to bleed** [bliːd] bluten III U2, 38

to blind [blaɪnd] blenden <III U1, 17>

blog [blɒg] Blog; Internettagebuch II

blouse [blaʊz] Bluse I

blue [bluː] blau I

the blue one [ðə ˈbluː ˌwʌn] der blaue II

board [bɔːd] Tafel I

on board [ˈɒn bɔːd] an Bord III U4, 84

boat [bəʊt] Boot II

boat trip [ˈbəʊt ˌtrɪp] Bootsfahrt; Schiffsfahrt II

body [ˈbɒdi] Körper III U5, 97

body lotion [ˈbɒdi ˌləʊʃn] Körperlotion III U5, 97

bodyguard [ˈbɒdigaːd] Leibwächter <III U3, 130>

book [bʊk] Buch; Heft I

exercise book [ˈeksəsaɪz ˌbʊk] Übungsheft I

to book [bʊk] buchen; reservieren <III U2, 44>

to bookmark [ˈbʊkmaːk] zu … hinfügen II

boot [buːt] Stiefel II

boring [ˈbɔːrɪŋ] langweilig I

***to be born** [bi: ˈbɔːn] geboren werden III U3, 52

to borrow [ˈbɒrəʊ] ausleihen II

boss [bɒs] Boss; Chef II

both [bəʊθ] beide <III U2, 128>

both … and … [ˈbəʊθ … ənd] sowohl … als auch … <III U1, 126>

a bottle of [ˈbɒtl] eine Flasche … I

bottle bank [ˈbɒtl bæŋk] Altglascontainer II

bought [bɔːt] simple past von *to buy* I; past participle von *to buy* II

bowl [bəʊl] Schale; Schälchen; Schüssel II

box [bɒks] Box; Kiste I

a box of [bɒks] eine Schachtel … I

telephone box [ˈtelɪfəʊn ˌbɒks] Telefonzelle II

boy [bɔɪ] Junge I

brand [brænd] Marke III U4, 81

brave [breɪv] tapfer; mutig III U3, 63

sliced **bread** [ˌslaɪst ˈbred] in Scheiben geschnittenes Brot III U4, 80

bread [bred] Brot II

at **break** [ət ˈbreɪk] in der Pause I

break of dawn [ˌbreɪk əv ˈdɔːn] Tagesanbruch <III U5, 101>

to take a break [ˌteɪk ə ˈbreɪk] Pause machen II

***to break** [breɪk] brechen; kaputt machen II

breakfast [ˈbrekfəst] Frühstück I

bed and breakfast (B & B) [ˌbed ən ˈbrekfəst] Frühstückspension III U3, 58

to have breakfast [ˌhæv ˈbrekfəst] frühstücken I

to breathe [briːð] atmen III U1, 22

bridge [brɪdʒ] Brücke II

briefcase [ˈbriːfkeɪs] Aktenkoffer; Aktentasche III U2, 45

brilliant [ˈbrɪlɪənt] toll I

***to bring** [brɪŋ] bringen; mitbringen II

British [ˈbrɪtɪʃ] britisch II

brochure [ˈbrəʊʃə] Broschüre; Prospekt III U1, 31

broke [brəʊk] simple past von *to break* II

broken [ˈbrəʊkn] past participle von *to break* II

brother [ˈbrʌðə] Bruder I

brother-in-law [ˈbrʌðər ˌɪn lɔː] Schwager <III U1, 126>

brought [brɔːt] simple past von *to bring* II

brown [braʊn] braun I

bruise [bruːz] Bluterguss; blauer Fleck <III U2, 187>

speech **bubble** [ˈspiːtʃ ˌbʌbl] Sprechblase <III U2, 47>

buffet [ˈbʊfeɪ] Büfett III U3, 58

***to build** [bɪld] bauen II

builder [ˈbɪldə] Bauarbeiter; Bauarbeiterin II

ship builder [ˈʃɪp ˌbɪldə] Schiffsbauer; Schiffsbauerin III U4, 84

building [ˈbɪldɪŋ] Gebäude II

built [bɪlt] simple past, past participle von *to build* II

light **bulb** [ˈlaɪt ˌbʌlb] Glühbirne III U3, 57

burger [ˈbɜːgə] Hamburger II

***to burn** [bɜːn] verbrennen; brennen III U2, 39

burnt [bɜːnt] simple past, past participle von *to burn* III U2, 39

bus [bʌs] Bus I

bus stop [ˈbʌs ˌstɒp] Bushaltestelle II

on the bus [ˌɒn ðə ˈbʌs] im Bus II

busy [ˈbɪzi] beschäftigt I; belebt <III U1, 30>

a busy day [ə ˌbɪzi ˈdeɪ] ein ausgefüllter Tag I

but [bʌt] aber I

butcher's ['bʊtʃəz] Metzgerei III U1, 13

butter ['bʌtə] Butter I
   peanut butter [ˌpiːnʌt 'bʌtə] Erdnussbutter III U4, 81

*to **buy** [baɪ] kaufen I

by [baɪ] von II; vorbei <III U1, 17>; bis
   (spätestens) III U5, 100
   to go by (train) [ˌgəʊ baɪ ('treɪn)]
   mit (dem Zug) fahren I

Bye! [baɪ] Tschüss! I

C

cabbage ['kæbɪdʒ] Kohl; Kraut II

caber ['keɪbə] Baumstamm
   <III U3, 130>
   caber toss ['keɪbə ˌtɒs] Baumstammwerfen <III U3, 130>

cache [kæʃ] Cache (Geheimschatz) I
   cache box ['kæʃ ˌbɒks] Schatzkiste
   beim Geocaching I

café ['kæfeɪ] Café I

cafeteria [kæfə'tɪəriə] Cafeteria;
   Mensa I

cage [keɪdʒ] Käfig I

cake [keɪk] Kuchen I

calculator ['kælkjəleɪtə] (Taschen-)
   Rechner I

calendar ['kæləndə] Kalender
   <III U2, 129>

call [kɔːl] Anruf; Ruf III U5, 104
   phone call ['fəʊn ˌkɔːl] Telefonanruf I

to **call** [kɔːl] rufen; anrufen II; nennen <III U1, 17>
   to be called [bi: 'kɔːld] heißen;
   genannt werden II
   call me ['kɔːl ˌmi] nenne mich I

caller ['kɔːlə] Anrufer; Anruferin
   III U2, 38

calm [kɑːm] ruhig; friedlich
   <III U4, 77>

came [keɪm] simple past von to
   come I

camel ['kæml] Kamel III U4, 82

camera ['kæmrə] Fotoapparat;
   Kamera <III U1, 27>

camp [kæmp] Camp; Lager II

camper ['kæmpə] Wohnmobil
   <III U3, 194>

camping ['kæmpɪŋ] Camping; Zelten
   III U2, 36
   to go camping [ˌgəʊ 'kæmpɪŋ]
   campen gehen; zelten II

campsite ['kæmpsaɪt] Campingplatz;
   Zeltplatz III U3, 58

a **can** of [kæn] eine Dose … I

can't [kɑːnt] nicht können I
   can [kæn; kən] können I
   Can I come back for it later? [kæn
   aɪ kʌm ˌbæk fərˌɪt 'leɪtə] Kann ich
   später nochmal wiederkommen? I
   Can you say that again, please?
   [kæn juː ˌseɪ ðæt ə'gen pliːs] Könntest du das bitte wiederholen? I
   Can you tell me the way to …?
   [kæn juː ˌtel mi ðə 'weɪ tə] Kannst
   du mir sagen, wie ich … komme? I
   I can't find … [aɪ kɑːnt 'faɪnd] ich
   kann … nicht finden I
   I can't wait [aɪ ˌkɑːnt 'weɪt] ich
   kann es kaum erwarten III U5, 100

canary [kə'neəri] Kanarienvogel
   III U1, 20

candle ['kændl] Kerze I

cannon ['kænən] Kanone II
   cannon ball ['kænən ˌbɔːl] Kanonenkugel II

cannot ['kænɒt] nicht können
   III U2, 45

canoeing [kə'nuːɪŋ] Kanufahren I

cap [kæp] Kappe; Mütze I

capital (city) ['kæpɪtl (ˌsɪti)] Hauptstadt III U2, 33

captain ['kæptɪn] Kapitän; Kapitänin I

caption ['kæpʃn] Untertitel; Bildun-
   terschrift <II>

car [kɑː] Auto I
   car park ['kɑː ˌpɑːk] Parkplatz
   <III U4, 86>

caravan ['kærəvæn] Wohnwagen
   III U3, 59

static caravan ['stætɪk ˌkærəvæn]
   Mobilheim (großer, fest stehender
   Wohnwagen) <III U3, 194>

card [kɑːd] Karte; Spielkarte II
   prompt card ['prɒmt ˌkɑːd] Stich-
   wortkarte <II>

cardboard ['kɑːdbɔːd] Pappe; Karton
   III U3, 55

to **care** (for) ['keə (fɔː)] sich kümmern
   (um) III U5, 95

*to be **careful** [bi: 'keəfl] vorsichtig
   sein II

caretaker ['keəˌteɪkə] Hausmeister;
   Hausmeisterin I

carnival ['kɑːnɪvl] Karneval;
   Fasching I

carpenter ['kɑːpəntə] Zimmermann;
   Zimmerin; Tischler; Tischlerin II

carpet ['kɑːpɪt] Teppich I

carrot ['kærət] Karotte II
   carrot pudding ['kærət ˌpʊdɪŋ]
   indische Nachspeise I

to **carry** ['kæri] tragen III U5, 103

pencil **case** ['pensl ˌkeɪs] Federmäppchen I

cast [kɑːst] Gips III U2, 39

castle ['kɑːsl] Schloss; Burg II

cat [kæt] Katze I

catering college ['keɪtərɪŋ ˌkɒlɪdʒ]
   Hotelfachschule II

Catholic ['kæθlɪk] Katholik; Katholikin; katholisch III U4, 74

to **cause** [kɔːz] verursachen
   <III U4, 132>

'**cause** (= because) [kɒz] weil
   <III U5, 101>

cave [keɪv] Höhle II

CD [ˌsiː'diː] CD I

ceiling ['siːlɪŋ] Zimmerdecke I

to **celebrate** ['seləbreɪt] feiern I

Celt [kelt] Kelte; Keltin <III U5, 134>

Celtic ['keltɪk] keltisch <III U5, 134>

centimetre (cm) ['sentɪˌmiːtə] Zentimeter (cm) I

centre ['sentə] Zentrum; Mitte; Center
   III U1, 16
   activity centre [æk'tɪvəti ˌsentə]
   Jugendzentrum III U2, 34

city centre [ˌsɪti ˈsentə] Stadtzentrum; Stadtmitte III U2, 33

shopping centre [ˈʃɒpɪŋ ˌsentə] Einkaufszentrum I

in the centre of [ɪn ðə ˈsentər ˌəv] in der Mitte von III U1, 16

century [ˈsenʃri] Jahrhundert III U1, 25

cereal [ˈsɪəriəl] Müsli; Cornflakes III U5, 96

chain [tʃeɪn] Kette <III U3, 131>

chair [tʃeə] Stuhl I

chamber of horrors [ˌtʃeɪmbər ˌəv ˈhɒrəz] Kammer des Schreckens <III U1, 30>

chance [tʃɑːns] Chance; Gelegenheit; Möglichkeit II

change [tʃeɪndʒ] Münzgeld; Wechselgeld II

to **change** [tʃeɪndʒ] wechseln II; ändern <III U1, 127>; (sich) ändern; verändern III U3, 54; umsteigen III U5, 100

to change one's mind [ˌtʃeɪndʒ wʌnz ˈmaɪnd] seine Meinung ändern <III U2, 44>; III U4, 81

charades [ʃəˈrɑːdz] Scharaden <II>

charger [ˈtʃɑːdʒə] Ladegerät III U5, 97

charity [ˈtʃærɪti] Wohltätigkeitsorganisation <III U2, 128>

chart [tʃɑːt] Tabelle; Diagramm <II>

video **chat** [ˈvɪdiəʊ ˌtʃæt] Video-Chat III U3, 67

to **chat** [tʃæt] chatten; plaudern II

cheap [tʃiːp] billig II

to **check** [tʃek] überprüfen; kontrollieren III U4, 81

to check in [ˌtʃek ˈɪn] einchecken III U3, 59

to check out [tʃek ˈaʊt] auschecken III U3, 59

checklist [ˈtʃeklɪst] Checkliste <I>

checkpoint [ˈtʃekpɔɪnt] Kontrollpunkt <I>

cheeky [ˈtʃiːki] frech III U2, 34

to **cheer** sb up [tʃɪər ˈʌp] jmdn. aufheitern; jmdn. aufmuntern III U5, 105

cheese [tʃiːz] Käse I

cheesecake [ˈtʃiːskeɪk] Käsekuchen II

chef [ʃef] Koch; Köchin II

head chef [ˈhed ˌʃef] Chefkoch II

chewing gum [ˈtʃuːɪŋ ˌɡʌm] Kaugummi I

chic [ʃɪk] schick; elegant I

chicken [ˈtʃɪkɪn] Huhn I; Hühnchen II

children (pl) [ˈtʃɪldrən] Kinder II

chilli [ˈtʃɪli] Chili II

chilli con carne [ˌtʃɪli kɒn ˈkɑːni] Chili con carne II

the **Chinese** [ðə ˈtʃaɪniːz] die Chinesen <III U1, 24>

chips (pl) [tʃɪps] Pommes I

fish and chips [ˌfɪʃ ən ˈtʃɪps] Pommes mit Fisch I

chocolate [ˈtʃɒklət] Schokolade I

*to **choose** [tʃuːz] wählen; auswählen II

chorus [ˈkɔːrəs] Refrain <I>

chose [tʃəʊz] simple past von to choose II

chosen [ˈtʃəʊzn] past participle von to choose II

Christianity [ˌkrɪstiˈænəti] Christentum <III U5, 134>

Christmas [ˈkrɪsməs] Weihnachten I

church [tʃɜːtʃ] Kirche II

cinema [ˈsɪnəmə] Kino I

circle [ˈsɜːkl] Kreis; Ring III U1, 10

city [ˈsɪti] Stadt; Großstadt II

city centre [ˌsɪti ˈsentə] Stadtzentrum; Stadtmitte III U2, 33

clan [klæn] Clan; Stamm <III U3, 130>

class [klɑːs] Klasse III U2, 36; Unterricht III U5, 102

classmate [ˈklɑːsmeɪt] Klassenkamerad; Klassenkameradin; Mitschüler; Mitschülerin <II>

classroom [ˈklɑːsrʊm] Klassenzimmer I

to **clean** [kliːn] sauber machen; putzen I

clean [kliːn] sauber III U3, 53

to **clear** the table [ˌklɪə ðə ˈteɪbl] den Tisch abräumen II

clever [ˈklevə] schlau; klug; intelligent II

to **click** [klɪk] klicken I

climb [klaɪm] Steigflug <III U3, 73>

to **climb** [klaɪm] besteigen; steigen; klettern III U2, 34

rock **climber** [ˈrɒk ˌklaɪmə] Kletterer; Kletterin <III U3, 72>

clock [klɒk] Uhr II

alarm clock [əˈlɑːm ˌklɒk] Wecker I

clock tower [ˈklɒk ˌtaʊə] Uhrenturm II

o'clock [əˈklɒk] Uhr (Zeitangabe bei vollen Stunden) I

to **close** [kləʊz] schließen; zumachen I

close [kləʊs] in der Nähe; nahe III U1, 17

clothes (pl) [kləʊðz] Kleider (Pl.); Kleidung I

cloud [klaʊd] Wolke III U2, 42

cloudy [ˈklaʊdi] wolkig I

club [klʌb] Klub; Verein II

clue [kluː] Hinweis; Spur I

coach [kəʊtʃ] Trainer; Trainerin <III U2, 36>

coal [kəʊl] Kohle III U1, 16

coast [kəʊst] Küste III U2, 33

on the coast [ɒn ðə ˈkəʊst] an der Küste III U1, 17

coat [kəʊt] Jacke I

coffee [ˈkɒfi] Kaffee <III U3, 68>

coin [kɔɪn] Münze III U4, 79

coke [kəʊk] Cola I

cold [kəʊld] kalt I

to get cold [ˌget ˈkəʊld] frieren III U3, 60

collar [ˈkɒlə] Halsband I

to **collect** [kəˈlekt] sammeln I

catering **college** [ˈkeɪtərɪŋ ˌkɒlɪdʒ] Hotelfachschule II

colour [ˈkʌlə] Farbe I

colourful [ˈkʌləfl] bunt II

comb [ˈkəʊm] Kamm III U5, 97

combination [ˌkɒmbɪˈneɪʃn] Kombination II

*to **come** [kʌm] kommen I

to come out [kʌm ˈaʊt] hervorkommen II

Come on! [kʌm ˈɒn] Komm jetzt! I

s six • **z** zoo • **ʃ** she • **ʒ** revision • **h** her • **m** me • **n** no • **ŋ** sing • **iə** hear • **l** let • **r** red • **j** yes

217

come

comedy [ˈkɒmədi] Komödie III U2, 50

comfortable [ˈkʌmftəbl] bequem; angenehm II

comic [ˈkɒmɪk] Comic(heft) II

comment [ˈkɒment] Kommentar II

company [ˈkʌmpəni] Firma; Gesellschaft II

to **compare** [kəmˈpeə] vergleichen I

to **compete (against)** [kəmˈpiːt] konkurrieren (gegen); sich messen (gegen) <III U3, 130>

competition [ˌkɒmpəˈtɪʃn] Wettbewerb; Turnier III U5, 95

competitor [kəmˈpetɪtə] Mitbewerber; Mitbewerberin; Teilnehmer; Teilnehmerin <III U3, 131>

to **complete** [kəmˈpliːt] vervollständigen I

complete [kəmˈpliːt] vollständig <III U3, 131>

computer [ˌkəmˈpjuːtə] Computer I

computer game [ˌkəmˈpjuːtə geɪm] Computerspiel I

concert [ˈkɒnsət] Konzert II

conclusion [kənˈkluːʒn] Schlussfolgerung; Schluss III U2, 50

confident [ˈkɒnfɪdnt] selbstsicher; selbstbewusst III U4, 77

confused [kənˈfjuːzd] verwirrt; wirr III U1, 25

Congratulations! [kənˌgrætʃuˈleɪʃnz] Glückwunsch! II

to **connect** [kəˈnekt] verbinden III U3, 67

connecting [kəˈnektɪŋ] verbindend <II>

conquest [ˈkɒŋkwest] Eroberung <III U1, 126>

content [ˈkɒntent] Inhalt III U2, 50

to **control** [kənˈtrəʊl] kontrollieren <III U1, 17>

to **cook** [kʊk] kochen II

to **cool** [kuːl] kühlen III U2, 39

cool [kuːl] cool; super; kühl I

to **keep cool** [ˌkiːp ˈkuːl] Ruhe bewahren <III U1, 27>

copy [ˈkɒpi] Kopie II; Abschrift <III U2, 51>

to **copy** [ˈkɒpi] kopieren II; abschreiben <III U2, 35>

corner [ˈkɔːnə] Ecke III U4, 92

corner shop [ˈkɔːnə ˌʃɒp] Tante-Emma-Laden I

film corner [ˈfiːlm ˌkɔːnə] Filmecke <I>

reading corner [ˈriːdɪŋ ˌkɔːnə] Leseecke <I>

Cornish [ˈkɔːnɪʃ] Cornish; aus Cornwall II

to **correct** [kəˈrekt] verbessern I

correct [kəˈrekt] richtig; korrekt <III U1, 25>

corridor [ˈkɒrɪdɔː] Gang; Flur; Korridor III U2, 42

cost [kɒst] Preis; Kosten <III U1, 30>

*to **cost** [kɒst] kosten III U4, 75

cost [kɒst] simple past, past participle von *to cost* III U4, 75

costume [ˈkɒstjuːm] Kostüm I

cosy [ˈkəʊzi] gemütlich III U3, 58

cottage [ˈkɒtɪdʒ] Häuschen III U3, 53

holiday cottage [ˈhɒlədeɪ ˌkɒtɪdʒ] Ferienhäuschen <III U3, 194>

cotton [ˈkɒtn] Baumwolle III U3, 55

to **cough** [kɒf] husten III U1, 21

could [kʊd] konnte III U1, 21; könnten III U3, 58

country [ˈkʌntri] ländliche Gegend; Land I

countryside [ˈkʌntrɪsaɪd] Landschaft; Land III U3, 53

course [kɔːs] Kurs III U5, 95

main course [ˌmeɪn ˈkɔːs] Hauptgericht II

of course [əv ˈkɔːs] natürlich; selbstverständlich II

court [kɔːt] Spielfeld III U4, 87

cousin [ˈkʌzn] Cousin; Cousine II

to **cover** [ˈkʌvə] überziehen <III U3, 66>

cow [kaʊ] Kuh III U1, 16

crazy [ˈkreɪzi] verrückt I

to **drive sb crazy** [draɪv … ˈkreɪzi] jmdn. verrückt machen III U4, 76

credit card [ˈkredɪt ˌkaːd] Kreditkarte <III U4, 86>

crew [kruː] Crew; Besatzung; Mannschaft III U4, 84

cricket [ˈkrɪkɪt] Kricket II

crime [kraɪm] Verbrechen <III U4, 77>

financial crisis [faɪˌnænʃl ˈkraɪsɪs] Wirtschaftskrise <III U5, 135>

crisp [krɪsp] Kartoffelchip I

crisp [krɪsp] knusprig; kross <III U3, 66>

crocodile [ˈkrɒkədaɪl] Krokodil I

to **cross** [krɒs] überqueren III U1, 12

crowd [kraʊd] Menschenmenge II

to **cry** [kraɪ] weinen; rufen; schreien <III U4, 77>

CU (See you!) [ˈsiː ˌjuː] Bis später! II

cuddly [ˈkʌdli] knuddelig III U2, 39

cuddly toy [ˈkʌdli ˌtɔɪ] Kuscheltier III U2, 39

cuju [ˈtsuju] Cuju *(asiatischer Vorgänger des Fußballs)* <III U1, 24>

culture [ˈkʌltʃə] Kultur <I>

cup [kʌp] Tasse II

cupboard [ˈkʌbəd] Schrank III U5, 98

curry [ˈkʌri] Curry II

custard [ˈkʌstəd] Vanillesauce II

customer [ˈkʌstəmə] Kunde; Kundin III U4, 80

cut [kʌt] Schnittverletzung <III U2, 187>

*to **cut** [kʌt] schneiden III U2, 39

cut [kʌt] simple past, past participle von *to cut* III U2, 39

cute [kjuːt] niedlich; süß II

cycling [ˈsaɪklɪŋ] Radfahren III U3, 61

D

dad [dæd] Papa; Vati I

daily [ˈdeɪli] täglich III U5, 101

dance [daːns] Tanz III U5, 100

to **dance** [daːns] tanzen I

dancer [ˈdaːnsə] Tänzer; Tänzerin I

dancing [ˈdaːnsɪŋ] Tanzen; Tanz- <III U3, 131>

danger [ˈdeɪndʒə] Gefahr <III U2, 128>

dangerous [ˈdeɪndʒrəs] gefährlich III U2, 34

the **dark** [ðə 'dɑːk] Dunkelheit III U1, 20

dark [dɑːk] dunkel I

darkness ['dɑːknəs] Dunkelheit <III U5, 101>

date [deɪt] Zeitpunkt; Datum I

daughter ['dɔːtə] Tochter I

break of **dawn** [ˌbreɪk ˌəv 'dɔːn] Tagesanbruch <III U5, 101>

day [deɪ] Tag I

a busy day [ə ˌbɪzi 'deɪ] ein ausgefüllter Tag I

all day [ɔːl 'deɪ] den ganzen Tag III U3, 58

lucky day [ˌlʌki 'deɪ] Glückstag II

one day [wʌn 'deɪ] eines Tages III U1, 21

four hours a day [ˌfɔːr aʊəzˌə 'deɪ] vier Stunden täglich I

dead [ded] tot III U1, 22

deadly ['dedli] tod-; tödlich III U1, 20

deaf [def] gehörlos; schwerhörig; taub III U3, 54

Dear …, [dɪə] Liebe(r) …, (Anrede in Briefen) I

oh dear [əʊ 'dɪə] oje III U4, 80

debit card ['debɪt ˌkɑːd] EC-Karte <III U4, 86>

December [dɪ'sembə] Dezember I

to **decide** [dɪ'saɪd] (sich) entscheiden III U3, 58

deep fried [ˌdiːp'fraɪd] frittiert; in Fett ausgebacken <III U3, 66>

definition [ˌdefi'nɪʃn] Definition <III U3, 59>

delicious [dɪ'lɪʃəs] köstlich II

department [dɪ'pɑːtmənt] Abteilung II

department store [dɪ'pɑːtmənt ˌstɔː] Kaufhaus II

to **describe** [dɪ'skraɪb] beschreiben <I>

design [dɪ'zaɪn] Design; Gestaltung <III U3, 69>

Design Technology (DT) [dɪˌzaɪn tek'nɒlədʒi, ˌdiː'tiː] Technik I

to **design** [dɪ'zaɪn] entwerfen; gestalten <III U3, 69>

information **desk** [ˌɪnfə'meɪʃn ˌdesk] Information II

dessert [dɪ'zɜːt] Nachspeise II

detail ['diːteɪl] Detail; Einzelheit <II>

detective [dɪ'tektɪv] Detektiv; Detektivin <I>

dialogue ['daɪəlɒg] Dialog; Gespräch <I>

diamond ['daɪəmənd] Diamant <II>

diary ['daɪəri] Tagebuch I

dictionary ['dɪkʃnri] Wörterbuch <III U3, 73>

did [dɪd] simple past von to do I

to **die** [daɪ] sterben III U1, 21

difficult ['dɪfɪklt] schwierig II

dining room ['daɪnɪŋ ˌrʊm] Esszimmer I

dinner ['dɪnə] Mittagessen; Abendessen II

directions [dɪ'rekʃnz] Anweisungen; Wegbeschreibung <III U1, 15>

director [dɪ'rektə] Regisseur; Regisseurin II

dirty ['dɜːti] dreckig; schmutzig I

to **disagree** [ˌdɪsə'griː] anderer Meinung sein; nicht einverstanden sein II

disagreement [ˌdɪsə'griːmnt] Meinungsverschiedenheit; Streit <III U4, 132>

disaster [dɪ'zɑːstə] Katastrophe; Desaster; Unglück III U4, 84

to **discover** [dɪ'skʌvə] entdecken <III U1, 30>

dish [dɪʃ] Gericht; Speise II

*to **do** [duː] machen; tun I

to do homework [ˌduː 'həʊmwɜːk] Hausaufgabe(n) machen I

to do the right thing [ˌduː ðə 'raɪt θɪŋ] das Richtige tun III U2, 38

to do the shopping [ˌduː ðə 'ʃɒpɪŋ] Einkäufe machen; Besorgungen machen II

to do the washing up [ˌduː ðə 'wɒʃɪŋ ʌp] abspülen II

dos and don'ts [ˌduːzˌən 'dəʊnts] Verhaltensregel <III U2, 44>

doctor ['dɒktə] Arzt; Ärztin II

document ['dɒkjəmənt] Dokument <III U5, 206>

dog [dɒg] Hund I

dog biscuit ['dɒg ˌbɪskɪt] Hundekeks II

to take the dog for a walk [ˌteɪk ðə dɒg fɔːrˌə 'wɔːk] den Hund ausführen I

dome [dəʊm] Kuppel II

dos and **don'ts** [ˌduːzˌən 'dəʊnts] Verhaltensregeln <III U2, 44>

done [dʌn] past participle von to do II

door [dɔː] Tür II

doorbell ['dɔːbel] Türklingel I

down [daʊn] entlang; herunter; hinunter III U1, 12

down [daʊn] traurig III U4, 77

to **download** [ˌdaʊn'ləʊd] herunterladen II

Dr ['dɒktə] Dr. (Anrede) III U4, 85

draft [drɑːft] Entwurf <II>

drama ['drɑːmə] Theater II; Drama III U2, 51

drank [dræŋk] simple past von to drink II

*to **draw** [drɔː] zeichnen II

drawn [drɔːn] past participle von to draw II

dreadful ['dredfl] furchtbar III U4, 77

dream [driːm] Traum II

*to **dream** [driːm] träumen III U1, 25

dreamt [dremt] simple past, past participle von to dream III U1, 25

dress [dres] Kleid II

fancy dress [ˌfænsi 'dres] Verkleidung; Kostüm I

dressed [drest] angezogen (wie); verkleidet (als) III U5, 105

*to get **dressed** [ˌget 'drest] sich anziehen II

drew [druː] simple past von to draw II

drink [drɪŋk] Getränk II

*to **drink** [drɪŋk] trinken II

anything to drink ['eniθɪŋ tə 'drɪŋk] etwas zu trinken II

drive [draɪv] Fahrt; Autofahrt III U1, 17

drive

s six • **z** zoo • **ʃ** she • **ʒ** revision • **h** her • **m** me • **n** no • **ŋ** sing • **iə** hear • **l** let • **r** red • **j** yes

219

drive

*to **drive** [draɪv] treiben <III U5, 134>
  to drive sb crazy [draɪv … 'kreɪzi] jmdn. verrückt machen III U4, 76
driver ['draɪvə] Fahrer; Fahrerin III U5, 102
  lorry driver ['lɒri ˌdraɪvə] LKW-Fahrer; LKW-Fahrerin II
to **drown** [draʊn] ertrinken <III U5, 134>
drumming ['drʌmɪŋ] Trommeln- III U5, 100
drunk [drʌŋk] past participle von *to drink* II
dry [draɪ] trocken III U2, 35
duke [djuːk] Herzog <III U1, 126>
dumpling ['dʌmplɪŋ] Kloß II
duration [djʊ'reɪʃn] Dauer <III U1, 30>
during ['djʊərɪŋ] während III U1, 11
on **duty** [ɒn 'djuːti] im Dienst <III U3, 68>
DVD [ˌdiːviː'diː] DVD I

E

each [iːtʃ] jede <III U4, 79>
  each other [iːtʃ'ʌðə] einander; sich; sich gegenseitig III U2, 34
each [iːtʃ] pro Stück II
ear [ɪə] Ohr II
early ['ɜːli] früh III U3, 60
  early settler [ˌɜːli 'setlə] früher Siedler; frühe Siedlerin <III U5, 134>
east [iːst] Osten III U1, 17
eastbound ['iːstbaʊnd] in Richtung Osten <III U5, 207>
easy ['iːzi] einfach; leicht I
*to **eat** [iːt] essen I
eaten ['iːtn] past participle von *to eat* II
economy [ɪ'kɒnəmi] Wirtschaft <III U5, 135>
egg [eg] Ei II
  scrambled egg [ˌskræmbld 'eg] Rührei II
Eid [iːd] Eid *(muslimisches Fest)* I
eight [eɪt] acht I
eighteen [eɪ'tiːn] achtzehn I
eighty ['eɪti] achtzig I

not … **either** [nɒt … 'aɪðə] auch nicht III U3, 58
electricity [ˌelɪk'trɪsəti] Strom, Elektrizität III U3, 53
elephant ['elɪfənt] Elefant I
eleven [ɪ'levn] elf I
e-mail ['iːmeɪl] E-Mail II
embarrassed [ɪm'bærəst] verlegen II
emergency [ɪ'mɜːdʒnsi] Notfall III U2, 38
  emergency call [ɪ'mɜːdʒnsi ˌkɔːl] Notruf III U2, 38
  emergency service [ɪ'mɜːdʒnsi ˌsɜːvɪs] Notdienst; Rettungsdienst III U2, 38
to **emigrate** ['emɪgreɪt] auswandern <III U5, 135>
end [end] Ende; Schluss II
  in the end [ɪn ði 'end] schließlich; zum Schluss II
to **end** [end] enden <II>
ending ['endɪŋ] Schluss; Ende III U2, 45
enemy ['enəmi] Feind; Feindin III U2, 50
steam **engine** ['stiːm ˌendʒɪn] Dampfmaschine III U3, 57
engineer [ˌendʒɪ'nɪə] Ingenieur; Ingenieurin; Techniker; Technikerin II
English ['ɪŋglɪʃ] Englisch I
the **English** [ði 'ɪŋglɪʃ] die Engländer III U1, 11
to **enjoy** [ɪn'dʒɔɪ] mögen III U2, 50; genießen III U3, 53
enough [ɪ'nʌf] genug; genügend III U2, 34
enough [ɪ'nʌf] genug; genügend <III U1, 127>
entry ['entri] Eintrag <III U3, 73>
  entry form ['entri ˌfɔːm] Anmeldeformular II
equipment [ɪ'kwɪpmənt] Ausrüstung III U2, 34
Victorian **era** [vɪkˌtɔːriən 'ɪərə] viktorianisches Zeitalter III U1, 25
eraser [ɪ'reɪzə] Radiergummi I
escalator ['eskəleɪtə] Rolltreppe II

to **escape** [ɪ'skeɪp] entkommen; fliehen; entfliehen; flüchten <III U3, 72>
euro ['jʊərəʊ] Euro *(Währung)* III U5, 94
European [ˌjʊərə'piːən] europäisch <III U5, 135>
even ['iːvn] noch; sogar II
evening ['iːvnɪŋ] Abend I
  in the evenings [ɪn ði 'iːvnɪŋz] abends III U4, 76
event [ɪ'vent] Ereignis; Veranstaltung <III U2, 129>; <III U4, 88>
ever ['evə] jemals II
every ['evri] jede I
every ['evri] alle III U4, 75
everyone ['evriwʌn] jeder I; zusammen; alle II
everything ['evriθɪŋ] alles II
exact [ɪg'zækt] exakt; genau III U4, 81
example [ɪg'zɑːmpl] Beispiel <III U3, 69>
except [ɪk'sept] außer III U5, 96
exchange [ɪks'tʃeɪndʒ] Austausch <III U5, 106>
to **exchange** [ɪks'tʃeɪndʒ] tauschen; austauschen <III U2, 41>
excited [ɪk'saɪtɪd] aufgeregt; begeistert II
exciting [ɪk'saɪtɪŋ] spannend; aufregend I
Excuse me. [ɪk'skjuːz mi] Entschuldigung. I
exercise book ['eksəsaɪz ˌbʊk] Übungsheft I
exhausted [ɪg'zɔːstɪd] erschöpft III U2, 35
to **expect** [ɪk'spekt] erwarten III U2, 45
expensive [ɪk'spensɪv] teuer II
experiment [ɪk'sperɪmənt] Versuch II
to **explain** [ɪk'spleɪn] erklären III U5, 104
to **explode** [ɪk'spləʊd] explodieren III U1, 20
to **explore** [ɪk'splɔː] erkunden; erforschen II
explosion [ɪk'spləʊʒn] Explosion III U1, 20

p pen • **b** bed • **t** ten • **d** dad • **k** cat • **g** grey • **tʃ** chair • **dʒ** joke • **f** fan • **v** very • **θ** three • **ð** the

extra [ˈekstrə] Extra; Zusatz
<III U5, 206>

extra [ˈekstrə] zusätzlich; Zusatz- II
extra practice [ˌekstrə ˈpræktɪs]
Zusatzübungen <I>

eye [aɪ] Auge II
I couldn't believe my eyes. [aɪ
ˌkʊdnt bɪˌliːv maɪ ˈaɪz] Ich traute
meinen Augen nicht. III U5, 105

F

fable [ˈfeɪbl] Fabel; Märchen
III U5, 105

face [feɪs] Gesicht I

fact [fækt] Fakt; Tatsache II

factory [ˈfæktri] Fabrik; Werk III U1, 16

fair [feə] gerecht; fair <III U1, 24>

***to fall** [fɔːl] fallen; hinfallen I
to fall (over) [fɔːl ˈəʊvə] fallen;
hinfallen; umfallen III U2, 38
to fall apart [fɔːl əˈpaːt] zusam-
menbrechen <III U4, 77>
to fall asleep [fɔːl əˈsliːp] einschlafen III U1, 25
to fall in love (with) [fɔːl ɪn ˈlʌv]
sich verlieben (in) III U2, 50

family [ˈfæmli] Familie I
host family [ˈhəʊst ˌfæmli] Gastfamilie <III U5, 99>

famine [ˈfæmɪn] Hungersnot
<III U5, 135>

famous [ˈfeɪməs] berühmt I

fan [fæn] Fan I

fancy dress [ˌfænsi ˈdres] Verkleidung;
Kostüm I

fantastic [fænˈtæstɪk] fantastisch;
großartig II

fantasy [ˈfæntəsi] Fantasie; Fantasy II
fantasy trip [ˈfæntəsi ˌtrɪp] Fantasieausflug I

far [faː] weit III U1, 12

fare [feə] Fahrpreis III U5, 100

farewell speech [feəˈwel spiːtʃ]
Abschiedsrede II

farm [faːm] Bauernhof I
wind farm [ˈwɪndfaːm] Windpark
III U3, 53

farmer [ˈfaːmə] Bauer; Bäuerin;
Landwirt; Landwirtin I

fashionable [ˈfæʃnəbl] modisch II

fast [faːst] schnell II
fast food restaurant [ˌfaːst fuːd
ˈrestrɒnt] Fastfood-Restaurant I
the fastest [ðə ˈfaːstɪst] der/die/
das schnellste I

father [ˈfaːðə] Vater I

It was my **fault**. [ɪt wəz ˌmaɪ ˈfɔːlt] Es
war meine Schuld. II

favourite [ˈfeɪvrɪt] Lieblings- I

fear [fɪə] Angst; Furcht <III U4, 77>

feature [ˈfiːtʃə] Merkmal <III U4, 88>

February [ˈfebruri] Februar I

fed [fed] simple past von to feed I;
past participle von to feed II

***to be fed up (with)** [bi: fed ˈʌp (wɪð)]
die Nase voll haben (von); sauer
sein III U4, 76

***to feed** [fiːd] füttern I

feedback [ˈfiːdbæk] Feedback; Rück-
meldung <II>

***to feel** [fiːl] (sich) fühlen II
to feel sorry [ˌfiːl ˈsɒri fə] Mitleid
haben mit; bedauern III U5, 105
to make sb feel like sth [ˌmeɪk …
ˈfiːl laɪk] jmdm. das Gefühl geben,
etw. zu sein III U2, 43

feeling [ˈfiːlɪŋ] Gefühl <III U4, 87>

foot (sg) [fʊt], **feet** (pl) [fiːt] Fuß I

fell [fel] simple past von to fall I

felt-tip [ˌfelt'tɪp] Filzstift I

felt [felt] simple past von to feel II

female [ˈfiːmeɪl] weiblich <III U1, 24>

ferry [ˈferi] Fähre <III U5, 207>

a **few** [ə ˈfjuː] ein paar; wenige;
einige III U3, 58

science **fiction** [ˌsaɪəns ˈfɪkʃn] Science-
Fiction I

fifteen [ˌfɪfˈtiːn] fünfzehn I

fifty [ˈfɪfti] fünfzig I

fight [faɪt] Kampf; Streit III U2, 50

***to fight** [faɪt] kämpfen; (sich) strei-
ten III U3, 52

fighting [ˈfaɪtɪŋ] Kämpfen; Kämpfe
<III U4, 132>

file [faɪl] Datei II

to fill [fɪl] (sich) füllen <III U1, 17>

film [fɪlm] Film I
film corner [ˈfiːlm ˌkɔːnə] Filmecke
<I>
film maker [ˈfɪlm ˌmeɪkə] Filmemacher; Filmemacherin <III U5, 107>

to film [fɪlm] filmen; drehen
<III U1, 26>

finally [ˈfaɪnli] schließlich; zum
Schluss II

financial crisis [faɪˌnænʃl ˈkraɪsɪs]
Wirtschaftskrise <III U5, 135>

***to find** [faɪnd] finden; herausfin-
den I
to find out [ˌfaɪndˈaʊt] herausfinden I
I can't find … [aɪ kaːnt ˈfaɪnd] ich
kann … nicht finden I

fine [faɪn] gut; in Ordnung; schön II
I'm fine. [aɪm ˈfaɪn] Mir geht es
gut. II

finger [ˈfɪŋə] Finger III U2, 39

fingerprint [ˈfɪŋəprɪnt] Fingerabdruck II

to finish [ˈfɪnɪʃ] beenden; enden;
aufhören; fertigstellen; vervollständigen II

fire [faɪə] Feuer II
fire engine [ˈfaɪərˌendʒɪn] Feuerwehrauto II

first [fɜːst] zuerst; als Erstes; erste I
first name [ˌfɜːst ˈneɪm] Vorname
<III U1, 127>
the first time [ðə ˌfɜːst ˈtaɪm] das
erste Mal I

fish (sg) [fɪʃ], **fish** (pl) [fɪʃ] Fisch I
fish and chips [ˌfɪʃ ən ˈtʃɪps] Pom-
mes mit Fisch I

to fit [fɪt] passen II

fit [fɪt] fit; in Form III U2, 34

five [faɪv] fünf I

flag [flæg] Flagge; Fahne II

flamingo [fləˈmɪŋgəʊ] Flamingo I

flare [fleə] Leuchtsignal; Leuchtfa-
ckel <III U5, 101>

flat [flæt] Wohnung I
holiday flat [ˈhɒlədeɪ ˌflæt] Ferienwohnung <III U3, 194>

flat

flavour ['fleɪvə] Geschmack; Geschmacksrichtung; Sorte <III U4, 200>

flew [fluː] simple past von *to fly* II

flip flop ['flɪp flɒp] Flipflop <III U2, 44>

floor [flɔː] Stockwerk II; <III U1, 30>

flour [flaʊə] Mehl I

flower ['flaʊə] Blume III U5, 104

flown [fləʊn] past participle von *to fly* II

fluent ['fluːənt] fließend; flüssig III U2, 33

*to **fly** [flaɪ] fliegen II; wehen <III U1, 30>

flyer ['flaɪə] Flyer; Faltblatt II

flying ['flaɪɪŋ] Fliegen <III U1, 30>

foggy ['fɒgi] neblig I

to **follow** ['fɒləʊ] befolgen; folgen III U5, 102

food [fuːd] Essen; Lebensmittel I
food stall ['fuːd ˌstɔːl] Essensstand II

foot *(sg)* [fʊt], **feet** *(pl)* [fiːt] Fuß I
to go on foot [ˌgəʊ ˌɒn ˈfʊt] zu Fuß gehen I

football ['fʊtbɔːl] Fußball I
association football ['əsəʊsieɪʃn ˌfʊtbɔːl] Assoziationsfußball *(offizieller Name von Fußball)* <III U1, 24>
football association ['fʊtbɔːl ˌəsəʊsieɪʃn] Fußballverband <III U1, 24>

for [fɔː; fə] lang <III U5, 134>
for example [fər ˌɪgˈzɑːmpl] zum Beispiel <III U1, 24>
for five months [fə ˌfaɪv ˈmʌnθs] fünf Monate lang
for fun [fə ˈfʌn] zum Spaß III U2, 43
for service [fə ˈsɜːvɪs] um bedient zu werden <III U4, 86>

for [fɔː] für I; seit <III U2, 129>

foreground ['fɔːgraʊnd] Vordergrund III U4, 92
in the foreground [ɪn ðə ˈfɔːgraʊnd] im Vordergrund III U4, 92

to **foretell** [fɔːˈtel] vorhersagen III U5, 105

forever [fəˈrevə] für immer; ewig II

*to **forget** [fəˈget] vergessen I

forgot [fəˈgɒt] simple past von *to forget* II

forgotten [fəˈgɒtn] past participle von *to forget* II

fork [fɔːk] Gabel II

form [fɔːm] Form <III U5, 98>
entry form ['entri ˌfɔːm] Anmeldeformular II

forty ['fɔːti] vierzig I

fought [fɔːt] simple past, past participle von *to fight* III U3, 52

found [faʊnd] simple past von *to find* II

four [fɔː] vier I

fourteen [ˌfɔːˈtiːn] vierzehn I

fourth [fɔːθ] vierte I

free [friː] kostenlos III U4, 75
free range [ˌfriː ˈreɪndʒ] Freiland- II
free time [ˌfriː ˈtaɪm] Freizeit I

*to **freeze** [friːz] frieren; gefrieren III U3, 58

freeze frame ['friːz ˌfreɪm] Standbild <II>

French [frentʃ] Französisch I

French [frenʃ] französisch <III U1, 130>

fresh [freʃ] frisch II

Friday ['fraɪdeɪ] Freitag I

fridge [frɪdʒ] Kühlschrank III U5, 96

deep **fried** [ˌdiːpˈfraɪd] frittiert; in Fett ausgebacken <III U3, 66>

fried [fraɪd] (in der Pfanne) gebraten II

friend [frend] Freund; Freundin I
to make friends [ˌmeɪk ˈfrendz] Freundschaften schließen I

friendly ['frendli] freundlich; nett III U2, 35

frisbee ['frɪzbi] Frisbeescheibe I

from [frɒm] aus; von I
I'm from … ['aɪm ˌfrɒm] ich komme aus … I
Where are you from? [ˌweər ə ju ˈfrɒm] Woher kommst du? I

in **front of** [ɪn ˈfrʌnt ˌəv] vor; davor <III U4, 93>

froze [frəʊz] simple past von *to freeze* III U3, 58

frozen ['frəʊzn] past participle von *to freeze* III U3, 58

fruit [fruːt] Frucht; Obst I

to **fry** [fraɪ] frittieren <III U3, 66>

full service [ˌfʊl ˈsɜːvɪs] Komplettservice <III U3, 68>

fun [fʌn] Freude; Spaß I
for fun [fə ˈfʌn] zum Spaß III U2, 43

fundraising ['fʌndˌreɪzɪŋ] Spendenaktionen <III U2, 128>

funny ['fʌni] merkwürdig; komisch; lustig; witzig I

furious ['fjʊəriəs] wütend III U4, 77

future ['fjuːtʃə] Zukunft <II>

G

game [geɪm] Spiel I
computer game [ˌkəmˈpjuːtə geɪm] Computerspiel I

gamer ['geɪmə] Spieler *(Computer)*; Spielerin *(Computer)* II

garage ['gærɑːʒ] Werkstatt; Tankstelle <III U3, 68>

garden ['gɑːdn] Garten I

garlic ['gɑːlɪk] Knoblauch II

gas [gæs] Gas III U1, 20

gave [geɪv] simple past von *to give* II

gel [dʒel] Gel III U5, 97
hair gel ['heə ˌdʒel] Haargel III U5, 97
shower gel ['ʃaʊə ˌdʒel] Duschgel III U5, 97

gently ['dʒentli] sanft <III U4, 86>

geocaching ['dʒiːəʊkæʃɪŋ] Geocaching *(eine Art elektronische Schatzsuche)* I

Geography [dʒiˈɒgrəfi] Geografie; Erdkunde I

German ['dʒɜːmən] Deutsch I

German ['dʒɜːmən] deutsch; aus Deutschland III U5, 98

*to **get** [get] bekommen I; verstehen III U4, 80

to get a job wrong [ˌget ə dʒɒb ˈrɒŋ] einen Auftrag vermasseln III U2, 50

to get around [ˌget əˈraʊnd] herumkommen III U5, 100

to get back [ˌget ˈbæk] zurückkommen <III U2, 128>

to get cold [ˌget ˈkəʊld] frieren III U3, 60

to get dressed [ˌget ˈdrest] sich anziehen II

to get in [ˈget ˌɪn] hereinkommen I

to get into trouble [ˌget ˌɪntə ˈtrʌbl] in Schwierigkeiten geraten <III U2, 128>

to get married [ˌget ˈmærɪd] heiraten II

to get off [ˌget ˈɒf] aussteigen II

to get out [ˌget ˈaʊt] herauskommen III U1, 22

to get ready [ˌget ˈredi] sich vorbereiten; sich fertig machen <III U1, 27>; <III U2, 44>

to get to [ˈget tə] hinkommen zu; gelangen <III U2, 128>

to get to know [ˌget tə ˈnəʊ] kennen lernen II

to get up [ˌget ˈʌp] aufstehen I

ghost [ɡəʊst] Geist II

giant [dʒaɪənt] Riese III U4, 75

giraffe [dʒɪˈrɑːf] Giraffe I

girl [ɡɜːl] Mädchen I

*to **give** [ɡɪv] geben I

to give a talk [ɡɪv ə ˈtɔːk] einen Vortrag halten <III U1, 19>

to give reasons [ɡɪv ˈriːznz] Gründe nennen; Gründe angeben III U2, 51

to give sth a miss [ɡɪv sʌmθɪŋ ə ˈmɪs] auf etw. verzichten; etw. bleiben lassen III U2, 50

to give up [ɡɪv ˈʌp] aufgeben III U3, 63

glad [ɡlæd] froh II

glass [ɡlɑːs] Glas II

glove [ɡlʌv] Handschuh <III U2, 44>

to **glow** [ɡləʊ] leuchten <III U5, 101>

glue [ɡluː] Klebstoff I

*to **go** [ɡəʊ] gehen; fahren I

to go beach combing [ɡəʊ ˈbiːtʃ ˌkəʊmɪŋ] den Strand nach Strandgut absuchen II

to go by (train) [ˌɡəʊ baɪ (ˈtreɪn)] mit (dem Zug) fahren I

to go camping [ɡəʊ ˈkæmpɪŋ] campen gehen; zelten II

to go for a walk [ɡəʊ fər ə ˈwɔːk] spazieren gehen I

to go on foot [ˌɡəʊ ɒn ˈfʊt] zu Fuß gehen I

to go shopping [ɡəʊ ˈʃɒpɪŋ] einkaufen gehen II

to go sightseeing [ɡəʊ ˈsaɪtsiːɪŋ] eine Besichtigungstour machen II

to go swimming [ɡəʊ ˈswɪmɪŋ] schwimmen gehen I

to go to bed [ɡəʊ tə ˈbed] ins Bett gehen I

goat [ɡəʊt] Ziege III U1, 16

goggles *(pl)* [ˈɡɒɡlz] Schutzbrille <III U2, 44>

gold [ɡəʊld] Gold III U5, 104

gold [ɡəʊld] golden; Gold- III U5, 104

gone [ɡɒn] past participle von *to go* II

gonna (= going to) [ˈɡɒnə] werden III U4, 77

good [ɡʊd] gut I

to be good at [bi ˈɡʊd ˌət] gut sein in; gut sein bei I

Good morning. [ˌɡʊd ˈmɔːnɪŋ] Guten Morgen. II

good luck [ˌɡʊd ˈlʌk] viel Glück II

Goodbye. [ɡʊdˈbaɪ] Auf Wiedersehen. I

gooey [ˈɡuːi] zähflüssig <III U3, 66>

got [ɡɒt] simple past von *to get* I

GPS *(Global Positioning System)* [ˌdʒiːpiːˈes] GPS *(ein satellitengestütztes System zur weltweiten Positionsbestimmung)* I

gr8 (great) [ɡreɪt] großartig; toll II

to **grab** [ɡræb] schnappen; greifen; ergreifen III U5, 105

grammar [ˈɡræmə] Grammatik <I>

grandad [ˈɡrændæd] Opa III U4, 75

great-great-grandad [ɡreɪt ɡreɪt ˈɡrændæd] Ururopa I

grandfather [ˈɡrænˌfɑːðə] Großvater II

grandma [ˈɡrænmɑː] Oma II

grandmother [ˈɡrænˌmʌðə] Großmutter II

grandparents *(pl)* [ˈɡrænˌpeərənts] Großeltern II

grave [ɡreɪv] Grab III U1, 11

great [ɡreɪt] großartig; toll I; groß; riesig <III U5, 135>

green [ɡriːn] grün I

greengrocer's [ˈɡriːnˌɡrəʊsəz] Obst- und Gemüseladen III U1, 13

grew [ɡruː] simple past von *to grow* <III U5, 135>

grew up [ˌɡruːˈʌp] simple past von *to grow up* III U3, 54

grey [ɡreɪ] grau I

ground [ɡraʊnd] Boden; Erdboden III U3, 64

group [ɡruːp] Gruppe I

group skills [ˈɡruːp ˌskɪlz] Fertigkeit Kooperatives Lernen <I>

tutor group [ˈtjuːtə ˌɡruːp] Klasse I

*to **grow** [ɡrəʊ] wachsen <III U5, 135>

to grow up [ɡrəʊ ˈʌp] aufwachsen III U3, 54

grown up [ˌɡrəʊn ˈʌp] past participle von *to grow up* III U3, 54

to **guess** [ɡes] erraten; raten; überlegen II

Guess what? [ɡes ˈwɒt] Weißt du was? I

guest [ɡest] Gast III U2, 33

guinea pig [ˈɡɪni ˌpɪɡ] Meerschweinchen II

guitar [ɡɪˈtɑː] Gitarre III U5, 95

guys [ɡaɪz] Leute II

gymnasium [dʒɪmˈneɪziəm] Fitnessraum III U4, 84

gymnasium

H

had [hæd] simple past von *to have* I; past participle von *to have* II

had to ['hæd tə] simple past von *to have to* II

haggis ['hægɪs] Haggis *(schottisches Gericht aus Schafsinnereien)* III U3, 60

hair gel ['heə ˌdʒel] Haargel III U5, 97

hair [heə] Haar; Haare III U5, 98
hair straightener ['heə ˌstreɪtnə] Haarglätter I

hairbrush ['heəbrʌʃ] Haarbürste III U5, 97

haircut ['heəkʌt] Haarschnitt II
to have a haircut ['heəkʌt] sich die Haare schneiden lassen II

hairdresser ['heəˌdresə] Friseur; Friseurin II

hairdryer ['heəˌdraɪə] Fön III U5, 97

half *(sg)* [hɑːf], **halves** *(pl)* [hɑːvz] (die) Hälfte III U4, 84

half past (two) [ˌhɑːf 'pɑːst] halb (drei) I

half [hɑːf] halb III U1, 16
half a million [ˌhɑːf ə 'mɪljən] eine halbe Million III U1, 16

Halloween [ˌhæləʊ'iːn] Halloween I

ham [hæm] Schinken II

hammer throw ['hæmə ˌθrəʊ] Hammerwurf <III U3, 131>

hand [hænd] Hand III U2, 40

handball ['hændbɔːl] Handball <III U2, 186>

*to **hang** [hæŋ] hängen II

to **happen** ['hæpn] geschehen; passieren II

happy ['hæpi] glücklich; froh I
Happy birthday! [ˌhæpi 'bɜːθdeɪ] Alles Gute zum Geburtstag! I

harbour ['hɑːbə] Hafen II

hard [hɑːd] hart; schwer; schwierig II

hat [hæt] Hut II

to **hate** [heɪt] hassen; nicht mögen III U4, 76

*to **have** [hæv] haben; besitzen I

to have a haircut ['heəkʌt] sich die Haare schneiden lassen II
to have a look [ˌhæv ə 'lʊk] anschauen II
to have breakfast [ˌhæv 'brekfəst] frühstücken I
to have to ['hæv tə] müssen II
have you got [ˌhæv ju: 'gɒt] hast du II
Have you ever been to …? [hæv ju ˌevə 'biːn tə] Warst du schon in …? II
Have you finished yet? [ˌhæv ju: 'fɪnɪʃt jet] Seid ihr schon fertig? II

he [hiː] er I

head [hed] Kopf II
head chef ['hed ˌʃef] Chefkoch II
head first ['hed fɜːst] kopfüber III U1, 18

headache ['hedeɪk] Kopfschmerzen; Kopfweh II

heading ['hedɪŋ] Überschrift; Titel <III U1, 22>

headline ['hedlaɪn] Schlagzeile <III U4, 79>

headteacher [ˌhed'tiːtʃə] Schulleiter; Schulleiterin <III U4, 88>

*to **hear** [hɪə] hören I

heard [hɜːd] simple past von *to hear* I; past participle von *to hear* II

heart [hɑːt] Herz <III U3, 66>

heavy ['hevi] schwer; stark II

height [haɪt] Höhe II

held [held] simple past, past participle von *to hold* III U2, 43

helicopter ['helɪkɒptə] Helikopter; Hubschrauber I

Hello. [hə'ləʊ] Hallo. I

helm [helm] Steuermann <III U2, 129>

helmet ['helmət] Helm I

help [help] Hilfe II

to **help** [help] helfen I
to help oneself [ˌhelp wʌn'self] sich bedienen III U5, 96
Help yourselves! [ˌhelp jɔː'selvz] Bedient euch!; Bedienen Sie sich! II

How can I help you? [ˌhaʊ kæn aɪ 'help ˌjuː] Was kann ich für dich tun? I
I couldn't help but … [ˌaɪ kʊdnt 'help bʌt] Ich konnte nicht anders als … III U5, 105

her [hɜː] ihr I

here [hɪə] hier I
Here you are. [ˌhɪə ju ˌɑː] Bitte schön. I
Here's your change. [ˌhɪəz jɔː 'tʃeɪndʒ] Hier ist dein Wechselgeld. I

hero *(sg)* ['hɪərəʊ], **heroes** *(pl)* ['hɪərəʊz] Held III U3, 64

hers [hɜːz] ihre II

herself [hɜː'self] sie selbst; sich selbst III U2, 152

Hi. [haɪ] Hi.; Hallo. I
Say hi to … [seɪ 'haɪ tə] Grüße … von mir. I

hid [hɪd] simple past von *to hide* III U2, 50

hidden ['hɪdn] past participle von *to hide* III U2, 50

*to **hide** [haɪd] (sich) verstecken III U2, 50

high [haɪ] hoch; groß I
high jump ['haɪ ˌdʒʌmp] Hochsprung <III U2, 186>
high school ['haɪ ˌskuːl] High School *(weiterführende Schule, Oberstufe)* <III U2, 129>

highlight ['haɪlaɪt] Highlight; Höhepunkt <III U5, 134>

highlighted ['haɪlaɪtɪd] markiert <III U1, 31>

to **hike** [haɪk] wandern II

hiking ['haɪkɪŋ] Wandern III U3, 58

him [hɪm] ihn; ihm I

himself [hɪm'self] er selbst; sich (selbst) III U2, 34

hip hop ['hɪphɒp] Hip-Hop *(Musik)* III U5, 95

his [hɪz] sein I; seins; seiner II

History ['hɪstri] Geschichte I

history ['hɪstri] Geschichte III U1, 12

hit [hɪt] Hit; Treffer <III U3, 73>

*to **hit** [hɪt] treffen; schlagen II; (sich) stoßen; anstoßen III U2, 40; gegen etw. fahren III U4, 84

hit [hɪt] simple past, past participle von *to hit* II

hobby ['hɒbi] Hobby III ZI 9

*to **hold** [həʊld] halten; festhalten III U2, 43

hole [həʊl] Loch I

holiday ['hɒlədeɪ] Ferien; Urlaub II

  holiday cottage ['hɒlədeɪ ˌkɒtɪdʒ] Ferienhäuschen <III U3, 194>

  holiday flat ['hɒlədeɪ ˌflæt] Ferienwohnung <III U3, 194>

home [həʊm] Zuhause; Heim I

  at home [ət 'həʊm] zu Hause I

  back home [bæk 'həʊm] zu Hause II

*to be **homesick** [bi: 'həʊmsɪk] Heimweh haben III U5, 104

*to do **homework** [ˌduː 'həʊmwɜːk] Hausaufgabe(n) machen I

honey ['hʌni] Honig <III U4, 200>

hood [hʊd] Kapuze <III U1, 17>

Hooray! [hʊ'reɪ] Hurra! III U3, 65

to **hoover** ['huːvə] staubsaugen II

to **hope** [həʊp] hoffen II

hopeful ['həʊpfl] hoffnungsvoll III U4, 77

horrible ['hɒrəbl] schrecklich; furchtbar III U4, 77

chamber of **horrors** [ˌtʃeɪmbər ˌəv 'hɒrəz] Kammer des Schreckens <III U1, 30>

horse [hɔːs] Pferd I

  horse riding ['hɔːs ˌraɪdɪŋ] Reiten I

hospital ['hɒspɪtl] Krankenhaus I

host family ['həʊst ˌfæmli] Gastfamilie <III U5, 99>

hostel ['hɒstl] Herberge III U3, 59

hot [hɒt] heiß I

  hot air balloon [ˌhɒt ˌeə bə'luːn] Heißluftballon <III U2, 44>

hotel [həʊ'tel] Hotel II

40 kilometres an **hour** [kɪ'lɒmiːtəz ən ˌaʊə] 40 Kilometer pro Stunde I

house [haʊs] Haus I

around the house [əˌraʊnd ðə 'haʊs] zu Hause I

tree house ['triː ˌhaʊs] Baumhaus I

how [haʊ] wie I

  How are you? [ˌhaʊ 'ɑː jə] Wie geht es dir? I

  How can I help you? [ˌhaʊ kæn aɪ 'help ju:] Was kann ich für dich tun? I

  How do I get there? [ˌhaʊ du aɪ 'get ðeə] Wie komme ich dahin? III U1, 12

  how many [ˌhaʊ 'meni] wie viele II

  How much (is/are) …? [ˌhaʊ 'mʌtʃ ɪz/ɑː] Wie viel (kostet/kosten) …? I

  How old are you? [haʊ ˌ'əʊld ə ju:] Wie alt bist du? I

  How to … ['haʊ tə] Wie man … II

however [haʊ'evə] jedoch III U4, 85

huge [hjuːdʒ] riesig; riesengroß III U1, 17; gewaltig <III U3, 72>

a/one **hundred** ['hʌndrəd] einhundert; hundert I

hung [hʌŋ] simple past von *to hang* II

hungry ['hʌŋgri] hungrig I

to **hurry** ['hʌri] sich beeilen III U2, 38

*to **hurt** [hɜːt] weh tun; verletzen II

hurt [hɜːt] simple past, past participle von *to hurt* II

I

I [aɪ] ich I

  I can't wait [aɪ ˌkɑːnt 'weɪt] ich kann es kaum erwarten III U5, 100

  I don't know! [aɪ dəʊnt 'nəʊ] Ich weiß (es) nicht! I

  I don't like [aɪ ˌdəʊnt 'laɪk] ich mag nicht; gefällt mir nicht I

  I like [aɪ 'laɪk] ich mag; gefällt mir I

  I spy with my little eye … [aɪ spaɪ wɪð ˌmaɪ lɪtl 'aɪ] Ich sehe was, was du nicht siehst … I

  I wouldn't like (to) … [aɪ 'wʊdnt laɪk (tə)] ich möchte nicht …; ich würde nicht gerne … I

  I'd like (to) … (= I would like to) [aɪd 'laɪk (tə)] ich möchte …; ich würde gerne … I

  I'd rather [aɪd 'rɑːðə] ich würde lieber III U1, 25

  I'm fine. [aɪm 'faɪn] Mir geht es gut. II

  I'm from … ['aɪm ˌfrɒm] ich komme aus … I

  I've (I have) got [aɪv 'gɒt] ich habe II

ice skating ['aɪs ˌskeɪtɪŋ] Schlittschuhlaufen <III U2, 186>

  ice cream [aɪs 'kriːm] Eiscreme; Eis II

iceberg ['aɪsbɜːg] Eisberg III U4, 84

ID [aɪ'diː] Ausweis; Personalausweis III U5, 97

idea [aɪ'dɪə] Idee I

  Any idea? [ˌeni 'aɪdɪə] Irgendeine Idee? I

identity card [aɪ'dentəti ˌkɑːd] Ausweis; Personalausweis <III U5, 206>

if [ɪf] wenn II

ill [ɪl] krank; schlecht II

important [ɪm'pɔːtnt] wichtig; einflussreich III U2, 33

impossible [ɪm'pɒsəbl] unmöglich III U3, 62

to **impress** [ɪm'pres] beeindrucken III U5, 107

in [ɪn] in; im I

  in August [ɪn 'ɔːgəst] im August I

  in front of [ɪn 'frʌnt ˌəv] vor; davor <III U4, 93>

  in need [ɪn 'niːd] bedürftig; in Not <III U4, 77>

  in the background [ɪn ðə 'bækgraʊnd] im Hintergrund III U4, 92

  in the foreground [ɪn ðə 'fɔːgraʊnd] im Vordergrund III U4, 92

  in the middle [ɪn ðə 'mɪdl] in der Mitte III U4, 92

  in vain [ɪn 'veɪn] umsonst; vergeblich <III U5, 101>

in

include

in the centre of [ɪn ðə 'sentər‿əv] in der Mitte von III U1, 16

in the end [ɪn ði 'end] schließlich; zum Schluss II

in the evenings [ɪn ði 'iːvnɪŋz] abends III U4, 76

in the south of [ɪn ðə 'saʊθ‿əv] im Süden von III U1, 10

in the world [ɪn ðə 'wɜːld] auf der Welt II

to include [ɪn'kluːd] enthalten <III U3, 66>

Indian ['ɪndiən] indisch II

indoor [ˌɪn'dɔː] Hallen-; Innen- III U2, 34

Industrial Revolution [ɪnˌdʌstriəl revlˈuːʃn] industrielle Revolution III U1, 11

industry ['ɪndəstri] Industrie III U1, 11

information desk [ɪnfə'meɪʃn ˌdesk] Information II

informative [ɪn'fɔːmətɪv] informativ <III U1, 27>

ingredient [ɪn'griːdiənt] Zutat II

inhabitant [ɪn'hæbɪtnt] Einwohner; Einwohnerin; Bewohner; Bewohnerin III U1, 16

injection [ɪn'dʒekʃn] Spritze III U2, 39

insect ['ɪnsekt] Insekt III U3, 58

inside [ˌɪn'saɪd] in … hinein II

inside [ˌɪn'saɪd] in; innen in; im Innern III U1, 31

institution [ˌɪnstɪ'tjuːʃn] Einrichtung; Organisation; Institution <III U2, 128>

instructor [ɪn'strʌktə] Lehrer; Lehrerin III U2, 35

intelligent [ɪn'telɪdʒnt] intelligent; klug; vernünftig III U4, 77

*to be interested in [bi: 'ɪntrəstɪd ɪn] sich interessieren für; interessiert sein an III U1, 12

interesting ['ɪntrəstɪŋ] interessant I

internet ['ɪntənet] Internet II

to surf the internet [ˌsɜːf ði 'ɪntənet] im Internet surfen II

interview ['ɪntəvjuː] Interview; Befragung II

to interview ['ɪntəvjuː] interviewen; befragen I

into ['ɪntə] in; drin <III U1, 17>

introduction [ˌɪntrə'dʌkʃn] Einleitung; Einführung III U2, 50

to invade [ɪn'veɪd] einmarschieren (in); eindringen (in) III U1, 11

to invent [ɪn'vent] erfinden III U3, 54

invention [ɪn'venʃn] Erfindung III U3, 54

inventor [ɪn'ventə] Erfinder; Erfinderin III U3, 52

invitation [ˌɪnvɪ'teɪʃn] Einladung I

to invite [ɪn'vaɪt] einladen I

Irish ['aɪrɪʃ] irisch; Irisch III U5, 94

is [ɪz] ist I

… is 99p [ɪz ˌnaɪntinaɪn 'pens] … kostet 99 Pence I

is something wrong [ɪz 'sʌmθɪŋ rɒŋ] stimmt etwas nicht II

island ['aɪlənd] Insel II

isn't it? ['ɪznt‿ɪt] nicht wahr?; stimmt's? II

it [ɪt] es I

it isn't up to you [ɪt‿ˌɪznt‿ʌp tə 'juː] es ist nicht deine Sache <III U1, 17>

It was my fault. [ɪt wəz ˌmaɪ 'fɔːlt] Es war meine Schuld. II

It's me! [ɪts 'miː] Ich bin es! I

It's time to go. [ɪts ˌtaɪm tə 'gəʊ] Es ist Zeit zu gehen. I

IT (Information Technology) [ˌaɪ'tiː] Informatik; Informationstechnik I

its [ɪts] sein; ihr III U3, 52

itself [ɪt'self] (sich) selbst III U2, 152

J

jacket ['dʒækɪt] Jacke II

jacket potato [ˌdʒækɪt pə'teɪtəʊ] Ofenkartoffel II

jam [dʒæm] Marmelade; Konfitüre III U4, 80

Jamaican [dʒə'meɪkən] jamaikanisch II

January ['dʒænjuri] Januar I

jar [dʒaː] Glas III U4, 80

javelin ['dʒævlɪn] Speerwerfen <III U2, 186>

jealous ['dʒeləs] eifersüchtig; neidisch II

jeans (pl) [dʒiːnz] Jeans I

jerk [dʒɜːk] *in Gewürzen mariniertes und über Holzfeuer gegrilltes Essen* II

jeweller's ['dʒuːələz] Juwelierladen III U1, 13

jewellery ['dʒuːəlri] Schmuck II

job [dʒɒb] Job; Aufgabe; Tätigkeit; Arbeit; Beruf II

jogging ['dʒɒgɪŋ] Joggen <III U2, 186>

to join [dʒɔɪn] Mitglied werden in <III U2, 129>; sich anschließen III U5, 96

joke [dʒəʊk] Witz I

journey ['dʒɜːni] Fahrt; Reise III U5, 100

to joust [dʒaʊst] einen Turnierzweikampf austragen; turnieren III U2, 43

jousting ['dʒaʊstɪŋ] Turnierzweikampf III U2, 43

judge [dʒʌdʒ] Juror; Jurorin II

to judge [dʒʌdʒ] beurteilen; bewerten <III U4, 77>

juice [dʒuːs] Saft II

July [dʒʊ'laɪ] Juli I

on 7th July [ɒn ðə ˌsevnθ əv 'dʒʊlaɪ] am 7. Juli I

jumble sale ['dʒʌmbl ˌseɪl] Flohmarkt II

high jump ['haɪ ˌdʒʌmp] Hochsprung <III U2, 186>

long jump ['lɒŋ ˌdʒʌmp] Weitsprung <III U2, 186>

to jump [dʒʌmp] zusammenzucken; erschrecken III U2, 42

June [dʒuːn] Juni I

just [dʒʌst] gerade (eben); soeben; nur II

K

kayak [ˈkaɪæk] Kajak <III U2, 128>

kayaking [ˈkaɪækɪŋ] Kajakfahren
<III U2, 128>

*to keep [kiːp] halten II
to keep cool [ˌkiːp ˈkuːl] Ruhe
bewahren <III U1, 27>
to keep in touch [ˌkiːp ɪn ˈtʌtʃ] in
Verbindung bleiben II
to keep out [ˌkiːp ˈaʊt] draußen
halten III U3, 62

kept [kept] simple past, past participle von *to keep* II

ketchup [ˈketʃʌp] Ketchup II

kid [kɪd] Kind II

to kill [kɪl] töten III U1, 20

7 kilograms a day [ˌkɪləgræmz ə ˈdeɪ]
sieben Kilogramm täglich I

40 kilometres an hour [kɪˈlɒmiːtəz
ən ˈaʊə] 40 Kilometer pro Stunde I

kilt [kɪlt] Schottenrock; Kilt III U3, 53

king [kɪŋ] König III U1, 11

kiss [kɪs] Kuss II

kitchen [ˈkɪtʃin] Küche I

knee [niː] Knie III U2, 39

knife *(sg)* [naɪf], **knives** *(pl)* [naɪvz]
Messer II

knight [naɪt] Ritter III U2, 42

*to know [nəʊ] kennen; wissen I
to get to know [ˌget tə ˈnəʊ] kennen lernen II
I don't know! [aɪ dəʊnt ˈnəʊ] Ich
weiß (es) nicht! I

L

to label [ˈleɪbl] beschriften <III U2, 43>

lace [leɪs] Schnürsenkel <III U1, 17>

ladder [ˈlædə] Leiter I

laid [leɪd] simple past, past participle von *to lay* II

lake [leɪk] See III U3, 53

lamb [læm] Lamm II

lamp [læmp] Lampe I

land [lænd] Land II

landlord [ˈlændlɔːd] Eigentümer II

language [ˈlæŋgwɪdʒ] Sprache II

language tip [ˌlæŋgwɪdʒ ˈtɪp]
Grammatikhinweis <I>
sign language [ˈsaɪn ˌlæŋgwɪdʒ]
Gebärdensprache; Zeichensprache
III U5, 95

large [lɑːdʒ] groß II

lasagne [ləˈzænjə] Lasagne II

last [lɑːst] letzte I
at last [ət ˈlɑːst] endlich; zu guter
Letzt II

late [leɪt] (zu) spät II

later [ˈleɪtə] später I

to laugh [lɑːf] lachen II
LOL (Laugh out loud!) [ˈlɑːf aʊt
ˌlaʊd] Laut lachen! II

laundry basket [ˈlɔːndri ˌbɑːskɪt]
Wäschekorb <III U4, 86>

*to lay [leɪ] decken; legen II
to lay the table [ˌleɪ ðə ˈteɪbl] den
Tisch decken II

*to lead [liːd] anführen; leiten
<III U2, 129>

leader [ˈliːdə] Führer; Führerin;
Anführer; Anführerin III U3, 65

to learn [lɜːn] lernen II
to learn about sth [ˌlɜːn əˈbaʊt]
etwas erfahren über III U1, 12

leather [ˈleðə] Leder III U3, 55

leave [liːv] abfahren; verlassen;
lassen II

leaving [ˈliːvɪŋ] Abschieds- II

left [left] simple past, past participle
von *to leave* II

left [left] links III U1, 12
to turn left (into …) [ˌtɜːn ˈleft]
(nach) links abbiegen I
on the left [ɒn ðə ˈleft] auf der
linken Seite; links I

leg [leg] Bein II

legend [ˈledʒənd] Legende; Sage
<III U3, 130>

lemon [ˈlemən] Zitrone II

lemonade [ˌleməˈneɪd] Limonade II

*to lend [lend] leihen; verleihen II

lent [lent] simple past von *to lend* II

less [les] weniger III U4, 80

lesson [ˈlesn] Schulstunde; Unterricht I

*to let go [ˌlet ˈgəʊ] loslassen
<III U3, 131>
let us [ˈlet ʌs] lass(t) uns <III U2, 44>
let's (= let us) [lets] lass(t) uns I

letter [ˈletə] Buchstabe; Brief III U4, 80

lettuce [ˈletɪs] Kopfsalat II

library [ˈlaɪbri] Bibliothek; Bücherei
III U1, 15

life *(sg)* [laɪf], **lives** *(pl)* [laɪvz] Leben I
school **life** [ˈskuːˌlaɪf] Schulalltag <I>

lifeboat [ˈlaɪfbəʊt] Rettungsboot
III U2, 33

light [laɪt] Licht <III U1, 17>
light bulb [ˈlaɪt ˌbʌlb] Glühbirne
III U3, 57
traffic light [ˈtræfɪk ˌlaɪt]
(Verkehrs-)Ampel <III U1, 178>

*to light up [ˌlaɪt ˈʌp] (sich) erhellen;
anzünden <III U5, 101>

light [laɪt] leicht; hell <III U3, 193>

to like [laɪk] mögen; gern haben I
would like [wʊd ˈlaɪk] würde(n)
gern; hätte(n) gern II
I don't like [aɪ ˌdəʊnt ˈlaɪk] ich mag
nicht; gefällt mir nicht I
I like [aɪ ˈlaɪk] ich mag; gefällt mir I
I wouldn't like (to) … [aɪ ˈwʊdnt
laɪk (tə)] ich möchte nicht …; ich
würde nicht gerne … I
I'd like (to) … (= I would like to)
[aɪd ˈlaɪk (tə)] ich möchte …; ich
würde gerne … I
Would you like (to)…? [ˌwʊd jə
ˈlaɪk (tə)] Möchtest du? I

like [laɪk] wie II
like that [laɪk ˈðæt] so I
like this [laɪk ˈðɪs] so; auf diese
Weise III U3, 62
What must you be like? [wɒt ˌmʌst
ju ˈbiː laɪk] Wie musst du sein?
III U2, 37

line [laɪn] Zeile <I>; Linie III U5, 100

lines [laɪnz] Text II

lion [ˈlaɪən] Löwe I

list [lɪst] Liste II
shopping list [ˈʃɒpɪŋ ˌlɪst] Einkaufszettel I

list

to **listen** (to) ['lɪsn (tə)] hören; anhören; zuhören I

listening ['lɪsnɪŋ] Hörverstehen <I>
listening skills ['lɪsnɪŋ ˌskɪlz] Fertigkeit Hören <I>

little ['lɪtl] klein II
a little [ə 'lɪtl] ein bisschen II

to **live** [lɪv] wohnen; leben I

liver ['lɪvə] Leber <III U3, 66>

living room ['lɪvɪŋ ˌrʊm] Wohnzimmer I

loaf *(sg)* [ləʊf], **loaves** *(pl)* [ləʊvz] Brotlaib III U4, 80

local ['ləʊkl] hiesig; örtlich; lokal III U3, 58

location [ləʊ'keɪʃn] Drehort; Lage III U2, 50

LOL (Laugh out loud!) ['lɑːf aʊt ˌlaʊd] Laut lachen! II

lonely ['ləʊnli] einsam III U4, 76

long [lɒŋ] lang I
long jump ['lɒŋ ˌdʒʌmp] Weitsprung <III U2, 186>

*to **have** a **look** [ˌhæv ə 'lʊk] anschauen II

to **look** [lʊk] (nach)schauen I; aussehen; sehen II
to look after [lʊk ˌ'ɑːftə] aufpassen; hüten II
to look at ['lʊk ˌət] anschauen I
to look for ['lʊk ˌfə] suchen I
Well, look … [wel 'lʊk] Na ja, schau mal … nach. I

lookout point ['lʊkaʊt ˌpɔɪnt] Aussichtspunkt II

loose [luːs] locker; lose II

lorry driver ['lɒri ˌdraɪvə] LKW-Fahrer; LKW-Fahrerin II

*to **lose** [luːz] verlieren II

lost [lɒst] simple past von *to lose* II; past participle von *to lose* III U3, 62

a **lot** [ə'lɒt] viel I; sehr II
a lot of [ə 'lɒt ˌəv] eine Menge; viel I; viel; eine Menge III U1, 16

body **lotion** ['bɒdi ˌləʊʃn] Körperlotion III U5, 97

lots [lɒts] viel; jede Menge III U2, 43
lots of ['lɒts ˌəv] viel; jede Menge I

loud [laʊd] laut III U2, 35

*to **fall** in **love** (with) [ˌfɔːl ɪn 'lʌv] sich verlieben (in) III U2, 50

to **love** [lʌv] lieben; gern mögen I

lovely ['lʌvli] schön; herrlich; hübsch II

low [ləʊ] niedrig II

lower ['ləʊə] untere III U4, 92

*to **be** lucky [bi: 'lʌki] Glück haben <III U3, 72>
lucky day [ˌlʌki 'deɪ] Glückstag II

luminous ['luːmɪnəs] leuchtend <III U5, 101>

lunch [lʌnʃ] Mittagessen I
packed lunch [ˌpækt 'lʌnʃ] Lunchpaket; Vesper II

lunchtime ['lʌnʃtaɪm] Mittagszeit; Mittagspause I

lung [lʌŋ] Lunge <III U3, 66>

lyrics ['lɪrɪks] Liedtext <II>

M

machine [mə'ʃiːn] Automat; Maschine II
payment machine ['peɪmənt ˌməʃiːn] Bezahlautomat II

made [meɪd] past participle von *to make* II
to be made of [bi: 'meɪd ˌəv] hergestellt sein aus III U3, 54

magazine [ˌmægə'ziːn] Zeitschrift I

magic ['mædʒɪk] Magie; Zauberei II

magical ['mædʒɪkl] zauberhaft; magisch <III U3, 68>

main [meɪn] Haupt- <III U4, 88>
main course [ˌmeɪn 'kɔːs] Hauptgericht II

*to **make** [meɪk] erstellen; machen; tun I
to make a reservation [ˌmeɪk ə ˌrezə'veɪʃn] reservieren III U3, 59
to make friends [ˌmeɪk 'frendz] Freundschaften schließen I
to make sb feel like sth [ˌmeɪk … 'fiːl laɪk] jmdm. das Gefühl geben, etw. zu sein III U2, 43

it's **made** with [ˌɪts 'meɪd wɪð] es wird aus gemacht II

film **maker** ['fɪlm ˌmeɪkə] Filmemacher; Filmemacherin <III U5, 107>

mama ['mæmə] Mama II

man *(sg)* [mæn], **men** *(pl)* [men] Mann I

many ['meni] viele II
how many [ˌhaʊ 'meni] wie viele II

map [mæp] Stadtplan; Landkarte I

March [mɑːtʃ] März I

market ['mɑːkɪt] Markt II

*to **get** married [ˌget 'mærɪd] heiraten II

mashed potatoes [ˌmæʃt pə'teɪtəʊz] Kartoffelbrei II

to **match** [mætʃ] zuordnen I

material [mə'tɪəriəl] Material; Stoff <III U3, 55>

Maths [mæθs] Mathe I

It doesn't **matter**. [ɪt ˌdʌznt 'mætə] Es ist egal. II

won't **matter** [ˌwəʊnt 'mætə] wird nicht von Bedeutung sein; wird nichts ausmachen <III U5, 101>

May [meɪ] Mai I

may [meɪ] vielleicht; dürfen; können II

maybe ['meɪbi] vielleicht II

mayonnaise [ˌmeɪə'neɪz] Mayonnaise II

me [miː] ich; mich; mir I
Excuse me. [ɪk'skjuːz mi] Entschuldigung. I
call me ['kɔːl ˌmi] nenne mich I
It's me! [ɪts 'miː] Ich bin es! I

meal [miːl] Essen; Mahlzeit II

*to **mean** [miːn] bedeuten; meinen III U2, 33

meaning ['miːnɪŋ] Bedeutung; Sinn <III U3, 73>

meant [ment] simple past, past participle von *to mean* III U2, 33

meat [miːt] Fleisch I

mechanic [mə'kænɪk] Mechaniker; Mechanikerin <III U3, 68>

mediation [ˌmiː'di'eɪʃn] Sprachmittlung <I>

mediation skills [ˌmiːdiˈeɪʃn ˌskɪlz] Fertigkeit Sprachmitteln <I>

medicine [ˈmedsn] Medikamente; Medizin III U2, 39

*to **meet** [miːt] kennen lernen I; (sich) treffen II

meeting [ˈmiːtɪŋ] Treffen; Treff- <III U1, 30>

meeting point [ˈmiːtɪŋ ˌpɔɪnt] Treffpunkt <III U1, 30>

member [ˈmembə] Mitglied <III U1, 30>; <III U2, 128>

menu [ˈmenjuː] Speisekarte II

mess [mes] Unordnung; Durcheinander I

message [ˈmesɪdʒ] Nachricht; SMS II; Botschaft <III U3, 69>

text message [ˈtekst ˌmesɪdʒ] Textnachricht (SMS) I

met [met] simple past von to meet I

metal [ˈmetl] Metall III U3, 54

metre [ˈmiːtə] Meter I

microwave [ˈmaɪkrəweɪv] Mikrowelle II

middle [ˈmɪdl] Mitte III U4, 92

in the middle [ɪn ðə ˈmɪdl] in der Mitte III U4, 92

midnight [ˈmɪdnaɪt] Mitternacht III U4, 84

mild [maɪld] mild I

mile [maɪl] Meile II

milk [mɪlk] Milch II

milkshake [ˈmɪlkˌʃeɪk] Milchmischgetränk; Milchshake III U4, 76

million [ˈmɪljən] Million III U1, 11

half a million [ˌhaːf ə ˈmɪljən] eine halbe Million III U1, 16

mind [maɪnd] Geist; Verstand <III U1, 17>

mind map [ˈmaɪnd ˌmæp] Wörternetz <III U4, 88>

Never **mind.** [ˌnevə ˈmaɪnd] Macht nichts.; Schon gut.; Mach dir nichts draus. II

mine [maɪn] Bergwerk III U1, 16

mine [maɪn] meins; meine II

of mine [əv ˈmaɪn] von mir II

miner [ˈmaɪnə] Bergarbeiter; Bergarbeiterin III U1, 20

mineral water [ˈmɪnrl ˌwɔːtə] Mineralwasser III U4, 81

prime **minister** [ˌpraɪm ˈmɪnɪstə] Premierminister; Ministerpräsident; Ministerpräsidentin; Premierministerin <III U5, 135>

minute [ˈmɪnɪt] Minute II

mirror [ˈmɪrə] Spiegel <III U3, 193>; III U5, 97

miserable [ˈmɪzrəbl] elend; armselig; jämmerlich III U5, 105

*to give sth a **miss** [ˌgɪv sʌmθɪŋ ə ˈmɪs] auf etw. verzichten; etw. bleiben lassen III U2, 50

to **miss** [mɪs] vermissen II

to **mix** [mɪks] mischen <III U2, 46>

mixed [mɪkst] gemischt <III U4, 133>

mobile (phone) [ˈməʊbaɪl (ˌfəʊn)] Handy I

modern [ˈmɒdn] modern I

moment [ˈməʊmənt] Moment; Augenblick II

Monday [ˈmʌndeɪ] Montag I

money [ˈmʌni] Geld I

monkey [ˈmʌŋki] Affe I

monster [ˈmɒnstə] Ungeheuer; Monster III U3, 58

month [mʌnθ] Monat I

monthly [ˈmʌnθli] monatlich III U5, 101

monument [ˈmɒnjəmənt] Denkmal II

moon [muːn] Mond <III U5, 101>

moped [ˈməʊped] Moped <III U5, 207>

more [mɔː] mehr <I>; mehr II

once more [ˈwʌns ˌmɔː] noch einmal II

morning [ˈmɔːnɪŋ] Morgen; Vormittag I

Good morning. [gʊd ˈmɔːnɪŋ] Guten Morgen. II

mosque [mɒsk] Moschee II

most [məʊst] die meisten; die Mehrheit <III U1, 127>

the most famous [ðə ˈməʊst ˌfeɪməs] der berühmteste II

mother [ˈmʌðə] Mutter I

motorbike [ˈməʊtəbaɪk] Motorrad I

mountain [ˈmaʊntɪn] Berg III U1, 17

mouse (sg) [maʊs], **mice** (pl) [maɪs] Maus I

moussaka [muˈsɑːkə] Moussaka II

mouth [maʊθ] Mund II

move [muːv] Bewegung III U5, 100

to **move** [muːv] (sich) bewegen III U2, 39

to **move** (house) [muːv] umziehen II

movie [ˈmuːvi] Film I

Mr [ˈmɪstə] Herr (Anrede) I

Mrs [ˈmɪsɪz] Frau (Anrede) I

Ms [mɪz] Frau (Anrede) I

much [mʌtʃ] viel I

so much [ˌsəʊ ˈmʌtʃ] so sehr III U4, 76

too much [tuː ˈmʌtʃ] zu sehr II

How much (is/are) …? [ˌhaʊ ˈmʌtʃ ɪz/ɑː] Wie viel (kostet/kosten) …? I

mud [mʌd] Schlamm; Matsch I

stuck in the mud [ˌstʌk ɪn ðə ˈmʌd] im Schlamm festgesteckt I

mum [mʌm] Mama; Mutti I

mural [ˈmjʊərəl] Wandgemälde III U4, 74

murderer [ˈmɜːdrə] Mörder; Mörderin III U2, 50

museum [mjuːˈziːəm] Museum II

music [ˈmjuːzɪk] Musik I

musical [ˈmjuːzɪkl] Musical <III U3, 73>

musical [ˈmjuːzɪkl] Musik-; musikalisch III U5, 95

Muslim [ˈmʊzlɪm] Muslim; Muslimin I

must not/never [ˌmʌst ˈnɒt/ˈnevə] nicht/nie dürfen III U3, 63

must [mʌst] müssen I

mustard [ˈmʌstəd] Senf II

mustn't [ˈmʌsnt] nicht dürfen III U5, 100

my [maɪ] mein I

My name is … [maɪ ˈneɪm ˌɪz] Ich heiße … I

myself [maɪˈself] selbst; selber III U2, 34

mystery [ˈmɪstri] Rätsel; Geheimnis I

mystery

N

to **nag** [næg] nörgeln; meckern III U4, 76

nail [neɪl] Nagel III U5, 97

nail scissors ['neɪl ˌsɪzəz] Nagelschere III U5, 97

name [neɪm] Name I

first name [ˌfɜːst 'neɪm] Vorname <III U1, 127>

My name is … [maɪ 'neɪm ˌɪz] Ich heiße … I

napkin ['næpkɪn] Serviette II

narrator [nə'reɪtə] Erzähler; Erzählerin I

national ['næʃnl] National-; national III U5, 104

nature ['neɪtʃə] Natur III U3, 53

naughty ['nɔːti] frech; böse III U2, 43

near [nɪə] nah III U1, 15

near [nɪə] in der Nähe von I

to **need** [niːd] brauchen II

needn't ['niːdnt] nicht brauchen; nicht müssen I

with special **needs** [wɪθ ˌspeʃl 'niːdz] mit Behinderung; mit besonderen Bedürfnissen III U5, 95

neighbour ['neɪbə] Nachbar; Nachbarin III U3, 67

nervous ['nɜːvəs] nervös; aufgeregt II

netball ['netbɔːl] Korbball I

never ['nevə] nie; niemals I

Never mind. [ˌnevə 'maɪnd] Macht nichts.; Schon gut.; Mach dir nichts draus. II

new [njuː] neu I

news [njuːz] Neuigkeit(en); Nachricht(en) II

newsagent's ['njuːzˌeɪdʒnts] Zeitschriftenladen III U1, 13

newspaper ['njuːsˌpeɪpə] Zeitung <I>

next [nekst] nächste I

next to ['nekst tə] neben I

next [nekst] als Nächstes II

nice [naɪs] nett; schön I; lecker; gut III U3, 58

Nice to meet you. [ˌnaɪs tə 'miːt juː] Nett, dich kennen zu lernen. I

nickname ['nɪkneɪm] Spitzname <III U1, 127>

niece [niːs] Nichte III U4, 80

night [naɪt] Nacht I

night walk ['naɪt wɔːk] Nachtwanderung I

nine [naɪn] neun I

nineteen [ˌnaɪn'tiːn] neunzehn I

ninety ['naɪnti] neunzig I

no [nəʊ] kein; keine; nein I

no one ['nəʊ wʌn] niemand I

No way! [ˌnəʊ 'weɪ] Auf keinen Fall!; Was?!; Echt?! III U3, 58

no vacancies [ˌnəʊ 'veɪknsiz] kein Zimmer frei <III U4, 86>

nobody ['nəʊbədi] niemand III U3, 58

noise [nɔɪz] Geräusch I

noisy ['nɔɪzi] laut III U1, 16

non [nɒn] nicht <III U4, 86>

Norman ['nɔːmən] Normanne; Normannin III U1, 11

the **Normans** [ðə 'nɔːmənz] die Normannen III U1, 11

Norman ['nɔːmən] normannisch <III U1, 126>

north [nɔːθ] Norden III U1, 10

northbound ['nɔːθbaʊnd] in Richtung Norden <III U5, 207>

northwest [ˌnɔːθ'west] Nordwesten III U1, 16

northwest of [ˌnɔːθ'west ˌəv] nordwestlich III U4, 75

nose [nəʊz] Nase I

not [nɒt] nicht I

not … any [ˌnɒt … eni] kein II

not … any more [ˌnɒt … eni 'mɔː] nicht mehr III U4, 76

not … either [nɒt … 'aɪðə] auch nicht III U3, 58

not … yet [nɒt … 'jet] noch nicht II

note [nəʊt] Geldschein II

*to take **notes** [ˌteɪk 'nəʊts] sich Notizen machen I

nothing ['nʌθɪŋ] nichts III U1, 21

noun [naʊn] Nomen; Hauptwort <I>

November [nə'vembə] November I

now [naʊ] jetzt; nun I; heutzutage II

right now [ˌraɪt 'naʊ] gerade; jetzt gleich; sofort III U5, 98

nowadays ['naʊədeɪz] heutzutage <III U1, 24>

number ['nʌmbə] Nummer; Zahl I

phone number ['fəʊn ˌnʌmbə] Telefonnummer III U2, 38

nurse [nɜːs] Krankenschwester; Krankenpfleger II

nut [nʌt] Nuss I

O

o'clock [ə'klɒk] Uhr (Zeitangabe bei vollen Stunden) I

oat [əʊt] Hafer III U3, 53

oatmeal ['əʊtmiːl] Haferflocken <III U3, 66>

object ['ɒbdʒɪkt] Objekt; Gegenstand <III U5, 105>

October [ɒk'təʊbə] Oktober I

the **odd** one out [ˌɒd wʌn 'aʊt] das Wort, das nicht in die Gruppe passt <III U5, 101>

a photo **of** [ə 'fəʊtəʊ ˌəv] ein Foto von I

to be made of [biː 'meɪd ˌəv] hergestellt sein aus III U3, 54

of course [əv 'kɔːs] natürlich; selbstverständlich II

of mine [əv 'maɪn] von mir II

offer ['ɒfə] Angebot <III U3, 68>

special offer [ˌspeʃl 'ɒfə] Sonderangebot III U4, 80

office ['ɒfɪs] Büro II

post office ['pəʊst ˌɒfɪs] Postamt I

police **officer** [pə'liːs ˌɒfɪsə] Polizeibeamter; Polizeibeamtin I

often ['ɒfn] oft; häufig I

oh [əʊ] null (bei Uhrzeiten und Telefonnummern) I

oh dear [ˌəʊ 'dɪə] oje III U4, 80

oil [ɔɪl] Öl <III U3, 66>

OK [əʊ'keɪ] okay I

old [əʊld] alt I

How old are you? [haʊ ˌəʊld ə ˌjuː] Wie alt bist du? I

on [ɒn] auf; an; am I

on board [ˈɒn bɔːd] an Bord
III U4, 84

on duty [ɒn ˈdjuːti] im Dienst
<III U3, 68>

on time [ɒn ˈtaɪm] pünktlich
III U5, 100

on weekdays [ɒn ˈwiːkdeɪz] unter
der Woche; an Werktagen III U5, 96

to try on [ˌtraɪ ˈɒn] anprobieren II

on purpose [ɒn ˈpɜːpəs] absichtlich
II

on Saturdays [ɒn ˈsætədeɪz] samstags I

on 7th July [ɒn ðə ˌsevnθ əv ˈdʒʊlaɪ]
am 7. Juli I

on the bus [ɒn ðə ˈbʌs] im Bus II

on the left [ɒn ðə ˈleft] auf der
linken Seite; links I

on the right [ɒn ðə ˈraɪt] auf der
rechten Seite; rechts I

on Tuesday [ˌɒn ˈtjuːzdeɪ] am
Dienstag I

once [wʌns] einst; einmal III U5, 105

once more [ˈwʌns ˌmɔː] noch
einmal II

one [wʌn] eins I

a/one hundred [ˈhʌndrəd] einhundert; hundert I

no one [ˈnəʊ wʌn] niemand I

one day [wʌn ˈdeɪ] eines Tages
III U1, 21

one(s) [wʌn(z)] *Platzhalter für ein
Nomen* III U4, 80

the blue one [ðə ˈbluː ˌwʌn] der
blaue II

to help oneself [help wʌnˈself] sich
bedienen III U5, 96

onion [ˈʌnjən] Zwiebel II

online [ɒnˈlaɪn] online II

only [ˈəʊnli] einzige II; nur; bloß; erst
III U1, 16

to open [ˈəʊpn] öffnen; aufmachen I

operation [ˌɒpəˈreɪʃn] Operation
III U2, 39

operator [ˈɒpreɪtə] Vermittlung
III U2, 38

opinion [əˈpɪnjən] Meinung III U2, 50

opposite [ˈɒpəzɪt] gegenüber I;
Gegenteil <II>

optimistic [ˌɒptɪˈmɪstɪk] optimistisch
III U4, 77

or [ɔː] oder I

orange [ˈɒrɪndʒ] orange; Orange I

orchestra [ˈɔːkɪstrə] Orchester
III U5, 94

order [ˈɔːdə] Reihenfolge <III U2, 47>

to order [ˈɔːdə] bestellen II

ordinal number [ˌɔːdɪnəl ˈnʌmbə]
Ordinalzahl I

to organize [ˈɔːgənaɪz] organisieren II

other [ˈʌðə] andere I

each other [iːtʃˈʌðə] einander;
sich; sich gegenseitig III U2, 34

others [ˈʌðəz] anderen II

our [aʊə] unser I

ours [aʊəz] unsere III U5, 96

ourselves [ˌaʊəˈselvz] selber; selbst
III U2, 152

out [aʊt] heraus II

to keep out [ˌkiːp ˈaʊt] draußen
halten III U3, 62

out and about [ˌaʊt ən əˈbaʊt] unterwegs I

out of [ˈaʊt əv] aus … heraus I

outdoor [ˌaʊtˈdɔː] Freiluft-; Outdoor-
III U2, 34

outfit [ˈaʊtfɪt] Outfit; Kleidung
III U5, 105

outline Skizze; Kontur; Überblick
<III U5, 105>

outside [ˌaʊtˈsaɪd] draußen; im Freien
III U3, 58

over [ˈəʊvə] über <III U4, 93>

over there [ˌəʊvə ˈðeə] da drüben;
dort drüben II

to own [əʊn] besitzen II

own [əʊn] eigene <I>; eigene II

P

p.m. [ˌpiːˈem] nachmittags II

to pack [pæk] packen; einpacken II

to pack up [ˌpæk ˈʌp] packen;
einpacken II

packed lunch [ˌpækt ˈlʌnʃ] Lunchpaket; Vesper II

a packet of [ˈpækɪt] eine Packung …;
eine Tüte … I

paddle [ˈpædl] Paddel <III U2, 186>

paid [peɪd] simple past, past participle von *to pay* II

to paint [peɪnt] streichen; anmalen;
malen II

pair [peə] Paar <III U2, 41>

a pair of [ə ˈpeər əv] ein Paar II

palace [ˈpælɪs] Palast <III U1, 30>

pancake [ˈpænkeɪk] Pfannkuchen II

to panic [ˈpænɪk] panisch werden II

pantomime [ˈpæntəmaɪm] Weihnachtstheaterstück II

paper [ˈpeɪpə] Papier III U3, 55

parade [pəˈreɪd] Parade; Umzug
III U5, 104

paragraph [ˈpærəgraːf] Paragraph;
Absatz <III U5, 104>

Pardon? [ˈpɑːdn] Wie bitte? I

parents (pl) [ˈpeərnts] Eltern II

park [pɑːk] Park I

theme park [ˈθiːm ˌpɑːk] Freizeitpark I

part [pɑːt] Rolle; Teil II

to take part (in) [ˌteɪk ˈpɑːt] teilnehmen (an) III U5, 100

partner [ˈpɑːtnə] Partner; Partnerin
III U5, 99

party [ˈpɑːti] Party; Feier I

to pass [pɑːs] reichen II

passenger [ˈpæsndʒə] Passagier;
Passagierin II

passport [ˈpɑːspɔːt] (Reise-)Pass
<III U5, 206>

simple past [ˌsɪmpl ˈpɑːst] einfache
Vergangenheit <III U2, 41>

past [pɑːst] Vergangenheit III U1, 16

past [pɑːst] nach (bei Uhrzeitangaben) I; vorbei (an) III U1, 12

half past (two) [ˌhɑːf ˈpɑːst] halb
(drei) I

pasta [ˈpæstə] Pasta; Nudeln II

pasta bake [ˌpæstə ˈbeɪk] Nudelauf-
lauf II

to paste [peɪst] einfügen II

paste

pasty ['pæsti] Pastete II

patient ['peɪʃnt] Patient; Patientin II

patient ['peɪʃnt] geduldig III U2, 35

patron saint [ˌpeɪtrn 'seɪnt] Schutzheiliger; Schutzheilige <III U5, 134>

patterned ['pætənd] gemustert II

*to **pay** [peɪ] bezahlen II

    to pay back [ˌpeɪ 'bæk] zurückzahlen II

    to pay the bill [ˌpeɪ ðə 'bɪl] die Rechnung bezahlen III U3, 59

pay phone ['peɪ fəʊn] Münztelefon III U3, 67

payment machine ['peɪmənt ˌməʃi:n] Bezahlautomat II

PE (Physical Education) [ˌpi:'i:, ˌfɪzɪkl edʒʊ'keɪʃn] Sportunterricht I

peace [pi:s] Frieden III U3, 65

peach [pi:tʃ] Pfirsich I

peanut butter [ˌpi:nʌt 'bʌtə] Erdnussbutter III U4, 81

pen [pen] Füller; Stift I

pence *(pl)* [pens], **penny** *(sg)* ['peni] Pence *(brit. Währungseinheit)* I

    … is 99p [ɪz ˌnaɪntinaɪn 'pens] … kostet 99 Pence I

pencil ['pensl] Bleistift I

    pencil case ['pensl ˌkeɪs] Federmäppchen I

    pencil sharpener ['pensl ˌʃɑ:pnə] Anspitzer I

penguin ['peŋgwɪn] Pinguin I

people ['pi:pl] Leute; Menschen I; Volk <III U5, 134>

pepper ['pepə] Pfeffer II

per [pɜ:] pro <III U2, 128>

percent (%) [pə'sent] Prozent <III U4, 86>

present perfect [ˌpreznt 'pɜ:fɪkt] das Perfekt <III U2, 41>

perfume ['pɜ:fju:m] Parfüm III U5, 97

person ['pɜ:sn] Person; Mensch II

personal ['pɜ:snl] persönlich III U5, 97

pet [pet] Haustier I

    pet shop ['pet ʃɒp] Tierhandlung III U1, 13

petrol ['petrl] Benzin <III U3, 68>

Phew! [fju:] Puh! III U4, 75

mobile (phone) ['məʊbaɪl (ˌfəʊn)] Handy I

phone [fəʊn] Telefon II

    to answer the phone [ˌɑ:nsə ðə 'fəʊn] ans Telefon gehen III U2, 45

    pay phone ['peɪ fəʊn] Münztelefon III U3, 67

    phone call ['fəʊn ˌkɔ:l] Telefonanruf I

    phone number ['fəʊn ˌnʌmbə] Telefonnummer III U2, 38

to phone [fəʊn] anrufen; telefonieren I

photo ['fəʊtəʊ] Foto I

    to take a photo [ˌteɪk ə 'fəʊtəʊ] ein Foto machen I

phrase [freɪz] Ausdruck <III U1, 17>; Redewendung; Satz <III U4, 79>

to pick up [ˌpɪk ˈʌp] aufheben III U1, 22

picnic ['pɪknɪk] Picknick I

picture ['pɪktʃə] Bild I

pie [paɪ] Kuchen; Pastete II

piece [pi:s] Stück II

pierogi [pjɜ'rɒgi] Pirogge II

pig [pɪg] Schwein <III U1, 127>

pinch [pɪntʃ] Prise II

pineapple ['paɪnæpl] Ananas III U5, 107

pink [pɪŋk] pink; rosa I

pipe [paɪp] Rohr III U3, 67

pirate ['paɪrət] Pirat; Piratin I

pizza ['pi:tsə] Pizza I

place [pleɪs] Platz; Stelle; Ort I

    to take place [ˌteɪk 'pleɪs] stattfinden <III U3, 130>; <III U4, 89>

plain [pleɪn] schlicht; einfach II

plan [plæn] Plan II

to plan [plæn] planen II

plane [pleɪn] Flugzeug II

plant [plɑ:nt] Pflanze III U2, 33

plantain ['plænteɪn] Kochbanane II

plaster ['plɑ:stə] Pflaster III U2, 39

plastic ['plæstɪk] Plastik; Kunststoff III U3, 54

plate [pleɪt] Teller II

play [pleɪ] Theaterstück II

to play [pleɪ] spielen I

player ['pleɪə] Spieler; Spielerin II

playground ['pleɪgraʊnd] Schulhof; Pausenhof; Spielplatz I

please [pli:z] bitte I

poem ['pəʊɪm] Gedicht III U5, 105

lookout point ['lʊkaʊt ˌpɔɪnt] Aussichtspunkt II

    meeting point ['mi:tɪŋ ˌpɔɪnt] Treffpunkt <III U1, 30>

    starting point ['stɑ:tɪŋ ˌpɔɪnt] Ausgangspunkt <III U5, 101>

poison ['pɔɪzn] Gift <III U2, 187>

pole [pəʊl] Pfahl; Stange <III U3, 130>

police [pə'li:s] Polizei III U2, 38

    police officer [pə'li:s ˌɒfɪsə] Polizeibeamter; Polizeibeamtin I

polite [pə'laɪt] höflich II

swimming pool ['swɪmɪŋ ˌpu:l] Schwimmbad I

poor [pɔ:] arm <III U5, 135>

popcorn ['pɒpkɔ:n] Popcorn I

popular ['pɒpjələ] beliebt III U2, 33

pork [pɔ:k] Schweinefleisch II

porridge ['pɒrɪdʒ] Haferbrei III U3, 53

positive ['pɒzətɪv] positiv III U4, 76

possessive pronoun [pə'sesɪv ˌprəʊnaʊn] Possessivpronomen <III U5, 99>

post office ['pəʊst ˌɒfɪs] Postamt I

to post [pəʊst] aufgeben *(einen Brief)*; abschicken *(einen Brief)* III U4, 80

postcard ['pəʊstkɑ:d] Postkarte I

poster ['pəʊstə] Poster I

postman ['pəʊsmən] Postbote <III U2, 129>

pot [pɒt] Topf III U5, 104

potato *(sg)* [pə'teɪtəʊ], **potatoes** *(pl)* [pə'teɪtəʊz] Kartoffel II

    jacket potato [ˌdʒækɪt pə'teɪtəʊ] Ofenkartoffel II

    mashed potatoes [ˌmæʃt pə'teɪtəʊz] Kartoffelbrei II

pound [paʊnd] Pfund *(brit. Währungseinheit)* I

practice ['præktɪs] Training; Übung I

to practise ['præktɪs] üben; trainieren III U5, 96

to **prefer** [prɪˈfɜː] vorziehen II
  I prefer working [aɪ prɪˈfɜː ˌwɜːkɪŋ]
  ich arbeite lieber II
to **prepare** [prɪˈpeə] zubereiten;
  vorbereiten III U5, 96
present [ˈpreznt] Geschenk I
  present perfect [ˌpreznt ˈpɜːfɪkt]
  das Perfekt <III U2, 41>
  present progressive [ˌpreznt
  prəˈgresɪv] Verlaufsform der
  Gegenwart <III U4, 93>
  simple present [ˌsɪmpl ˈpreznt]
  Gegenwart; Präsens <III U5, 98>
to **present** [prɪˈzent] präsentieren I
presentation [ˌpreznˈteɪʃn] Präsentation; Vortrag <III U5, 104>
presenter [prɪˈzentə] Moderator;
  Moderatorin <III U1, 26>
pretty [ˈprɪti] hübsch II
price [praɪs] Preis II
prime minister [ˌpraɪm ˈmɪnɪstə] Premierminister; Ministerpräsident;
  Ministerpräsidentin; Premierministerin <III U5, 135>
prison [ˈprɪzn] Gefängnis II
private [ˈpraɪvɪt] Privat-; privat
  <III U4, 86>
prize [praɪz] Preis II
probably [ˈprɒbəbli] wahrscheinlich
  III U4, 75
problem [ˈprɒbləm] Problem I
process [ˈprəʊses] Prozess <III U5, 135>
product [ˈprɒdʌkt] Produkt <III U3, 68>
profile [ˈprəʊfaɪl] Profil; Steckbrief <I>
present **progressive** [ˌpreznt
  prəˈgresɪv] Verlaufsform der
  Gegenwart <III U4, 93>
project [ˈprɒdʒekt] Projekt III U5, 98
prompt card [ˈprɒmt ˌkaːd] Stichwort-
  karte <II>
possessive **pronoun** [pəˈsesɪv
  ˌprəʊnaʊn] Possessivpronomen
  <III U5, 99>
prop [prɒp] Requisit III U2, 45
to **protect** [prəˈtekt] schützen III U3, 53
Protestant [ˈprɒtɪstnt] Protestant;
  Protestantin; protestantisch
  III U4, 74

proud (of) [praʊd (əv)] stolz (auf)
  III U3, 65
pub [pʌb] Kneipe; Gasthaus III U5, 94
public transport [ˌpʌblɪk ˈtrænspɔːt]
  öffentliche Verkehrsmittel
  III U5, 100
pudding [ˈpʊdɪŋ] Nachspeise; Pudding II
to **pull** [pʊl] ziehen I
purple [ˈpɜːpl] lila; violett I
on **purpose** [ɒn ˈpɜːpəs] absichtlich II
to **push** [pʊʃ] schieben I; schubsen;
  drängeln III U5, 102
*to **put** [pʊt] setzen; legen; stellen II
  to put in [pʊtˈɪn] einsetzen I
  to put in the right order [pʊtˌɪn ðə
  ˈraɪt ɔːdə] in die richtige Reihenfolge bringen I
  to put on [pʊtˈɒn] anlegen; anziehen III U2, 39
  to put up [pʊtˈʌp] hochhalten
  <III U2, 128>
  Put your hands up. [pʊt jɔː ˌhændz
  ˈʌp] Meldet euch. I
put [pʊt] simple past von to put II

Q

quarter past [ˈkwɔːtə paːst] Viertel
  nach I
  quarter to [ˈkwɔːtə tə] Viertel vor I
queen [kwiːn] Königin III U1, 31
question [ˈkwestʃən] Frage I
queue [kjuː] Warteschlange II
quick [kwɪk] schnell III U2, 34
quickly [ˈkwɪkli] schnell II
quiet [ˈkwaɪət] ruhig; leise; still
  III U1, 16
quite [kwaɪt] ziemlich; ganz; völlig
  III U2, 34

R

raccoon [rəˈkuːn] Waschbär I
race [reɪs] Wettrennen; Rennen I
racket [ˈrækɪt] Schläger <III U2, 186>
radio [ˈreɪdiəʊ] Radio III U3, 67
rafting [ˈraːftɪŋ] Rafting III U2, 33

to **rain** [reɪn] regnen I
rainbow [ˈreɪnbəʊ] Regenbogen
  III U5, 104
raincoat [ˈreɪnkəʊt] Regenmantel
  III U5, 97
ran [ræn] simple past von to run
  III U4, 75
rang [ræŋ] simple past von to ring II
rap [ræp] Rap <I>
to **rap** [ræp] rappen II
rapper [ˈræpə] Rapper; Rapperin
  III U5, 98
raspberry [ˈraːzbri] Himbeere
  III U4, 80
to **rate** [reɪt] bewerten; einstufen
  III U2, 51
I'd **rather** [aɪd ˈraːðə] ich würde lieber
  III U1, 25
rating [ˈreɪtɪŋ] Bewertung <III U2, 51>
*to **read** [riːd] lesen I
reading [ˈriːdɪŋ] Lesen <I>
  reading corner [ˈriːdɪŋ ˌkɔːnə]
  Leseecke <I>
  reading skills [ˈriːdɪŋ ˌskɪlz] Fertigkeit Lesen <I>
ready [ˈredi] fertig; bereit I
  to get ready [ˌget ˈredi] sich
  vorbereiten; sich fertig machen
  <III U1, 27>; <III U2, 44>
real [rɪəl] echt; richtig; wirklich II
really [ˈrɪəli] echt II
Really? [ˈrɪəli] Wirklich? I
reason [ˈriːzn] Grund III U2, 51
  to give reasons [gɪv ˈriːznz]
  Gründe nennen; Gründe angeben
  III U2, 51
receipt [rɪˈsiːt] Quittung II
recipe [ˈresɪpi] Rezept II
to **record** [rɪˈkɔːd] aufnehmen
  <III U2, 43>
recording [rɪˈkɔːdɪŋ] Aufnahme
  <III U2, 43>
recyclable [riːˈsaɪkləbl] wiederver-
  wertbar; recycelbar <III U3, 193>
red [red] rot I
registration [ˌredʒɪˈstreɪʃn] Überprü-
  fung der Anwesenheit I; Anmel-
  dung II

relaxed [rɪ'lækst] entspannt; locker; gelassen II

religion [rɪ'lɪdʒn] Religion <III U4, 132>

RE (Religious Education) [ˌɑː ˌriː, rɪˌlɪdʒəsˌedʒʊ'keɪʃn] Religionsunterricht I

to **remember** [rɪ'membə] sich merken; sich erinnern (an) II

rent [rent] Miete II

to **rent** [rent] mieten III U3, 58

to **repair** [rɪ'peə] reparieren III U3, 67

to **repeat** [rɪ'piːt] wiederholen III U4, 80

report [rɪ'pɔːt] Bericht <I>

reporter [rɪ'pɔːtə] Reporter; Reporterin III U2, 42

republic [rɪ'pʌblɪk] Republik III U5, 94

are **required** [ˌɑː rɪ'kwaɪəd] werden gebeten <III U4, 86>

animal **rescue** shelter [ˌænɪml 'reskjuː ˌʃeltə] Tierheim I

rescue ['reskjuː] Rettung <III U2, 128>

to **rescue** ['reskjuː] retten <III U2, 128>

rescued ['reskjuːd] gerettet <III U2, 129>

reservation [ˌrezə'veɪʃn] Reservierung III U3, 59

to make a reservation [ˌmeɪk ə 'rezəveɪʃn] reservieren III U3, 59

to **rest** [rest] rasten; ausruhen; liegen II

restaurant ['restrɒnt] Restaurant II

fast food restaurant [ˌfɑːst fuːd 'restrɒnt] Fastfood-Restaurant I

result [rɪ'zʌlt] Ergebnis II

return ticket [rɪ'tɜːn ˌtɪkɪt] Hin- und Rückfahrkarte III U5, 101

review [rɪ'vjuː] Kritik III U2, 50

Industrial **Revolution** [ɪnˌdʌstriəl revl'uːʃn] industrielle Revolution III U1, 11

rice [raɪs] Reis II

rich [rɪtʃ] reich III U3, 54

ridden ['rɪdn] past participle von *to ride* II

ride [raɪd] Fahrt; Ritt II

*to **ride** [raɪd] fahren; reiten II

horse **riding** ['hɔːs ˌraɪdɪŋ] Reiten I

right [raɪt] richtig; korrekt I; rechts III U1, 12

all **right** [ˌɔːl 'raɪt] in Ordnung; alles klar II

to be **right** [bi 'raɪt] recht haben II

to do the **right** thing [ˌduː ðə 'raɪt θɪŋ] das Richtige tun III U2, 38

to turn **right** (into …) [ˌtɜːn 'raɪt] rechts abbiegen I

on the **right** [ɒn ðə 'raɪt] auf der rechten Seite; rechts I

You're **right**. [jɔː 'raɪt] Du hast recht. I

right now [ˌraɪt 'naʊ] gerade; jetzt gleich; sofort III U5, 98

*to **ring** [rɪŋ] läuten; klingeln II

river ['rɪvə] Fluss I

road [rəʊd] Straße I

rock [rɒk] Fels; Stein III U2, 38

rock climber ['rɒk ˌklaɪmə] Kletterer; Kletterin <III U3, 72>

rock climbing ['rɒk ˌklaɪmɪŋ] Klettern I

space **rocket** ['speɪs ˌrɒkɪt] Raumschiff <III U1, 30>

rode [rəʊd] simple past von *to ride* II

role play ['rəʊl ˌpleɪ] Rollenspiel <II>

roller coaster ['rəʊlə ˌkəʊstə] Achterbahn II

the **Romans** [ðə 'rəʊmənz] die Römer III U1, 10

romance ['rəʊmæns] Liebesgeschichte III U2, 51

roof [ruːf] Dach II

room [ruːm] Zimmer; Raum I

dining room ['daɪnɪŋ ˌrʊm] Esszimmer I

rope [rəʊp] Seil I

royal ['rɔɪəl] königlich II

rubber ['rʌbə] Gummi III U3, 55

rubbish ['rʌbɪʃ] Müll; Abfall II

rugby ['rʌgbi] Rugby III U2, 34

to **ruin** ['ruːɪn] ruinieren; zerstören II

rule [ruːl] Regel III U2, 34

ruler ['ruːlə] Lineal I

run [rʌn] Lauf <III U2, 129>

*to **run** [rʌn] rennen; laufen I; betreiben; leiten; führen III U4, 75

to **run** away [ˌrʌn ə'weɪ] weglaufen III U2, 50

to **run** out of [ˌrʌn 'aʊt ˌəv] ausgehen *(Ware)* III U4, 81

run [rʌn] past participle von *to run* III U4, 75

rung [rʌŋ] past participle von *to ring* III U5, 96

to **rush** [rʌʃ] eilen; sich beeilen; stürzen III U5, 105

S

sad [sæd] traurig III U3, 65

safe [seɪf] sicher; ungefährlich III U2, 35

safety ['seɪfti] Sicherheit <III U2, 128>

said [sed] simple past von *to say* I

to **sail** [seɪl] segeln <III U1, 126>

patron **saint** [ˌpeɪtrn 'seɪnt] Schutzheiliger; Schutzheilige <III U5, 134>

salad ['sæləd] Salat II

sale [seɪl] Schlussverkauf; Ausverkauf II; Verkauf <III U2, 129>

jumble sale ['dʒʌmbl ˌseɪl] Flohmarkt II

salt [sɔːlt] Salz II

the **same** [ðə 'seɪm] derselbe; gleich II

sand [sænd] Sand II

sandal ['sændl] Sandale <III U2, 44>

sandwich ['sænwɪdʒ] Sandwich; belegtes Brot I

sang [sæŋ] simple past von *to sing* II

sank [sæŋk] simple past von *to sink* III U4, 84

on **Saturdays** [ɒn 'sætədeɪz] samstags I

Saturday ['sætədeɪ] Samstag I

sauce [sɔːs] Soße II

sausage ['sɒsɪdʒ] Wurst; Bratwurst II

sausage roll [ˌsɒsɪdʒ 'rəʊl] *Blätterteig mit Wurstfüllung* II

to **save** [seɪv] speichern II; retten; bergen III U4, 85

saw [sɔː] simple past von *to see* I

saxophone ['sæksəfəʊn] Saxofon I

*to **say** [seɪ] nachsprechen; nennen; sagen; sprechen I

to say sorry [ˌseɪ ˈsɒri] sich entschuldigen II

Can you say that again, please? [kæn ju: ˌseɪ ðæt əˈgen pli:s] Könntest du das bitte wiederholen? I

Say hi to … [seɪ ˈhaɪ tə] Grüße … von mir. I

to **scan** [skæn] scannen; nach Details durchsuchen <III U1, 31>

to **scare** [skeə] erschrecken II

*to be **scared** [bi: ˈskeəd] Angst haben; erschrocken sein III U2, 34

scared [skeəd] verängstigt I

scarf (sg) [skɑːf], **scarves** (pl) [skɑːvz] Schal; Tuch II

scary [ˈskeəri] gruselig; beängstigend I

scene [si:n] Szene II

school [sku:l] Schule I

at school [ət ˈsku:l] in der Schule I

high school [ˈhaɪ ˌsku:l] High School (weiterführende Schule, Oberstufe) <III U2, 129>

school life [ˈsku: ˌlaɪf] Schulalltag <I>

Science [saɪəns] Wissenschaft; Naturwissenschaft I

science fiction [ˌsaɪəns ˈfɪkʃn] Science-Fiction I

scissors (pl) [ˈsɪzəz] Schere III U5, 97

nail scissors [ˈneɪl ˌsɪzəz] Nagelschere III U5, 97

scone [skɒn] Scone (eine Art süßes Brötchen) II

Scot [skɒt] Schotte; Schottin III U3, 53

Scottish [ˈskɒtɪʃ] schottisch III U3, 53

scrambled egg [ˌskræmbld ˈeg] Rührei II

script [skrɪpt] Drehbuch; Skript <III U1, 27>

sea [si:] Meer I

search [sɜːtʃ] Suche <III U3, 73>

to **search** [sɜːtʃ] durchsuchen <III U3, 65>

seasick [ˈsiːsɪk] seekrank <III U2, 128>

at the **seaside** [ət ðə ˈsiːsaɪd] am Meer I

second [ˈseknd] Sekunde II

second [ˈseknd] zweite I

secret [ˈsiːkrət] Geheimnis II

secret [ˈsiːkrət] geheim II

section [sekʃn] Abschnitt <III U1, 22>

*to **see** [si:] sehen I

CU (See you!) [ˈsi: ju:] Bis später! II

See you! [ˈsi: ju:] Tschüss!; Bis bald! I

See you soon! [ˌsi: ju: ˈsu:n] Bis bald! I

seen [si:n] past participle von to see II

self [self] selbst; sich III U2, 34

*to **sell** [sel] verkaufen III U1, 13

*to **send** [send] schicken; senden I

sent [sent] simple past von to send I; past participle von to send II

sentence [ˈsentəns] Satz <I>

to **separate** [ˈsepreɪt] trennen <III U4, 133>

separate [ˈseprət] getrennt; separat; verschieden <III U4, 132>

September [sepˈtembə] September I

series (no pl) [ˈsɪəri:z] Serie <III U4, 133>

serious [ˈsɪəriəs] ernst III U3, 58

Are you **serious**? [ˌɑː ju ˈsɪəriəs] Im Ernst? III U3, 58

to **serve** [sɜːv] servieren <III U3, 66>

service [ˈsɜːvɪs] Dienst III U2, 38

emergency service [ɪˈmɜːdʒnsi ˌsɜːvɪs] Notdienst; Rettungsdienst III U2, 38

full service [ˌfʊl ˈsɜːvɪs] Komplettservice <III U3, 68>

for service [fə ˈsɜːvɪs] um bedient zu werden <III U4, 86>

*to **set** free [set ˈfri:] freilassen <III U4, 77>

to set off [set ˈɒf] auslösen <III U3, 72>

to **settle** (in) [ˈsetl] besiedeln; sich niederlassen (in) <III U4, 132>

early **settler** [ˌɜːli ˈsetlə] früher Siedler; frühe Siedlerin <III U5, 134>

seven [ˈsevn] sieben I

seventeen [ˌsevnˈtiːn] siebzehn I

seventy [ˈsevnti] siebzig I

shampoo [ʃæmˈpu:] Shampoo III U5, 96

shamrock [ˈʃæmrɒk] Kleeblatt III U5, 104

shape [ʃeɪp] Form <III U5, 105>

to **share** [ʃeə] teilen III U5, 96

shark [ʃɑːk] Hai I

pencil **sharpener** [ˈpensl ˌʃɑːpnə] Anspitzer I

she [ʃi:] sie I

sheep (sg) [ʃi:p], **sheep** (pl) [ʃi:p] Schaf I

shelf (sg) [ʃelf], **shelves** (pl) [ʃelvz] Regal; Regalbrett I

animal rescue **shelter** [ˌænɪml ˈreskju: ˌʃeltə] Tierheim I

*to **shine** [ʃaɪn] scheinen <III U5, 101>

ship [ʃɪp] Schiff I

ship builder [ˈʃɪp ˌbɪldə] Schiffsbauer; Schiffsbauerin III U4, 84

shipyard [ˈʃɪpjɑːd] Werft III U4, 84

shirt [ʃɜːt] Hemd; Shirt II

shoe [ʃu:] Schuh II

*to **shoot** (a film) [ˌʃu:t (ə ˈfɪlm)] (einen Film) drehen <III U5, 107>

shop [ʃɒp] Geschäft; Laden I

corner shop [ˈkɔːnə ˌʃɒp] Tante-Emma-Laden I

shop assistant [ˈʃɒp əˌsɪstnt] Verkäufer; Verkäuferin II

sports shop [ˈspɔːts ˌʃɒp] Sportgeschäft I

shopping [ˈʃɒpɪŋ] Einkaufen I

to do the shopping [ˌdu: ðə ˈʃɒpɪŋ] Einkäufe machen; Besorgungen machen II

to go shopping [ˌgəʊ ˈʃɒpɪŋ] einkaufen gehen II

shopping centre [ˈʃɒpɪŋ ˌsentə] Einkaufszentrum I

shopping list [ˈʃɒpɪŋ ˌlɪst] Einkaufszettel I

short [ʃɔːt] kurz II

shortly [ˈʃɔːtli] kurz III U4, 84

shorts (pl) [ʃɔːts] Shorts; kurze Hose I

shorts

should [ʃʊd] sollte III U2, 38

shout [ʃaʊt] Schrei I

to **shout** [ʃaʊt] schreien; rufen II

talent **show** [ˈtælənt ˌʃəʊ] Talentwettbewerb I

TV **show** [ˌtiːˈviː ˌʃəʊ] Fernsehsendung II

*to **show** [ʃəʊ] zeigen II

shower [ˈʃaʊə] Dusche III U5, 97

shower gel [ˈʃaʊə ˌdʒel] Duschgel III U5, 97

sick [sɪk] krank III U1, 11

to be sick [bi ˈsɪk] sich übergeben I

side [saɪd] Seite II

sight [saɪt] Sehenswürdigkeit II

*to go **sightseeing** [gəʊ ˈsaɪtsiːɪŋ] eine Besichtigungstour machen II

sign [saɪn] Schild; Zeichen III U2, 32

sign language [ˈsaɪn ˌlæŋgwɪdʒ] Gebärdensprache; Zeichensprache III U5, 95

to **sign** [saɪn] unterschreiben; unterzeichnen <III U5, 135>

signal [ˈsɪgnl] Empfang; Signal; Zeichen III U3, 67

silence [ˈsaɪləns] Stille; Schweigen; Ruhe III U1, 20

silent [ˈsaɪlənt] stumm; schweigsam III U1, 21

silk [sɪlk] Seide III U3, 55

silly [ˈsɪli] albern II; dumm; doof III U4, 76

similarity [ˌsɪmɪˈlærəti] Ähnlichkeit <III U1, 24>

simple [ˈsɪmpl] einfach III U3, 58

simple past [ˌsɪmpl ˈpɑːst] einfache Vergangenheit <III U2, 41>

simple present [ˌsɪmpl ˈpreznt] Gegenwart; Präsens <III U5, 98>

since [sɪns] seit <III U2, 128>; <III U3, 68>; seitdem <III U4, 132>

*to **sing** [sɪŋ] singen I

singer [ˈsɪŋə] Sänger; Sängerin I

single ticket [ˈsɪŋgl ˌtɪkɪt] einfache Fahrkarte III U5, 101

*to **sink** [sɪŋk] untergehen; sinken III U4, 84

siren [ˈsaɪrən] Sirene; Martinshorn <III U1, 17>

sister [ˈsɪstə] Schwester I

*to **sit** (down) [sɪt ˈdaʊn] sich (hin)setzen I

situation [ˌsɪtjuˈeɪʃn] Situation II

six [sɪks] sechs I

sixteen [ˌsɪkˈstiːn] sechzehn I

sixty [ˈsɪksti] sechzig I

size [saɪz] Größe II

skateboard [ˈskeɪtbɔːd] Skateboard III U2, 41

ice **skating** [ˈaɪs ˌskeɪtɪŋ] Schlittschuhlaufen <III U2, 186>

to **ski** [skiː] Ski fahren II

skiing [ˈskiːɪŋ] Skifahren III U2, 32

to **skim** [skɪm] überfliegen <III U1, 31>

skin [skɪn] Haut <III U2, 44>

skirt [skɜːt] Rock I

sleep [sliːp] Schlaf <III U1, 17>; III U2, 39

*to **sleep** [sliːp] schlafen I

sleepover [ˈsliːpˌəʊvə] Übernachtung I

slept [slept] simple past, past participle von to sleep II

sliced bread [ˌslaɪst ˈbred] in Scheiben geschnittenes Brot III U4, 80

slow [sləʊ] langsam III U2, 34

small [smɔːl] klein III U2, 35

smart [smɑːt] schlau; klug; intelligent III U4, 77

*to **smell** [smel] riechen III U1, 20

smelt [smelt] simple past, past participle von to smell III U1, 20

smoke [sməʊk] Rauch III U2, 42

smuggler [ˈsmʌglə] Schmuggler; Schmugglerin II

smurf [smɜːf] Schlumpf I

snack [snæk] Snack; Imbiss I

snake [sneɪk] Schlange I

snow [snəʊ] Schnee <III U3, 72>

snowboarding [ˈsnəʊbɔːdɪŋ] Snowboarden <III U2, 186>

so [səʊ] so II

so much [ˌsəʊ ˈmʌtʃ] so sehr III U4, 76

so [səʊ] deshalb; also I

soap [səʊp] Seife III U5, 97

soccer (AE) [ˈsɒkə] Fußball <III U1, 24>

sock [sɒk] Socke I

sofa [ˈsəʊfə] Sofa II

software [ˈsɒftweə] Software II

sold [səʊld] simple past, past participle von to sell III U1, 13

soldier [ˈsəʊldʒə] Soldat; Soldatin III U3, 62

solid [ˈsɒlɪd] fest III U3, 55

to **solve** [sɒlv] lösen I

some [sʌm] einige; etwas I

something [ˈsʌmθɪŋ] etwas I

sometimes [ˈsʌmtaɪmz] manchmal II

son [sʌn] Sohn III U3, 64

song [sɒŋ] Lied <I>

soon [suːn] bald II

See you soon! [si juː ˈsuːn] Bis bald! I

sore [sɔː] schmerzhaft; wund II

sore throat [ˌsɔː ˈθrəʊt] Halsschmerzen II

*to be **sorry** [bi ˈsɒri] leid tun III U4, 87

*to feel **sorry** [ˌfiːl ˈsɒri fə] Mitleid haben mit; bedauern III U5, 105

Sorry. [ˈsɒri] Tut mir leid.; Entschuldigung. I

to say sorry [ˌseɪ ˈsɒri] sich entschuldigen II

sort [sɔːt] Sorte; Art II

to **sort** [sɔːt] sortieren <III U1, 17>

sound [saʊnd] Laut; Ton Geräusch III U3, 54

to **sound** [saʊnd] klingen II

sounds [saʊndz] Laute <I>

soup [suːp] Suppe II

south [saʊθ] Süden III U1, 10

in the south of [ɪn ðə ˈsaʊθ ˌəv] im Süden von III U1, 10

southbound [ˈsaʊθbaʊnd] in Richtung Süden <III U5, 207>

souvenir [ˌsuːvnˈɪə] Souvenir; Andenken III U1, 12

souvenir shop [ˈsuːvnɪə ˌʃɒp] Souvenirladen III U1, 12

space rocket [ˈspeɪs ˌrɒkɪt] Raumschiff <III U1, 30>

spaghetti [spəˈgeti] Spaghetti II

*to **speak** [spi:k] sprechen III U1, 21

speaking ['spi:kɪŋ] Sprechen <I>
speaking skills ['spi:kɪŋ ˌskɪlz] Fertigkeit Sprechen <I>

special ['speʃl] besonders; speziell I
special offer [ˌspeʃl ˈɒfə] Sonderangebot III U4, 80

with **special** needs [wɪθ ˌspeʃl ˈni:dz] mit Behinderung; mit besonderen Bedürfnissen III U5, 95

speech [spi:tʃ] Sprache; Rede III U3, 54
farewell speech [feəˈwel spi:tʃ] Abschiedsrede II
speech bubble ['spi:tʃ ˌbʌbl] Sprechblase <III U2, 47>

*to **spell** [spel] buchstabieren I

spelling ['spelɪŋ] Rechtschreibung I

*to **spend** [spend] ausgeben (Geld); verbringen (Zeit) II

spent [spent] simple past, past participle von to spend II

spice [spaɪs] Gewürz II

spider ['spaɪdə] Spinne III U3, 63

*to **split** [splɪt] teilen; spalten <III U5, 135>

spoke [spəʊk] simple past von to speak III U1, 21

spoken ['spəʊkn] past participle von to speak III U1, 21

spoon [spu:n] Löffel II

sport [spɔ:t] Sport I; Sportart III U2, 33
sports shop ['spɔ:ts ˌʃɒp] Sportgeschäft I

to **spot** [spɒt] sehen; erkennen <III U2, 128>

to **sprain** [spreɪn] verstauchen; verrenken III U2, 39

spring roll [ˌsprɪŋ ˈrəʊl] Frühlingsrolle II

I **spy** with my little eye … [aɪ spaɪ wɪð ˌmaɪ lɪtl ˈaɪ] Ich sehe was, was du nicht siehst … I

square [skweə] Platz II

squash [skwɒʃ] Squash <III U2, 186>

stadium ['steɪdɪəm] Stadion II

stage [steɪdʒ] Bühne II

food **stall** ['fu:d ˌstɔ:l] Essensstand II

stallholder ['stɔ:lˌhəʊldə] Standinhaber; Standinhaberin II

stamp [stæmp] Briefmarke III U4, 80

*to **stand** [stænd] stehen II

star [stɑ:] Star I; Stern III U2, 50
You're a star. [jɔ:rə ˈstɑ:] Du bist fantastisch. II

start [stɑ:t] Start; Anfang III U2, 51

to **start** [stɑ:t] anfangen; beginnen; starten II; gründen III U3, 55
to start a band [ˌstɑ:t ə ˈbænd] eine Band gründen II
starting point ['stɑ:tɪŋ ˌpɔɪnt] Ausgangspunkt <III U5, 101>

static caravan ['stætɪk ˌkærəvæn] Mobilheim (großer, fest stehender Wohnwagen) <III U3, 194>

station ['steɪʃn] Haltestelle; Station; Bahnhof III U5, 101

to **stay** [steɪ] übernachten; bleiben II

steam engine ['sti:mˌendʒɪn] Dampfmaschine III U3, 57

steel [sti:l] Stahl III U3, 55

steep [sti:p] steil <III U3, 73>

step [step] Schritt III U5, 102; Stufe II

sticker ['stɪkə] Aufkleber II

sticky ['stɪki] klebrig <III U3, 66>

still [stɪl] dennoch III U2, 43

to **stir** [stɜ:] rühren; umrühren II

stocks [stɒks] Pranger III U2, 43

stomach ['stʌmək] Magen; Bauch II
stomach ache ['stʌmək ˌeɪk] Bauchweh; Bauchschmerzen II

stone [stəʊn] Stein III U1, 10
stone put ['stəʊn ˌpʊt] Steinwurf <III U3, 131>

stood [stʊd] simple past, past participle von to stand II

stop [stɒp] Haltestelle; Halt III U5, 100
bus stop ['bʌs ˌstɒp] Bushaltestelle II
Stop it! ['stɒp ɪt] Hör(t) auf! II

department **store** [dɪˈpɑ:tmənt ˌstɔ:] Kaufhaus II

storm [stɔ:m] Sturm I

story ['stɔ:ri] Geschichte I

straight on [streɪt ˈɒn] geradeaus I

hair **straightener** ['heə ˌstreɪtnə] Haarglätter I

strange [streɪndʒ] merkwürdig; seltsam II

stranger ['streɪndʒə] Fremder; Fremde <III U1, 17>

straw [strɔ:] Trinkhalm II

strawberry ['strɔ:bri] Erdbeere II

stream [stri:m] Bach II

street [stri:t] Straße III U1, 15
back street ['bæk stri:t] Hinterhof <III U1, 17>

striking ['straɪkɪŋ] bemerkenswert; auffallend III U5, 100

strong [strɒŋ] stark III U2, 34

structure ['strʌktʃə] Struktur; Aufbau <III U2, 51>

*to be **stuck** [bi ˈstʌk] feststecken; nicht weg können I
stuck in the mud [ˌstʌk ɪn ðə ˈmʌd] im Schlamm festgesteckt I

student ['stju:dnt] Schüler; Schülerin I

TV **studio** [ˌti:ˈvi: ˌstju:diəʊ] Fernsehstudio II

study skills [ˌstʌdi ˈskɪlz] Fertigkeit Lern- und Arbeitstechniken <I>

style [staɪl] Stil III U5, 95

subject ['sʌbdʒɪkt] Schulfach I

submarine [ˌsʌbmrˈi:n] U-Boot I

success [səkˈses] Erfolg III U3, 54

successful [səkˈsesfl] erfolgreich III U2, 35

such as ['sʌtʃ ˌəz] wie <III U1, 24>

suddenly ['sʌdnli] plötzlich; auf einmal II

suit [su:t] Anzug <III U2, 44>

to **suit** [su:t] stehen; passen II

suitcase ['su:tkeɪs] Koffer II

summary ['sʌmri] Zusammenfassung <III U1, 25>

summer ['sʌmə] Sommer II

sun [sʌn] Sonne III U1, 11

to **sunbathe** ['sʌnbeɪð] sonnenbaden II

Sunday ['sʌndeɪ] Sonntag I

sunglasses (pl) ['sʌnˌglɑ:sɪz] Sonnenbrille II

sunglasses

sunk [sʌŋk] past participle von *to sink* III U4, 84

sunny ['sʌni] sonnig I

superman ['su:pəmæn] Superman I

supermarket ['su:pə͵ma:kɪt] Supermarkt II

sure [ʃʊə] sicher II
sure of oneself ['ʃʊər͵əv ͵wʌnself] selbstsicher III U4, 77

to surf [sɜ:f] surfen; wellenreiten II
to surf the internet [͵sɜ:f ði 'ɪntənet] im Internet surfen II

surfing ['sɜ:fɪŋ] Wellenreiten; Surfen <III U2, 186>

surname ['sɜ:neɪm] Nachname; Familienname <III U1, 127>

surprise [sə'praɪz] Überraschung I

surprised [sə'praɪzd] überrascht II

surprising [sə'praɪzɪŋ] überraschend <III U4, 133>

survey ['sɜ:veɪ] Umfrage II

to survive [sə'vaɪv] überleben III U4, 84

swam [swæm] simple past von *to swim* II

sweater ['swetə] Pullover <III U5, 206>

sweatshirt ['swetʃɜ:t] Sweatshirt I

*__to sweep__ [swi:p] fegen II; mitreißen <III U3, 72>
to sweep through [͵swi:p 'θru:] durchziehen <III U3, 73>

sweet [swi:t] Süßigkeit; Bonbon I

sweet [swi:t] süß III U5, 96

swept [swept] simple past, past participle von *to sweep* II

*__to swim__ [swɪm] schwimmen II

*__to go swimming__ [͵gəʊ 'swɪmɪŋ] schwimmen gehen I
swimming pool ['swɪmɪŋ ͵pu:l] Schwimmbad I
swimming things ['swɪmɪŋ ͵θɪŋz] Schwimmsachen <III U5, 206>

*__to swing__ [swɪŋ] schwingen; schwenken <III U3, 131>

sword [sɔ:d] Schwert III U2, 43

swum [swʌm] past participle von *to swim* II

T

table ['teɪbl] Tisch I; Tabelle <III ZI, 9>
table tennis ['teɪbl ͵tenɪs] Tischtennis II

tablespoon ['teɪblspu:n] Esslöffel II

tablet ['tæblət] Tablette II

tactic ['tæktɪk] Taktik; Vorgehensweise <III U3, 64>

take [teɪk] Aufnahme <III U1, 27>

*__to take__ [teɪk] nehmen; mitnehmen; bringen; mitbringen; hinbringen II; dauern III U1, 10
to take a break [͵teɪk ͵ə 'breɪk] Pause machen II
to take a photo [͵teɪk ͵ə 'fəʊtəʊ] ein Foto machen I
to take a trip [͵teɪk ͵ə 'trɪp] eine Fahrt machen III U2, 34
to take notes [͵teɪk 'nəʊts] sich Notizen machen I
to take off [͵teɪk ͵'ɒf] ausziehen III U5, 96
to take out [͵teɪk ͵'aʊt] herausnehmen I
to take part (in) [͵teɪk 'pa:t] teilnehmen (an) III U5, 100
to take place [͵teɪk 'pleɪs] stattfinden <III U3, 130>; <III U4, 89>
to take turns [͵teɪk 'tɜ:nz] sich abwechseln <II>
to take the dog for a walk [͵teɪk ðə dɒg fɔ:r͵ə 'wɔ:k] den Hund ausführen I

takeaway ['teɪkəweɪ] Essen zum Mitnehmen II

taken ['teɪkn] past participle von *to take* II

talent show ['tælənt ͵ʃəʊ] Talentwettbewerb I
What's your talent? [wɒts jɔ: 'tælənt] Was ist dein Talent? I

talented ['tæləntɪd] talentiert III U2, 35

talk [tɔ:k] Vortrag; Rede <III U1, 19>
to give a talk [͵gɪv ͵ə 'tɔ:k] einen Vortrag halten <III U1, 19>

to talk (to) [tɔ:k] sprechen (mit); reden (mit) I
to talk about ['tɔ:k ͵ə͵baʊt] sprechen über II
TTYL (Talk to you later!) ['tɔ:k tə ju ͵leɪtə] Wir reden später! II
don't talk [͵dəʊnt 'tɔ:k] sei still; rede nicht I

tall [tɔ:l] groß; hoch II

tapestry ['tæpɪstri] Wandteppich <III U1, 127>

task [ta:sk] Aufgabe; Auftrag <I>

tasty ['teɪsti] lecker; schmackhaft III U4, 80

taxi ['tæksi] Taxi II

tea bag ['ti: ͵bæg] Teebeutel <III U4, 200>

tea [ti:] Tee; (frühes) Abendessen I

teacher ['ti:tʃə] Lehrer; Lehrerin I

team [ti:m] Team; Gruppe I

teamwork ['ti:mwɜ:k] Teamwork II

tear [tɪə] Träne <III U4, 77>

teaspoon ['ti:spu:n] Teelöffel II

Design Technology (DT) [dɪ͵zaɪn tek'nɒlədʒi, ͵di:'ti:] Technik I

technology [tek'nɒlədʒi] Technologie <III U1, 30>

teen [ti:n] Jugend-; Teenager; Jugendliche; Jugendlicher II

teenage ['ti:neɪdʒ] jugendlich <III U2, 128>

teenager ['ti:n͵eɪdʒə] Teenager; Teenagerin; Jugendliche; Jugendlicher III U2, 33

telephone ['telɪfəʊn] Telefon III U3, 54
telephone box ['telɪfəʊn ͵bɒks] Telefonzelle II

*__to tell__ [tel] erzählen; sagen I
Can you tell me the way to …? [kæn ju: ͵tel mi ðə 'weɪ tə] Kannst du mir sagen, wie ich … komme? I

ten [ten] zehn I

tennis ['tenɪs] Tennis I

tent [tent] Zelt III U3, 61

to test [test] testen; prüfen II

text [tekst] Text II
text message ['tekst ͵mesɪdʒ] Textnachricht (SMS) I

to **text** [tekst] texten; eine SMS schreiben II

texter [ˈtekstə] SMS-Schreiber; SMS-Schreiberin II

than [ðæn] als II

Thank you. [ˈθæŋk ju] Danke. I

Thanks. [θæŋks] Danke. I

that [ðæt] dass III U1, 22

that [ðæt] das I

after that [ˌɑːftə ˈðæt] danach I

that's £2.24 [ðæts ˌtuː paʊndz twentiˈfɔː] das macht 2 Pfund und 24 Pence I

the [ðə] der; die; das I

the same [ðə ˈseɪm] derselbe; gleich II

theatre [ˈθɪətə] Theater II

their [ðeə] ihr I

theirs [ðeəz] ihre III U5, 99

them [ðem] sie II

theme park [ˈθiːm ˌpɑːk] Freizeitpark I

themselves [ðəmˈselvz] selber; sie selbst; sich selbst; selbst III U2, 152

then [ðen] dann; danach I; damals III U1, 10

there [ðeə] da; dort I

over there [ˌəʊvə ˈðeə] da drüben; dort drüben II

there are [ðeərˈɑː] da sind; es gibt I

there is (= there's) [ðeəˈɪz] da ist; es gibt I

these [ðiːz] diese II

they [ðeɪ] sie (Pl.) I

thing [θɪŋ] Sache; Ding II

*to **think** [θɪŋk] denken I

to think of [ˈθɪŋk ˌəv] sich ausdenken; sich etwas einfallen lassen <III U3, 68>

I don't think so. [ˌaɪ dəʊnt ˈθɪŋk səʊ] Ich glaube nicht. II

I think so. [ˌaɪ ˈθɪŋk səʊ] Ich glaube. II

third [θɜːd] dritte I

thirsty [ˈθɜːsti] durstig II

thirteen [θɜːˈtiːn] dreizehn I

thirty [ˈθɜːti] dreißig I

this [ðɪs] das; dies I

like this [laɪk ˈðɪs] so; auf diese Weise III U3, 62

this way [ðɪs ˈweɪ] in diese Richtung II

those [ðəʊz] jene II

though [ðəʊ] jedoch <III U1, 24>

thought [θɔːt] simple past, past participle von to think II

a/one **thousand** [əˈwʌn ˈθaʊznd] eintausend; tausend II

three [θriː] drei I

throat [θrəʊt] Hals II

sore throat [ˌsɔː ˈθrəʊt] Halsschmerzen II

through [θruː] durch II

Thursday [ˈθɜːzdeɪ] Donnerstag I

ticket [ˈtɪkɪt] Karte II; Fahrschein; Eintrittskarte III U1, 15

return ticket [rɪˈtɜːn ˌtɪkɪt] Hin- und Rückfahrkarte III U5, 101

single ticket [ˈsɪŋl ˌtɪkɪt] einfache Fahrkarte III U5, 101

to **tidy** (up) [ˌtaɪdi ˈʌp] aufräumen; in Ordnung bringen II

tiger [ˈtaɪgə] Tiger I

tight [taɪt] eng; fest II

time [taɪm] Zeit; Uhrzeit I; Mal III U1, 21

free time [ˌfriː ˈtaɪm] Freizeit I

on time [ɒn ˈtaɪm] pünktlich III U5, 100

time travel [ˈtaɪm ˌtrævl] Zeitreise III U4, 79

It's time to go. [ɪts ˌtaɪm tə ˈgəʊ] Es ist Zeit zu gehen. I

the first time [ðə ˌfɜːst ˈtaɪm] das erste Mal I

What time is it? [wɒt ˈtaɪm ˌɪz ɪt] Wie spät ist es?; Wie viel Uhr ist es? I

timetable [ˈtaɪmˌteɪbl] Stundenplan I; Fahrplan III U5, 100

tiny [ˈtaɪni] klein; winzig III U1, 17

tip [tɪp] Tipp III U3, 58; Ratschlag <I>

language tip [ˈlæŋgwɪdʒ ˈtɪp] Grammatikhinweis <I>

tired [taɪəd] müde I

tissue [ˈtɪʃuː] Taschentuch III U4, 81

title [ˈtaɪtl] Titel; Überschrift <II>

to [tuː] in; nach; zu; vor (bei Uhrzeitangaben) I

to [tʊ] bis II

to [tuː] um zu <III U1, 24>

today [təˈdeɪ] heute I

together [təˈgeðə] zusammen; gemeinsam I

toiletries [ˈtɔɪlɪtriz] Toilettenartikel; Hygieneartikel <III U5, 206>

told [təʊld] simple past von to tell I

tomato (sg) [təˈmɑːtəʊ], **tomatoes** (pl) [təˈmɑːtəʊz] Tomate II

tomorrow [təˈmɒrəʊ] morgen II

tongue twister [ˈtʌŋ ˌtwɪstə] Zungenbrecher <III U1, 13>

tonne [tʌn] Tonne II

too [tuː] auch I; zu II

too much [ˌtuː ˈmʌtʃ] zu sehr II

took [tʊk] simple past von to take II

tool [tuːl] Werkzeug II

tooth (sg) [tuːθ], **teeth** (pl) [tiːθ] Zahn III U2, 39

toothbrush [ˈtuːθbrʌʃ] Zahnbürste III U5, 96

toothpaste [ˈtuːθpeɪst] Zahnpasta III U5, 97

toothpick [ˈtuːθpɪk] Zahnstocher II

top [tɒp] Top; Oberteil II

topic [ˈtɒpɪk] Thema <II>

torch [tɔːtʃ] Taschenlampe I

tornado [tɔːˈneɪdəʊ] Tornado <III U3, 73>

caber **toss** [ˈkeɪbə ˌtɒs] Baumstammwerfen <III U3, 130>

*to keep in **touch** [ˌkiːp ɪn ˈtʌtʃ] in Verbindung bleiben II

tough [tʌf] hart III U2, 34

tour [tʊə] Tour; Fahrt; Reise; Rundgang <III U1, 30>

tourist [ˈtʊərɪst] Tourist; Touristin I

Tourist Information Centre [ˌtʊərɪst ˌɪnfəˈmeɪʃn ˌsentə] Touristeninformation I

to **tow** away [ˈtəʊ əweɪ] abschleppen <III U4, 86>

towel [ˈtaʊəl] Handtuch III U5, 96

towel

tower

tower ['taʊə] Turm II
 clock tower ['klɒk ˌtaʊə] Uhrenturm II
town [taʊn] Stadt I
toy [tɔɪ] Spielzeug III U2, 39
 cuddly toy ['kʌdli ˌtɔɪ] Kuscheltier III U2, 39
tractor ['træktə] Traktor I
tradition [trə'dɪʃn] Tradition III U3, 53
traffic light ['træfɪk ˌlaɪt] (Verkehrs-) Ampel <III U1, 178>
traffic ['træfɪk] Verkehr III U1, 16
train [treɪn] Zug I
 to go by (train) [ˌgəʊ baɪ ('treɪn)] mit (dem Zug) fahren I
trained [treɪnd] ausgebildet <III U1, 126>
trainer ['treɪnə] Turnschuh I
training ['treɪnɪŋ] Training III U2, 41
tram [træm] Straßenbahn III U5, 100
public **transport** [ˌpʌblɪk 'trænspɔːt] öffentliche Verkehrsmittel III U5, 100
time **travel** ['taɪm ˌtrævl] Zeitreise III U4, 79
to **travel** ['trævl] reisen II; fahren III U5, 103
traveller ['trævlə] Reisender; Reisende <III U1, 17>
tray [treɪ] Tablett II
treasure ['treʒə] Schatz II
treat [triːt] Leckerbissen <III U3, 66>
tree [triː] Baum I
 tree house ['triː ˌhaʊs] Baumhaus I
trick [trɪk] Trick; Streich I; Kunststück III U2, 41
 Trick or treat! [ˌtrɪk ə 'triːt] Süßes, sonst gibt's Saures! I
trip [trɪp] Ausflug I; Trip; Fahrt III U2, 34; Reise III U3, 58
 boat trip ['bəʊt ˌtrɪp] Bootsfahrt; Schiffsfahrt II
 to take a trip [ˌteɪk ə 'trɪp] eine Fahrt machen III U2, 34
trouble ['trʌbl] Schwierigkeiten; Problem; Ärger III U2, 33

to get into trouble [ˌget ˌɪntə 'trʌbl] in Schwierigkeiten geraten <III U2, 128>
trousers (pl) ['traʊzəz] Hose I
truck [trʌk] Wagen; Karre III U1, 21
true [truː] wahr II
truth [truːθ] Wahrheit <III U4, 77>
to **try** [traɪ] ausprobieren III U2, 33
 to try on [ˌtraɪ 'ɒn] anprobieren II
 to try out [ˌtraɪ 'aʊt] ausprobieren III U2, 43
T-shirt ['tiːʃɜːt] T-Shirt I
TTYL (Talk to you later!) ['tɔːk tə ju ˌleɪtə] Wir reden später! II
tube [tjuːb] Schlauch; Rohr III U3, 55
Tuesday ['tjuːzdeɪ] Dienstag I
 on Tuesday [ˌɒn 'tjuːzdeɪ] am Dienstag I
tuna ['tjuːnə] Thunfisch II
tunnel ['tʌnl] Tunnel III U1, 20
(wind) **turbine** [(wɪnd) 'tɜːbaɪn] Windrad III U3, 53
Your turn. [jɔː 'tɜːn] Du bist dran. <I>
to **turn** [tɜːn] abbiegen III U1, 12
 to turn left (into …) [ˌtɜːn 'left] (nach) links abbiegen I
 to turn right (into …) [ˌtɜːn 'raɪt] rechts abbiegen I
*to take **turns** [ˌteɪk 'tɜːnz] sich abwechseln <II>
tutor ['tjuːtə] Klassenlehrer; Klassenlehrerin I
 tutor group ['tjuːtə ˌgruːp] Klasse I
TV [ˌtiː'viː] Fernseher I
 TV show [ˌtiː'viː ˌʃəʊ] Fernsehsendung II
 TV studio [ˌtiː'viː ˌstjuːdiəʊ] Fernsehstudio II
 to watch TV [ˌwɒtʃ tiː'viː] fernsehen I
tweet [twiːt] Pieps III U1, 22
twelve [twelv] zwölf I
twenty ['twenti] zwanzig I
 twenty-one [ˌtwenti'wʌn] einundzwanzig I
to **twist** [twɪst] verdrehen; verzerren II
two [tuː] zwei I

type [taɪp] Sorte; Typ; Art III U1, 31
to **type** [taɪp] tippen <III U2, 47>
typically ['tɪpɪkli] typisch <III U3, 66>
tyre [taɪə] Reifen III U3, 55

U

umbrella [ʌm'brelə] Regenschirm II
umpire ['ʌmpaɪə] Schiedsrichter; Schiedsrichterin <III U5, 109>
uncle ['ʌŋkl] Onkel II
uncomfortable [ʌn'kʌmftəbl] unbequem; unangenehm II
under ['ʌndə] unter I
underground ['ʌndəgraʊnd] U-Bahn II
underlined [ʌndə'laɪnd] unterstrichen <III U3, 73>
*to **understand** [ʌndə'stænd] verstehen II
understood [ʌndə'stʊd] simple past, past participle von to understand II
unemployment (no pl) [ˌʌnɪm'plɔɪmənt] Arbeitslosigkeit <III U4, 133>
unfair [ʌn'feə] unfair III U1, 16
unfashionable [ʌn'fæʃnəbl] unmodisch II
unfriendly [ʌn'frendli] unfreundlich III U2, 35
unhappy [ʌn'hæpi] unglücklich II
uniform ['juːnɪfɔːm] Uniform I
unit ['juːnɪt] Lektion; Kapitel <I>
unreal [ʌn'rɪəl] irreal <III U5, 101>
untied [ʌn'taɪd] nicht zugebunden <III U1, 17>
until [ʌn'tɪl] bis I
up [ʌp] hinauf; oben II
to **upload** ['ʌpləʊd] ins Internet stellen; hochladen II
upper ['ʌpə] obere III U4, 92
us [ʌs] uns I
to **use** [juːz] benutzen; verwenden II
used to (live) ['juːst tə] (wohnte) früher III U1, 16
useful ['juːsfl] nützlich; hilfreich III U4, 76

p pen • **b** bed • **t** ten • **d** dad • **k** cat • **g** grey • **tʃ** chair • **dʒ** joke • **f** fan • **v** very • **θ** three • **ð** the

usually [ˈjuːʒli] normalerweise; gewöhnlich II

V

no **vacancies** [ˌnəʊ ˈveɪknsɪz] kein Zimmer frei <III U4, 86>

in **vain** [ɪn ˈveɪn] umsonst; vergeblich <III U5, 101>

valid [ˈvælɪd] gültig III U5, 100

van [væn] Lieferwagen; Transporter III U4, 93

vegetable (veg) [ˈvedʒtəbl] Gemüse II

vegetarian [ˌvedʒɪˈteəriən] Vegetarier; Vegetarierin I

veggie bean cake [ˌvedʒi ˈbiːn keɪk] vegetarisches Bohnengericht II

vehicle [ˈvɪəkl] Fahrzeug <III U4, 86>

version [ˈvɜːʃn] Version <III U1, 27>

very [ˈveri] sehr I

vet [vet] Tierarzt; Tierärztin II

Victorian era [vɪkˌtɔːriən ˈɪərə] viktorianisches Zeitalter III U1, 25

video [ˈvɪdiəʊ] Video II

video chat [ˈvɪdiəʊ ˌtʃæt] Video-Chat III U3, 67

viewing [ˈvjuːɪŋ] Hör-/Sehverstehen <I>

viewing skills [ˈvjuːɪŋ ˌskɪlz] Fertigkeit Hör-/Sehverstehen <I>

the **Vikings** [ðə ˈvaɪkɪŋz] die Wikinger III U1, 11

Viking [ˈvaɪkɪŋ] Wikinger; Wikingerin <III U5, 134>

village [ˈvɪlɪdʒ] Dorf III U1, 16

violence (no pl) [ˈvaɪələns] Gewalt <III U4, 133>

violent [ˈvaɪələnt] gewaltsam; gewalttätig; brutal <III U4, 132>

visa [ˈviːzə] Visum; Einreisebewilligung <III U5, 206>

to **visit** [ˈvɪzɪt] besuchen II

visitor [ˈvɪzɪtə] Besucher; Besucherin II

voice [vɔɪs] Stimme III U1, 22

volleyball [ˈvɒlibɔːl] Volleyball II

volunteer [ˌvɒlənˈtɪə] Freiwilliger; Freiwillige; ehrenamtlicher Helfer; ehrenamtliche Helferin III U2, 33

voyage [ˈvɔɪɪdʒ] Reise; Fahrt III U4, 84

W

to **wait** [weɪt] warten II

to wait for [weɪt ˈfɔː] warten auf II

I can't wait [aɪ ˌkɑːnt ˈweɪt] ich kann es kaum erwarten III U5, 100

waiter [ˈweɪtə] Kellner II

*to **wake up** [ˌweɪk ˈʌp] aufwachen II

walk [wɔːk] Spaziergang III U3, 61

to go for a walk [ˌgəʊ fər ə ˈwɔːk] spazieren gehen I

night walk [ˈnaɪt wɔːk] Nachtwanderung I

a five minute walk [ə ˌfaɪv mɪnɪt ˌwɔːk] fünf Minuten zu Fuß III U1, 12

to take the dog for a walk [teɪk ðə dɒg fɔːr ə ˈwɔːk] den Hund ausführen I

to **walk** [wɔːk] gehen; laufen I

walking [ˈwɔːkɪŋ] Wandern III U3, 61

wall [wɔːl] Mauer; Wand II

to **want** (to) [ˈwɒnt] wollen I

wardrobe [ˈwɔːdrəʊb] Kleiderschrank I

warm [wɔːm] warm I

was [wɒz] simple past von to be I

to **wash** [wɒʃ] (sich) waschen; spülen III U5, 98

washable [ˈwɒʃəbl] waschbar <III U3, 193>

*to do the **washing** up [ˌduː ðə ˈwɒʃɪŋ ˌʌp] abspülen II

to **watch** [wɒtʃ] anschauen I; aufpassen auf; zuschauen; beobachten II

to watch TV [wɒtʃ tiːˈviː] fernsehen I

bird **watching** [ˈbɜːd ˌwɒtʃɪŋ] Vogelbeobachtung III U3, 61

mineral **water** [ˈmɪnrl ˌwɔːtə] Mineralwasser III U4, 81

water [ˈwɔːtə] Wasser III U2, 33

waterproofs [ˈwɔːtəpruːfs] Regenbekleidung <III U2, 186>

wave [weɪv] Welle I; <III U3, 72>

to **wave** [weɪv] winken II

wax [wæks] Wachs <III U1, 30>

way [weɪ] Weg; Art und Weise III U1, 12

No way! [ˌnəʊ ˈweɪ] Auf keinen Fall!; Was?!; Echt?! III U3, 58

way in [ˌweɪ ˈɪn] Einstieg <I>

asking the way [ˌɑːskɪŋ ðə ˈweɪ] nach dem Weg fragen I

Can you tell me the way to …? [kæn juː ˌtel mi ðə ˈweɪ tə] Kannst du mir sagen, wie ich … komme? I

this way [ðɪs ˈweɪ] in diese Richtung II

way to go [ˈweɪ tə ˌgəʊ] super II

we [wiː; wi] wir I

weak [wiːk] schwach III U2, 35

wealth [welθ] Reichtum III U5, 105

*to **wear** [weə] tragen I

weather [ˈweðə] Wetter I

web [web] Spinnennetz; Netz III U3, 63

website [ˈwebsaɪt] Website II

wedding [ˈwedɪŋ] Hochzeit II

Wednesday [ˈwenzdeɪ] Mittwoch I

week [wiːk] Woche I

on **weekdays** [ɒn ˈwiːkdeɪz] unter der Woche; an Werktagen III U5, 96

weekend [ˈwiːkend] Wochenende I

at the weekend [ət ðə ˌwiːkˈend] am Wochenende I

weekly [ˈwiːkli] wöchentlich III U5, 101

to **weigh** [weɪ] wiegen II

to **welcome** [ˈwelkəm] willkommen heißen <III U4, 132>

You're welcome. [jɔː ˈwelkəm] Gern geschehen. I

welcome (to) [ˈwelkəm tʊ] willkommen (bei/in) I

well [wel] gut II

Well done! [ˌwel ˈdʌn] Gut gemacht! I

well [wel] na ja I

Well, look … [wel ˈlʊk] Na ja, schau mal … nach. I

well

Welsh [welʃ] Walisisch; walisisch; Waliser; Waliserin III U2, 32

went [went] simple past von *to go* I

were [wɜ:] simple past von *to be* I

west [west] Westen III U1, 17

westbound ['wesbaʊnd] in Richtung Westen <III U5, 207>

wet [wet] nass I

what [wɒt] was I; welche II; wie III U1, 12

What about you? [ˌwɒt‿əbaʊt 'ju:] Und du? II

What must you be like? [wɒt ˌmʌst ju 'bi: laɪk] Wie musst du sein? III U2, 37

what sth was like [ˌwɒt … 'wəz laɪk] wie etwas war III U1, 12

What time is it? [ˌwɒt 'taɪm‿ɪz‿ɪt] Wie spät ist es?; Wie viel Uhr ist es? I

What to … ['wɒt tə] Was man … II

What's your name? [ˌwɒts jə 'neɪm] Wie heißt du? I

What's wrong? [ˌwɒts 'rɒŋ] Was ist los?; Was stimmt nicht? II

wheel [wi:l] Rad III U3, 55

big wheel [ˌbɪg 'wi:l] Riesenrad II

wheelchair ['wi:ltʃeə] Rollstuhl III U2, 43

when [wen] wenn; als II

when [wen] wann I

where [weə] wo; wohin; woher I

Where are you from? [ˌweər‿ə ju 'frɒm] Woher kommst du? I

wherever [weə'revə] wo(hin) auch immer; egal wo(hin); überall wo(hin) III U5, 107

which [wɪtʃ] welche II

which [wɪtʃ] die; der; dem; den; das III U3, 54

while [waɪl] während II

white [waɪt] weiß I

who [hu:] wer I

who [hu:] die; welche II; der; dem; den III U3, 54

whose [hu:z] dessen; deren III U3, 54

why [waɪ] warum II

will [wɪl] werden II

*to **win** [wɪn] gewinnen; siegen I

wind [wɪnd] Wind I

wind farm ['wɪnd fɑ:m] Windpark III U3, 53

window ['wɪndəʊ] Fenster I

windowsill ['wɪndəʊsɪl] Fenstersims <III U1, 17>

windsurfing ['wɪndsɜ:fɪŋ] Windsurfen <III U2, 186>

windy ['wɪndi] windig I

winner ['wɪnə] Gewinner; Gewinnerin I

winter ['wɪntə] Winter I

wish [wɪʃ] Wunsch <III U3, 61>

Best wishes, [ˌbest 'wɪʃɪz] Mit den besten Wünschen, I

to **wish** [wɪʃ] wünschen III U1, 25

witch [wɪtʃ] Hexe I

with [wɪð] mit I

with special needs [wɪθ ˌspeʃl 'ni:dz] mit Behinderung; mit besonderen Bedürfnissen III U5, 95

without [wɪ'ðaʊt] ohne III U4, 76

woke up [ˌwəʊk‿'ʌp] simple past von *to wake up* II

woman *(sg)* ['wʊmən], **women** *(pl)* ['wɪmɪn] Frau II

women's national team [ˌwɪmɪnz 'næʃnl ti:m] Frauen-Nationalmannschaft <III U1, 24>

won [wʌn] past participle von *to win* II

It **won't** be long. [ɪt ˌwəʊnt bi 'lɒŋ] Es wird nicht lange dauern. II

won't (= will not) [wəʊnt] nicht werden II

won't matter [ˌwəʊnt 'mætə] wird nicht von Bedeutung sein; wird nichts ausmachen <III U5, 101>

wonderful ['wʌndəfl] wunderbar III U5, 105

wood [wʊd] Holz III U3, 54; Wald II

wool [wʊl] Wolle I

word [wɜ:d] Wort <I>

wore [wɔ:] simple past von *to wear* I

work [wɜ:k] Arbeit I

to **work** [wɜ:k] arbeiten I

worker ['wɜ:kə] Arbeiter; Arbeiterin II

workshop ['wɜ:kʃɒp] Workshop II

acting workshop ['æktɪŋ ˌwɜ:kʃɒp] Schauspielworkshop II

world [wɜ:ld] Welt II

in the world [ɪn ðə 'wɜ:ld] auf der Welt II

worried ['wʌrid] beunruhigt; besorgt II

to **worry** ['wʌri] sich Sorgen machen I

Don't worry. [dəʊnt 'wʌri] Mach dir keine Sorgen. II

worst [wɜ:st] schlimmste; schlechteste III U1, 16

would [wʊd] würde(n) II

would like [wʊd 'laɪk] würde(n) gern; hätte(n) gern II

I wouldn't like (to) … [aɪ 'wʊdnt laɪk (tə)] ich möchte nicht …; ich würde nicht gerne … I

Would you like (to)…? [ˌwʊd jə 'laɪk (tə)] Möchtest du? I

wound [wu:nd] Wunde; Verletzung <III U2, 187>

wrap [ræp] Wrap II

*to **write** [raɪt] schreiben I

to write down [raɪt 'daʊn] aufschreiben <III U1, 24>

writer ['raɪtə] Schriftsteller; Schriftstellerin II; Verfasser; Verfasserin; Autor; Autorin III U2, 50

writing ['raɪtɪŋ] Schreiben <I>

wrong [rɒŋ] falsch I

to get a job wrong [ˌget ə dʒɒb 'rɒŋ] einen Auftrag vermasseln III U2, 50

is something wrong [ɪz 'sʌmθɪŋ rɒŋ] stimmt etwas nicht II

What's wrong? [ˌwɒts 'rɒŋ] Was ist los?; Was stimmt nicht? II

wrote [rəʊt] simple past von *to write* II

Y

yeah *(infml)* [jeə] ja II

year [jɪə] Jahr; Jahrgangsstufe; Klasse I

yellow ['jeləʊ] gelb I

yes [jes] ja I
yesterday ['jestədeɪ] gestern I
yet [jet] schon II
    not … yet [nɒt … 'jet] noch nicht II
yogurt ['jɒgət] Joghurt II
you [juː] du; Sie; ihr; dich; euch; dir;
    Ihnen I
    Would you like (to)…? [ˌwʊd jə
    'laɪk (tə)] Möchtest du? I
    You're right. [jɔː ˌ'raɪt] Du hast
    recht. I
    You're welcome. [jɔː 'welkəm] Gern
    geschehen. I
young [jʌŋ] jung II
Your turn. [jɔː 'tɜːn] Du bist dran. II
your [jɔː] dein; euer I
    Your turn. [jɔː 'tɜːn] Du bist dran.
    <I>
yours [jɔːz] deine; eure; Ihre II
yourself [jɔː'self] dich selbst II
yourselves [jɔː'selvz] selber; ihr/euch/
    Sie/sich (selbst) III U2, 152
    Help yourselves! [ˌhelp jɔː'selvz]
    Bedient euch!; Bedienen Sie sich!
    II
youth (no pl) [juːθ] Jugend; Jugend-
    III U5, 94

Z

zebra ['zebrə] Zebra I
zero ['zɪərəʊ] null I
zip line ['zɪp ˌlaɪn] Seilrutsche
    III U2, 32
zoo [zuː] Zoo; Tierpark I
    at the zoo [ət ðə 'zuː] im Zoo I
zookeeper ['zuːˌkiːpə] Tierpfleger;
    Tierpflegerin I
to **zoom** in ['zuːm ˌɪn] heranzoomen
    <I>

Boys' names
Alan ['ælən] III U5, 103
Alex ['ælɪks] II
Ashley ['æʃli] III U4, 76
Barry ['bæri] I
Bart [bɑːt] III U1, 21

Ben [ben] I
Bertie ['bɜːti] <III U5, 135>
Billy ['bɪli] III U1, 20
Brad [bræd] II
Conor ['kɒnə] III U5, 96
Dan [dæn] III U4, 80
Dave [deɪv] I
Desmond ['dezmənd] I
Dylan ['dɪlən] III ZI 9
Edward ['edwəd] <III U1, 126>
Frank [fræŋk] I
Fred [fred] I
George [dʒɔːdʒ] III U4, 75
Harold ['hærəld] <III U1, 126>
Harry ['hæri] III U3, 58
Howard ['haʊəd] III U2, 129
Ian ['iːən] III U4, 80
Jahangir ['dʒəhæŋgɪr] I
Jake [dʒeɪk] III U3, 58
Jamie ['dʒeɪmi] I
Jay [dʒeɪ] I
Jim [dʒɪm] I
Jinsoo ['dʒɪnsuː] I
Joe [dʒəʊ] II
John [dʒɒn] <III U2, 129>
John [dʒɒn] III U4, 85
Jonas ['dʒəʊnəs] III U1, 20
Keith [kiːθ] III U5, 95
Leo ['liːəʊ] III U5, 96
Lewis ['lʊɪs] III ZI 9
Luke [luːk] I
Malcolm ['mælkəm] <III U3, 130>
Mark [mɑːk] III U2, 34
Marley ['mɑːli] I
Nathan ['neɪθn] I
Nick [nɪk] II
Patrick ['pætrɪk] III ZI 9
Richard ['rɪtʃəd] III U2, 42
Sam [sæm] I
Sean [ʃɔːn] III U4, 87
Seb [seb] III U4, 79
Shahid ['ʃɑːhɪd] I
Sid [sɪd] I
Simon ['saɪmən] I
Steve [stiːv] III U4, 79
Tim [tɪm] I
Tom [tɒm] I
William ['wɪljəm] <III U1, 126>

Girls' names
Abby ['æbi] III U3, 58
Alicia [ə'lɪʃə] I
Alva ['ælvə] III U3, 67
Beth [beθ] III U2, 34
Billy ['bɪli] III U5, 104
Carol ['kærl] III U4, 79
Ciara ['kɪərə] III U5, 107
Claire [kleə] I
Daisy ['deɪzi] III U1, 16
Dianne [daɪ'æn] <III U3, 59>
Ellie ['eli] III U2, 43
Emily ['emɪli] III ZI 9
Gwen [gwen] II
Hannah ['hænə] I
Hayley ['heɪli] III U5, 107
Helen ['helɪn] III U5, 103
Holly ['hɒli] I
Irina [i'riːnə] I
Jamila [dʒə'miːlə] II
Janet ['dʒænɪt] I
Julie ['dʒuːli] III U4, 74
Kate [keɪt] III U5, 103
Katie ['keɪti] III U3, 58
Kim [kɪm] III U2, 41
Laura ['lɔːrə] I
Lucy ['luːsi] I
Maddy ['mædi] III U5, 96
Maggie ['mægi] III U4, 75
Maisie ['meɪzi] II
Mary ['meəri] I
Megan ['megən] III U2, 40
Mina ['miːnə] II
Molly ['mɒli] II
Niamh [niːv] III U5, 104
Nichola ['nɪklə] II
Nisha ['nɪʃə] III U5, 104
Olivia [ɒl'ɪviə] I
Pamela ['pæmələ] II
Parule ['pəruːl] I
Polly ['pɒli] II
Rachel ['reɪtʃl] I
Rosie ['rəʊzi] I
Sally ['sæli] I
Sarah ['seərə] III U4, 74
Sharon ['ʃærən] III U1, 13
Sonya ['sɒnjə] III U5, 104

Sonya

Sophie ['səʊfi] III ZI 9
Susan ['su:zn] <III U2, 129>
Violet ['vaɪələt] III U1, 25

Surnames

Adams ['ædəmz] III U2, 38
Ahern [ə'hɜ:n] <III U5, 135>
Archer ['ɑ:tʃə] <III U1, 127>
Azad ['æzæd] I
Becket ['bekɪt] III U2, 45
Brown [braʊn] III U4, 74
Burgess ['bɜ:dʒəs] II
Darcy ['dɑ:si] <III U1, 127>
Elliot ['eliət] I
Fox [fɒks] III U1, 20
Fraser ['freɪzə] I
Green [gri:n] II
Hanley ['hænli] III U5, 95
Hardy ['hɑ:di] II
Jenkins ['dʒeŋkɪnz] III U1, 12
Kapoor ['kæpɔ:] I
Link [lɪŋk] III U2, 129
MacGowan [mə'gaʊən] III U3, 61
McCane [mə'keɪn] II
Merchant ['mɜ:tʃnt] <III U2, 129>
Miller ['mɪlə] I
Nair [neə] II
O'Brian [ə'braɪən] III U5, 96
Preston ['prestən] I
Reedman ['ri:dmən] II
Richardson ['rɪtʃədsn] I
Safi ['sæfi] I
Simpson ['sɪmsən] III U4, 85
Smith [smɪθ] III U2, 42
Swindon ['swɪndən] I
Taylor ['teɪlə] <III U2, 129>
Thomas ['tɒməs] III U2, 38
Thompson ['tɒmpsn] III U4, 80
Warren ['wɒrn] I
Welch [weltʃ] I
Yeates [jeɪts] III U2, 42

Place names

Africa ['æfrɪkə] Afrika I
America [ə'merɪkə] Amerika II
Australia [ɒs'treɪliə] Australien I

Ballyronan [ˌbælɪ'rəʊnən] *Ort in Nord-irland* III U4, 80
Bannockburn ['bænəkbɜ:n] *Ort in Schottland* III U3, 64
Bavaria [bə'veəriə] Bayern II
Belfast [bel'fɑ:st] *Hauptstadt von Nordirland* III U4, 74
Berlin [bɜ:'lɪn] Berlin II
Birmingham ['bɜ:mɪŋəm] *Stadt in der Mitte Englands* II
Boston ['bɒstən] *Stadt in den USA* III U3, 54
Bramford ['bræmfəd] *Dorf in Nord-england* III U1, 16
Brighton ['braɪtn] *Küstenort in Südengland* II
Bristol ['brɪstl] *Stadt in Südwesteng-land* II
The **British Isles** [ðə ˌbrɪtɪʃ 'aɪlz] die Britischen Inseln III ZI 8
Cambridge ['keɪmbrɪdʒ] *Stadt in Ostengland* <III U1, 24>
Canada ['kænədə] Kanada III U3, 54
Cardiff ['kɑ:dɪf] *Hauptstadt von Wales* III U2, 33
Cork ['kɔ:k] *Stadt in Irland* III U5, 95
Cornwall ['kɔ:nwɔ:l] *Grafschaft in Südwestengland* II
Culloden [kə'lɒdn] *Ort in Schottland* III U3, 64
Denmark ['denmɑ:k] Dänemark III U1, 11
Devon ['devn] *Grafschaft in Südwest-england* I
Donegal [ˌdɒnɪ'gɔ:l] *Ort in Irland* III U5, 104
Dublin ['dʌblɪn] *Hauptstadt von Irland* III U4, 76
Edinburgh ['edɪnbrə] *Hauptstadt von Schottland* III U3, 52
England ['ɪŋglənd] England I
Europe ['jʊərəp] Europa II
France [frɑ:ns] Frankreich III U1, 11
Germany ['dʒɜ:məni] Deutschland I
Glasgow ['glɑ:zgəʊ] *Stadt in Schott-land* III U3, 61
Goldenbridge [ˌgəʊldn'brɪdʒ] *Stadtteil von Dublin* III U5, 100

Great Britain [ˌgreɪt 'brɪtn] Großbri-tannien III ZI 8
Greenwich ['grenɪdʒ] *Stadtteil im Südosten Londons* I
Hastings ['heɪstɪŋz] *Stadt in Südost-england* III U1, 11
India ['ɪndiə] Indien I
Inverness [ˌɪnvə'nes] *Ort in Nord-schottland* III U3, 58
Isle of Skye [ˌaɪl əv 'skaɪ] *Insel in Nordwestschottland* III U3, 61
Isle of Wight ['aɪl əv ˌwaɪt] *Insel süd-lich von England* II
Italy ['ɪtəli] Italien II
Jamaica [dʒə'meɪkə] Jamaika II
Lisburn ['lɪzbɜ:n] *Stadt in Nordirland* III U4, 92
Llandudno [læn'dɪdnəʊ] *Küstenort in Wales* III U2, 38
London ['lʌndən] *Hauptstadt von England* I
Manchester ['mæntʃɪstə] *Stadt im Norden von England* II
Margate ['mɑ:geɪt] *Ausflugsort in England* I
Milltown ['mɪltaʊn] *Stadtteil von Dublin* III U5, 101
New York [ˌnju: 'jɔ:k] *Großstadt in den USA* III U4, 84
Newcastle ['nju:ˌkɑ:sl] *Stadt in Nord-ostengland* III U1, 16
Northampton [ˌnɔ:'θæmtən] *Stadt in Mittelengland* III U5, 104
Northern Ireland [ˌnɔ:ðn̩ˈaɪələnd] Nordirland III ZI 8
Norway ['nɔ:weɪ] Norwegen III U1, 11
Paris ['pærɪs] Paris II
Poland ['pəʊlənd] Polen II
Powys ['pəʊɪs] *Stadt in Wales* III U2, 34
Randalstown ['rændlztaʊn] *Ort in Nordirland* III U4, 75
The **Republic of Ireland** [ðə rɪˌpʌblɪkˌ əvˈaɪələnd] Irland III ZI 8
Rugby ['rʌgbi] *Stadt in Mittelengland* <III U1, 24>
Scotland ['skɒtlənd] Schottland II
Senlac Hill [ˌsenlæk 'hɪl] *Ort in der Nähe von Hastings* <III U1, 126>

Snowdonia [snəʊ'dəʊniə] *National-park in Nordwales* III U2, 36

South Pole ['saʊθ ˌpəʊl] *Südpol* II

Southampton [saʊ'θæmtən] *Hafen-stadt in Südengland* III U4, 84

Spain [speɪn] *Spanien* II

Stamford Bridge ['stæmfəd ˌbrɪdʒ] *Ort in Nordengland* <III U1, 126>

Stirling ['stɜ:lɪŋ] *Ort in Schottland* III U3, 64

Turkey ['tɜ:ki] *Türkei* II

The United Kingdom [ðə ju:ˌnaɪtɪd 'kɪŋdəm] *Vereinigtes Königreich von Großbritannien und Nordir-land* III ZI 8

USA (United States of America) [ju:es'eɪ (ju:ˌnaɪtɪd ˌsteɪts əv ə'merɪkə)] *USA (Vereinigte Staaten von Amerika)* III U3, 54

Wales [weɪlz] *Wales* III ZI 8

York [jɔ:k] *Stadt in Nordengland* III U1, 11

Other names

Abbey Street ['æbi ˌstri:t] *Straße in Dublin* III U5, 100

Arsenal ['ɑ:snl] *Name einer Fußball-mannschaft* <III U1, 24>

The Baker [ðə 'beɪkə] *Filmname* III U2, 50

Baker Street ['beɪkə ˌstri:t] *Straßen-name* I

Bayeux Tapestry [ˌbaɪjɜ: 'tæpɪstri] *Bayeuxteppich* <III U1, 127>

Alexander Graham Bell [ˌælɪgzɑ:ndə 'greɪəm bel] *Erfinder des Telefons* III U3, 54

Ben Nevis [ˌben 'nevɪs] *höchster Berg Schottlands* <III U3, 72>

Big Ben [ˌbɪg 'ben] *Sehenswürdigkeit in London* II

Bollywood ['bɒliwʊd] *indische Filmin-dustrie: Bombay + Hollywood* II

Bond Street ['bɒnd ˌstri:t] *Londoner Straßenname* II

Brandenburg Gate ['brændənbɜ:g ˌgeɪt] *Brandenburger Tor* II

Buckingham Palace [ˌbʌkɪŋəm 'pælɪs] *Buckingham-Palast* <III U1, 30>

The Busy Bookworm [ðə ˌbɪzi 'bʊkwɜ:m] *Name einer Buchhand-lung* III U1, 14

Caldicot Castle ['kɑ:ldɪkɒt ˌkɑ:sl] *Burgruine in Wales* III U2, 42

Camden Market [ˌkæmdən 'mɑ:kɪt] *Markt im Londoner Stadtteil Camden* II

Captain Sparrow [ˌkæptɪn 'spærəʊ] *Filmfigur* II

Cats [kæts] *Musicalname* <III U3, 73>

The Channel Tunnel [ðə ˌtʃænl 'tʌnl] *Ärmelkanaltunnel* III ZI 8

Chelsea ['tʃelsi] *Name einer Fußball-mannschaft* <III U1, 24>

Lewis Clarke [ˌlʊɪs 'klɑ:k] *Personen-name* II

Connolly ['kɒnli] *Bahnhof in Dublin* III U5, 101

Cutty Sark [ˌkʌti 'sɑ:k] *Museumsschiff in Greenwich* I

Duke of Normandy [ˌdju:k əv 'nɔ:məndi] *Herzog der Normandie* <III U1, 126>

Edward I [ˌedwəd ðə 'fɜ:st] *König von England (1272-1307)* III U3, 62

Elizabeth Tower [ɪˌlɪzəbəθ 'taʊə] *Sehenswürdigkeit in London* II

European Union [ˌjʊərəpi:ən 'ju:njən] *Europäische Union* III U5, 94

George's Dock ['dʒɔ:dʒɪz ˌdɒk] *Hafen in Dublin* III U5, 101

Giant's Causeway [ˌdʒaɪənts 'kɔ:zweɪ] *Sehenswürdigkeit in Nordirland* III U4, 74

The Globe Theatre [ðə ˌgləʊb 'θɪətə] *das Globe-Theater* II

Green Park [ˌgri:n 'pɑ:k] *Park in Lon-don* <III U1, 30>

Greenwich Market ['grenɪdʒ ˌmɑ:kɪt] *überdachter Markt in Greenwich* I

Greenwich Park ['grenɪdʒ ˌpɑ:k] *Park in Greenwich* I

Greenwich Shopping Park [ˌgrenɪdʒ 'ʃɒpɪŋ pɑ:k] *Einkaufszentrum in Greenwich* II

Hadrian's Wall [ˌheɪdriənz 'wɔ:l] *Sehenswürdigkeit in Nordengland* III U1, 10

Harley Street ['hɑ:li ˌstri:t] *Londoner Straßenname* II

Harrods ['hærədz] *Kaufhaus in London* II

Henry II [ˌhenri ðə 'seknd] *König von England (1154-1189)* <III U5, 134>

Henry VIII [ˌhenri ði 'eɪtθ] *König von England (1509-1547)* <III U5, 134>

High Road ['haɪ ˌrəʊd] *Straßenname* II

the Highlands [ðə 'haɪləndz] *Bergre-gion in Schottland* III U3, 58

Hollywell School ['hɒliwel ˌsku:l] *Schulname* <III U4, 88>

Hollywood ['hɒliwʊd] *Zentrum der amerikanischen Filmindustrie (in Los Angeles)* II

Hyde Park [ˌhaɪd 'pɑ:k] *Park in Lon-don* <III U1, 30>

Irish Sea ['aɪrɪʃ ˌsi:] *Irische See* III U5, 105

Jedward ['dʒedwəd] *irische Popgruppe* <III U5, 101>

John Dunlop [ˌdʒɒn 'dʌnlɒp] *Erfinder der Gummireifen* III U3, 55

John Lewis ['dʒɒn ˌlu:ɪs] *Name einer Kaufhauskette* II

Kilkenny [kɪl'keni] *Tiername* III U1, 18

Lancelot ['lɑ:nsəlɒt] *Name eines Ritters* III U2, 42

Lionheart ['laɪənhɑ:t] *Löwenherz* III U2, 42

Loch Ness [ˌlɒk 'nes] *See in Schottland* III U3, 58

The London Eye [ðə ˌlʌndən 'aɪ] *Rie-senrad in London* II

London Underground ['lʌndən ˌʌndəgraʊnd] *Londoner U-Bahn* II

Lough Neagh [ˌlɒx 'neɪ] *See in Nordir-land* III U4, 75

Madame Tussauds [ˌmædəm tʊ'sɔ:dz] *Wachsfigurenmuseum in London* <III U1, 30>

Manchester City [ˌmæntʃɪstə 'sɪti] *Name einer Fußballmannschaft* III U1, 16

Mount

Mount Snowdon [ˌmaʊnt ˈsnəʊdn] *höchster Berg in Wales* III U2, 32

Nessie [ˈnesi] *Ungeheuer, das angeblich in Loch Ness wohnt* III U3, 58

Nessie's Nest [ˌnesiz ˈnest] *Name einer Frühstückspension* III U3, 61

No Tree Hostel [ˌnəʊ tri: ˈhɒstl] *Name einer Herberge* III U3, 61

Norman Conquest [ˌnɔ:mən ˈkɒŋkwest] *Normannische Eroberung Englands* <III U1, 126>

Notting Hill Carnival [ˌnɒtɪŋ hɪl ˈkɑ:nɪvl] *jährlicher Karneval im Londoner Stadtteil Notting Hill* I

The O2 [ði ˈəʊˌtu:] *Konzertarena in London* II

O'Connell Street [əˈkɒnl ˌstri:t] *Straße in Dublin* III U5, 100

Paddy [ˈpædi] *Kosename für Patrick* III U5, 105

Portobello Road Market [ˌpɔ:təbeləʊ rəʊd ˈmɑ:kɪt] *Straßenmarkt in London* <III U1, 30>

Prince George Theatre [ˌprins dʒɔ:dʒ ˈθɪətə] *Theater in London* II

Red Line [ˈred ˌlaɪn] *Straßenbahnlinie in Dublin* III U5, 100

Red Nose Day [red nəʊz ˈdeɪ] *Spendenmarathon* I

River Humber [ˌrɪvə ˈhʌmbə] *Fluss im Nordosten Englands* II

River Severn [ˈrɪvə ˌsevn] *Fluss im Südwesten Englands* II

River Thames [ˌrɪvə ˈtemz] *Fluss in London* II

RNLI (Royal National Lifeboat Institution) [ˈɑ:rˌen el ˌaɪ] *britische Seenotrettungsorganisation* <III U2, 128>

Robert the Bruce [ˈrɒbət də ˌbru:s] *König von Schottland (1306–1329)* III U3, 52

Rushy Park Coal Mine [ˌrʌʃi pɑ:k ˈkəʊl maɪn] *Name eines Kohlebergwerks* III U1, 20

Sackville Place [ˈsækvɪl ˌpleɪs] *Straßenname in Dublin* III U5, 100

Saint Patrick [snt ˈpætrɪk] *Schutzheiliger von Irland* <III U5, 134>

Selfridges [ˈselfrɪdʒɪz] *Name einer Kaufhauskette* II

William Shakespeare [ˌwɪljəm ˈʃeɪkspɪə] *englischer Schriftsteller* II

The Shambles [ðə ˈʃæmblz] *Einkaufsstraße in York* III U1, 12

The Shard [ðə ˈʃɑ:d] *Name eines Gebäudes in London* II

Sherlock [ˈʃɜ:lɒk] *Tiername* I

South Kensington [saʊθ ˈkenzɪŋtən] *Londoner U-Bahn-Haltestelle* <III U1, 30>

Spiderman [ˈspaɪdəmæn] *Spiderman* II

The Spire [ðə ˈspaɪə] *Monument und Wahrzeichen von Dublin* III U5, 100

St Patrick's Day [sn ˈpætrɪks ˌdeɪ] *Feiertag in Irland am 17. März* III U5, 95

St Paul's Cathedral [sənt ˈpɔ:lz ˌkəθi:drəl] *St.-Pauls-Kathedrale* II

Stonehenge [ˌstəʊnˈhendʒ] *Sehenswürdigkeit in Südwestengland* III U1, 10

Thomas Tallis School [ˌtɒməs ˈtælɪs ˌsku:l] *Schulname* I

Tigerboy III [ˈtaɪgəˌbɔɪ ˈθri:] *Filmname* III U4, 79

Titanic [taɪˈtænɪk] *Schiffsname* III U4, 75

The Tower of London [ðə ˌtaʊərˌəv ˈlʌndən] *Sehenswürdigkeit in London* II

Victoria Station [vɪkˌtɔ:riə ˈsteɪʃn] *Londoner Bahnhof* <III U1, 25>

Victoria Station [vɪkˌtɔ:riə ˈsteɪʃn] *Londoner Bahnhof* III U5, 107

Viking Centre [ˈvaɪkɪŋ ˌsentə] *Wikingermuseum in York* III U1, 12

The Voice of Ireland [ðə ˌvɔɪs ˌəv ˈaɪələnd] *Name einer Fernsehsendung* III U5, 95

Emma Watson [ˌemə ˈwɒtsn] *Schauspielerin* II

Wembley [ˈwembli] *Name eines Fußballstadions in London* II

Westminster Abbey [ˈwestmɪnstərˌæbi] *Kirche im Londoner Stadtteil Westminster* II

Westminster Cathedral [ˈwestmɪnstə ˌkəθi:drəl] *Dom im Londoner Stadtteil Westminster* II

The White Star Line [ðə ˌwaɪt stɑ: ˈlaɪn] *Baufirma der Titanic* III U4, 84

Whitelee [ˌwaɪtˈli:] *Name eines Windparks in Schottland* III U3, 53

Zip World [ˈzɪp ˌwɜ:ld] *Erlebniswelt in Nordwales* <III U2, 44>

A

abbiegen to turn III U1, 12
Abend evening I
Abendessen dinner II
(frühes) Abendessen tea I
abends in the evenings III U4, 76
Abenteuer adventure III U2, 32
aber but I
abfahren leave II
Abfall rubbish II
den Tisch **abräumen** to clear the
   table II
abschicken *(einen Brief)* to post
   III U4, 80
Abschieds- leaving II
Abschiedsrede farewell speech II
absichtlich on purpose II
abspülen *to do the washing up II
Abteilung department II
acht eight I
Achterbahn roller coaster II
achtzehn eighteen I
achtzig eighty I
Adapter adaptor III U5, 96
Adresse address II
Affe monkey I
Aktenkoffer briefcase III U2, 45
Aktentasche briefcase III U2, 45
Aktivität activity I
albern silly II
alle all I
alle everyone II; every III U4, 75
Allergie allergy II
allergisch gegen allergic to II
alles klar all right II
alles everything II
Alphabet alphabet I
als than; as II
als when II
als Nächstes next II
also so I
alt old I
   Wie alt bist du? How old are you? I
Alter age I
Altglascontainer bottle bank II
Aluminium aluminium III U3, 55
am on; at I

am Wochenende at the weekend I
am 7. Juli on 7th July I
am Dienstag on Tuesday I
an on; at I
   an Bord on board III U4, 84
Ananas pineapple III U5, 107
Andenken souvenir III U1, 12
andere other I
   ein andere another II
anderen others II
anderer Meinung sein to disagree II
(sich) ändern to change III U3, 54
   seine Meinung ändern to change
   one's mind III U4, 81
Anfang start III U2, 51; beginning
   III U5, 105
anfangen to start II
Anführer leader III U3, 65
Anführerin leader III U3, 65
angenehm comfortable II
angezogen (wie) dressed III U5, 105
Angst haben *to be scared III U2, 34
Angst haben *to be afraid II
ängstlich afraid II
anhören to listen (to) I
ankommen to arrive II
Ankündigung announcement II
anlegen *to put on III U2, 39
anmalen to paint II
Anmeldeformular entry form II
anprobieren to try on II
Anruf call III U5, 104
anrufen to call II; to phone I
Anrufer caller III U2, 38
Anruferin caller III U2, 38
anschauen to watch; to look at I; *to
   have a look II
sich **anschließen** to join III U5, 96
Anspitzer pencil sharpener I
anstoßen *to hit III U2, 40
Antwort answer I
antworten to answer I
anziehen *to put on III U2, 39
   sich anziehen to get dressed II
Apfel apple I
April April I
Arbeit work I; job II
arbeiten to work I

Arbeiter worker II
Arbeiterin worker II
Archiv archive II
Ärger trouble III U2, 33
Armee army III U3, 62
armselig miserable III U5, 105
Art sort II; type III U1, 31
Art und Weise way III U1, 12
Arzt doctor II
Ärztin doctor II
atmen to breathe III U1, 22
auch too I
   auch nicht not … either III U3, 58
auf on; at I
   auf diese Weise like this III U3, 62
   auf einmal suddenly II
   Auf Wiedersehen. Goodbye. I
   auf der Welt in the world II
   Auf keinen Fall! No way! III U3, 58
auffallend striking III U5, 100
Aufgabe job II
aufgeben *to give up III U3, 63
aufgeben *(einen Brief)* to post
   III U4, 80
aufgeregt excited; nervous II
aufheben to pick up III U1, 22
jmdn. **aufheitern** to cheer sb up
   III U5, 105
aufhören to stop I; to finish II
   Hör(t) auf! Stop it! II
Aufkleber sticker II
aufmachen to open I
jmdn. **aufmuntern** to cheer sb up
   III U5, 105
aufpassen to look after II
   aufpassen auf to watch II
aufräumen to tidy (up) II
aufregend exciting I
aufstehen *to get up I
einen **Auftrag vermasseln** *to get a
   job wrong III U2, 50
aufwachen *to wake up II
aufwachsen *to grow up III U3, 54
Auge eye II
   Ich traute meinen Augen nicht. I
   couldn't believe my eyes. III U5, 105
Augenblick moment II
August August I

im August in August I
aus from I
    aus Deutschland German III U5, 98
    hergestellt sein aus to be made of
    III U3, 54
auschecken to check out III U3, 59
Auseinandersetzung argument II
Ausflug trip I
den Hund **ausführen** to take the dog
    for a walk I
ausgeben *(Geld)* *to spend II
ein **ausgefüllter** Tag a busy day I
ausgehen *(Ware)* *to run out of
    III U4, 81
ausleihen to borrow II
ausprobieren to try III U2, 33; to try
    out III U2, 43
ausruhen to rest II
Ausrüstung equipment III U2, 34
aussehen to look II
außer except III U5, 96
Außerirdische alien I
Außerirdischer alien I
Aussichtspunkt lookout point II
aussteigen *to get off II
einen Turnierzweikampf **austragen**
    to joust III U2, 43
Ausverkauf sale II
auswählen *to choose II
Ausweis ID III U5, 97
Auto car I
Autofahrt drive III U1, 17
Automat machine II
Autor writer III U2, 50
Autorin writer III U2, 50

B

Bach stream II
Bäcker baker III U2, 50
Bäckerei baker's III U1, 13
Bäckerin baker III U2, 50
Bad(ezimmer) bathroom I
Bahnhof station I
bald soon II
Bis **bald**! See you!; See you soon! I
Ball ball II
Banane banana I

Band band II
Bank bench III U4, 87
Basketball basketball II
Bauarbeiter builder II
Bauarbeiterin builder II
Bauch stomach II
Bauchschmerzen stomach ache II
Bauchweh stomach ache II
bauen *to build II
Bauer farmer I
Bäuerin farmer I
Bauernhof farm I
Baum tree I
Baumhaus tree house I
Baumwolle cotton III U3, 55
beängstigend scary I
beantworten to answer I
bedauern *to feel sorry III U5, 105
bedeuten *to mean III U2, 33
Bedienen Sie sich! Help yourselves!
    II
    sich bedienen to help oneself
    III U5, 96
    Bedient euch! Help yourselves! II
mit besonderen **Bedürfnissen** with
    special needs III U5, 95
sich **beeilen** to hurry III U2, 38; to
    rush III U5, 105
beeindrucken to impress III U5, 107
beenden to finish II
befolgen to follow III U5, 102
befragen to interview I
Befragung interview II
begeistert excited II
Beginn beginning III U5, 105
beginnen to start II
mit **Behinderung** with special needs
    III U5, 95
bei at I
    bei Bewusstsein awake III U2, 38
Bein leg II
beinahe almost III U1, 25
bekommen *to get I
beliebt popular III U2, 33
bemerkenswert striking III U5, 100
benutzen to use II
beobachten to watch II
bequem comfortable II

bereit ready I
bereits already II
Berg mountain III U1, 17
Bergarbeiter miner III U1, 20
Bergarbeiterin miner III U1, 20
bergen to save III U4, 85
Bergwerk mine III U1, 16
Beruf job II
berühmt famous I
Besatzung crew III U4, 84
beschäftigt busy I
eine **Besichtigungstour** machen *to
    go sightseeing II
besitzen *to have I; to own II
mit **besonderen** Bedürfnissen with
    special needs III U5, 95
besonders special I
besorgt worried II
Besorgungen machen *to do the
    shopping II
beste best II
besteigen to climb III U2, 34
bestellen to order II
die **besten** the best II
besuchen to visit II
Besucher visitor II
Besucherin visitor II
betreiben *to run III U4, 75
Bett bed I
    ins Bett gehen to go to bed I
beunruhigt worried II
bevor before II
(sich) **bewegen** to move III U2, 39
Bewegung move III U5, 100
bewerten to rate III U2, 51
Bewohner inhabitant III U1, 16
Bewohnerin inhabitant III U1, 16
bei **Bewusstsein** awake III U2, 38
Bezahlautomat payment machine II
bezahlen *to pay II
Bibliothek library III U1, 15
Bild picture I
billig cheap II
Biologie Biology I
bis to II
    bis zu before II
bis (spätestens) by III U5, 100
Bis bald! See you!; See you soon! I

bis until I
ein **bisschen** a little; a bit II
bitte please I
　Bitte schön. Here you are. I
blau blue I
der **blaue** the blue one II
bleiben to stay II
　etw. bleiben lassen to give sth a
　miss III U2, 50
　in Verbindung bleiben to keep in
　touch II
Bleistift pencil I
Blog blog II
bloß only III U1, 16
Blume flower III U5, 104
Bluse blouse I
bluten *to bleed III U2, 38
Boden ground III U3, 64
Bonbon sweet I
Boot boat II
Bootsfahrt boat trip II
an **Bord** on board III U4, 84
böse angry II; bad III U2, 38; naughty
　III U2, 43
Boss boss II
Box box I
Bratwurst sausage II
brauchen to need II
　nicht brauchen needn't I
braun brown I
brechen *to break II
brennen *to burn III U2, 39
Brief letter III U4, 80
Briefmarke stamp III U4, 80
bringen *to bring II
britisch British II
Broschüre brochure III U1, 31
belegtes **Brot** sandwich I
Brot bread II
Brotlaib loaf III U4, 80
Brücke bridge II
Bruder brother I
Buch book I
Bücherei library III U1, 15
Buchstabe letter III U4, 80
buchstabieren *to spell I
Büfett buffet III U3, 58
Bühne stage II

bunt colourful II
Burg castle II
Büro office II
Bus bus I
　im Bus on the bus II
Bushaltestelle bus stop II
Butter butter I

C

Cache *(Geheimschatz)* cache I
Café café I
Cafeteria cafeteria I
Camp camp II
campen gehen *to go camping II
Camping camping III U2, 36
Campingplatz campsite III U3, 58
Center centre III U1, 16
Chance chance II
chatten to chat II
Chef boss II
Chefkoch head chef II
Chili chilli II
circa about II
Cola coke I
Comic(heft) comic II
Computer computer I
Computerspiel computer game I
cool cool I
Cousin cousin II
Cousine cousin II
Crew crew III U4, 84
Curry curry II

D

da there I
　da drüben over there II
da because I
Dach roof II
Dachboden attic I
damals then III U1, 10
Dampfmaschine steam engine
　III U3, 57
danach then; after that; after
　III U4, 84
Danke. Thanks.; Thank you. I
dann then I

das the I
das this; that I; which III U3, 54
dass that III U1, 22
Datei file II
Datum date I
dauern *to take III U1, 10
decken *to lay II
dein your I
deine yours II
dem who; which III U3, 54
den who; which III U3, 54
denken *to think I
Denkmal monument II
dennoch still III U2, 43
der the I
der who; which III U3, 54
deren whose III U3, 54
derselbe the same II
Desaster disaster III U4, 84
deshalb so I
dessen whose III U3, 54
Deutsch German I
deutsch German III U5, 98
Deutschland Germany I
Dezember December I
dich you I
　dich selbst yourself II
die the I
die who II; which III U3, 54
Dienst service III U2, 38
Dienstag Tuesday I
　am Dienstag on Tuesday I
dies this I
diese these II
Ding thing II
dir you I
Donnerstag Thursday I
doof silly III U4, 76
Dorf village III U1, 16
dort there I
　dort drüben over there II
eine **Dose** … a can of I
Dr. *(Anrede)* Dr III U4, 85
Drama drama III U2, 51
drängeln to push III U5, 102
draußen halten *to keep out III U3, 62
draußen outside III U3, 58
dreckig dirty I

dreckig

Drehort location III U2, 50

drei three I

dreißig thirty I

dreizehn thirteen I

dritte third I

du you I

Dudelsack bagpipes *(pl)* III U3, 53

dumm silly III U4, 76

dunkel dark I

Dunkelheit dark III U1, 20

durch through II

Durcheinander mess I

Durchsage announcement II

dürfen may II

    nicht/nie **dürfen** must not/never

    III U3, 63

    nicht **dürfen** mustn't III U5, 100

durstig thirsty II

Dusche shower III U5, 97

Duschgel shower gel III U5, 97

DVD DVD II

E

echt real II

Echt?! No way! III U3, 58

echt really II

Ecke corner III U4, 92

Es ist **egal**. It doesn't matter. II

egal wo(hin) wherever III U5, 107

ehrenamtliche Helferin volunteer

    III U2, 33

ehrenamtlicher Helfer volunteer

    III U2, 33

Ei egg II

eifersüchtig jealous II

eigene own II

eigentlich actually III U5, 105

Eigentümer landlord II

eilen to rush III U5, 105

ein a; an I

    ein bisschen a bit II

    ein paar a few III U3, 58

    ein wenig a bit II

einander each other III U2, 34

einchecken to check in III U3, 59

eindringen (in) to invade III U1, 11

eine a; an I

einfach easy I; plain II; simple

    III U3, 58

einfache Fahrkarte single ticket

    III U5, 101

einflussreich important III U2, 33

einfügen to paste II

einhundert a/one hundred I

einige some I

einige a few III U3, 58

Einkäufe machen *to do the shop-

    ping II

Einkaufen shopping I

einkaufen gehen *to go shopping II

Einkaufszentrum shopping centre I

Einkaufszettel shopping list I

einladen to invite I

Einladung invitation I

einmal once III U5, 105

    auf einmal suddenly II

    noch einmal again; once more II

einmarschieren (in) to invade

    III U1, 11

einpacken to pack; to pack up II

eins one I

einsam lonely III U4, 76

einschlafen *to fall asleep III U1, 25

einsetzen *to put in I

einst once III U5, 105

einstufen to rate III U2, 51

Eintrittskarte ticket III U1, 15

nicht **einverstanden** sein to disagree

    II

Einwohner inhabitant III U1, 16

Einwohnerin inhabitant III U1, 16

einzige only II

Eis ice cream II

Eisberg iceberg III U4, 84

Eiscreme ice cream II

Elefant elephant I

elegant chic I

Elektrizität electricity III U3, 53

elend miserable III U5, 105

elf eleven I

Eltern parents *(pl)* II

E-Mail e-mail II

Empfang signal III U3, 67

Ende end II; ending III U2, 45

enden to finish II

endlich at last II

eng tight II

aus **England** English I

die **Engländer** the English III U1, 11

Englisch English I

entfernt away II

entlang down III U1, 12

entlang along I

(sich) **entscheiden** to decide III U3, 58

sich **entschuldigen** *to say sorry II

Entschuldigung. Sorry.; Excuse me. I

entspannt relaxed II

er he I

    er selbst himself III U2, 34

Erdbeere strawberry II

Erdboden ground III U3, 64

Erdkunde Geography I

Erdnussbutter peanut butter III U4, 81

etwas **erfahren** über to learn about

    sth III U1, 12

erfinden to invent III U3, 54

Erfinder inventor III U3, 52

Erfinderin inventor III U3, 52

Erfindung invention III U3, 54

Erfolg success III U3, 54

erfolgreich successful III U2, 35

erforschen to explore II

Ergebnis result II

ergreifen to grab III U5, 105

sich **erinnern** (an) to remember II

erklären to explain III U5, 104

erkunden to explore II

ernst serious III U3, 58

    Im Ernst? Are you serious? III U3, 58

erraten to guess II

erschöpft exhausted III U2, 35

erschrecken to scare II; to jump

    III U2, 42

erschrocken sein *to be scared

    III U2, 34

erst only III U1, 16

erstaunlich amazing III U3, 63

erste first I

    das erste Mal the first time I

als **Erstes** first I

Erwachsene adult III U4, 75

Erwachsener adult III U4, 75

erwarten to expect III U2, 45

ich kann es kaum erwarten I can't wait III U5, 100

erzählen *to tell I

Erzähler narrator I

Erzählerin narrator I

es it I

Mir geht es gut. I'm fine. II

es gibt there is (= there's); there are I

Essen food I; meal II

Essen zum Mitnehmen takeaway II

essen *to eat I

Essensstand food stall II

Esslöffel tablespoon II

Esszimmer dining room I

etwa about II

etwas something; some I

euch you I

euer your I

eure yours II

Euro *(Währung)* euro III U5, 94

ewig forever II

exakt exact III U4, 81

explodieren to explode III U1, 20

Explosion explosion III U1, 20

F

Fabel fable III U5, 105

Fabrik factory III U1, 16

Fahne flag II

fahren *to go I; *to ride II; to travel III U5, 103

gegen etw. fahren to hit III U4, 84

mit (dem Zug) fahren to go by (train) I

Fahrer driver III U5, 102

Fahrerin driver III U5, 102

einfache **Fahrkarte** single ticket III U5, 101

Fahrplan timetable III U5, 100

Fahrpreis fare III U5, 100

Fahrrad bike I

Fahrschein ticket III U1, 15

Fahrt ride II; drive III U1, 17; trip III U2, 34; journey III U5, 100; voyage III U4, 84

eine Fahrt machen to take a trip III U2, 34

Fakt fact II

fallen *to fall I; *to fall (over) III U2, 38

falsch wrong I

Faltblatt flyer II

Familie family I

Fan fan I

Fantasie fantasy II

Fantasieausflug fantasy trip I

fantastisch fantastic II

Du bist fantastisch. You're a star. II

Fantasy fantasy II

Farbe colour I

Fasching carnival I

fast almost III U1, 25

Fastfood-Restaurant fast food restaurant I

Februar February I

Federmäppchen pencil case I

fegen *to sweep II

Feier party I

feiern to celebrate I

Feind enemy III U2, 50

Feindin enemy III U2, 50

Fels rock III U2, 38

Fenster window I

Ferien holiday II

fernsehen to watch TV I

Fernseher TV I

Fernsehsendung TV show II

Fernsehstudio TV studio II

fertig ready I

fertigstellen to finish II

fest tight II; solid III U3, 55

festhalten *to hold III U2, 43

feststecken *to be stuck I

Feuer fire II

Feuerwehrauto fire engine II

Film film; movie I

Filzstift felt-tip I

finden *to find I

ich kann … nicht finden I can't find … I

Finger finger III U2, 39

Fingerabdruck fingerprint II

Firma company II

Fisch fish I

Pommes mit Fisch fish and chips I

fit fit III U2, 34

Fitnessraum gymnasium III U4, 84

Flagge flag II

Flamingo flamingo I

eine **Flasche** … a bottle of I

Fledermaus bat I

Fleisch meat I

fliegen *to fly II

fließend fluent III U2, 33

Flohmarkt jumble sale II

Flughafen airport II

Flugzeug plane II

Flur corridor III U2, 42

Fluss river I

flüssig fluent III U2, 33

Flyer flyer II

folgen to follow III U5, 102

Fön hairdryer III U5, 97

in **Form** fit III U2, 34

Foto photo I

ein Foto machen to take a photo I

Frage question I

fragen to ask I

Frankreich France III U1, 11

Französisch French I

Frau woman II

Frau *(Anrede)* Mrs; Ms I

frech cheeky III U2, 34; naughty III U2, 43

im **Freien** outside III U3, 58

Freiland- free range II

Freiluft- outdoor III U2, 34

Freitag Friday I

Freiwillige volunteer III U2, 33

Freiwilliger volunteer III U2, 33

Freizeit free time I

Freizeitpark theme park I

Freude fun I

Freund friend I

Freundin friend I

freundlich friendly III U2, 35

Freundschaften schließen *to make friends I

Frieden peace III U3, 65

frieren *to freeze III U3, 58; *to get cold III U3, 60

Frisbeescheibe frisbee I

frisch fresh II

Friseur hairdresser II

Friseurin hairdresser II

froh happy I; glad II

Frucht fruit I

früh early III U3, 60

(wohnte) früher used to (live)
III U1, 16

Frühlingsrolle spring roll II

Frühstück breakfast I

frühstücken *to have breakfast I

Frühstückspension bed and breakfast (B & B) III U3, 58

(sich) fühlen *to feel II

führen *to run III U4, 75

Führer leader III U3, 65

Führerin leader III U3, 65

Füller pen I

fünf five I

fünfzehn fifteen I

fünfzig fifty I

für for I

für immer forever II

furchtbar awful I; horrible; dreadful
III U4, 77

sich fürchten *to be afraid II

Fuß foot I

zu Fuß gehen to go on foot I

Fußball football I

Fußgelenk ankle II

Fußknöchel ankle II

füttern *to feed I

G

Gabel fork II

Gang corridor III U2, 42

ganz quite III U2, 34

den ganzen Tag all day III U3, 58

Garten garden I

Gas gas III U1, 20

Gast guest III U2, 33

Gasthaus pub III U5, 94

Gebärdensprache sign language
III U5, 95

Gebäude building II

es gibt there is (= there's); there are I

geben *to give I

jmdm. das Gefühl geben, etw.
zu sein to make sb feel like sth
III U2, 43

geboren werden *to be born III U3, 52

(in der Pfanne) gebraten fried II

Geburtstag birthday I

Alles Gute zum Geburtstag! Happy
birthday! I

Gedicht poem III U5, 105

geduldig patient III U2, 35

gefährlich dangerous III U2, 34

gefällt mir I like I

gefällt mir nicht I don't like I

Gefängnis prison II

gefrieren *to freeze III U3, 58

jmdm. das Gefühl geben, etw. zu
sein *to make sb feel like sth
III U2, 43

gegen against III U1, 11; around
III U5, 96

gegen etw. fahren to hit III U4, 84

sich gegenseitig each other III U2, 34

gegenüber opposite I

geheim secret II

Geheimnis mystery I; secret II

gehen *to go; to walk I

campen gehen to go camping II

gehen um to be about III U1, 31

ins Bett gehen to go to bed I

spazieren gehen to go for a walk I

zu Fuß gehen to go on foot I

Wie geht es dir? How are you? I

gehörlos deaf III U3, 54

Mir geht es gut. I'm fine. II

Geist ghost II

Gel gel III U5, 97

gelassen relaxed II

gelb yellow I

Geld money I

Geldschein note II

Gelegenheit chance II

gemeinsam together I

Gemüse vegetable (veg) II

Obst- und Gemüseladen
greengrocer's III U1, 13

gemustert patterned II

gemütlich cosy III U3, 58

genau exact III U4, 81

genießen to enjoy III U3, 53

genug enough III U2, 34

genügend enough III U2, 34

Geografie Geography I

gerade right now III U5, 98

geradeaus straight on I

Geräusch noise I; sound III U3, 54

Gericht dish II

gern haben to like I

Gern geschehen. You're welcome. I

ich würde gerne … I'd like (to) …
(= I would like to) I

Geschäft shop I

geschehen to happen II

Geschenk present I

Geschichte History; story I; history
III U1, 12

Gesellschaft company II

Gesicht face I

gestern yesterday I

Getränk drink II

gewinnen *to win I

Gewinner winner I

Gewinnerin winner I

gewöhnlich usually II

Gewürz spice II

Gips cast III U2, 39

Giraffe giraffe I

Gitarre guitar III U5, 95

Glas glass II; jar III U4, 80

glauben to believe II

Ich glaube nicht. I don't think so. II

Ich glaube. I think so. II

gleich the same II

jetzt gleich right now III U5, 98

Glocke bell II

viel Glück good luck II

glücklich happy I

Glückstag lucky day II

Glückwunsch! Congratulations! II

Glühbirne light bulb III U3, 57

Gold gold III U5, 104

Gold- gold III U5, 104

golden gold III U5, 104

Grab grave III U1, 11

grau grey I

greifen to grab III U5, 105

Grill barbecue I

groß high; big I; tall; large II
großartig great I; fantastic II
Größe size II
Großeltern grandparents *(pl)* II
Großmutter grandmother II
Großstadt city II
Großvater grandfather II
grün green I
Grund reason III U2, 51
    Gründe angeben to give reasons
    III U2, 51
    Gründe nennen to give reasons
    III U2, 51
gründen to start III U3, 55
Gruppe group; team I
gruselig scary I
Grüße … von mir. Say hi to … I
gültig valid III U5, 100
Gummi rubber III U3, 55
gut good I; fine II; nice III U3, 58
    Gut gemacht! Well done! I
    gut sein in to be good at I
    Guten Morgen. Good morning. II
    gut sein bei to be good at I
gut well II
Mir geht es **gut.** I'm fine. II

H

Haar hair III U5, 98
Haarbürste hairbrush III U5, 97
Haare hair III U5, 98
    sich die Haare schneiden lassen to
    have a haircut II
Haargel hair gel III U5, 97
Haarglätter hair straightener I
Haarschnitt haircut II
haben *to have I
    Angst haben to be scared III U2, 34
    hast du have you got II
    hätte(n) gern would like II
    Du hast recht. You're right. I
    Mitleid **haben** mit *to feel sorry
    III U5, 105
Hafen harbour II
Hafer oat III U3, 53
Haferbrei porridge III U3, 53
Hai shark I

halb half III U1, 16
    eine halbe Million half a million
    III U1, 16
halb (drei) half past (two) I
(die) Hälfte half III U4, 84
Hallen- indoor III U2, 34
Hallo. Hello.; Hi. I
Hals throat II
Halsband collar I
Halsschmerzen sore throat II
Halt stop III U5, 100
halten *to keep II; *to hold III U2, 43
Haltestelle stop II
Hamburger burger II
Hand hand III U2, 40
handeln von *to be about III U1, 31
Handtuch towel III U5, 96
Handy mobile (phone) I
hängen *to hang II
hart hard II; tough III U2, 34
hassen to hate I
hassen to hate III U4, 76
häufig often I
Hauptgericht main course II
Hauptstadt capital (city) III U2, 33
Haus house I
    zu Hause at home; around the
    house I
Hausaufgabe(n) machen *to do
    homework I
Häuschen cottage III U3, 53
Hausmeister caretaker I
Hausmeisterin caretaker I
Haustier pet I
Heer army III U3, 62
Heft book I
Heim home I
Heimweh haben *to be homesick
    III U5, 104
heiraten *to get married II
heiß hot I
heißen *to be called II
    Ich heiße … My name is … I
    Wie heißt du? What's your name? I
Held hero III U3, 64
helfen to help I
ehrenamtliche **Helferin** volunteer
    III U2, 33

ehrenamtlicher **Helfer** volunteer
    III U2, 33
Helikopter helicopter I
Helm helmet I
Hemd shirt II
heraus out II
herausfinden *to find; *to find out I
herauskommen *to get out III U1, 22
herausnehmen *to take out I
Herberge hostel III U3, 59
hereinkommen *to get in I
hergestellt sein aus *to be made of
    III U3, 54
Herr *(Anrede)* Mr I
herrlich lovely II
herum around III U1, 19
herumkommen *to get around
    III U5, 100
herunter down III U1, 12
herunterladen to download II
hervorkommen *to come out II
heute today I
heutzutage now II
Hexe witch I
hier here I
hiesig local III U3, 58
Hilfe help II
hilfreich useful III U4, 76
Himbeere raspberry III U4, 80
hinauf up II
hinbringen *to take II
in … hinein inside II
Hin- und Rückfahrkarte return ticket
    III U5, 101
hinfallen *to fall I; *to fall (over)
    III U2, 38
zu … hinfügen to bookmark II
hinter behind II
Hintergrund background III U4, 92
im Hintergrund in the background
    III U4, 92
hinunter down III U1, 12
Hinweis clue I
hinzufügen to add II
Hip-Hop *(Musik)* hip hop III U5, 95
Hobby hobby III ZI 9
hoch high I; tall II
hochladen to upload II

hochladen

Hochzeit wedding II
hoffen to hope II
hoffnungsvoll hopeful III U4, 77
höflich polite II
Höhe height II
Höhle cave II
Holz wood III U3, 54
hören to listen (to); *to hear I
Hose trousers (pl) I
   kurze Hose shorts (pl) I
Hotel hotel II
Hotelfachschule catering college II
hübsch beautiful I; pretty; lovely II
Hubschrauber helicopter I
Huhn chicken I
Hühnchen chicken II
Hund dog I
Hundekeks dog biscuit II
hundert a/one hundred I
hungrig hungry I
husten to cough III U1, 21
Hut hat II
hüten to look after II

I

ich I; me I
   ich mag I like I
   ich möchte … I'd like (to) … (= I
   would like to) I
   ich würde gerne … I'd like (to) …
   (= I would like to) I
   ich würde lieber I'd rather III U1, 25
   ich würde nicht gerne … I
   wouldn't like (to) … I
Idee idea I
   Irgendeine Idee? Any idea? I
ihm him I
ihn him I
Ihnen you I
ihr you; her; their I; its III U3, 52
ihre hers II; theirs III U5, 99
Ihre yours II
im in I
   im August in August I
   im Freien outside III U3, 58
   im Bus on the bus II

   im Süden von in the south of
   III U1, 10
Im Ernst? Are you serious? III U3, 58
Imbiss snack I
immer always I
   für immer forever II
in in; to; at I; inside III U1, 31
   in … hinein inside II
   in der Schule at school I
   in Form fit III U2, 34
   in Ordnung fine; all right II
   in der Mitte von in the centre of
   III U1, 16
Indien India I
indisch Indian II
Industrie industry III U1, 11
industrielle Revolution Industrial
   Revolution III U1, 11
Informatik IT (Information Technology) I
Information information desk II
Ingenieur engineer II
Ingenieurin engineer II
Inhalt content III U2, 50
innen in inside III U1, 31
Innen- indoor III U2, 34
im Innern inside III U1, 31
Insekt insect III U3, 58
Insel island II
intelligent clever II; smart; intelligent III U4, 77
interessant interesting I
sich **interessieren** für *to be interested in III U1, 12
interessiert sein an *to be interested
   in III U1, 12
Internet internet II
   im Internet surfen to surf the
   internet II
   ins Internet stellen to upload II
Internettagebuch blog II
Interview interview II
interviewen to interview I
irgendein any II
   Irgendeine Idee? Any idea? I
irgendetwas anything II
irgendwelche any II
Irisch Irish III U5, 94

irisch Irish III U5, 94

J

ja yes I; yeah (infml) II
Jacke coat I; jacket II
Jahr year I
Jahrgangsstufe year I
Jahrhundert century III U1, 25
jamaikanisch Jamaican II
jämmerlich miserable III U5, 105
Januar January I
Jeans jeans (pl) I
jede every I
jeder everyone I
jedoch however III U4, 85
jemals ever II
jene those II
jetzt now I
   jetzt gleich right now III U5, 98
Job job II
Joghurt yogurt II
Jugend youth (no pl) III U5, 94
Jugend- youth (no pl) III U5, 94
Jugend- teen II
Jugendliche teen II; teenager
   III U2, 33
Jugendlicher teen II; teenager
   III U2, 33
Jugendzentrum activity centre
   III U2, 34
Juli July I
   am 7. Juli on 7th July I
jung young II
Junge boy I
Juni June I
Juror judge II
Jurorin judge II
Juwelierladen jeweller's III U1, 13

K

Käfig cage I
kalt cold I
Kamel camel III U4, 82
Kamm comb III U5, 97
Kampf battle III U1, 11; fight III U2, 50
kämpfen *to fight III U3, 52

Kanarienvogel canary III U1, 20
Kanone cannon II
Kanonenkugel cannon ball II
Kanufahren canoeing I
Kapitän captain I
Kapitänin captain I
Kappe cap I
kaputt machen *to break II
Karneval carnival I
Karotte carrot II
Karre truck III U1, 21
Karte ticket; card II
Kartoffel potato II
Kartoffelbrei mashed potatoes II
Kartoffelchip crisp I
Karton cardboard III U3, 55
Käse cheese I
Käsekuchen cheesecake II
Katastrophe disaster III U4, 84
Katholik Catholic III U4, 74
Katholikin Catholic III U4, 74
katholisch Catholic III U4, 74
Katze cat I
kaufen *to buy I
Kaufhaus department store II
Kaugummi chewing gum I
kein no I
keine no I
kein not ... any II
Keks biscuit II
Kellner waiter II
kennen lernen *to meet I; *to get to
    know II
Kerze candle I
Ketchup ketchup II
sieben **Kilogramm** täglich 7 kilo-
    grams a day I
40 **Kilometer** pro Stunde 40 kilomet-
    res an hour I
Kilt kilt III U3, 53
Kind kid II
Kinder children *(pl)* II
Kinderzimmer bedroom I
Kino cinema I
Kirche church II
Kiste box I
alles **klar** all right II

Klasse year; tutor group I; class
    III U2, 36
Klassenlehrer tutor I
Klassenlehrerin tutor I
Klassenzimmer classroom I
Klebstoff glue I
Kleeblatt shamrock III U5, 104
Kleid dress II
Kleider *(Pl.)* clothes *(pl)* I
Kleiderschrank wardrobe I
Kleidung clothes *(pl)* I; outfit
    III U5, 105
klein little II; tiny III U1, 17; small
    III U2, 35
Klettern rock climbing I
klettern to climb III U2, 34
klicken to click I
klingeln *to ring II
klingen to sound II
Kloß dumpling II
Klub club II
klug clever II; smart; intelligent
    III U4, 77
Kneipe pub III U5, 94
Knie knee III U2, 39
Knoblauch garlic II
knuddelig cuddly III U2, 39
Koch chef II
Kochbanane plantain II
kochen to cook II
Köchin chef II
Koffer suitcase II
Kohl cabbage II
Kohle coal III U1, 16
Kombination combination II
komisch funny I
kommen *to come I
    ich komme aus ... I'm from ... I
    Kannst du mir sagen, wie ich ...
    komme? Can you tell me the way
    to ...? I
    Woher kommst du? Where are you
    from? I
Kommentar comment II
Komödie comedy III U2, 50
Konfitüre jam III U4, 80
König king III U1, 11
Königin queen III U1, 31

königlich royal II
können can I; may II
nicht weg **können** *to be stuck I
    nicht können can't I; cannot
    III U2, 45
    ich kann ... nicht finden I can't
    find ... I
    Ich konnte nicht anders als ... I
    couldn't help but ... III U5, 105
    Kannst du mir sagen, wie ich ...
    komme? Can you tell me the way
    to ...? I
    Könntest du das bitte wieder-
    holen? Can you say that again,
    please? I
konnte could III U1, 21
könnten could III U3, 58
kontrollieren to check III U4, 81
Konzert concert II
Kopf head II
Kopfsalat lettuce II
Kopfschmerzen headache II
kopfüber head first III U1, 18
Kopfweh headache II
Kopie copy II
kopieren to copy II
Korbball netball I
Körper body III U5, 97
Körperlotion body lotion III U5, 97
korrekt right I
Korridor corridor III U2, 42
kosten *to cost III U4, 75
    ... kostet 99 Pence ... is 99p I
    Wie viel (kostet/kosten) ...? How
    much (is/are) ...? I
kostenlos free III U4, 75
köstlich delicious II
Kostüm costume; fancy dress I
krank ill II; sick III U1, 11
Krankenhaus hospital I
Krankenpfleger nurse II
Krankenschwester nurse II
Krankenwagen ambulance III U2, 38
Kraut cabbage II
Kreis circle III U1, 10
Kricket cricket II
Kritik review III U2, 50
Krokodil crocodile I

Krokodil

Küche kitchen I
Kuchen cake I; pie II
Kuh cow III U1, 16
kühl cool I
kühlen to cool III U2, 39
Kühlschrank fridge III U5, 96
sich **kümmern** (um) to care (for)
III U5, 95
Kunde customer III U4, 80
Kundin customer III U4, 80
Kunst Art I
Künstler artist III U5, 98
Künstlerin artist III U5, 98
Kunststoff plastic III U3, 54
Kunststück trick III U2, 41
Kuppel dome II
Kurs course III U5, 95
kurz short II
kurze Hose shorts (pl) I
kurz shortly III U4, 84
Kuscheltier cuddly toy III U2, 39
Kuss kiss II
Küste coast III U2, 33
an der Küste on the coast III U1, 17

L

lachen to laugh II
Ladegerät charger III U5, 97
Laden shop I
Tante-Emma-Laden corner shop I
Lage location III U2, 50
Lager camp II
Lamm lamb II
Lampe lamp I
Land country I; land II; countryside
III U3, 53
Landkarte map I
ländliche Gegend country I
Landschaft countryside III U3, 53
Landwirt farmer I
Landwirtin farmer I
lang long I
langsam slow III U2, 34
langweilig boring I
Lasagne lasagne II
lassen leave II

etw. bleiben lassen to give sth a
miss III U2, 50
lass(t) uns let's (= let us) I
laufen *to run; to walk I
Laut sound III U3, 54
laut noisy III U1, 16; loud III U2, 35
läuten *to ring II
Leben life I
leben to live I
Lebensmittel food I
lecker nice III U3, 58; tasty III U4, 80
Leder leather III U3, 55
legen *to put II
Lehrer teacher I; instructor III U2, 35
Lehrerin teacher I; instructor
III U2, 35
leicht easy I
leid tun *to be sorry III U4, 87
Tut mir leid. Sorry. I
leihen *to lend II
leise quiet III U1, 16
leiten *to run III U4, 75
Leiter ladder I
lernen to learn II
kennen lernen to meet I; to get to
know II
lesen *to read I
letzte last I
Leute people I; guys II
Liebe(r) …, (Anrede in Briefen) Dear
…, I
lieben to love I
ich würde **lieber** I'd rather III U1, 25
Liebesgeschichte romance III U2, 51
Lieblings- favourite I
Lieferwagen van III U4, 93
liegen to rest II
lila purple I
Limonade lemonade II
Lineal ruler I
Linie line III U5, 100
links left III U1, 12
links on the left I
auf der linken Seite on the left I
Liste list II
LKW-Fahrer lorry driver II
LKW-Fahrerin lorry driver II
Loch hole I

locker relaxed; loose II
Löffel spoon II
lokal local III U3, 58
lose loose II
lösen to solve I
Löwe lion I
Luft air III U3, 55
Luftballon balloon I
Lunchpaket packed lunch II
lustig funny I

M

machen *to do; *to make I
ein Foto machen to take a photo I
Hausaufgabe(n) machen to do
homework I
kaputt machen to break II
sich Notizen machen to take
notes I
Mach dir keine Sorgen. Don't
worry. II
Mach dir nichts draus. Never
mind. II
Macht nichts. Never mind. II
Mädchen girl I
Magen stomach II
Magie magic II
Mahlzeit meal II
Mai May I
Mal time III U1, 21
das erste Mal the first time I
malen to paint II
Mama mum I; mama II
manchmal sometimes II
Mann man I
Mannschaft crew III U4, 84
Märchen fable III U5, 105
Marke brand III U4, 81
Markt market II
Marmelade jam III U4, 80
März March I
Maschine machine II
Mathe Maths I
Matsch mud I
Mauer wall II
Maus mouse I
Mayonnaise mayonnaise II

meckern to nag III U4, 76
Medikamente medicine III U2, 39
Medizin medicine III U2, 39
Meer sea I
  am Meer at the seaside I
Meerschweinchen guinea pig II
Mehl flour I
mehr more II
Meile mile II
mein my I
meine mine II
meinen *to mean III U2, 33
meins mine II
Meinung opinion III U2, 50
  seine Meinung ändern to change
  one's mind III U4, 81
  anderer Meinung sein to disagree
  II
eine **Menge** a lot of I
  jede Menge lots of I; lots III U2, 43
Mensa cafeteria I
Mensch person II
Menschenmenge crowd II
sich **merken** to remember II
merkwürdig funny I; strange II
Messer knife II
Metall metal III U3, 54
Meter metre I
Metzgerei butcher's III U1, 13
mich me I
Miete rent II
Mikrowelle microwave II
Milch milk II
Milchmischgetränk milkshake
  III U4, 76
Milchshake milkshake III U4, 76
mild mild I
Milliarde billion II
Million million III U1, 11
  eine halbe Million half a million
  III U1, 16
Mineralwasser mineral water
  III U4, 81
Minute minute II
mir me I
Mir geht es gut. I'm fine. II
mit with I

mit besonderen Bedürfnissen with
  special needs III U5, 95
Mit den besten Wünschen, Best
  wishes, I
mitbringen *to bring II
Mitleid haben mit *to feel sorry
  III U5, 105
Mittagessen lunch I; dinner II
Mittagspause lunchtime I
Mittagszeit lunchtime I
Mitte centre III U1, 16; middle
  III U4, 92
  in der Mitte in the middle III U4, 92
  in der Mitte von in the centre of
  III U1, 16
Mitternacht midnight III U4, 84
Mittwoch Wednesday I
modern modern I
modisch fashionable II
mögen to like I; to enjoy III U2, 50
  gern mögen to love I
  nicht mögen to hate III U4, 76
  ich mag I like I
  ich mag nicht I don't like I
  ich möchte nicht … I wouldn't like
  (to) … I
  ich möchte … I'd like (to) … (= I
  would like to) I
  Möchtest du? Would you like
  (to)…? I
Möglichkeit chance II
Moment moment II
Monat month I
monatlich monthly III U5, 101
Monster monster III U3, 58
Montag Monday I
Mörder murderer III U2, 50
Mörderin murderer III U2, 50
Morgen morning I
  Guten Morgen. Good morning. II
morgen tomorrow II
Moschee mosque II
Motorrad motorbike I
Moussaka moussaka II
müde tired I
Müll rubbish II
Mund mouth II
Münze coin III U4, 79

Münzgeld change II
Münztelefon pay phone III U3, 67
Museum museum II
Musik music I
Musik- musical III U5, 95
musikalisch musical III U5, 95
Musikgruppe band II
Müsli cereal III U5, 96
Muslim Muslim I
Muslimin Muslim I
müssen must I; *to have to II
  nicht müssen needn't I
mutig brave III U3, 63
Mutter mother I
Mutti mum I
Mütze cap I

N

na ja well I
  Na ja, schau mal … nach. Well,
  look … I
nach to; after I
nach (bei Uhrzeitangaben) past I
Nachbar neighbour III U3, 67
Nachbarin neighbour III U3, 67
Nachmittag afternoon I
  am Nachmittag in the afternoon I
nachmittags p.m. II
Nachricht message II
Nachricht(en) news II
Nachspeise dessert; pudding II
nachsprechen *to say I
nächste next I
als **Nächstes** next II
Nacht night II
Nachtwanderung night walk I
Nagel nail III U5, 97
Nagelschere nail scissors III U5, 97
nah near III U1, 15
in der **Nähe** close III U1, 17
  in der Nähe von near I
nahe close III U1, 17
Name name I
Nase nose I
  die Nase voll haben (von) to be
  fed up (with) III U4, 76
nass wet I

persönlich personal III U5, 97
Pfannkuchen pancake II
Pfeffer pepper II
Pferd horse I
Pfirsich peach I
Pflanze plant III U2, 33
Pflaster plaster III U2, 39
Pfund *(brit. Währungseinheit)*
    pound I
    das macht 2 Pfund und 24 Pence
    that's £2.24 I
Picknick picnic I
Pieps tweet III U1, 22
Pinguin penguin I
pink pink I
Pirat pirate I
Piratin pirate I
Pirogge pierogi II
Pizza pizza I
Plan plan II
planen to plan II
Plastik plastic III U3, 54
Platz place I; square II
plaudern to chat II
plötzlich suddenly II
Polizei police III U2, 38
Polizeibeamter police officer I
Polizeibeamtin police officer I
Pommes chips *(pl)* I
    Pommes mit Fisch fish and chips I
Popcorn popcorn I
positiv positive III U4, 76
Postamt post office I
Poster poster I
Postkarte postcard I
Pranger stocks III U2, 43
präsentieren to present I
Preis prize; price II
Prise pinch II
pro Stück each II
Problem problem I; trouble III U2, 33
Projekt project III U5, 98
Prospekt brochure III U1, 31
Protestant Protestant III U4, 74
Protestantin Protestant III U4, 74
protestantisch Protestant III U4, 74
prüfen to test II
Pudding pudding II

pünktlich on time III U5, 100
putzen to clean I

Q

Quittung receipt II

R

Rad wheel III U3, 55
Radfahren cycling III U3, 61
Radiergummi eraser I
Radio radio III U3, 67
Rafting rafting III U2, 33
rappen to rap II
Rapper rapper III U5, 98
Rapperin rapper III U5, 98
rasten to rest II
Rat advice III U2, 51
raten to guess II
Ratschlag advice III U2, 51
Rätsel mystery I
Rauch smoke III U2, 42
Raum room I
(Taschen-) **Rechner** calculator I
Rechnung bill III U3, 59
Du hast **recht**. You're right. I
    recht haben to be right II
rechts on the right I; right III U1, 12
    auf der rechten Seite on the right I
Rechtschreibung spelling I
Rede speech III U3, 54
reden (mit) to talk (to) I
Regal shelf I
Regalbrett shelf I
Regel rule III U2, 34
Regenbogen rainbow III U5, 104
Regenmantel raincoat III U5, 97
Regenschirm umbrella II
Regisseur director II
Regisseurin director II
regnen to rain I
reich rich III U3, 54
reichen to pass II
Reichtum wealth III U5, 105
Reifen tyre III U3, 55
in die richtige **Reihenfolge** bringen
    *to put in the right order I

Reis rice II
Reise trip III U3, 58; voyage III U4, 84;
    journey III U5, 100
reisen to travel II
Reiten horse riding I
reiten *to ride II
Religionsunterricht RE (Religious
    Education) I
Rennen race I
rennen *to run I
reparieren to repair III U3, 67
Reporter reporter III U2, 42
Reporterin reporter III U2, 42
Republik republic III U5, 94
Requisit prop III U2, 45
reservieren *to make a reservation
    III U3, 59
Reservierung reservation III U3, 59
Restaurant restaurant II
    Fastfood-Restaurant fast food
    restaurant I
retten to save III U4, 85
Rettungsboot lifeboat III U2, 33
Rettungsdienst emergency service
    III U2, 38
Rezept recipe II
richtig right I; real II
das **Richtige** tun *to do the right
    thing III U2, 38
in diese **Richtung** this way II
riechen *to smell III U1, 20
Riese giant III U4, 75
riesengroß huge III U1, 17
Riesenrad big wheel II
riesig huge III U1, 17
Rindfleisch beef II
Ring circle III U1, 10
Ritt ride II
Ritter knight III U2, 42
Rock skirt I
Rohr tube III U3, 55
Rolle part II
Rollstuhl wheelchair III U2, 43
Rolltreppe escalator II
die **Römer** the Romans III U1, 10
rosa pink I
rot red I

rot

Hin- und **Rückfahrkarte** return ticket III U5, 101
Ruf call III U5, 104
rufen to call; to shout II
Rugby rugby III U2, 34
Ruhe silence III U1, 20
ruhig quiet III U1, 16
Rührei scrambled egg II
rühren to stir II
ruinieren to ruin II
Rüstung armour III U2, 43

S

Sache thing II
Sack bag I
Saft juice II
sagen *to say; *to tell I
Salat salad II
Salz salt II
sammeln to collect I
Samstag Saturday I
samstags on Saturdays I
Sand sand II
Sandwich sandwich I
Sänger singer I
Sängerin singer I
sauber clean III U3, 53
   sauber machen to clean I
sauer sein *to be fed up (with) III U4, 76
Saxofon saxophone I
eine **Schachtel** … a box of I
Schaf sheep I
Schal scarf II
Schälchen bowl II
Schale bowl II
Schatz treasure II
(nach)**schauen** to look I
Schauspielen acting III U5, 95
Schauspieler actor II
Schauspielerei acting III U5, 95
Schauspielerin actor II
Schauspielworkshop acting workshop II
Schere scissors *(pl)* III U5, 97
schick chic I
schicken *to send I

schieben to push I
Schiff ship I
Schiffsbauer ship builder III U4, 84
Schiffsbauerin ship builder III U4, 84
Schiffsfahrt boat trip II
Schild sign III U2, 32
Schinken ham II
Schlacht battle III U1, 11
Schlaf sleep III U2, 39
schlafen *to sleep I; *to be asleep III U1, 25
Schlafzimmer bedroom I
schlagen *to hit II; *to beat III U3, 62
Schlamm mud I
Schlange snake I
schlau clever II; smart III U4, 77
Schlauch tube III U3, 55
schlecht ill II; bad III U2, 38
schlechteste worst III U1, 16
schlicht plain II
schließen to close I
schließlich in the end; finally II
schlimm bad III U2, 38
schlimmste worst III U1, 16
Schloss castle II
Schlumpf smurf I
Schluss end II; ending III U2, 45
   zum Schluss in the end; finally II
Schlussfolgerung conclusion III U2, 50
Schlussverkauf sale II
schmackhaft tasty III U4, 80
schmerzhaft sore II
Schmuck jewellery II
Schmuggler smuggler II
Schmugglerin smuggler II
schmutzig dirty I
Schnäppchen bargain II
schnappen to grab III U5, 105
schneiden *to cut III U2, 39
   sich die Haare schneiden lassen to have a haircut II
der/die/das **schnellste** the fastest I
schnell fast II; quick III U2, 34
schnell quickly II
Schokolade chocolate I
   eine Tafel Schokolade a bar of chocolate I

schön nice; beautiful I; fine; lovely II
schon already; yet II
Schon gut. Never mind. II
Schotte Scot III U3, 53
Schottenrock kilt III U3, 53
Schottin Scot III U3, 53
schottisch Scottish III U3, 53
Schrank cupboard III U5, 98
schrecklich awful I; horrible III U4, 77
Schrei shout I
schreiben *to write I
   eine SMS schreiben to text II
schreien to shout II
Schriftsteller writer II
Schriftstellerin writer II
Schritt step III U5, 102
schubsen to push III U5, 102
Schuh shoe II
Schule school I
   in der Schule at school I
Schüler student I
Schülerin student I
Schulfach subject I
Schulhof playground I
Schulstunde lesson I
Schüssel bowl II
schützen to protect III U3, 53
schwach weak III U2, 35
schwarz black I
Schweigen silence III U1, 20
schweigsam silent III U1, 21
Schweinefleisch pork II
schwer heavy; hard II
schwerhörig deaf III U3, 54
Schwert sword III U2, 43
Schwester sister I
schwierig difficult; hard II
Schwierigkeiten trouble III U2, 33
Schwimmbad swimming pool I
schwimmen *to swim II
   schwimmen gehen to go swimming I
Science-Fiction science fiction I
Scone *(eine Art süßes Brötchen)* scone II
sechs six I
sechzehn sixteen I
sechzig sixty I

See lake III U3, 53

sehen *to see I; to look II

Sehenswürdigkeit sight II

zu **sehr** too much II

sehr very I

    so sehr so much III U4, 76

Seide silk III U3, 55

Seife soap III U5, 97

Seil rope I

Seilrutsche zip line III U2, 32

sein *to be I

    hergestellt sein aus to be made of III U3, 54

    sauer sein to be fed up (with) III U4, 76

    sei still don't talk I

sein his I; its III U3, 52

seiner his II

seins his II

Seite side II

Sekunde second II

selber myself III U2, 34; ourselves; yourselves; themselves III U2, 152

ihr/euch/Sie/sich (**selbst**) yourselves III U2, 152

    dich selbst yourself II

    sie selbst herself; themselves III U2, 152

selbst myself; self III U2, 34

selbstbewusst confident III U4, 77

selbstsicher confident; sure of oneself III U4, 77

selbstverständlich of course II

seltsam strange II

senden *to send I

Senf mustard II

September September I

Serviette napkin II

setzen *to put II

    sich (hin)setzen to sit (down) I

Shampoo shampoo III U5, 96

Shirt shirt II

Shorts shorts (pl) I

sich each other; self III U2, 34

    sich (selbst) himself III U2, 34

    sich gegenseitig each other III U2, 34

    sich selbst herself III U2, 152

sicher sure II; safe III U2, 35

Sie you I

sie she I; them II

sie (Pl.) they I

    sie selbst herself III U2, 152

sieben seven I

siebzehn seventeen I

siebzig seventy I

siegen *to win I

Signal signal III U3, 67

singen *to sing I

sinken *to sink III U4, 84

Situation situation II

Sitzbank bench III U4, 87

Skateboard skateboard III U2, 41

Ski fahren to ski II

Skifahren skiing III U2, 32

SMS message II

    eine SMS schreiben to text II

Textnachricht (**SMS**) text message I

SMS-Schreiber texter II

SMS-Schreiberin texter II

Snack snack I

so like that I; so II

    so sehr so much III U4, 76

so … wie as … as II

so like this III U3, 62

Socke sock I

soeben just II

Sofa sofa II

sofort right now III U5, 98

Software software II

sogar even II

Sohn son III U3, 64

Soldat soldier III U3, 62

Soldatin soldier III U3, 62

sollte should III U2, 38

Sommer summer II

Sonderangebot special offer III U4, 80

Sonne sun III U1, 11

sonnenbaden to sunbathe II

Sonnenbrille sunglasses (pl) II

sonnig sunny I

Sonntag Sunday I

sich **Sorgen** machen to worry I

Mach dir keine **Sorgen**. Don't worry. II

Sorte sort II; type III U1, 31

Soße sauce II

Souvenir souvenir III U1, 12

Souvenirladen souvenir shop III U1, 12

Spaghetti spaghetti II

spannend exciting I

Spaß fun I

    zum Spaß for fun III U2, 43

Wie **spät** ist es? What time is it? I

    (zu) spät late II

später later I; after III U4, 84

spazieren gehen *to go for a walk I

Spaziergang walk III U3, 61

speichern to save II

Speise dish II

Speisekarte menu II

speziell special I

Spiegel mirror III U5, 97

Spiel game I

spielen to play I; to act II

Spieler player II

Spieler (Computer) gamer II

Spielerin player II

Spielerin (Computer) gamer II

Spielfeld court III U4, 87

Spielkarte card II

Spielplatz playground I

Spielzeug toy III U2, 39

Spinne spider III U3, 63

Spinnennetz web III U3, 63

Sport sport I

Sportart sport III U2, 33

Sportgeschäft sports shop I

Sportunterricht PE (Physical Education) I

Sprache language II; speech III U3, 54

sprechen *to say I; *to speak III U1, 21

sprechen (mit) to talk (to) I

    sprechen über to talk about II

Spritze injection III U2, 39

spülen to wash III U5, 98

Spur clue I

Stadion stadium II

Stadt town I; city II

Stadtmitte city centre III U2, 33

Stadtplan map I

Stadtzentrum city centre III U2, 33

Stahl steel III U3, 55

Stahl

Standinhaber stallholder II
Standinhaberin stallholder II
Star star I
stark heavy II
Start start III U2, 51
starten to start II
staubsaugen to hoover II
stehen to suit; *to stand II
steigen to climb III U2, 34
Stein rock III U2, 38; stone III U1, 10
Stelle place I
stellen *to put II
sterben to die III U1, 21
Stern star III U2, 50
Stiefel boot II
Stift pen I
Stil style III U5, 95
still quiet III U1, 16
Stille silence III U1, 20
Stimme voice III U1, 22
stimmt's? isn't it? II
Stockwerk floor II
stolz (auf) proud (of) III U3, 65
(sich) **stoßen** to hit III U2, 40
Strand beach I
 den Strand nach Strandgut
 absuchen to go beach combing II
Straße road I; street III U1, 15
Straßenbahn tram III U5, 100
Streich trick I
streichen to paint II
Streit argument II; fight III U2, 50
(sich) **streiten** *to fight III U3, 52
Strom electricity III U3, 53
Stück piece II
 pro Stück each II
Stufe step II
Stuhl chair I
stumm silent III U1, 21
40 Kilometer pro **Stunde** 40 kilomet-
 res an hour I
Stundenplan timetable I
Sturm storm I
stürzen to rush III U5, 105
suchen to look for I
Süden south III U1, 10
 im Süden von in the south of
 III U1, 10

super cool I; way to go II
Superman superman I
Supermarkt supermarket II
Suppe soup II
surfen to surf II
 im Internet surfen to surf the
 internet II
süß cute II; sweet III U5, 96
Süßes, sonst gibt's Saures! Trick or
 treat! I
Süßigkeit sweet I
Sweatshirt sweatshirt I
Szene scene II

T

Tablett tray II
Tablette tablet II
Tafel board I
 eine Tafel Schokolade a bar of
 chocolate I
Tag day I
 ein ausgefüllter Tag a busy day I
 eines Tages one day III U1, 21
 den ganzen Tag all day III U3, 58
Tagebuch diary I
täglich daily III U5, 101
 vier Stunden täglich four hours a
 day I
Taktik tactic III U3, 64
talentiert talented III U2, 35
Talentwettbewerb talent show I
Tante aunt II
tanzen to dance I
Tänzer dancer I
Tänzerin dancer I
tapfer brave III U3, 63
Tasche bag I
Taschenlampe torch I
Taschentuch tissue III U4, 81
Tasse cup II
Tätigkeit job II
Tatsache fact II
tatsächlich actually III U5, 105
taub deaf III U3, 54
tausend a/one thousand II
Taxi taxi II
Team team I

Teamwork teamwork II
Technik Design Technology (DT) I
Techniker engineer II
Technikerin engineer II
Tee tea I
Teelöffel teaspoon II
Teenager teen II; teenager III U2, 33
Teenagerin teenager III U2, 33
Teil part II
teilen to share III U5, 96
teilnehmen (an) *to take part (in)
 III U5, 100
Telefon phone II; telephone III U3, 54
 ans Telefon gehen to answer the
 phone III U2, 45
Telefonanruf phone call I
telefonieren to phone I
Telefonnummer phone number
 III U2, 38
Telefonzelle telephone box II
Teller plate II
Tennis tennis I
Teppich carpet I
testen to test II
teuer expensive II
Text lines; text II
texten to text II
Textnachricht (SMS) text message I
Theater theatre; drama II
Theaterstück play II
Thunfisch tuna II
Tier animal I
Tierarzt vet II
Tierärztin vet II
Tierhandlung pet shop III U1, 13
Tierheim animal rescue shelter I
Tierpark zoo I
Tierpfleger zookeeper I
Tierpflegerin zookeeper I
Tiger tiger I
Tipp tip III U3, 58
Tisch table I
 den Tisch decken to lay the table
 II
Tischler carpenter II
Tischlerin carpenter II
Tischtennis table tennis II
Tochter daughter I

tödlich deadly III U1, 20
toll great; brilliant I; amazing III U3, 63
Tomate tomato II
Ton sound III U3, 54
Tonne tonne II
Top top II
Topf pot III U5, 104
tot dead III U1, 22
töten to kill III U1, 20
Tourist tourist I
Touristin tourist I
Touristeninformation Tourist Information Centre I
Tradition tradition III U3, 53
tragen *to wear I; to carry III U5, 103
trainieren to practise III U5, 96
Training practice I; training III U2, 41
Traktor tractor I
Transporter van III U4, 93
Ich **traute** meinen Augen nicht. I couldn't believe my eyes. III U5, 105
Traum dream II
träumen *to dream III U1, 25
traurig sad III U3, 65; down III U4, 77
treffen *to hit II
(sich) **treffen** to meet II
Trick trick I
trinken *to drink II
Trinkhalm straw II
Trip trip III U2, 34
trocken dry III U2, 35
Trommel- drumming III U5, 100
Tschüss! Bye!; See you! I
T-Shirt T-shirt I
Tuch scarf II
tun *to do; *to make I
leid tun to be sorry III U4, 87
Tut mir leid. Sorry. I
Was kann ich für dich tun? How can I help you? I
Tunnel tunnel III U1, 20
Tür door II
Türkei Turkey II
Türklingel doorbell I
Turm tower II
Turnier competition III U5, 95
turnieren to joust III U2, 43

Turnierzweikampf jousting III U2, 43
einen Turnierzweikampf austragen to joust III U2, 43
Turnschuh trainer I
eine **Tüte** … a packet of I
Tüte bag I
Typ type III U1, 31

U

U-Bahn underground II
üben to practise III U5, 96
über about; across II
überall wo(hin) wherever III U5, 107
sich **übergeben** *to be sick I
überleben to survive III U4, 84
überlegen to guess II
übernachten to stay II
Übernachtung sleepover I
überprüfen to check III U4, 81
überqueren to cross III U1, 12
überrascht surprised II
Überraschung surprise I
U-Boot submarine I
Übung practice I
Übungsheft exercise book I
Uhr clock II
Wie viel Uhr ist es? What time is it? I
Uhr *(Zeitangabe bei vollen Stunden)* o'clock I
Uhrenturm clock tower II
Uhrzeit time I
um at I
umfallen *to fall (over) III U2, 38
Umfrage survey II
umher around III U1, 19
umrühren to stir II
umsteigen to change III U5, 100
umziehen to move (house) II
Umzug parade III U5, 104
unangenehm uncomfortable II
unbequem uncomfortable II
und and I
Und du? What about you? II
unfair unfair III U1, 16
Unfall accident III U2, 38
unfreundlich unfriendly III U2, 35

ungefähr about II
ungefähr um around III U5, 96
ungefährlich safe III U2, 35
Ungeheuer monster III U3, 58
unglaublich amazing III U3, 63
Unglück disaster III U4, 84
unglücklich unhappy II
Uniform uniform I
unmodisch unfashionable II
unmöglich impossible III U3, 62
Unordnung mess I
uns us I
unser our I
unsere ours III U5, 96
unter under I
untere lower III U4, 92
untergehen *to sink III U4, 84
Unterricht lesson I; class III U5, 102
unterwegs out and about I
Urlaub holiday II
Ururopa great-great-grandad I

V

Vanillesauce custard II
Vater father I
Vati dad I
Vegetarier vegetarian I
Vegetarierin vegetarian I
verändern to change III U3, 54
verängstigt scared I
verärgert angry II; annoyed III U4, 77
Verband bandage III U2, 39
verbessern to correct I
verbinden to connect III U3, 67
in **Verbindung** bleiben *to keep in touch II
verbrennen *to burn III U2, 39
verbringen *(Zeit)* *to spend II
verdrehen to twist II
Verein club II
Verfasser writer III U2, 50
Verfasserin writer III U2, 50
Vergangenheit past III U1, 16
vergessen *to forget I
vergleichen to compare I
verkaufen *to sell III U1, 13

Verkäufer shop assistant II; assistant III U4, 83

Verkäuferin shop assistant II; assistant III U4, 83

Verkehr traffic III U1, 16

öffentliche **Verkehrsmittel** public transport III U5, 100

verkleidet (als) dressed III U5, 105

Verkleidung fancy dress I

verlassen leave II

verlegen embarrassed II

verletzen *to hurt II

sich **verlieben** (in) *to fall in love (with) III U2, 50

verlieren *to lose II

einen Auftrag **vermasseln** *to get a job wrong III U2, 50

vermissen to miss II

Vermittlung operator III U2, 38

vernünftig intelligent III U4, 77

verrenken to sprain III U2, 39

verrückt crazy I

jmdn. verrückt machen to drive sb crazy III U4, 76

verstauchen to sprain III U2, 39

(sich) **verstecken** *to hide III U2, 50

verstehen *to understand II; *to get III U4, 80

Versuch experiment II

vervollständigen to complete I; to finish II

verwenden to use II

verwirrt confused III U1, 25

verzerren to twist II

auf etw. **verzichten** *to give sth a miss III U2, 50

Vesper packed lunch II

Video video II

Video-Chat video chat III U3, 67

viel much; lots of; a lot of I; lots III U2, 43

viel a lot of III U1, 16

viele many II

wie viele how many II

vielleicht may II

vielleicht maybe II

vier four I

vierte fourth I

Viertel nach quarter past I

Viertel vor quarter to I

vierzehn fourteen I

vierzig forty I

viktorianisches Zeitalter Victorian era III U1, 25

violett purple I

Vogel bird III U3, 61

Vogelbeobachtung bird watching III U3, 61

Volleyball volleyball II

völlig quite III U2, 34

von from I; by II

ein Foto von a photo of I

vor ago II

vor (bei Uhrzeitangaben) to I

vorbei (an) past III U1, 12

vorbereiten to prepare III U5, 96

Vordergrund foreground III U4, 92

im Vordergrund in the foreground III U4, 92

Vorgehensweise tactic III U3, 64

vorhaben *to be up to III U3, 67

vorher before II

vorhersagen to foretell III U5, 105

Vormittag morning I

vormittags a.m. II

vorsichtig sein *to be careful II

Vorsingen audition II

Vorspielen audition II

Vorsprechen audition II

Vortanzen audition II

vorziehen to prefer II

W

wach awake III U2, 38

Wagen truck III U1, 21

wählen *to choose II

wahr true II

während during III U1, 11

während while II

wahrscheinlich probably III U4, 75

Wald wood II

Waliser Welsh III U2, 32

Waliserin Welsh III U2, 32

walisisch Welsh III U2, 32

Walisisch Welsh III U2, 32

Wand wall II

Wandern hiking III U3, 58; walking III U3, 61

wandern to hike II

Wandgemälde mural III U4, 74

wann when I

warm warm I

warten to wait II

warten auf to wait for II

Warteschlange queue II

warum why II

was what I

Was kann ich für dich tun? How can I help you? I

Was man … What to … II

Was ist los? What's wrong? II

Was stimmt nicht? What's wrong? II

Was?! No way! III U3, 58

Waschbär raccoon I

(sich) **waschen** to wash III U5, 98

Wasser water III U2, 33

Website website II

Wechselgeld change II

Hier ist dein Wechselgeld. Here's your change. I

wechseln to change II

Wecker alarm clock I

Weg way III U1, 12

nach dem Weg fragen asking the way I

nicht **weg** können *to be stuck I

weg away II

wegen because of III U2, 37

weglaufen *to run away III U2, 50

weh tun *to hurt II

Weihnachten Christmas I

Weihnachtstheaterstück pantomime II

weil because I

auf diese **Weise** like this III U3, 62

weiß white I

weit far III U1, 12

welche which; what; who II

Welle wave I

wellenreiten to surf II

Welt world II

auf der Welt in the world II

ein **wenig** a bit II
wenige a few III U3, 58
weniger less III U4, 80
wenn when; if II
wer who I
werden will; *to become II
  nicht werden won't (= will not) II
Werft shipyard III U4, 84
Werk factory III U1, 16
an **Werktagen** on weekdays III U5, 96
Werkzeug tool II
Westen west III U1, 17
Wettbewerb competition III U5, 95
Wetter weather I
Wettrennen race I
wichtig important III U2, 33
wie like II
wie as II
  so … wie as … as II
wie how I; what III U1, 12
  wie viele how many II
  Wie alt bist du? How old are you? I
  Wie bitte? Pardon? I
  wie etwas war what sth was like
  III U1, 12
  Wie geht es dir? How are you? I
  Wie heißt du? What's your name? I
  Wie man … How to … II
  Wie musst du sein? What must
  you be like? III U2, 37
  Wie spät ist es? What time is it? I
  Wie viel (kostet/kosten) …? How
  much (is/are) …? I
  Wie viel Uhr ist es? What time is
  it? I
wieder again II
wiederholen to repeat III U4, 80
  Könntest du das bitte wieder-
  holen? Can you say that again,
  please? I
Auf **Wiedersehen.** Goodbye. I
wiegen to weigh II
die **Wikinger** the Vikings III U1, 11
willkommen (bei/in) welcome (to) I
Wind wind I
windig windy I
Windpark wind farm III U3, 53
Windrad (wind) turbine III U3, 53

winken to wave II
Winter winter I
winzig tiny III U1, 17
wir we I
wirklich real II
wirklich actually III U5, 105
Wirklich? Really? I
wirr confused III U1, 25
Ich **weiß** (es) nicht! I don't know! I
  Weißt du was? Guess what? I
Wissenschaft Science I
Witz joke I
witzig funny I
wo where I
  wo(hin) auch immer wherever
  III U5, 107
Woche week I
  unter der Woche on weekdays
  III U5, 96
Wochenende weekend I
  am Wochenende at the weekend I
wöchentlich weekly III U5, 101
woher where I
  Woher kommst du? Where are you
  from? I
wohin where I
wohnen to live I
Wohnung flat I
Wohnwagen caravan III U3, 59
Wohnzimmer living room I
Wolke cloud III U2, 42
wolkig cloudy I
Wolle wool I
wollen to want (to) I
Workshop workshop II
Wrap wrap II
wund sore II
Mit den besten **Wünschen,** Best
  wishes, I
wünschen to wish III U1, 25
würde(n) would II
  würde(n) gern would like II
  ich würde gerne … I'd like (to) …
  (= I would like to) I
  ich würde nicht gerne … I
  wouldn't like (to) … I
Wurst sausage II
wütend angry II; furious III U4, 77

Z

Zahl number I
Zahn tooth III U2, 39
Zahnbürste toothbrush III U5, 96
Zahnpasta toothpaste III U5, 97
Zahnstocher toothpick II
Zauberei magic II
Zebra zebra I
zehn ten I
Zeichen sign III U2, 32; signal III U3, 67
Zeichensprache sign language
  III U5, 95
zeichnen *to draw II
zeigen *to show II
Zeit time I
viktorianisches **Zeitalter** Victorian
  era III U1, 25
Zeitpunkt date I
Zeitreise time travel III U4, 79
Zeitschrift magazine I
Zeitschriftenladen newsagent's
  III U1, 13
Zelt tent II
Zelten camping III U2, 36
Zeltplatz campsite III U3, 58
Zentimeter (cm) centimetre (cm) I
Zentrum centre III U1, 16
zerstören to ruin II
Ziege goat III U1, 16
ziehen to pull I
ziemlich quite III U2, 34
Zimmer room I
Zimmerdecke ceiling I
Zimmerin carpenter II
Zimmermann carpenter II
Zitrone lemon II
Zoo zoo I
  im Zoo at the zoo I
zornig angry II
zu too II
  zu sehr too much II
zu to I
  zu Hause back home II
zubereiten to prepare III U5, 96
zuerst first I
Zug train I

mit (dem Zug) fahren to go by (train) I
Zuhause home I
zuhören to listen (to) I
zum Schluss finally II
    zum Spaß for fun III U2, 43
zumachen to close I
zuordnen to match I
zurück back III U2, 41

zurückzahlen *to pay back II
zusammen together I
zusammen everyone II
zusammenzucken to jump III U2, 42
Zusatz- extra II
zusätzlich extra II
zuschauen to watch II
zustimmen to agree II
Zutat ingredient II

zuvor before II
zwanzig twenty I
zwei two I
zweite second I
Zwiebel onion II
zwischen between II
zwölf twelve I

Lösungen Extra practice

Seite 28

1 Write the name of the places.
1. Hadrian's Wall, 2. York, 3. Manchester,
4. Stonhenge, 5. Hastings

2 Where do you go to . . .
1. baker's
2. sports shop
3. clothes shop
4. card shop
Which shop don't you need? shoe shop

3 Write Ben's sentences.
1. I never get up before 8 p.m.
2. I usually fly to different places.
3. But sometimes I also walk.
4. I always eat little animals for breakfast.
5. Cheese? No, I never have that.
6. I usually go to bed in the morning.

4 Write Ben's sentences.
1. Does your friend sometimes buy T-shirts at the new clothes shop?
2. Do you sometimes go shopping in the York Sweet Shop?
3. Do they often play football after school?
4. Does she usually buy bread at the baker's on the weekend?
5. Does the new shoe shop always open at 10 p.m.?
6. Does your family usually walk to the card shop?

Seite 29

5 Find the way.
a) 1. swimming pool
   2. park
   3. café
b) 1. opposite
   2. next to
   3. corner
   4. cross, right

6 Write sentences about Hannah.
1. Hannah didn't get up at 9 a.m. So she was late.
2. Hannah met her friend on the bus.
3. They went shopping and had lots of ice cream.
4. Hannah didn't call her mum at 4 p.m.
5. They went back home at 5 p.m. Hannah's mum was angry.
6. So they didn't go to the cinema in the evening.

7 Write the questions.
1. Did you forget your mobile?
2. Did you buy a new T-shirt?
3. Did you go to the library?
4. Did you have a good time together?
5. Did you buy cheese and tomatoes?

Seite 48

1 What's the word?
1. capital
2. canoeing, rafting
3. road signs
4. lifeboats
5. rugby
6. rules
7. volunteers
8. outdoor
9. rock climbing

2 What did the rock climbing instructor say?
1. carefully
2. loudly
3. good
4. hard
5. easy
6. slowly
7. careful
8. wet
9. tired

3 Match the parts of the dialogue.
1. F; 2. E; 3. D; 4. B; 5. A; 6. G; 7. C

Seite 49

4 Write about accidents.
a) 1. have an accident
   2. break my arm
   3. cut my finger
   4. twist my knee
   5. burnt my finger
   6. sprain my ankle

b) 1. I've had an accident.
   2. I've burnt my arm.
   3. I'v cut my finger.
   4. I've twisted my knee.
   5. I've burnt my finger.
   6. I've sprain my ankle.

5 **What have the people done? What haven't they done yet?**
1. Claire has bought some tablets. She hasn't taken them yet.
2. Nick has burnt his hand. He hasn't cooled it yet.
3. Molly has twisted her knee. She hasn't put a bandage on it yet.
4. Joe has gone to the doctor. He hasn't seen the doctor yet.

6 **Complete the text.**
Megan loves outdoor activities and sports. She has already tried many things (1). She has started (2) to play tennis when she was (3) ten years old. Two years ago she rode (4) her bike up Mount Snowdon. But canoeing is her favourite and she has already won (5) lots of prizes. Last year she had (6) an accident and broke (7) her arm. But it has got (8) better quickly and she has already been (9) on the river again this year. Have you ever gone (10) canoeing?

Seite 70

1 **Match the sentence parts.**
1. C; 2. F; 3. G; 4. B; 5. H; 6. E; 7. D; 8. A

2 **What's the material?**
1. This chair is made of wood.
2. This magazine is made of paper.
3. This fork is made of metal.
4. This bag is made of plastic.
5. This bag is made of leather.
6. This spoon is made of wood.
7. This eraser is made of rubber.
8. This T-shirt is made of cotton.

3 **Complete the sentences.**
1. A kilt is a skirt which is for men.
2. Robert the Bruce was a king who fought against the English.
3. Edinburgh is a Scottish city which is very old.
4. Porridge is a dish which has oats in it.
5. Scotland is a country which doesn't have much sun.
6. A cottage is a house which is small and often in the country.
7. An inventor is a person who invents machines and other things.

Seite 71

4 **Use whose to make one sentence out of two.**
1. Inventors are important persons whose ideas make life easies.
2. Bell was a famous inventor whose wife and his mother were both deaf.
3. Bell was a teacher whose wish was to help people who couldn't hear well.
4. Bell became a famous man whose invention changed the world forever.

5 **Complete the sentences.**
1. If we don't want to pay much, we will stay at a campsite.
2. We will freeze if we stay at a campsite.
3. There won't be any insects if we go to a cosy B & B.
4. If we are in a hotel, we will have our own bathroom.
5. We won't get nice food if we stay at a campsite.
6. If we choose a hotel, we won't have money for anything else.
7. We will take a cottage if a hotel room is too expensive.
8. If we see the Loch Ness monster, everyone will be happy.

6 Make sentences.
1. If I go to Scotland, I will visit Edinburgh.
2. If I see Nessie, I'll take a photo.
3. If I have money, Ill go shopping.
4. If I stay in a B&B, I'll eat porridge.
5. If it's wet tomorrow, I won't go into the mountains.
6. If I go to the museum, I'll learn about history.

Seite 90

1 Find the places.
1. Northern Ireland
2. bed and breakfast
3. Lough Neagh
4. Giant's Causeway
5. Maggie's shop
6. Belfast

2 Find the adjectives and make a new word.
1. smart
2. confident
3. fed up
4. furious
5. horrible
6. sad
7. optimistic
8. tourist

3 What would they do?
1. If Julie lived in a B&B, she would talk to the tourists.
2. If Sarah's parents had more time, it would be more fun.
3. If Sarah's mum didn't nag her, Sarah would feel better.
4. If Ashley didn't help Sarah, it would be horrible.
5. If Julie lived nearer, Sarah wouldn't miss her.
6. If Julie visited Sarah, she would ask silly questions.
7. If Sarah and her family lived in Belfast, Sarah would see her friend more often.

4 Complete the shopping dialogue.
1. like
2. jar
3. else
4. are
5. change
6. you

Seite 91

5 Write a shopping list.
two bottles of orange juice, two loaves of bread, a jar of strawberry jam, a bottle of mineral water, a jar of peanut butter, a packet if tissues

6 Compare the things.
1. Northern Ireland isn't as big as Scotland.
2. The train is faster than the car.
3. Rice is as good as pasta.
4. Rugby isn't as popular as football in Northern Ireland.
5. Belfast isn't as warm as Berlin today.
6. Orange juice is more expensive than mineral water.

7 Complete the dialogue in the supermarket.
1. any
2. some
3. some
4. any
5. some
6. any
7. any
8. some

Seite 110

1 Find the words.
1. competition
2. St Patrick's day; green
3. pubs
4. dance; courses
5. EU (European Union)
6. orchestra

2 What is it?
1. toothpaste
2. kitchen
3. bed
4. fridge
5. shampoo
6. tea
7. hairdryer

3 Put in the right forms.
1. 'm (am) doing
2. cooks
3. have
4. 's (is) practising
5. 's (is) wearing
6. uses
7. 's (is) shouting
8. rains

Seite 111

4 Match and make sentences.

a) 1. get off (around)
   2. public transport
   3. get around (off)
   4. bus timetable
   5. plan the journey
   6. pay the fare

b) 1. plan the journey
   2. get off
   3. pay the fare
   4. bus timetable
   5. public transport
   6. get around

5 Concert rules. Must or mustn't?

1. mustn't
2. must
3. mustn't
4. mustn't
5. must
6. mustn't
7. mustn't
8. mustn't

6 Put in the right word.

1. must
2. needn't
3. mustn't
4. must
5. needn't
6. mustn't
7. needn't
8. must

Lösungen Zoom in (Seite 8)

1. England, Wales, Scotland, Northern Ireland and the Republic of Ireland
2. England
3. The Republic of Ireland
4. Scotland
5. Northern Ireland
6. Scotland
7. London
8. The Republic of Ireland
9. England

Bildquellennachweis

Cover.1 plainpicture GmbH (Ableimages/Jutta Klee), Hamburg; **Cover.2** plainpicture GmbH (Bias), Hamburg; **2.1** plainpicture GmbH (Robert Harding), Hamburg; **3.1** Mauritius Images (Alamy), Mittenwald; **3.2** Getty Images (The Image Bank/Victoria Snowber), München; **4.1** plainpicture GmbH (Cultura), Hamburg; **4.2** Getty Images (Joe Daniel Price), München; **5.1** Alamy Images (GL Archive), Abingdon, Oxon; **9.1** plainpicture GmbH (Bias), Hamburg; **9.2** plainpicture GmbH (Design Pics/Wayne Hutchinson), Hamburg; **9.3** plainpicture GmbH (Westend61/lyzs), Hamburg; **9.4** plainpicture GmbH (Design Pics/The Irish Image Collection), Hamburg; **9.5** Corbis (Lola Akinmade Akerstrom/National Geographic Creative), Berlin; **9.6** Thinkstock (Jessica Hunnicutt), München; **9.7** iStockphoto (Guillermo Perales Gonzalez), Calgary, Alberta; **9.8** iStockphoto (kati1313), Calgary, Alberta; **9.9** Thinkstock (Brian Doty), München; **9.10** iStockphoto (jcarter), Calgary, Alberta; **10.1** plainpicture GmbH (Arcaid), Hamburg; **10.2** plainpicture GmbH (Robert Harding), Hamburg; **11.1** Getty Images (Iconica/Arctic-Images), München; **11.2** Alamy Images (Carolyn Clarke), Abingdon, Oxon; **11.3** Getty Images, München; **12.1** Alamy Images (Simon Dack), Abingdon, Oxon; **12.2** plainpicture GmbH (Robert Harding), Hamburg; **12.3** Alamy Images (Steve Morgan), Abingdon, Oxon; **12.4** shutterstock.com (Alastair Wallace), New York, NY; **16.1** plainpicture GmbH (alt6/Suzanne Rochette), Hamburg; **16.2** shutterstock.com (Julija Sapic), New York, NY; **19.1** Getty Images (Photodisc), München; **19.2** Klett-Archiv (Thomas Weccard), Stuttgart; **24.1** Corbis (Imaginechina), Berlin; **24.2** Getty Images (E+), München; **25.1** February Films, London; **25.2** February Films, London; **25.3** February Films, London; **27.1** Weccard, Thomas, Ludwigsburg; **28.1** plainpicture GmbH (Robert Harding), Hamburg; **28.2** Getty Images (Iconica/Arctic-Images), München; **28.3** Getty Images, München; **28.4** plainpicture GmbH (Arcaid), Hamburg; **28.5** plainpicture GmbH (Arcaid), Hamburg; **30.1** Corbis (Steven Vidler), Berlin; **30.2** Mauritius Images (Alamy), Mittenwald; **30.3** Getty Images (Brendan Hoffman), München; **30.4** Mauritius Images (Alamy), Mittenwald; **32.1** Getty Images (Cultura), München; **32.2** Mauritius Images (Alamy), Mittenwald; **33.1** Getty Images (Robert Harding), München; **33.2** Mauritius Images (Alamy), Mittenwald; **33.3** Corbis (Andrew Fox), Berlin; **34.1** Fotolia.com (goodluz), New York; **34.1** Getty Images (Cultura), München; **36.1** Alamy Images (John Robertson), Abingdon, Oxon; **36.2** Mauritius Images (Alamy), Mittenwald; **37.1** plainpicture GmbH (Johner), Hamburg; **37.1** shutterstock.com (Elena Elisseeva), New York, NY; **37.2** Thinkstock/iStock/Wojciech Gajda, Getty Images RF/PhotoDisc, shutterstock/Worytko Pawel; **39.1** shutterstock.com (PathDoc), New York, NY; **42.1** Fotolia.com (BasPhoto), New York; **42.2** Getty Images (Cultura), München; **43.1** Alamy Images (James Davies), Abingdon, Oxon; **43.2** Alamy Images (Cultura Creative), Abingdon, Oxon; **44.1** Corbis, Berlin; **45.1** February Films, London; **46.1** Corbis (Ed Bock), Berlin; **46.2** Corbis (Ed Bock), Berlin; **46.3** Corbis (Ed Bock), Berlin; **46.4** Corbis (Ed Bock), Berlin; **46.5** Corbis (Ed Bock), Berlin; **46.6** Corbis (Ed Bock), Berlin; **46.7** Corbis (Ed Bock), Berlin; **47.1** Corbis (Ed Bock), Berlin; **47.2** Corbis (Ed Bock), Berlin; **47.3** Corbis (Ed Bock), Berlin; **47.4** Corbis (Ed Bock), Berlin; **47.5** Corbis (Ed Bock), Berlin; **47.6** Corbis (Ed Bock), Berlin; **47.7** Corbis (Ed Bock), Berlin; **48.1** iStockphoto (MivPiv), Calgary, Alberta; **49.1** iStockphoto (saxifrag), Calgary, Alberta; **49.2** dreamstime.com (Maxximmm), Brentwood, TN; **49.3** iStockphoto (Steve Debenport), Calgary, Alberta; **49.4** Thinkstock (Ryan McVay), München; **49.5** Thinkstock (Wavebreakmedia Ltd), München; **52.1** Getty Images (John Lawson/Moment), München; **52.2** Getty Images (AWL Images), München; **53.1** CC-BY-SA-4.0 (Rosser1954/keine Änderungen), Mountain View; **53.2** Getty Images (2010 Billy Currie), München; **53.3** Getty Images (The Image Bank/Victoria Snowber), München; **54.1** Thinkstock (Photos.com), München; **54.2** Picture-Alliance (Everett Collection), Frankfurt; **54.3** Thinkstock (istock/passigatti), München; **54.4** iStockphoto (davincidig), Calgary, Alberta; **54.5** Thinkstock (istock/NatalyaAksenova), München; **54.6** Thinkstock (istock/TimZillion), München; **54.7** Thinkstock (istock/thumb), München; **54.8** Thinkstock (istock/rvlsoft), München; **57.1** Fotosearch Stock Photography (Eclecti Collection RF), Waukesha, WI; **57.2** Thinkstock (iStock/Digital Paws Inc.), München; **57.3** Fotolia.com (Diogo Barbosa), New York; **58.1** Avenue Images GmbH (Banana Stock), Hamburg; **60.1** iStockphoto (clubfoto), Calgary, Alberta; **60.2** Thinkstock (Eli Franssens), München; **61.1** Thinkstock (iStock/Nastco), München; **61.2** Klett-Archiv, Stuttgart; **61.3** Thinkstock (istock/ffolas), München; **61.4** Thinkstock (istock/Juliane Jacobs), München; **61.5** Thinkstock (istock/andreusK), München; **61.6** Thinkstock (iStock/JaySi), München; **66.1** Mauritius Images (Alamy), Mittenwald; **66.2** Mauritius Images (Alamy), Mittenwald; **66.2** Mauritius Images (Hüttner + Consorten), Mittenwald; **66.3** shutterstock.com (Gencay M. Emin), New York, NY; **66.4** Thinkstock (iStockphoto), München; **66.5** shutterstock.com (Gencay M. Emin), New York, NY; **66.6** Thinkstock (iStockphoto), München; **67.1** iStockphoto (davincidig), Calgary, Alberta; **68.1** Thinkstock (Smitt), München; **68.2** Fotolia.com (laralova), New York; **70.1** Thinkstock (iStock/saknakorn), München; **70.2** Thinkstock (iStock/prapann), München; **70.3** shutterstock.com (shnjr52), New York, NY; **70.4** shutterstock.com (MNI), New York, NY; **70.5** shutterstock.com (MaleWitch), New York, NY; **70.6** shutterstock.com (Diana Taliun), New York, NY; **70.7** shutterstock.com (spaxiax), New York, NY; **70.8** shutterstock.com (Komkrit Noenpoempisut), New York, NY; **71.1** shutterstock.com (Gencay M. Emin), New York, NY; **71.2** iStockphoto (gremlin), Calgary, Alberta; **71.3** Fotolia.com (bzyxx), New York; **71.4** shutterstock.com (Egorov Igor), New York, NY; **71.5** Thinkstock (iStock/MartinM303), München; **71.6** Fotolia.com (lupico), New York; **72.1** shutterstock.com (John A Cameron), New York, NY; **72.2** Alamy Images (Alex Ekins Adventure Photography), Abingdon, Oxon; **72.3** dreamstime.com (Micka), Brentwood, TN; **73.1** PONS GmbH, Stuttgart, Stuttgart; **74.1** Getty Images (John Molloy), München; **74.2** plainpicture GmbH (Design Pics), Hamburg; **74.3** plainpicture GmbH (Cultura), Hamburg; **75.1** Corbis (Jon Boyes/incamerastock), Berlin; **75.2** plainpicture GmbH (Stockwerk/Dirk Kugelmeier), Hamburg; **75.3** Corbis (Hugh Rooney/http:// www. eyeubiquitous. com/Eye Ubiquitous), Berlin; **76.1** Getty Images (John Molloy), München; **76.2** Getty Images (Stockbyte), München; **79.1** Alamy Images (Nikreates), Abingdon, Oxon; **87.1** February Films, London; **87.2** February Films, London; **87.3** February Films, London; **88.1** Fotolia.com (sharynos), New York; **89.1** Klett-Archiv (Peter Nierhoff), Stuttgart; **94.1** Getty Images (Joe Daniel Price), München; **94.2** Alamy Images (imageBROKER), Abingdon, Oxon; **95.1** shutterstock.com (TDC Photography), New York, NY; **95.2** plainpicture GmbH (Hero Images), Hamburg; **95.3** iStockphoto (Carmine Salvatore), Calgary, Alberta; **96.1** shutterstock.com (Tracy Whiteside), New York, NY; **96.2** shutterstock.com (RyFlip), New York, NY; **100.1** plainpicture GmbH (Westend61), Hamburg; **101.1** TRANSDEV Ireland, Dublin; **102.1** Thinkstock (Steeve ROCHE), München; **103.1** Thinkstock (istock/worac), München; **106.1** Picture-Alliance (Jens Kalaene/dpa), Frankfurt; **108.1** shutterstock.com (Aleksandar Mijatovic), New York, NY; **108.2** Thinkstock (iStockphoto), München; **108.3** shutterstock.com (ruskpp), New York, NY; **108.4** shutterstock.com (

Gencay M. Emin), New York, NY; **108.5** shutterstock.com (Jim Barber), New York, NY; **108.6** Thinkstock (iStockphoto), München; **110.1** iStockphoto (edfuentesg), Calgary, Alberta; **110.2** Thinkstock (CEZARY ZAREBSKI), München; **110.3** Alamy Images (Alex Segre), Abingdon, Oxon; **110.4** Thinkstock (Benis Arapovic), München; **110.5** Getty Images (Cultura), München; **110.6** shutterstock.com (Pavel L Photo and Video), New York, NY; **116.1** Thinkstock (Photos.com), München; **119.1** Thinkstock (iStock Editorial/IR_Stone), München; **119.2** Fotolia.com (Calin Bocian), New York; **119.3** shutterstock.com (Anneka), New York, NY; **119.4** Corbis (Steve Raymer/National Geographic Creative), Berlin; **119.5** shutterstock.com (Ilaszlo), New York, NY; **120.1** Thinkstock (iStock/Nastco), München; **120.2** Klett-Archiv, Stuttgart; **120.3** Thinkstock (istock/ffolas), München; **120.4** Thinkstock (istock/Juliane Jacobs), München; **120.5** Thinkstock (istock/andreusK), München; **120.6** Thinkstock (iStock/JaySi), München; **124.1** TRANSDEV Ireland, Dublin; **125.1** Thinkstock (istock/worac), München; **127.1** Alamy Images (GL Archive), Abingdon, Oxon; **128.1** shutterstock.com (antb), New York, NY; **128.1** Mauritius Images (Matthew Horwood/Alamy), Mittenwald; **128.2** shutterstock.com (Peter Raymond Llewellyn), New York, NY; **128.2** Mauritius Images (Jack Sullivan/Alamy), Mittenwald; **129.1** Getty Images (Moment), München; **129.2** plainpicture GmbH (Thorsten Rother), Hamburg; **129.3** Fotolia.com (PT Images), New York; **129.4** Thinkstock (umdash9), München; **130.1** Getty Images (Stockbyte), München; **130.2** Getty Images (Stockbyte), München; **131.1** Getty Images (The Image Bank), München; **131.2** iStockphoto (Liz Leyden), Calgary, Alberta; **131.3** Getty Images (Moment Open), München; **132.1** shutterstock.com (VanderWolf Images), New York, NY; **132.2** Getty Images (Stockbyte), München; **132.3** Getty Images (Christopher Pillitz), München; **133.1** Corbis (Artur Widak/NurPhoto), Berlin; **133.2** Corbis (Ralph White), Berlin; **133.2** Mauritius Images (Marco Secchi/Alamy), Mittenwald; **134.1** Getty Images (Matt Cardy), München; **134.2** Mauritius Images (Brickley Pix/Alamy), Mittenwald; **134.3** Getty Images (Universal Images Group), München; **134.4** Getty Images (Hulton Fine Art Collection), München; **134.5** Corbis, Berlin; **134.5** Alamy Images (imageBROKER/Dr. Wilfried Bahnmüller), Abingdon, Oxon; **135.1** Corbis, Berlin; **135.1** Mauritius Images (Ian Shipley IRE/Alamy), Mittenwald; **135.2** Alamy Images (jeremy sutton-hibbert), Abingdon, Oxon; **135.3** plainpicture GmbH (STOCK4B), Hamburg; **135.4** Getty Images (Cultura), München; **136.1** Klett-Archiv (Axel Reis), Stuttgart; **136.2** Klett-Archiv, Stuttgart; **136.3** Klett-Archiv (Axel Reis), Stuttgart; **136.4** Klett-Archiv (Axel Reis), Stuttgart; **136.5** Klett-Archiv (Axel Reis), Stuttgart; **137.1** Klett-Archiv (Axel Reis), Stuttgart; **137.2** Klett-Archiv (Axel Reis), Stuttgart; **137.3** Klett-Archiv (Axel Reis), Stuttgart; **137.4** Klett-Archiv (Axel Reis), Stuttgart; **137.5** Klett-Archiv, Stuttgart; **137.6** Klett-Archiv (Axel Reis), Stuttgart; **137.7** Klett-Archiv (Axel Reis), Stuttgart; **137.8** Klett-Archiv (Axel Reis), Stuttgart; **138.1** Thinkstock (Brand X Pictures/Jupiterimages), München; **138.2** Thinkstock (istock/Krzysztof Slusarczyk), München; **138.3** shutterstock.com (Leemonton), New York, NY; **138.4** Thinkstock (iStockphoto), München; **139.1** Thinkstock (iStock/blueringmedia), München; **139.2** Thinkstock (iStock/graphicsdunia4you), München; **144.1** Alamy Images (Ivy Close Images), Abingdon, Oxon; **172.1** dreamstime.com (Indos82), Brentwood, TN; **179.1** picturemaxx.net (RF), München; **179.2** Thinkstock (Medioimages/Photodisc), München; **179.3** Getty Images RF (Photodisc), München; **179.4** Thinkstock (iStockphoto), München; **186.1** Thinkstock (iStock/Michael Braun), München; **186.2** Thinkstock (Comstock), München; **186.3** Fotolia.com (Steve Lovegrove), New York; **186.4** Thinkstock (Lifesize), München; **186.5** Thinkstock (istockphoto), München; **186.6** Fotolia.com (Ints), New York; **186.7** Thinkstock (iStockphoto), München; **186.8** shutterstock.com (RF/McNally), New York, NY; **186.9** February Films (Elke Bock), London; **186.10** shutterstock.com, New York, NY; **186.11** Corbis RF (RF), Berlin; **186.12** Thinkstock (Comstock), München; **186.13** Fotolia.com (philippe Devanne), New York; **186.14** Thinkstock (mavrek), München; **186.15** iStockphoto (Liz Leyden), Calgary, Alberta; **186.16** Avenue Images GmbH (Image Source), Hamburg; **186.17** Avenue Images GmbH (Fancy RF), Hamburg; **186.18** shutterstock.com (Stefan Schurr), New York, NY; **186.19** dreamstime.com (Denyskuvaiev), Brentwood, TN; **186.20** Corbis (Gary Kufner), Berlin; **186.21** Getty Images RF (PhotoDisc), München; **186.22** Avenue Images GmbH (Ingram Publishing), Hamburg; **186.23** iStockphoto (Webphotographeer), Calgary, Alberta; **186.24** Thinkstock (iStockphoto), München; **186.25** creativ collection Verlag GmbH, Freiburg; **186.26** Avenue Images GmbH (image source), Hamburg; **186.27** Ingram Publishing, Tattenhall Chester; **186.28** Thinkstock (iStock/Ljupco), München; **186.29** Fotolia.com (mustgo), New York; **186.30** shutterstock.com (Cathleen A Clapper), New York, NY; **186.31** Thinkstock (Jupiterimages), München; **193.1** Klett-Archiv (Wolfgang Schaar, Grafing), Stuttgart; **194.1** shutterstock.com (Anneka), New York, NY; **194.2** iStockphoto (onfilm), Calgary, Alberta; **194.3** picturemaxx.net (RF), München; **194.4** Thinkstock (Medioimages/Photodisc), München; **194.5** Getty Images RF (Photodisc), München; **194.6** Thinkstock (iStockphoto), München; **206.1** shutterstock.com (Pack), New York, NY; **207.1** Thinkstock (iStockphoto), München; **207.2** iStockphoto (Lorraine Boogich), Calgary, Alberta; **207.3** iStockphoto (ollo), Calgary, Alberta; **207.4** shutterstock.com (Jordan Tan), New York, NY; **207.5** Fotolia.com (ang17a), New York; **207.6** Fotolia.com (david hughes), New York; **207.7** Avenue Images GmbH (Banana Stock), Hamburg; **207.8** Corbis RF, Berlin; **207.9** dreamstime.com, Brentwood, TN; **207.10** iStockphoto (Nick free), Calgary, Alberta; **207.11** panthermedia.net (dieschu), München; **207.12** Fotolia.com (godfer), New York; **207.13** shutterstock.com (William Attard McCarthy), New York, NY; **U00/Vorsatz hinten.1** Visit York, York

Sollte es in einem Einzelfall nicht gelungen sein, den korrekten Rechteinhaber ausfindig zu machen, so werden berechtigte Ansprüche selbstverständlich im Rahmen der üblichen Regelungen abgegolten.

Textquellennachweis
S. 17: The City, GOSLING, JAKE NATHAN/Sheeran, Edward Christopher © BDI Music Limited/Sony ATV Music Publishing (UK) Limited, Platz Musikverlage GmbH, Hamburg/Sony/ATV Music Publishing, (Germany) GmbH, Berlin
S. 77: Let your tears fall, FURLER, SIA KATE/Kurstin, Gregory Allen © EMI April Music Inc/EMI Music Publishing Ltd/Kurstin Music, EMI Music Publishing Germany GmbH, Berlin
S. 101: Luminous, Gustafsson, Johan/Haeggstam, Fredrik Folke Alexander/Lundberg, Sebastian Per Emil © Universal Music Publishing AB, Universal Music Publishing GmbH, Berlin
S. 140–143: Siobhan Dowd, The London Eye Mystery, Corgi Yearling (Verlag) © Siobhan Dowd, 2007